CASE CLOSED™

VOLUME 10

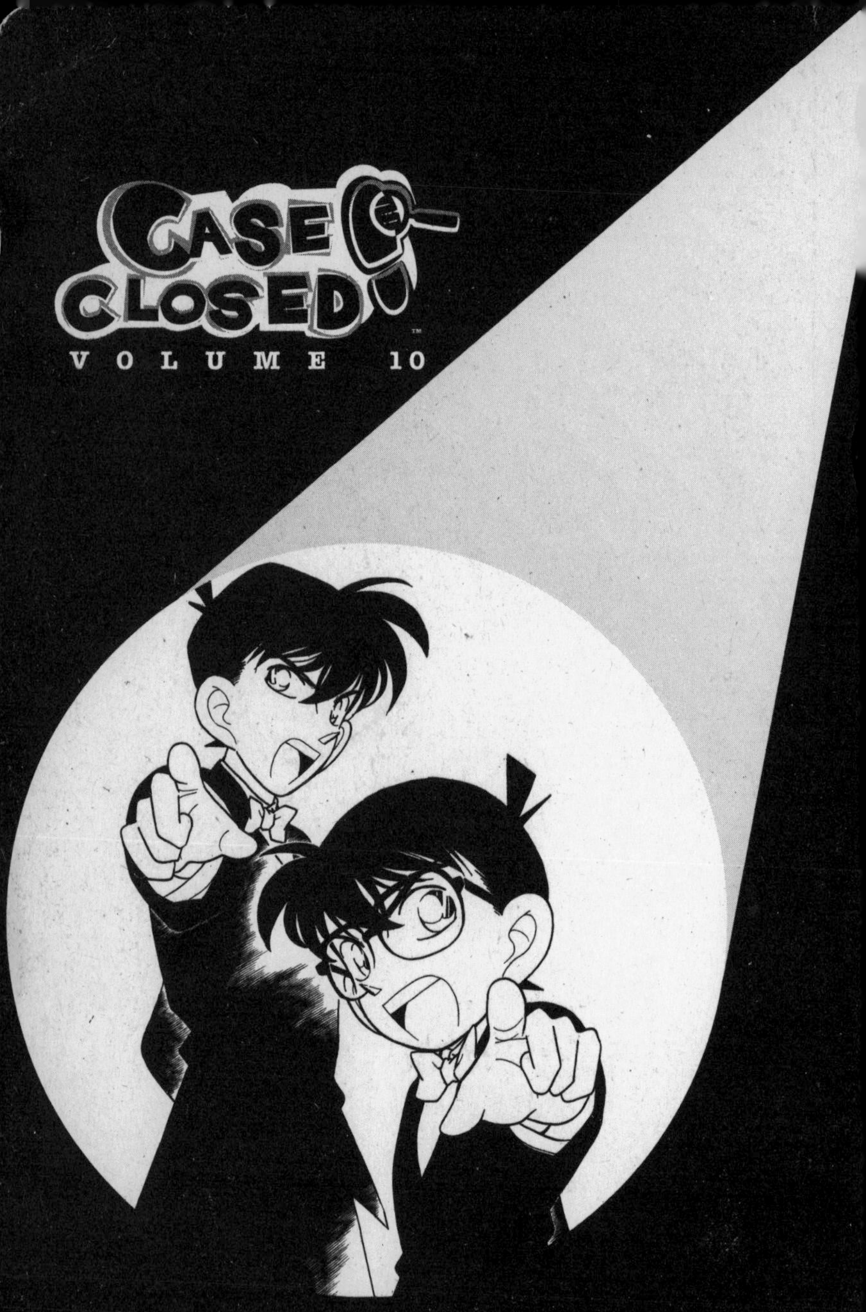

Gosho Aoyama

Case Briefing:

Subject: Jimmy Kudo, a.k.a. Conan Edogawa
Occupation: High School Student/Detective
Special Skills: Analytical thinking and deductive reasoning, Soccer
Equipment: Bow Tie Voice Transmitter, Super Sneakers, Homing Glasses, Stretchy Suspenders

The subject is hot on the trail of a pair of suspicious men in black when he is attacked from behind and administered a strange substance which physically transforms him into a first grader. When the subject confides in the eccentric inventor Dr. Agasa, they decide to keep the subject's true identity a secret for the safety of everyone around him. Assuming the new identity of first-grader Conan Edogawa, the subject continues to assist the police force on their most baffling cases. The only problem is that most crime-solving professionals won't take a little kid's advice!

Table of Contents

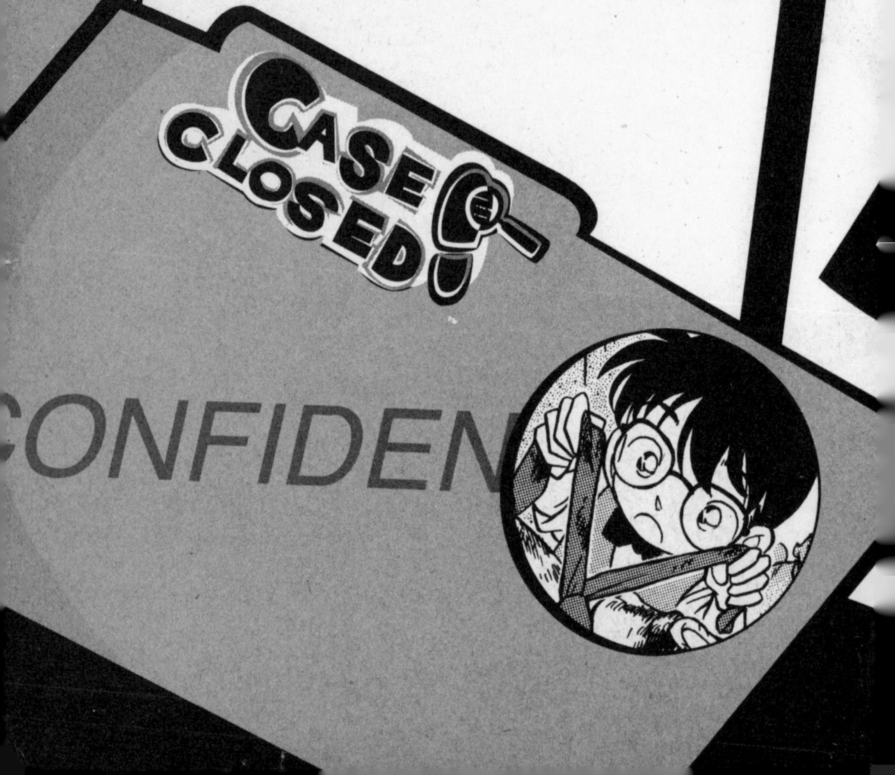

CASE CLOSED
CONFIDEN

CASE CLOSED
Volume 10 • Action Edition
GOSHO AOYAMA

English Adaptation
Naoko Amemiya

Translation
Joe Yamazaki

Touch-up & Lettering
Walden Wong

Cover & Interior Design
Andrea Rice

Editor
Urian Brown

Managing Editor **Annette Roman**
Director of Production **Noboru Watanabe**
Vice President of Publishing **Alvin Lu**
Sr. Director of Acquisitions **Rika Inouye**
Vice President of Sales & Marketing **Liza Coppola**
Publisher **Hyoe Narita**

store.viz.com

www.viz.com

Printed in the U.S.A.
Published by VIZ Media, LLC
P.O. Box 77010
San Francisco, CA 94107

10 9 8 7 6 5 4 3 2 1
First printing, March 2006

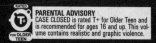

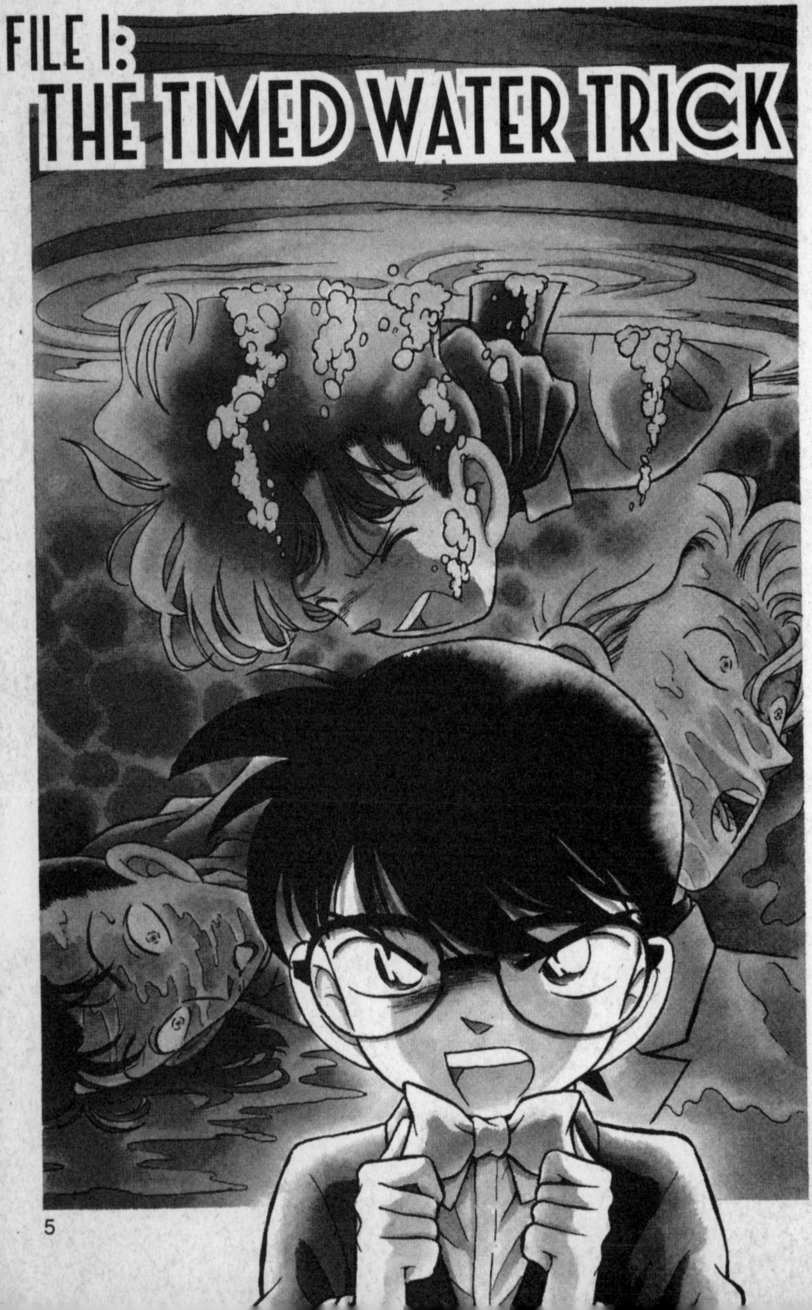
FILE 1:
THE TIMED WATER TRICK

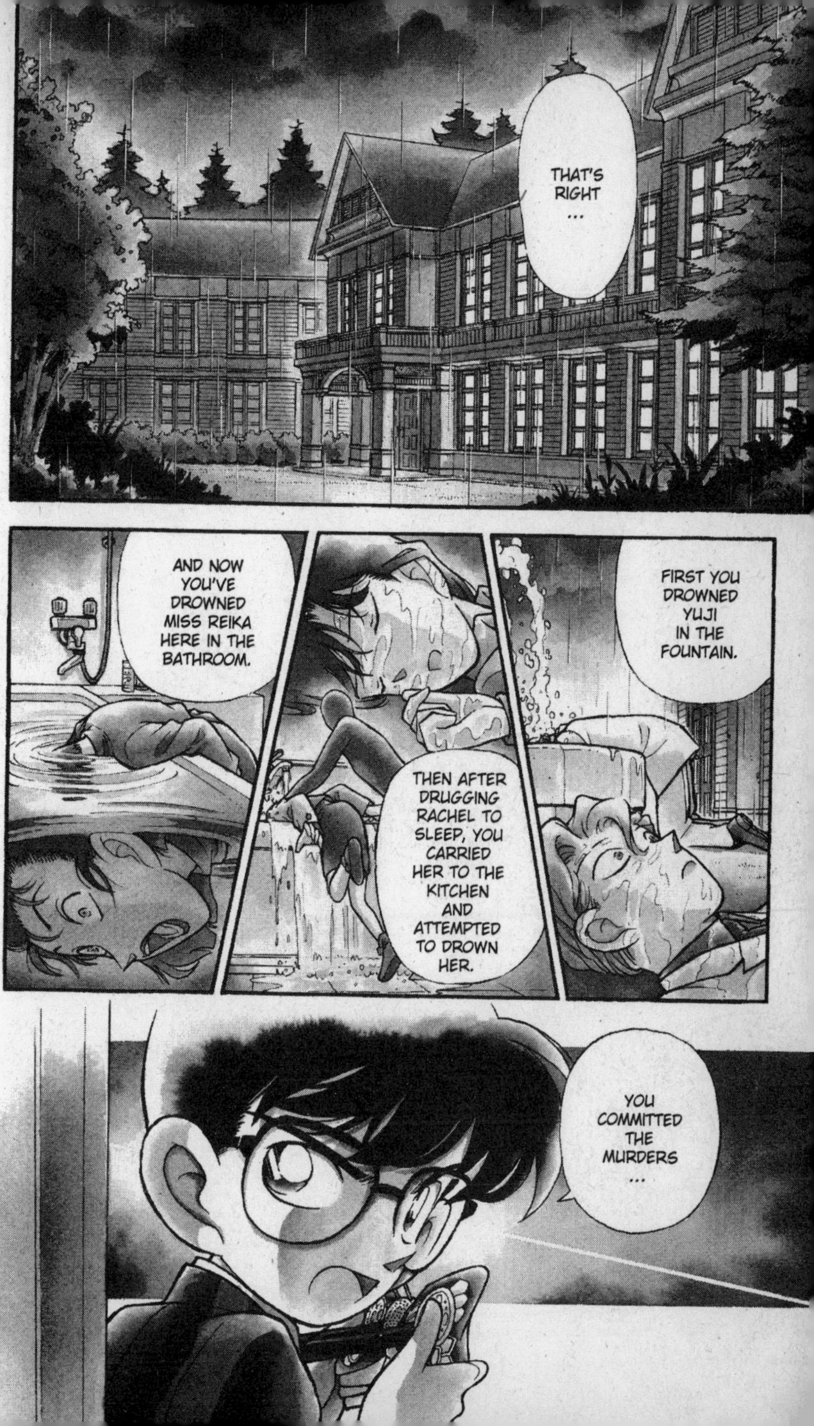
THAT'S RIGHT ...
FIRST YOU DROWNED YUJI IN THE FOUNTAIN.
THEN AFTER DRUGGING RACHEL TO SLEEP, YOU CARRIED HER TO THE KITCHEN AND ATTEMPTED TO DROWN HER.
AND NOW YOU'VE DROWNED MISS REIKA HERE IN THE BATHROOM.
YOU COMMITTED THE MURDERS ...

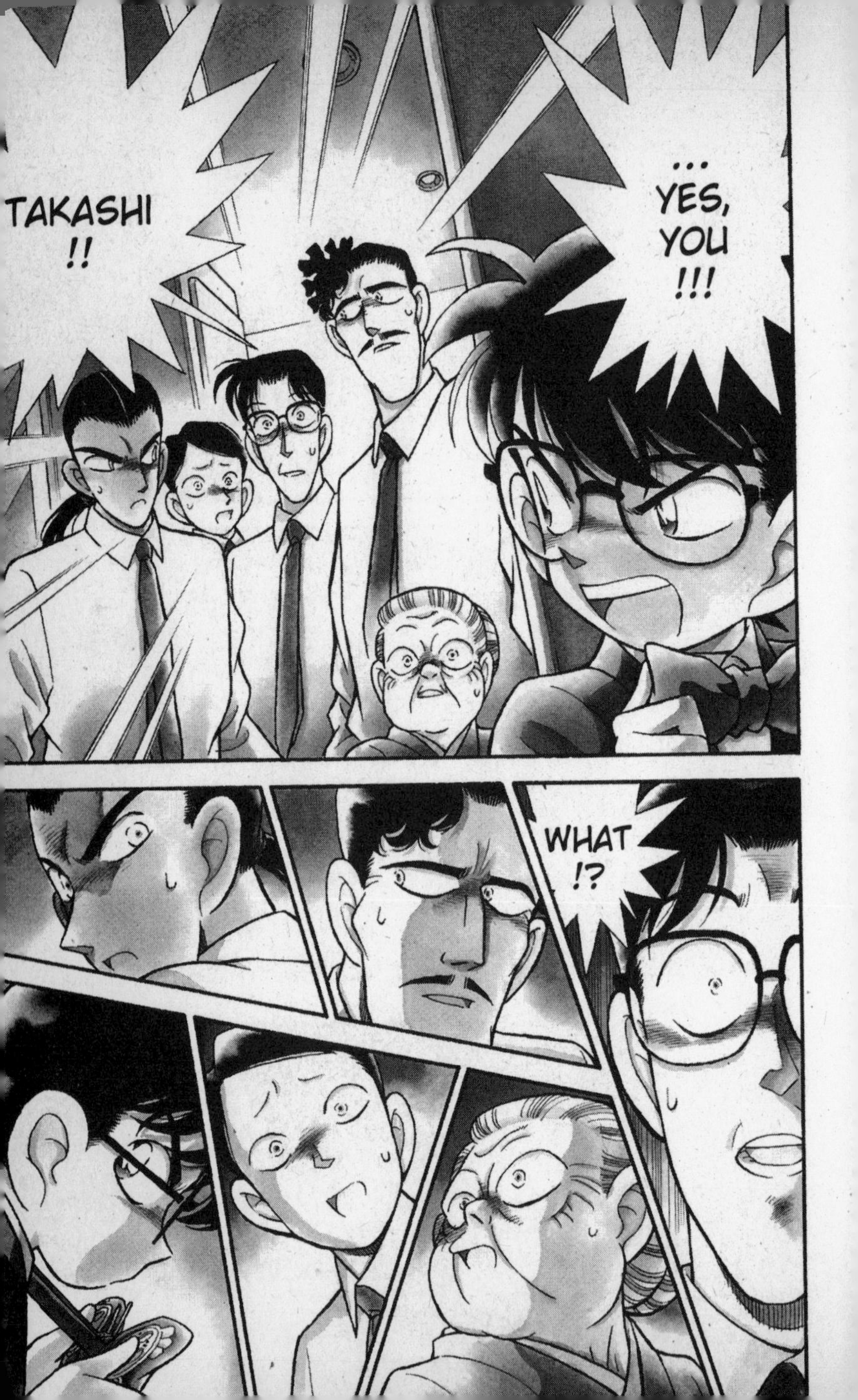
... YES, YOU !!!
TAKASHI !!
WHAT !?

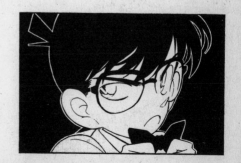

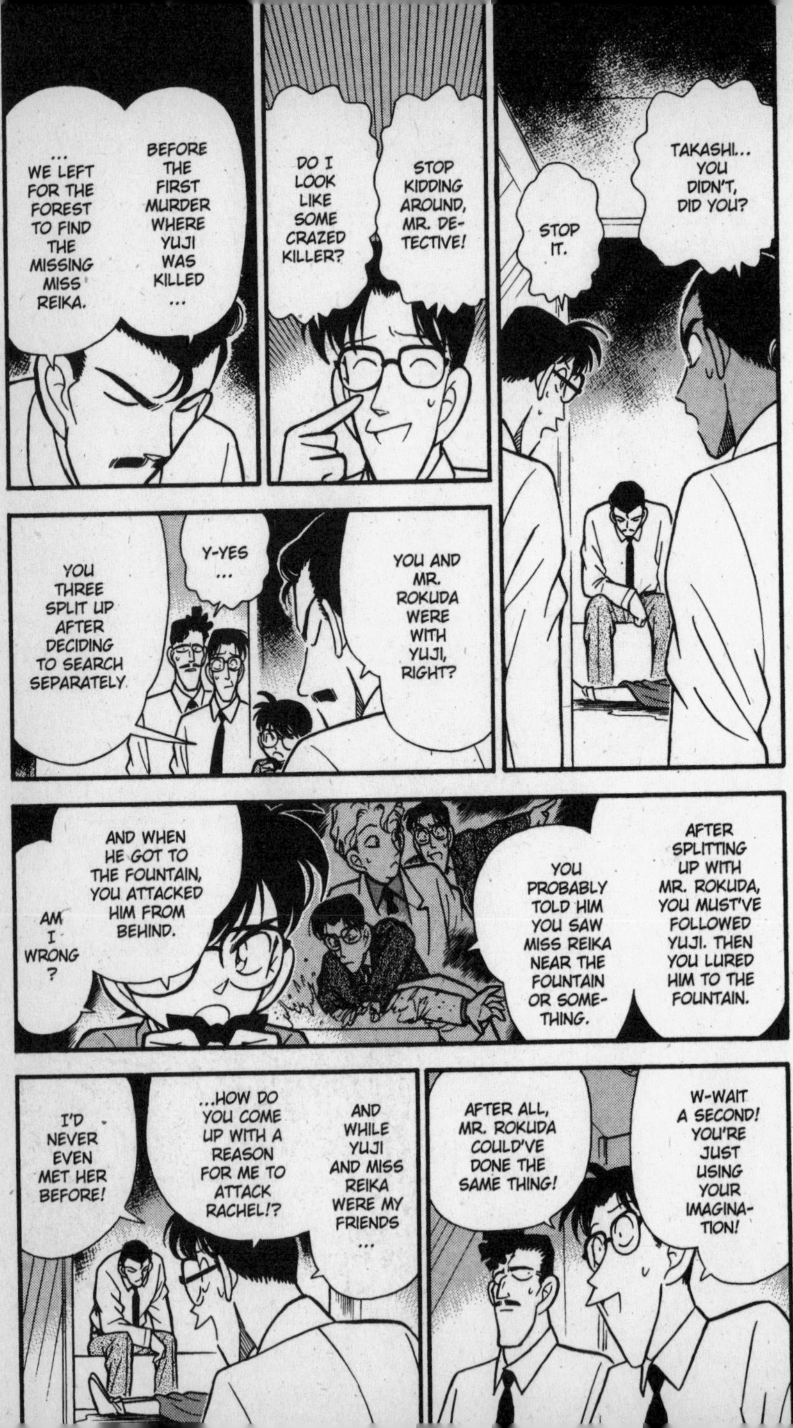
TAKASHI... YOU DIDN'T, DID YOU?
STOP IT.
STOP KIDDING AROUND, MR. DETECTIVE!
DO I LOOK LIKE SOME CRAZED KILLER?
BEFORE THE FIRST MURDER WHERE YUJI WAS KILLED ...
... WE LEFT FOR THE FOREST TO FIND THE MISSING MISS REIKA.
YOU AND MR. ROKUDA WERE WITH YUJI, RIGHT?
Y-YES ...
YOU THREE SPLIT UP AFTER DECIDING TO SEARCH SEPARATELY.
AFTER SPLITTING UP WITH MR. ROKUDA, YOU MUST'VE FOLLOWED YUJI. THEN YOU LURED HIM TO THE FOUNTAIN.
YOU PROBABLY TOLD HIM YOU SAW MISS REIKA NEAR THE FOUNTAIN OR SOMETHING.
AND WHEN HE GOT TO THE FOUNTAIN, YOU ATTACKED HIM FROM BEHIND.
AM I WRONG?
W-WAIT A SECOND! YOU'RE JUST USING YOUR IMAGINATION!
AFTER ALL, MR. ROKUDA COULD'VE DONE THE SAME THING!
AND WHILE YUJI AND MISS REIKA WERE MY FRIENDS ...
...HOW DO YOU COME UP WITH A REASON FOR ME TO ATTACK RACHEL!?
I'D NEVER EVEN MET HER BEFORE!

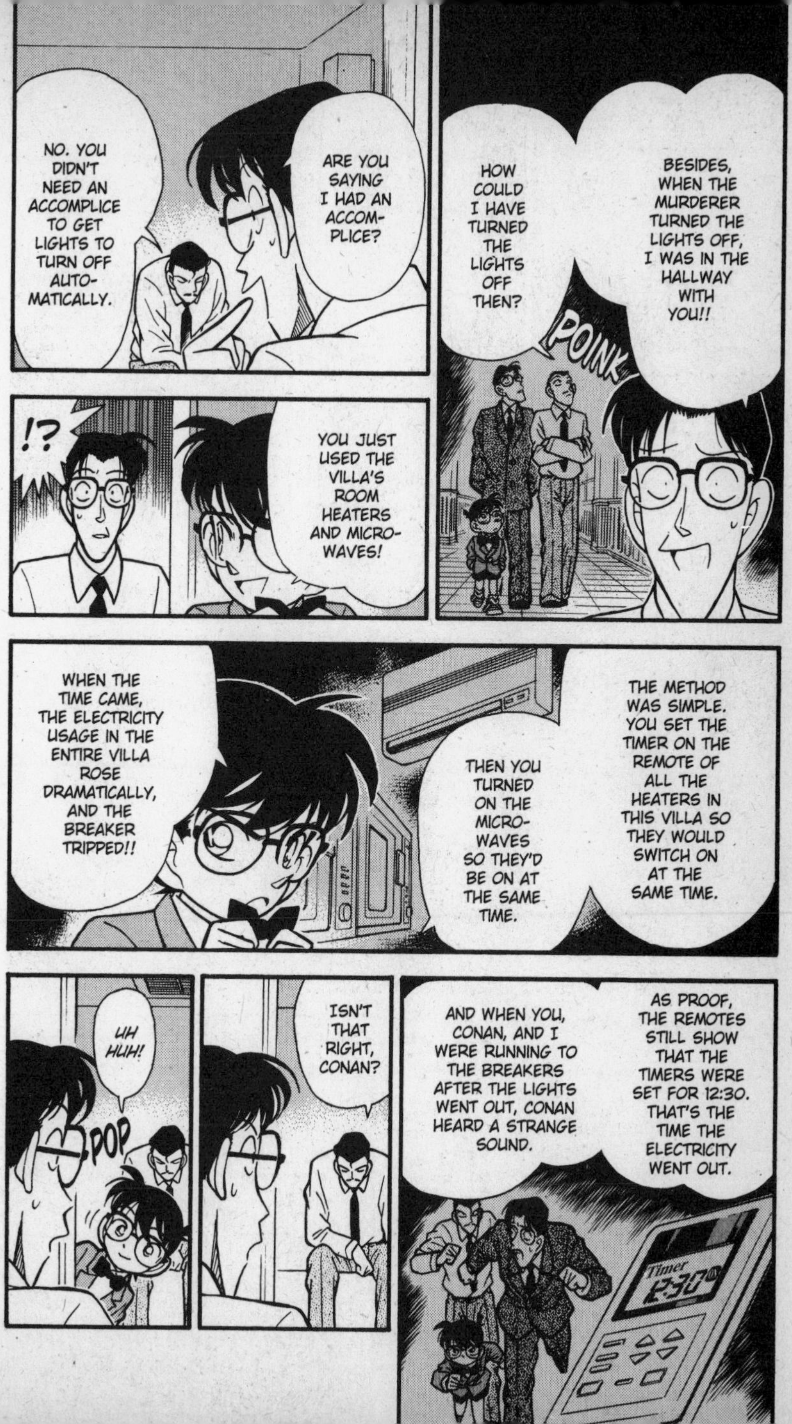
BESIDES, WHEN THE MURDERER TURNED THE LIGHTS OFF, I WAS IN THE HALLWAY WITH YOU!!
HOW COULD I HAVE TURNED THE LIGHTS OFF THEN?
POINK
ARE YOU SAYING I HAD AN ACCOMPLICE?
NO. YOU DIDN'T NEED AN ACCOMPLICE TO GET LIGHTS TO TURN OFF AUTOMATICALLY.
YOU JUST USED THE VILLA'S ROOM HEATERS AND MICROWAVES!
!?
THE METHOD WAS SIMPLE. YOU SET THE TIMER ON THE REMOTE OF ALL THE HEATERS IN THIS VILLA SO THEY WOULD SWITCH ON AT THE SAME TIME.
THEN YOU TURNED ON THE MICROWAVES SO THEY'D BE ON AT THE SAME TIME.
WHEN THE TIME CAME, THE ELECTRICITY USAGE IN THE ENTIRE VILLA ROSE DRAMATICALLY, AND THE BREAKER TRIPPED!!
AS PROOF, THE REMOTES STILL SHOW THAT THE TIMERS WERE SET FOR 12:30. THAT'S THE TIME THE ELECTRICITY WENT OUT.
AND WHEN YOU, CONAN, AND I WERE RUNNING TO THE BREAKERS AFTER THE LIGHTS WENT OUT, CONAN HEARD A STRANGE SOUND.
Timer
ISN'T THAT RIGHT, CONAN?
UH HUH!
POP

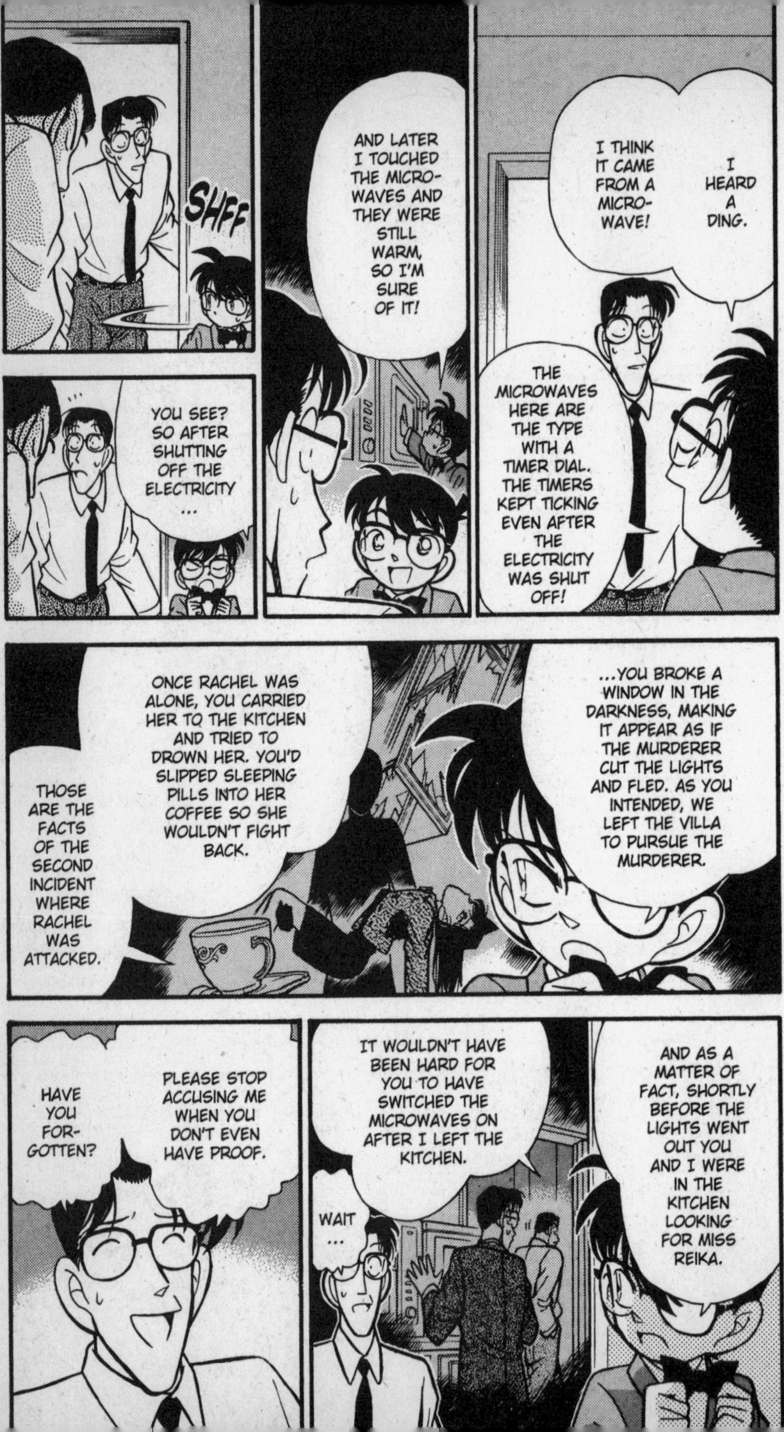
I HEARD A DING.
I THINK IT CAME FROM A MICROWAVE!
THE MICROWAVES HERE ARE THE TYPE WITH A TIMER DIAL. THE TIMERS KEPT TICKING EVEN AFTER THE ELECTRICITY WAS SHUT OFF!
AND LATER I TOUCHED THE MICROWAVES AND THEY WERE STILL WARM, SO I'M SURE OF IT!
SHFF
YOU SEE? SO AFTER SHUTTING OFF THE ELECTRICITY ...
...YOU BROKE A WINDOW IN THE DARKNESS, MAKING IT APPEAR AS IF THE MURDERER CUT THE LIGHTS AND FLED. AS YOU INTENDED, WE LEFT THE VILLA TO PURSUE THE MURDERER.
ONCE RACHEL WAS ALONE, YOU CARRIED HER TO THE KITCHEN AND TRIED TO DROWN HER. YOU'D SLIPPED SLEEPING PILLS INTO HER COFFEE SO SHE WOULDN'T FIGHT BACK.
THOSE ARE THE FACTS OF THE SECOND INCIDENT WHERE RACHEL WAS ATTACKED.
AND AS A MATTER OF FACT, SHORTLY BEFORE THE LIGHTS WENT OUT YOU AND I WERE IN THE KITCHEN LOOKING FOR MISS REIKA.
IT WOULDN'T HAVE BEEN HARD FOR YOU TO HAVE SWITCHED THE MICROWAVES ON AFTER I LEFT THE KITCHEN.
WAIT ...
PLEASE STOP ACCUSING ME WHEN YOU DON'T EVEN HAVE PROOF.
HAVE YOU FOR-GOTTEN?

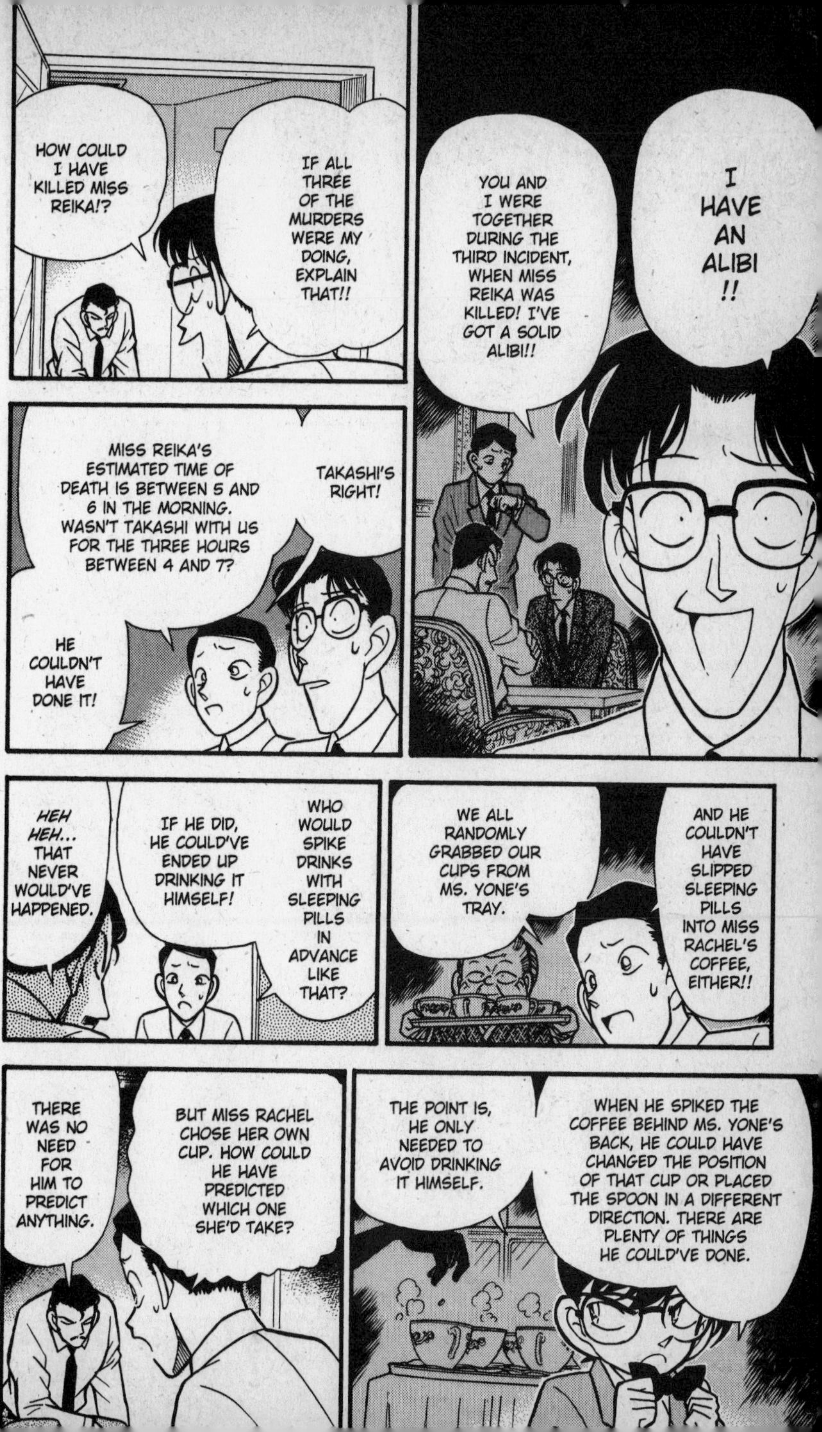
I HAVE AN ALIBI!!
YOU AND I WERE TOGETHER DURING THE THIRD INCIDENT, WHEN MISS REIKA WAS KILLED! I'VE GOT A SOLID ALIBI!!
IF ALL THREE OF THE MURDERS WERE MY DOING, EXPLAIN THAT!!
HOW COULD I HAVE KILLED MISS REIKA!?
TAKASHI'S RIGHT!
MISS REIKA'S ESTIMATED TIME OF DEATH IS BETWEEN 5 AND 6 IN THE MORNING. WASN'T TAKASHI WITH US FOR THE THREE HOURS BETWEEN 4 AND 7?
HE COULDN'T HAVE DONE IT!
AND HE COULDN'T HAVE SLIPPED SLEEPING PILLS INTO MISS RACHEL'S COFFEE, EITHER!!
WE ALL RANDOMLY GRABBED OUR CUPS FROM MS. YONE'S TRAY.
WHO WOULD SPIKE DRINKS WITH SLEEPING PILLS IN ADVANCE LIKE THAT?
IF HE DID, HE COULD'VE ENDED UP DRINKING IT HIMSELF!
HEH HEH... THAT NEVER WOULD'VE HAPPENED.
WHEN HE SPIKED THE COFFEE BEHIND MS. YONE'S BACK, HE COULD HAVE CHANGED THE POSITION OF THAT CUP OR PLACED THE SPOON IN A DIFFERENT DIRECTION. THERE ARE PLENTY OF THINGS HE COULD'VE DONE.
THE POINT IS, HE ONLY NEEDED TO AVOID DRINKING IT HIMSELF.
BUT MISS RACHEL CHOSE HER OWN CUP. HOW COULD HE HAVE PREDICTED WHICH ONE SHE'D TAKE?
THERE WAS NO NEED FOR HIM TO PREDICT ANYTHING.

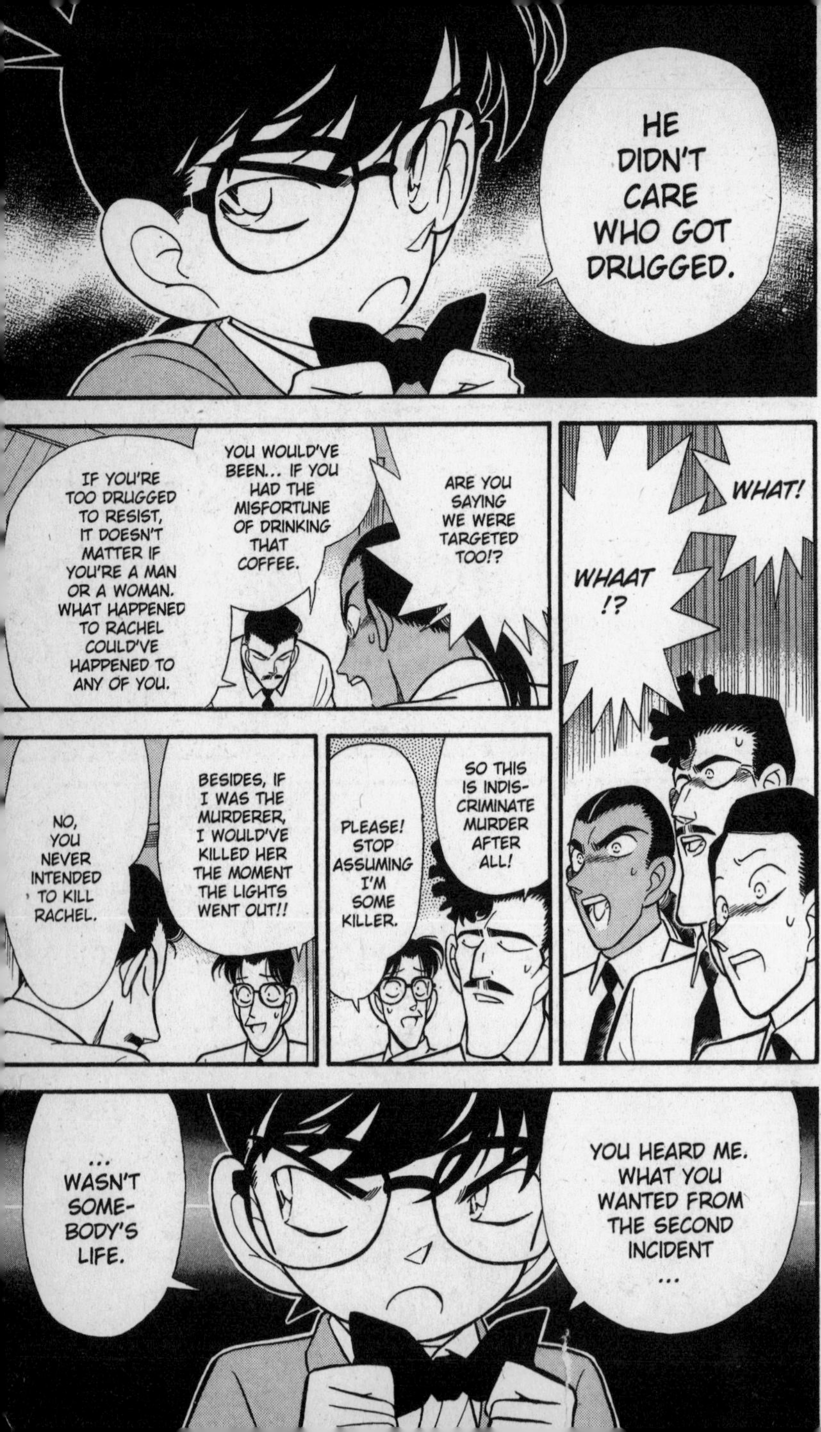
HE DIDN'T CARE WHO GOT DRUGGED.
WHAT!
WHAAT !?
ARE YOU SAYING WE WERE TARGETED TOO!?
YOU WOULD'VE BEEN... IF YOU HAD THE MISFORTUNE OF DRINKING THAT COFFEE.
IF YOU'RE TOO DRUGGED TO RESIST, IT DOESN'T MATTER IF YOU'RE A MAN OR A WOMAN. WHAT HAPPENED TO RACHEL COULD'VE HAPPENED TO ANY OF YOU.
SO THIS IS INDIS-CRIMINATE MURDER AFTER ALL!
PLEASE! STOP ASSUMING I'M SOME KILLER.
BESIDES, IF I WAS THE MURDERER, I WOULD'VE KILLED HER THE MOMENT THE LIGHTS WENT OUT!!
NO, YOU NEVER INTENDED TO KILL RACHEL.
YOU HEARD ME. WHAT YOU WANTED FROM THE SECOND INCIDENT ...
... WASN'T SOME-BODY'S LIFE.

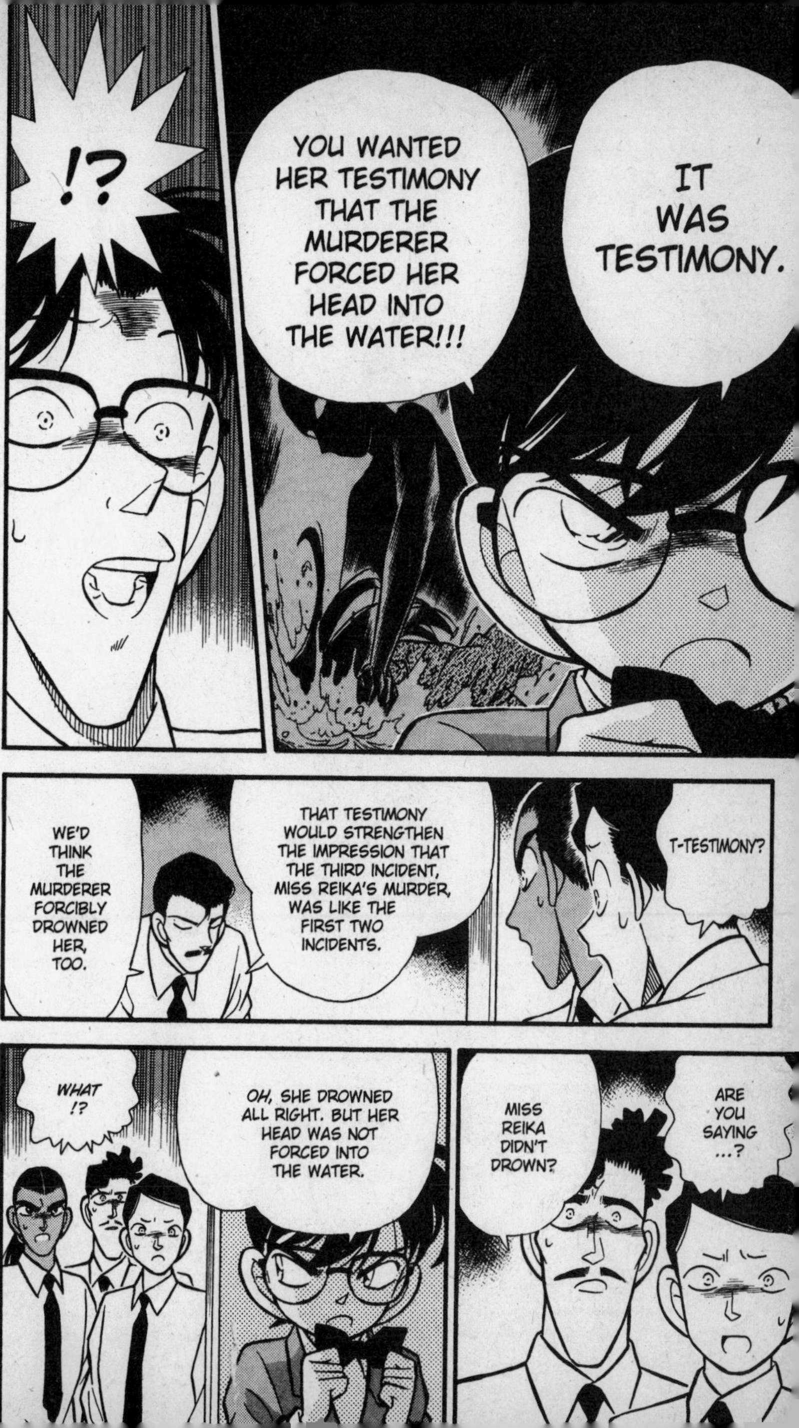
IT WAS TESTIMONY.
YOU WANTED HER TESTIMONY THAT THE MURDERER FORCED HER HEAD INTO THE WATER!!!
!?
T-TESTIMONY?
THAT TESTIMONY WOULD STRENGTHEN THE IMPRESSION THAT THE THIRD INCIDENT, MISS REIKA'S MURDER, WAS LIKE THE FIRST TWO INCIDENTS.
WE'D THINK THE MURDERER FORCIBLY DROWNED HER, TOO.
ARE YOU SAYING ...?
MISS REIKA DIDN'T DROWN?
OH, SHE DROWNED ALL RIGHT. BUT HER HEAD WAS NOT FORCED INTO THE WATER.
WHAT !?

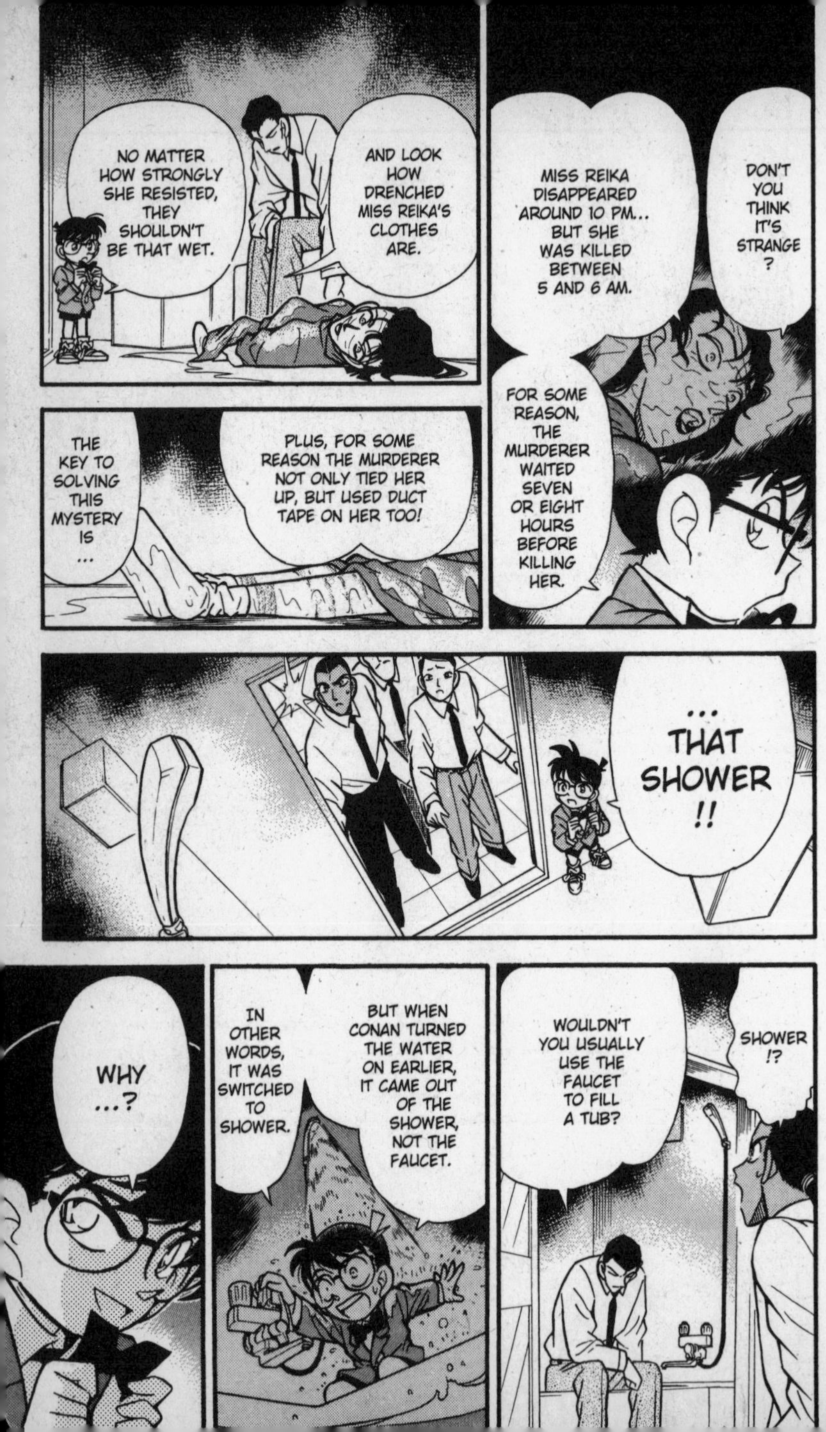
DON'T YOU THINK IT'S STRANGE?
MISS REIKA DISAPPEARED AROUND 10 PM... BUT SHE WAS KILLED BETWEEN 5 AND 6 AM.
FOR SOME REASON, THE MURDERER WAITED SEVEN OR EIGHT HOURS BEFORE KILLING HER.
AND LOOK HOW DRENCHED MISS REIKA'S CLOTHES ARE.
NO MATTER HOW STRONGLY SHE RESISTED, THEY SHOULDN'T BE THAT WET.
PLUS, FOR SOME REASON THE MURDERER NOT ONLY TIED HER UP, BUT USED DUCT TAPE ON HER TOO!
THE KEY TO SOLVING THIS MYSTERY IS ...
... THAT SHOWER !!
SHOWER !?
WOULDN'T YOU USUALLY USE THE FAUCET TO FILL A TUB?
BUT WHEN CONAN TURNED THE WATER ON EARLIER, IT CAME OUT OF THE SHOWER, NOT THE FAUCET.
IN OTHER WORDS, IT WAS SWITCHED TO SHOWER.
WHY ...?

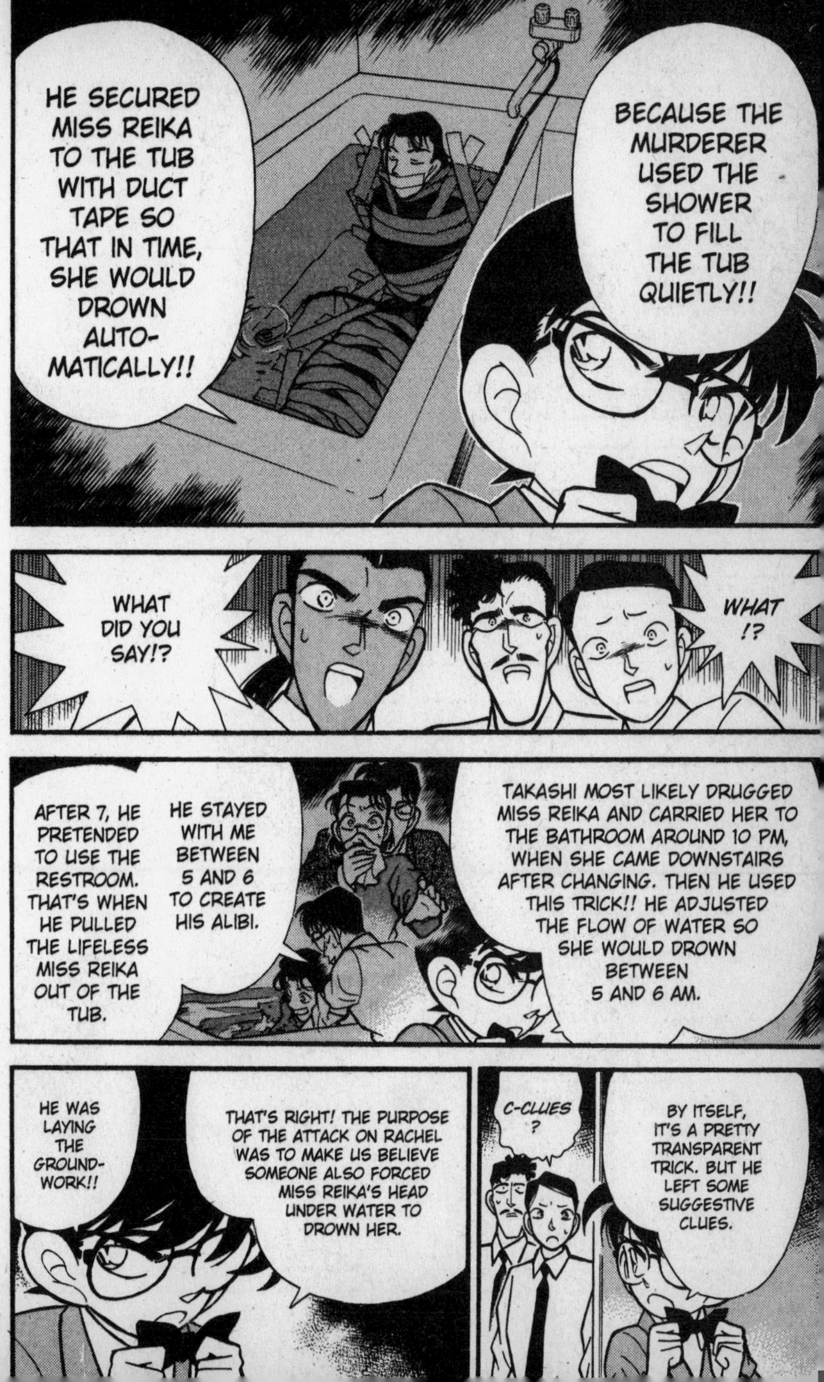
BECAUSE THE MURDERER USED THE SHOWER TO FILL THE TUB QUIETLY!!
HE SECURED MISS REIKA TO THE TUB WITH DUCT TAPE SO THAT IN TIME, SHE WOULD DROWN AUTO-MATICALLY!!
WHAT!?
WHAT DID YOU SAY!?
TAKASHI MOST LIKELY DRUGGED MISS REIKA AND CARRIED HER TO THE BATHROOM AROUND 10 PM, WHEN SHE CAME DOWNSTAIRS AFTER CHANGING. THEN HE USED THIS TRICK!! HE ADJUSTED THE FLOW OF WATER SO SHE WOULD DROWN BETWEEN 5 AND 6 AM.
HE STAYED WITH ME BETWEEN 5 AND 6 TO CREATE HIS ALIBI.
AFTER 7, HE PRETENDED TO USE THE RESTROOM. THAT'S WHEN HE PULLED THE LIFELESS MISS REIKA OUT OF THE TUB.
BY ITSELF, IT'S A PRETTY TRANSPARENT TRICK. BUT HE LEFT SOME SUGGESTIVE CLUES.
C-CLUES?
THAT'S RIGHT! THE PURPOSE OF THE ATTACK ON RACHEL WAS TO MAKE US BELIEVE SOMEONE ALSO FORCED MISS REIKA'S HEAD UNDER WATER TO DROWN HER.
HE WAS LAYING THE GROUND-WORK!!

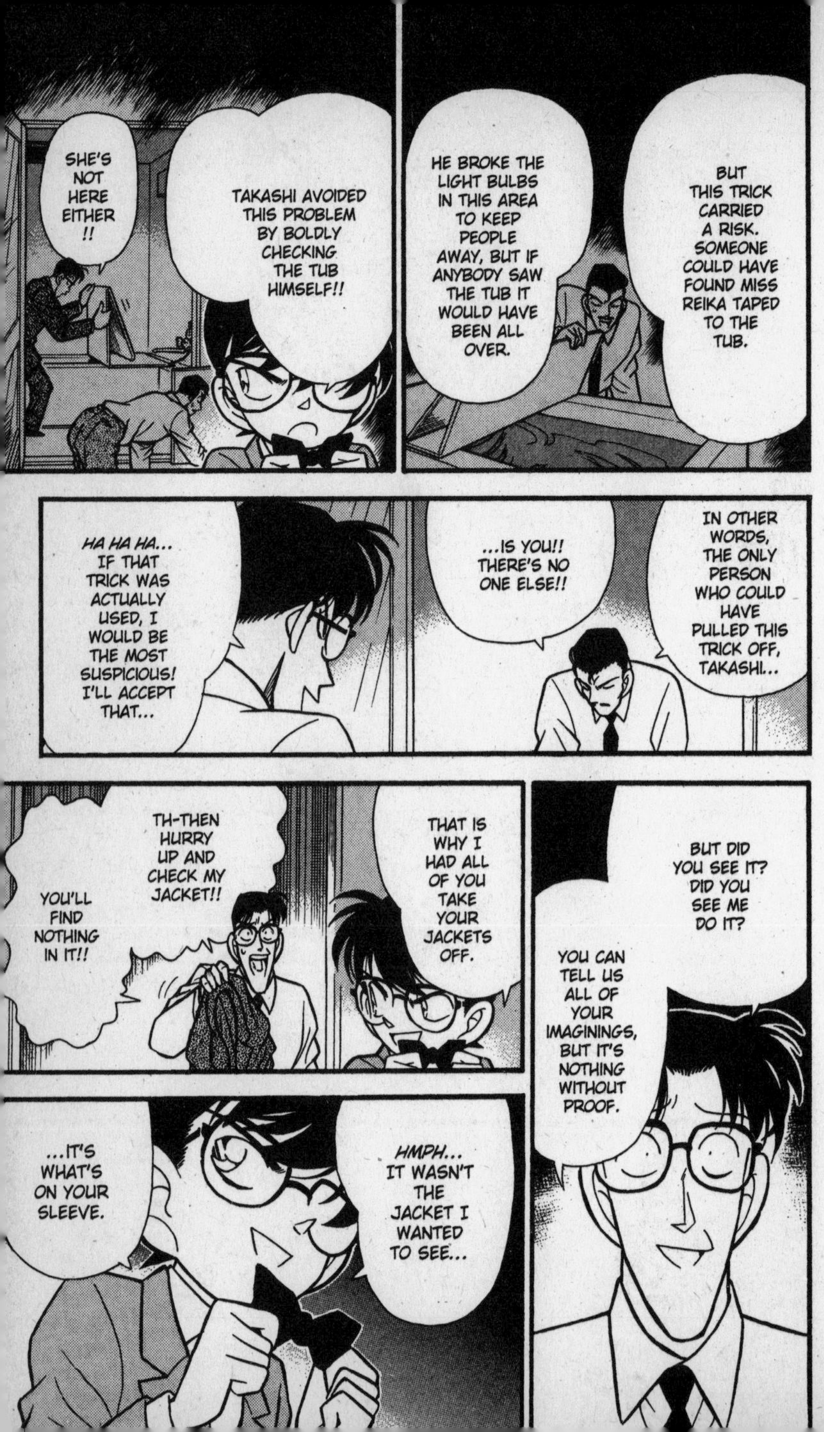
BUT THIS TRICK CARRIED A RISK. SOMEONE COULD HAVE FOUND MISS REIKA TAPED TO THE TUB.
HE BROKE THE LIGHT BULBS IN THIS AREA TO KEEP PEOPLE AWAY, BUT IF ANYBODY SAW THE TUB IT WOULD HAVE BEEN ALL OVER.
TAKASHI AVOIDED THIS PROBLEM BY BOLDLY CHECKING THE TUB HIMSELF!!
SHE'S NOT HERE EITHER!!
IN OTHER WORDS, THE ONLY PERSON WHO COULD HAVE PULLED THIS TRICK OFF, TAKASHI...
...IS YOU!! THERE'S NO ONE ELSE!!
HA HA HA... IF THAT TRICK WAS ACTUALLY USED, I WOULD BE THE MOST SUSPICIOUS! I'LL ACCEPT THAT...
BUT DID YOU SEE IT? DID YOU SEE ME DO IT?
YOU CAN TELL US ALL OF YOUR IMAGININGS, BUT IT'S NOTHING WITHOUT PROOF.
THAT IS WHY I HAD ALL OF YOU TAKE YOUR JACKETS OFF.
TH-THEN HURRY UP AND CHECK MY JACKET!!
YOU'LL FIND NOTHING IN IT!!
HMPH... IT WASN'T THE JACKET I WANTED TO SEE...
...IT'S WHAT'S ON YOUR SLEEVE.

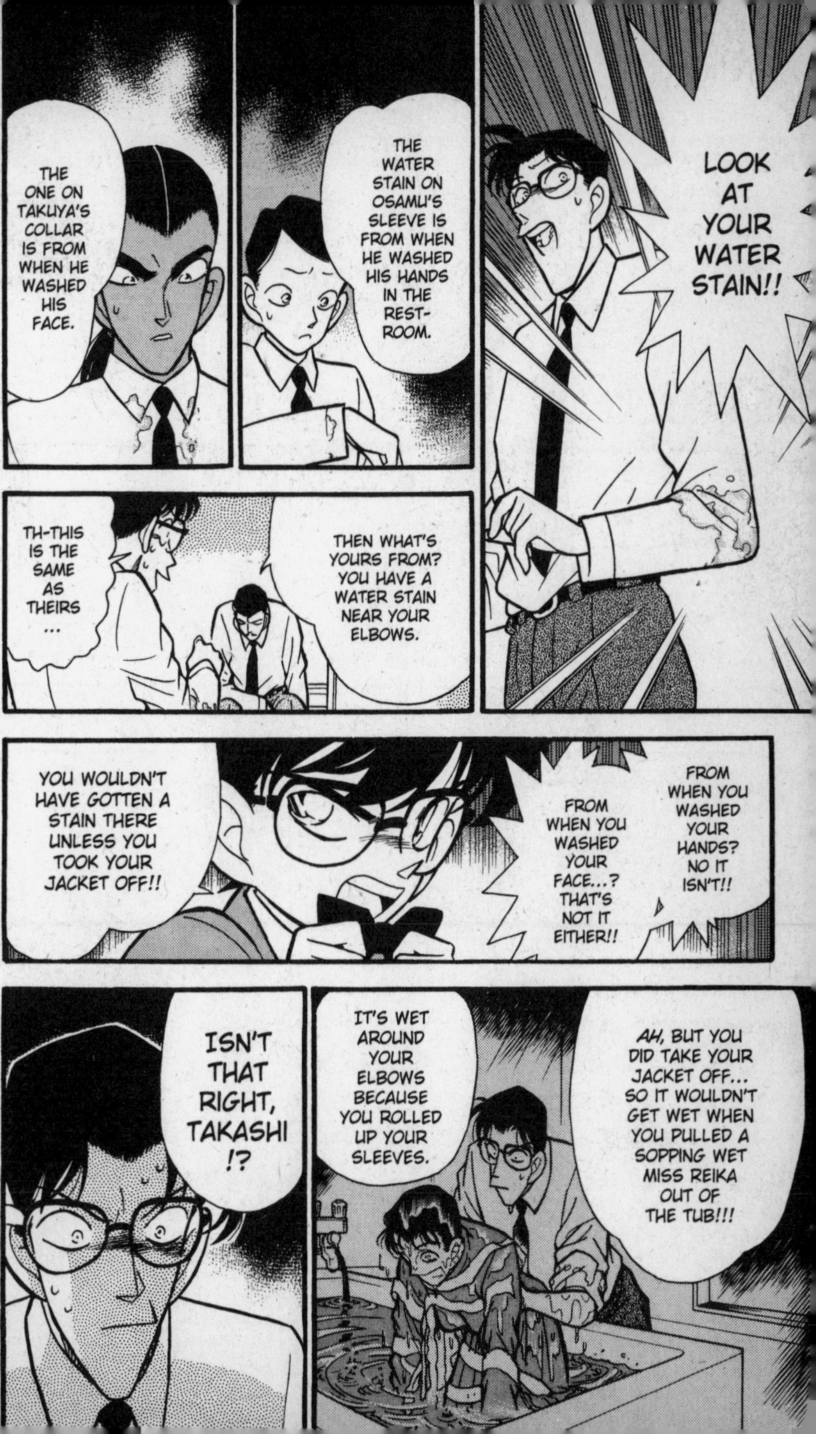
LOOK AT YOUR WATER STAIN!!
THE WATER STAIN ON OSAMU'S SLEEVE IS FROM WHEN HE WASHED HIS HANDS IN THE REST-ROOM.
THE ONE ON TAKUYA'S COLLAR IS FROM WHEN HE WASHED HIS FACE.
THEN WHAT'S YOURS FROM? YOU HAVE A WATER STAIN NEAR YOUR ELBOWS.
TH-THIS IS THE SAME AS THEIRS ...
FROM WHEN YOU WASHED YOUR HANDS? NO IT ISN'T!!
FROM WHEN YOU WASHED YOUR FACE...? THAT'S NOT IT EITHER!!
YOU WOULDN'T HAVE GOTTEN A STAIN THERE UNLESS YOU TOOK YOUR JACKET OFF!!
AH, BUT YOU DID TAKE YOUR JACKET OFF... SO IT WOULDN'T GET WET WHEN YOU PULLED A SOPPING WET MISS REIKA OUT OF THE TUB!!!
IT'S WET AROUND YOUR ELBOWS BECAUSE YOU ROLLED UP YOUR SLEEVES.
ISN'T THAT RIGHT, TAKASHI !?

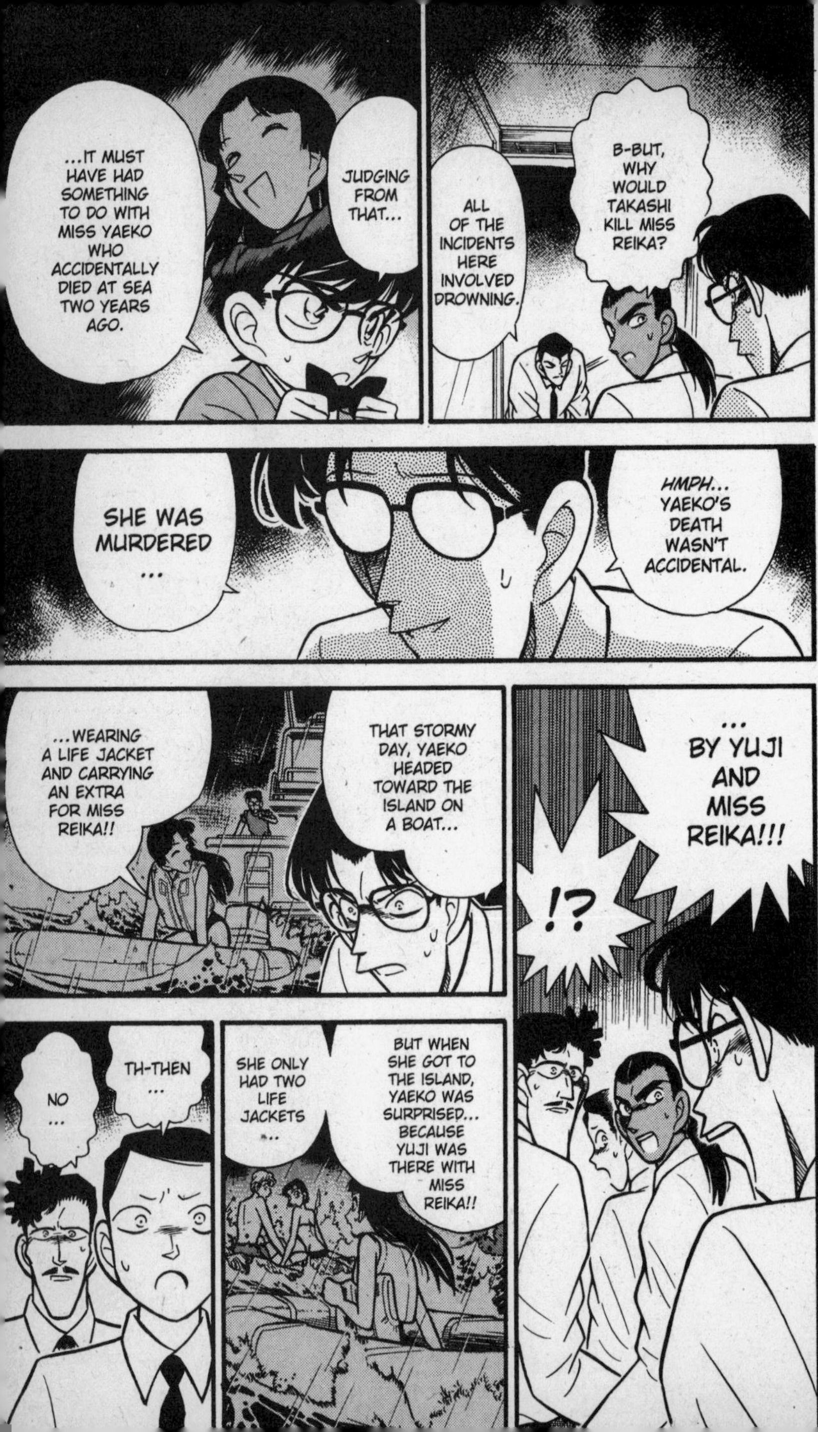
B-BUT, WHY WOULD TAKASHI KILL MISS REIKA?
ALL OF THE INCIDENTS HERE INVOLVED DROWNING.
JUDGING FROM THAT...
...IT MUST HAVE HAD SOMETHING TO DO WITH MISS YAEKO WHO ACCIDENTALLY DIED AT SEA TWO YEARS AGO.
HMPH... YAEKO'S DEATH WASN'T ACCIDENTAL.
SHE WAS MURDERED ...
... BY YUJI AND MISS REIKA!!!
!?
THAT STORMY DAY, YAEKO HEADED TOWARD THE ISLAND ON A BOAT...
...WEARING A LIFE JACKET AND CARRYING AN EXTRA FOR MISS REIKA!!
BUT WHEN SHE GOT TO THE ISLAND, YAEKO WAS SURPRISED... BECAUSE YUJI WAS THERE WITH MISS REIKA!!
SHE ONLY HAD TWO LIFE JACKETS ...
TH-THEN ...
NO ...

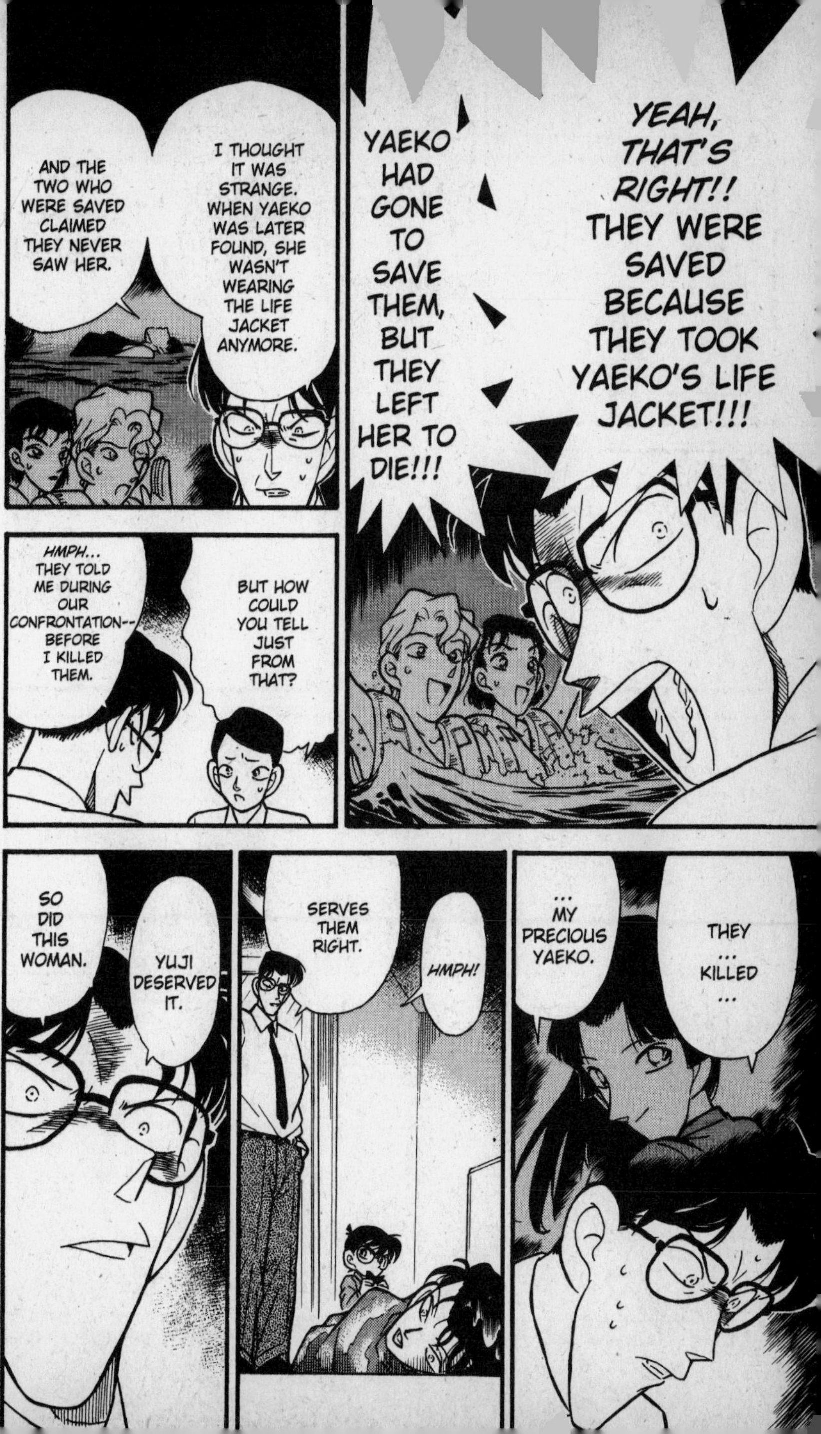
YEAH, THAT'S RIGHT!! THEY WERE SAVED BECAUSE THEY TOOK YAEKO'S LIFE JACKET!!!
YAEKO HAD GONE TO SAVE THEM, BUT THEY LEFT HER TO DIE!!!
I THOUGHT IT WAS STRANGE. WHEN YAEKO WAS LATER FOUND, SHE WASN'T WEARING THE LIFE JACKET ANYMORE.
AND THE TWO WHO WERE SAVED CLAIMED THEY NEVER SAW HER.
BUT HOW COULD YOU TELL JUST FROM THAT?
HMPH... THEY TOLD ME DURING OUR CONFRONTATION-- BEFORE I KILLED THEM.
THEY ... KILLED ...
... MY PRECIOUS YAEKO.
HMPH!
SERVES THEM RIGHT.
YUJI DESERVED IT.
SO DID THIS WOMAN.

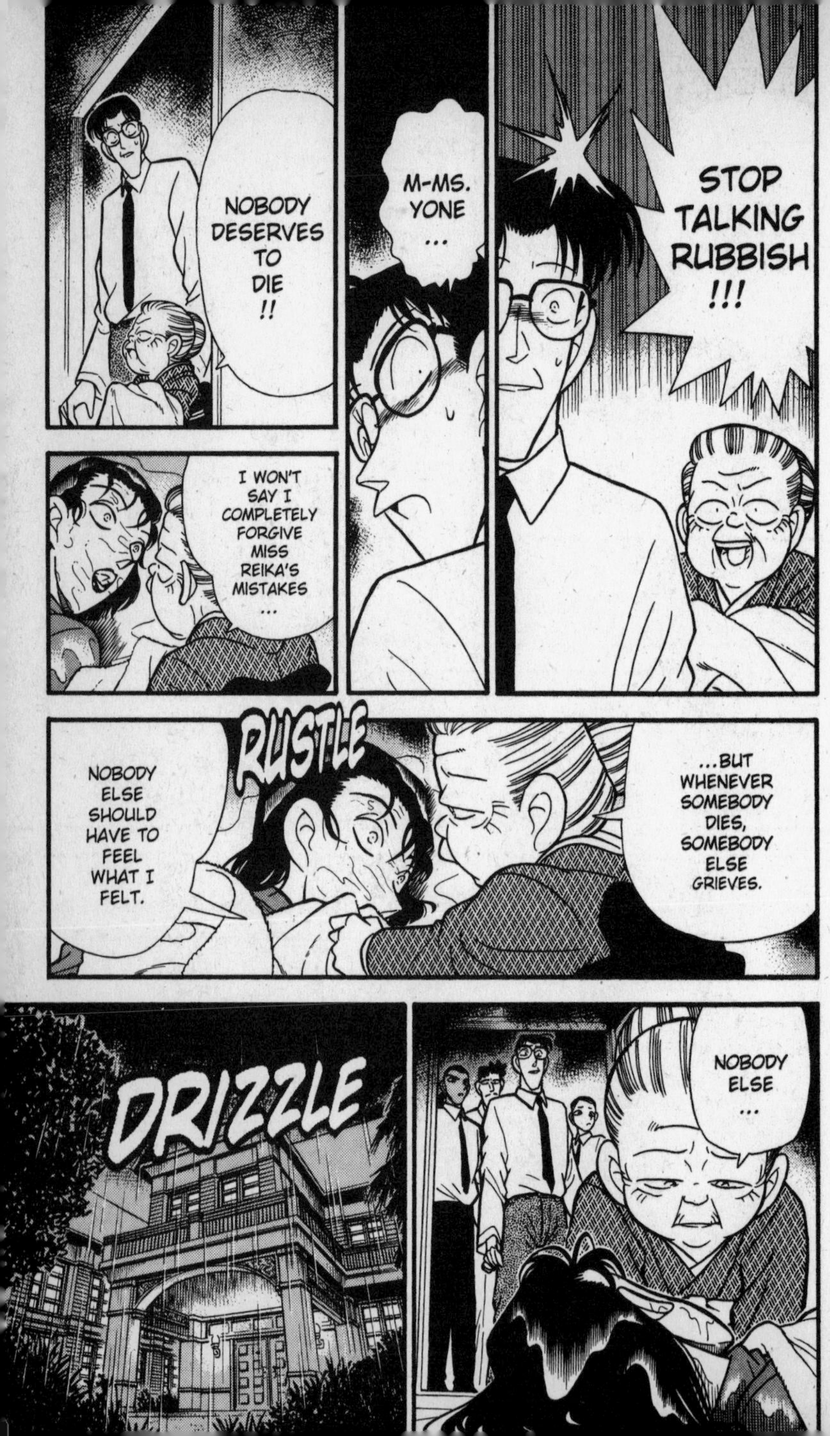
STOP TALKING RUBBISH !!!
M-MS. YONE ...
NOBODY DESERVES TO DIE !!
I WON'T SAY I COMPLETELY FORGIVE MISS REIKA'S MISTAKES ...
...BUT WHENEVER SOMEBODY DIES, SOMEBODY ELSE GRIEVES.
RUSTLE
NOBODY ELSE SHOULD HAVE TO FEEL WHAT I FELT.
NOBODY ELSE ...
DRIZZLE

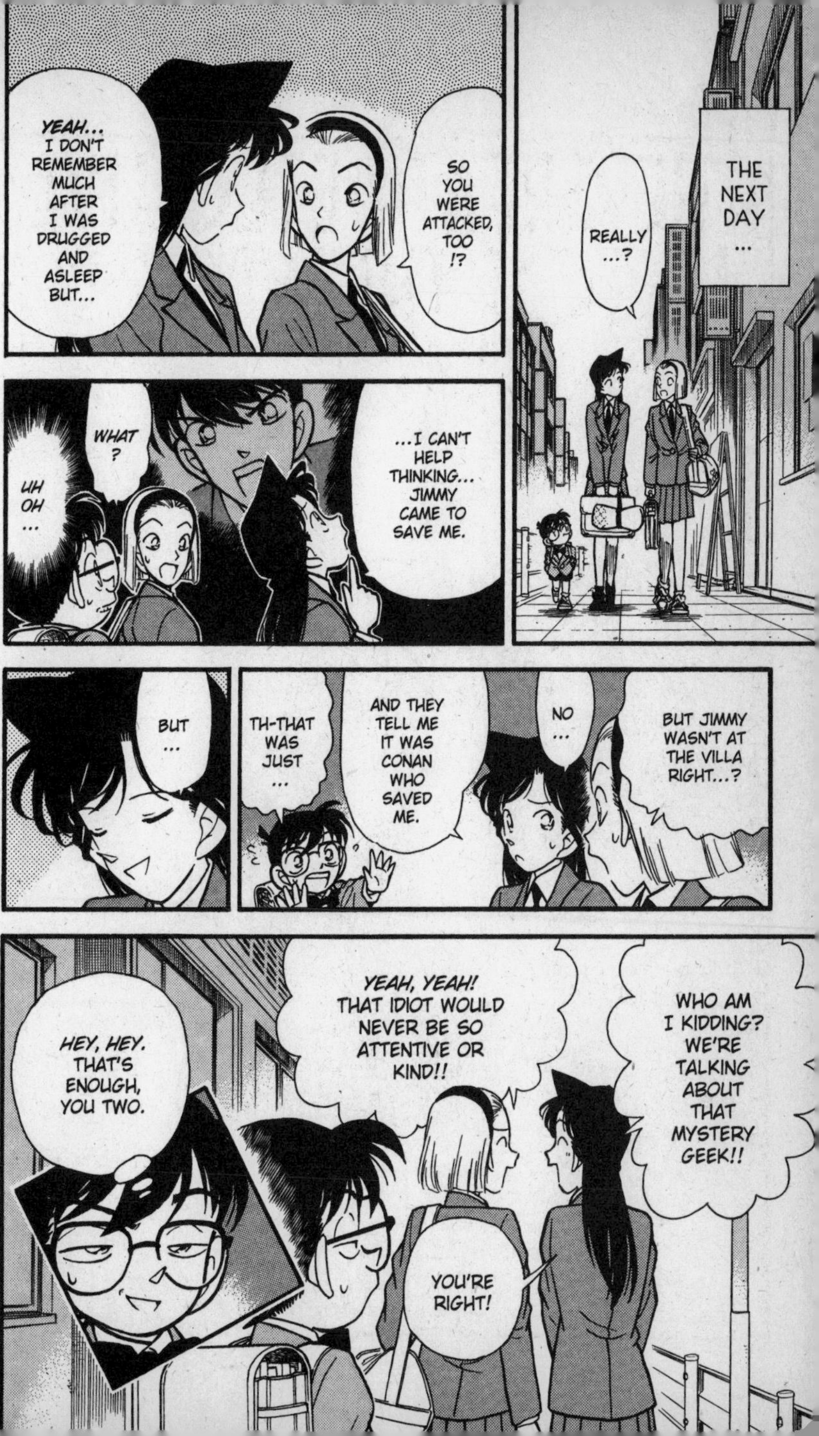
THE NEXT DAY...
REALLY...?
SO YOU WERE ATTACKED, TOO!?
YEAH... I DON'T REMEMBER MUCH AFTER I WAS DRUGGED AND ASLEEP BUT...
...I CAN'T HELP THINKING... JIMMY CAME TO SAVE ME.
WHAT?
UH OH...
BUT JIMMY WASN'T AT THE VILLA RIGHT...?
NO...
AND THEY TELL ME IT WAS CONAN WHO SAVED ME.
TH-THAT WAS JUST...
BUT...
WHO AM I KIDDING? WE'RE TALKING ABOUT THAT MYSTERY GEEK!!
YEAH, YEAH! THAT IDIOT WOULD NEVER BE SO ATTENTIVE OR KIND!!
YOU'RE RIGHT!
HEY, HEY. THAT'S ENOUGH, YOU TWO.

FILE 2:

THE GREAT DETECTIVE OF THE WEST

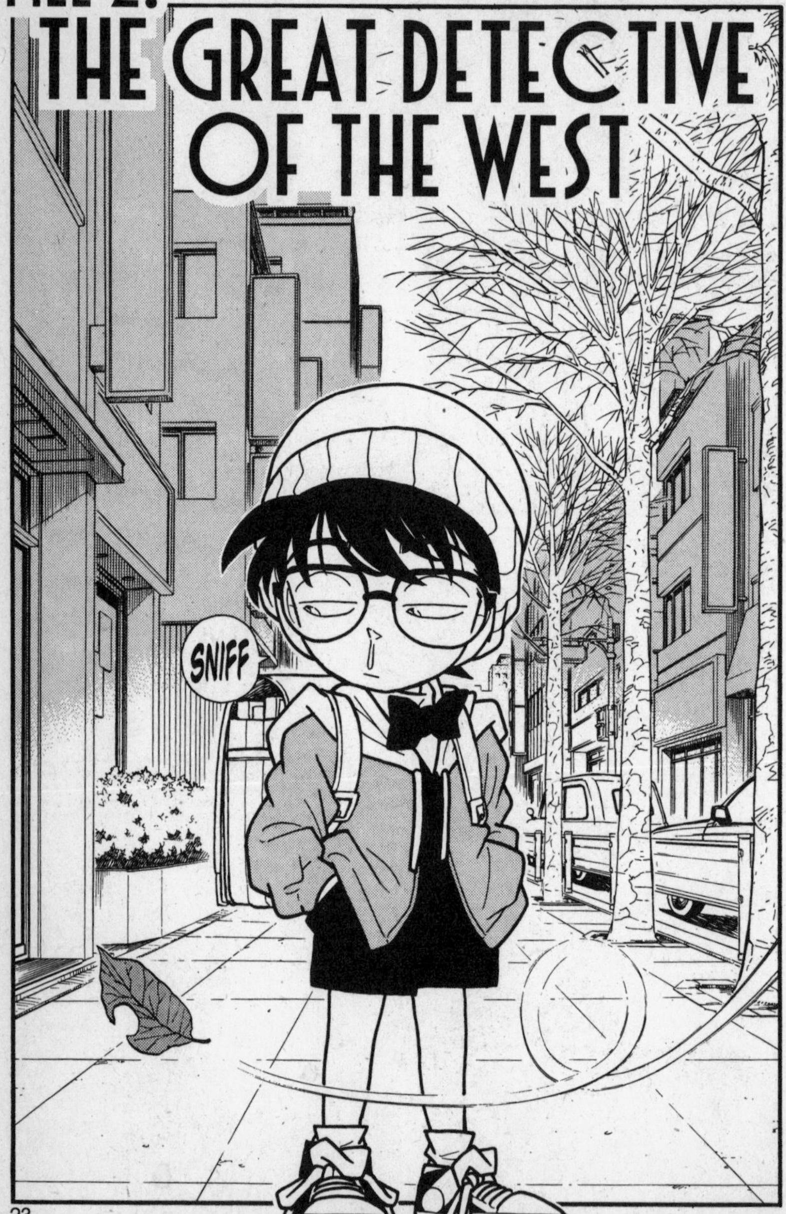
SNIFF

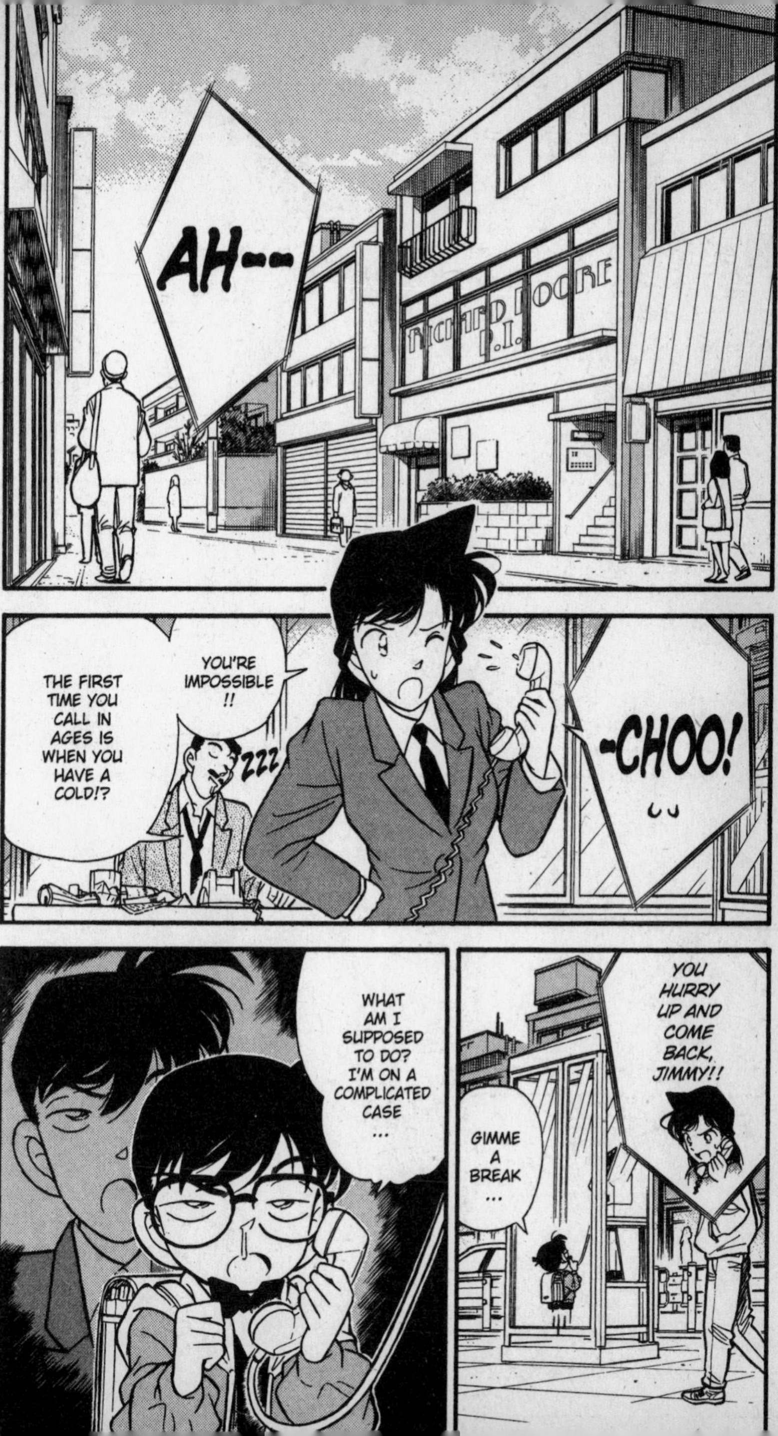
AH--
RICHARD MOORE P.I.
-CHOO!
YOU'RE IMPOSSIBLE!!
THE FIRST TIME YOU CALL IN AGES IS WHEN YOU HAVE A COLD!?
ZZZ
YOU HURRY UP AND COME BACK, JIMMY!!
GIMME A BREAK ...
WHAT AM I SUPPOSED TO DO? I'M ON A COMPLICATED CASE ...

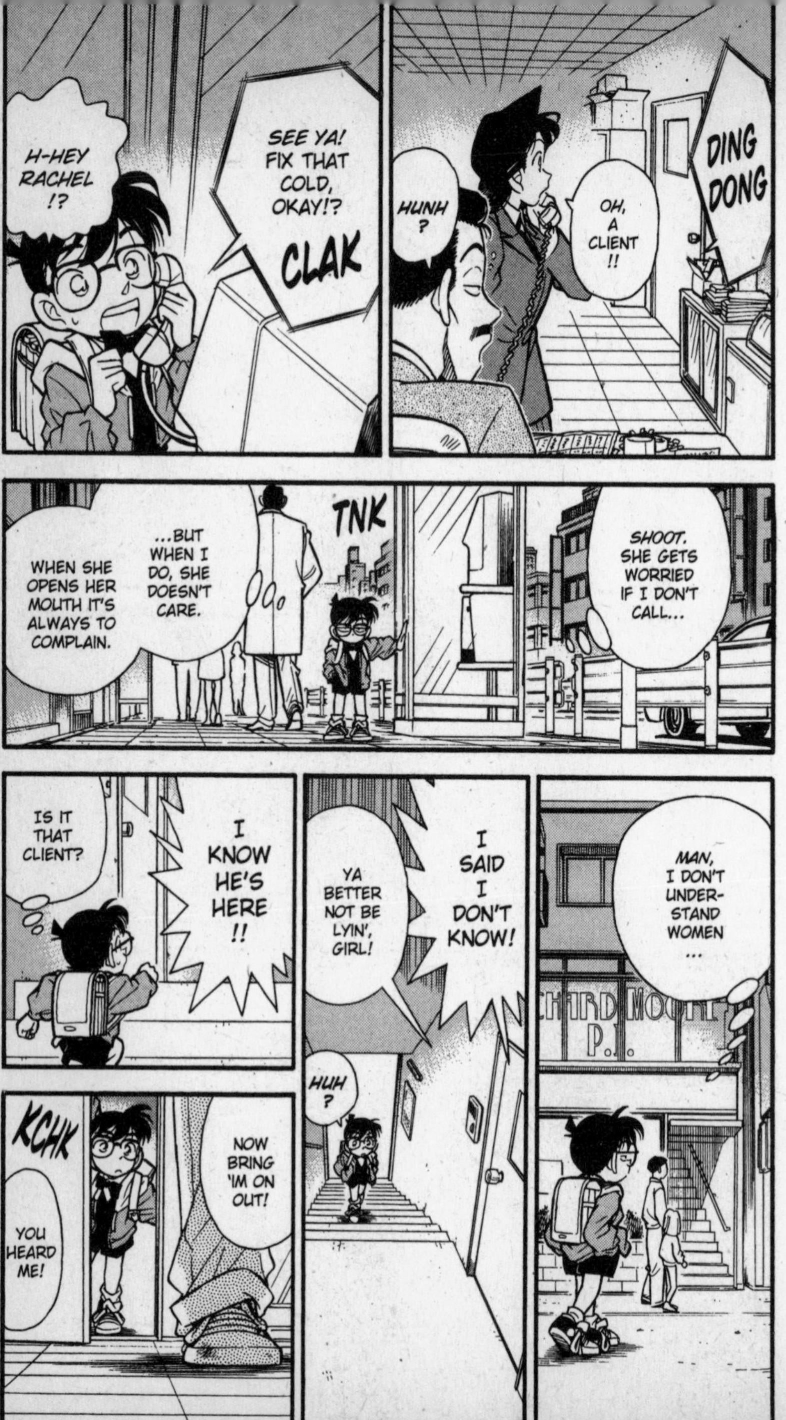
DING DONG
OH, A CLIENT!!
HUNH ?
SEE YA! FIX THAT COLD, OKAY!?
CLAK
H-HEY RACHEL !?
SHOOT. SHE GETS WORRIED IF I DON'T CALL...
TNK
...BUT WHEN I DO, SHE DOESN'T CARE.
WHEN SHE OPENS HER MOUTH IT'S ALWAYS TO COMPLAIN.
MAN, I DON'T UNDER-STAND WOMEN ...
I SAID I DON'T KNOW!
YA BETTER NOT BE LYIN', GIRL!
HUH ?
I KNOW HE'S HERE !!
IS IT THAT CLIENT?
NOW BRING 'IM ON OUT!
KCHK
YOU HEARD ME!

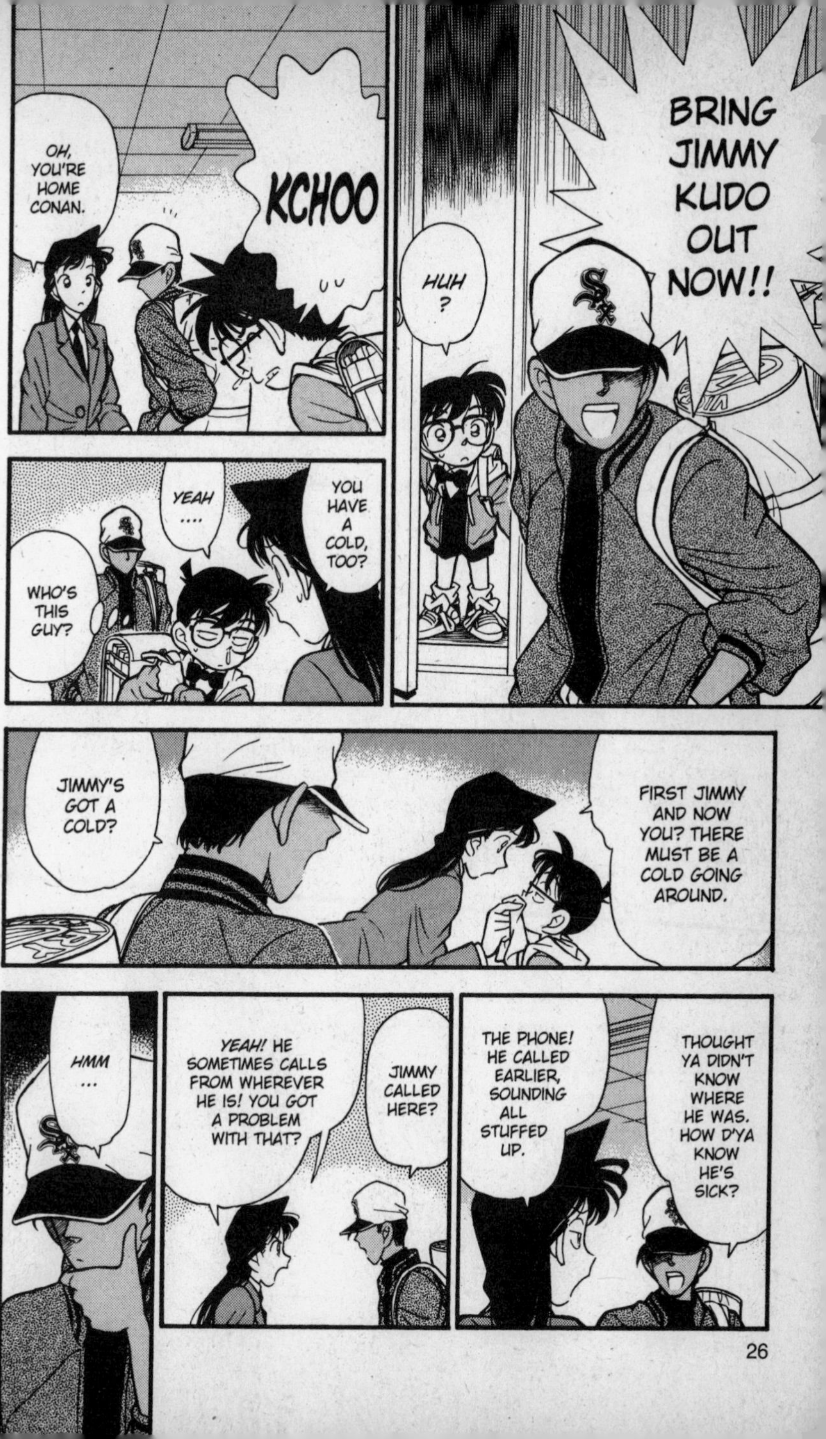

BRING JIMMY KUDO OUT NOW!!
HUH?
KCHOO
OH, YOU'RE HOME CONAN.
YOU HAVE A COLD, TOO?
YEAH ....
WHO'S THIS GUY?
FIRST JIMMY AND NOW YOU? THERE MUST BE A COLD GOING AROUND.
JIMMY'S GOT A COLD?
THOUGHT YA DIDN'T KNOW WHERE HE WAS. HOW D'YA KNOW HE'S SICK?
THE PHONE! HE CALLED EARLIER, SOUNDING ALL STUFFED UP.
JIMMY CALLED HERE?
YEAH! HE SOMETIMES CALLS FROM WHEREVER HE IS! YOU GOT A PROBLEM WITH THAT?
HMM ...

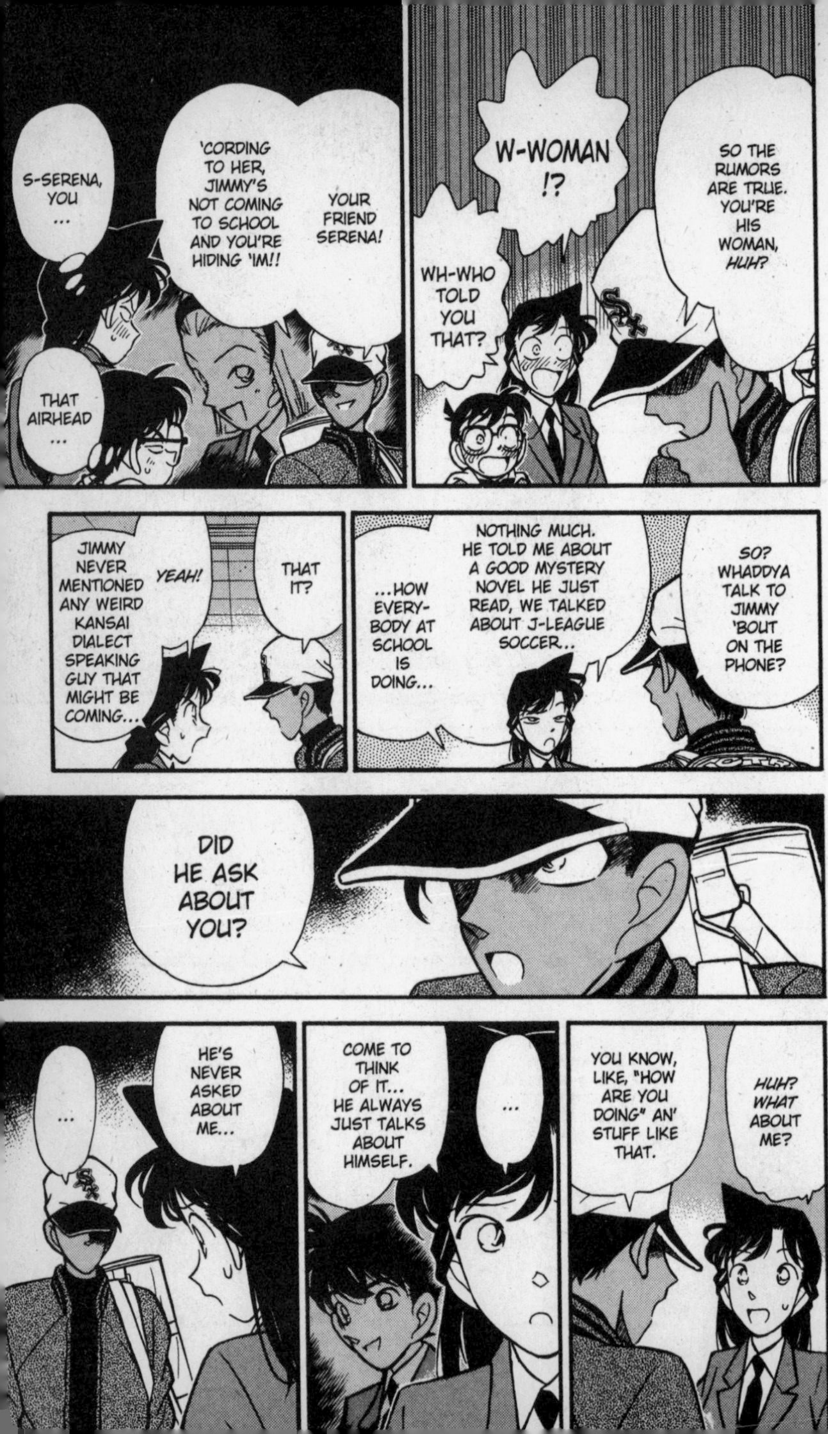
SO THE RUMORS ARE TRUE. YOU'RE HIS WOMAN, HUH?
W-WOMAN !?
WH-WHO TOLD YOU THAT?
YOUR FRIEND SERENA!
'CORDING TO HER, JIMMY'S NOT COMING TO SCHOOL AND YOU'RE HIDING 'IM!!
S-SERENA, YOU ...
THAT AIRHEAD ...
SO? WHADDYA TALK TO JIMMY 'BOUT ON THE PHONE?
NOTHING MUCH. HE TOLD ME ABOUT A GOOD MYSTERY NOVEL HE JUST READ, WE TALKED ABOUT J-LEAGUE SOCCER...
...HOW EVERY-BODY AT SCHOOL IS DOING...
THAT IT?
YEAH!
JIMMY NEVER MENTIONED ANY WEIRD KANSAI DIALECT SPEAKING GUY THAT MIGHT BE COMING...
DID HE ASK ABOUT YOU?
HUH? WHAT ABOUT ME?
YOU KNOW, LIKE, "HOW ARE YOU DOING" AN' STUFF LIKE THAT.
...
COME TO THINK OF IT... HE ALWAYS JUST TALKS ABOUT HIMSELF.
HE'S NEVER ASKED ABOUT ME...
...

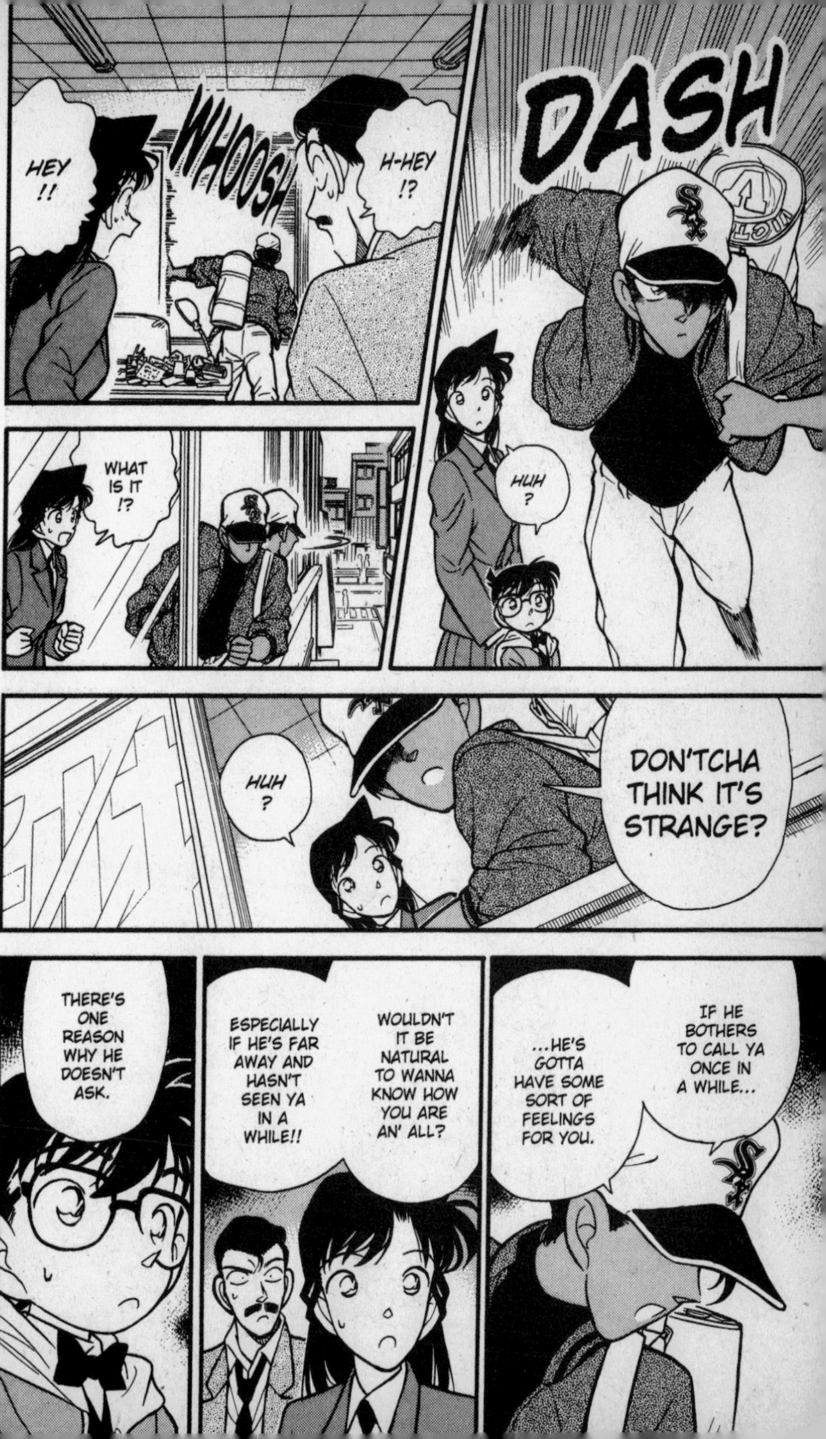
DASH
HUH ?
HEY !!
WHOOSH
H-HEY !?
WHAT IS IT !?
DON'TCHA THINK IT'S STRANGE?
HUH ?
IF HE BOTHERS TO CALL YA ONCE IN A WHILE...
...HE'S GOTTA HAVE SOME SORT OF FEELINGS FOR YOU.
WOULDN'T IT BE NATURAL TO WANNA KNOW HOW YOU ARE AN' ALL?
ESPECIALLY IF HE'S FAR AWAY AND HASN'T SEEN YA IN A WHILE!!
THERE'S ONE REASON WHY HE DOESN'T ASK.

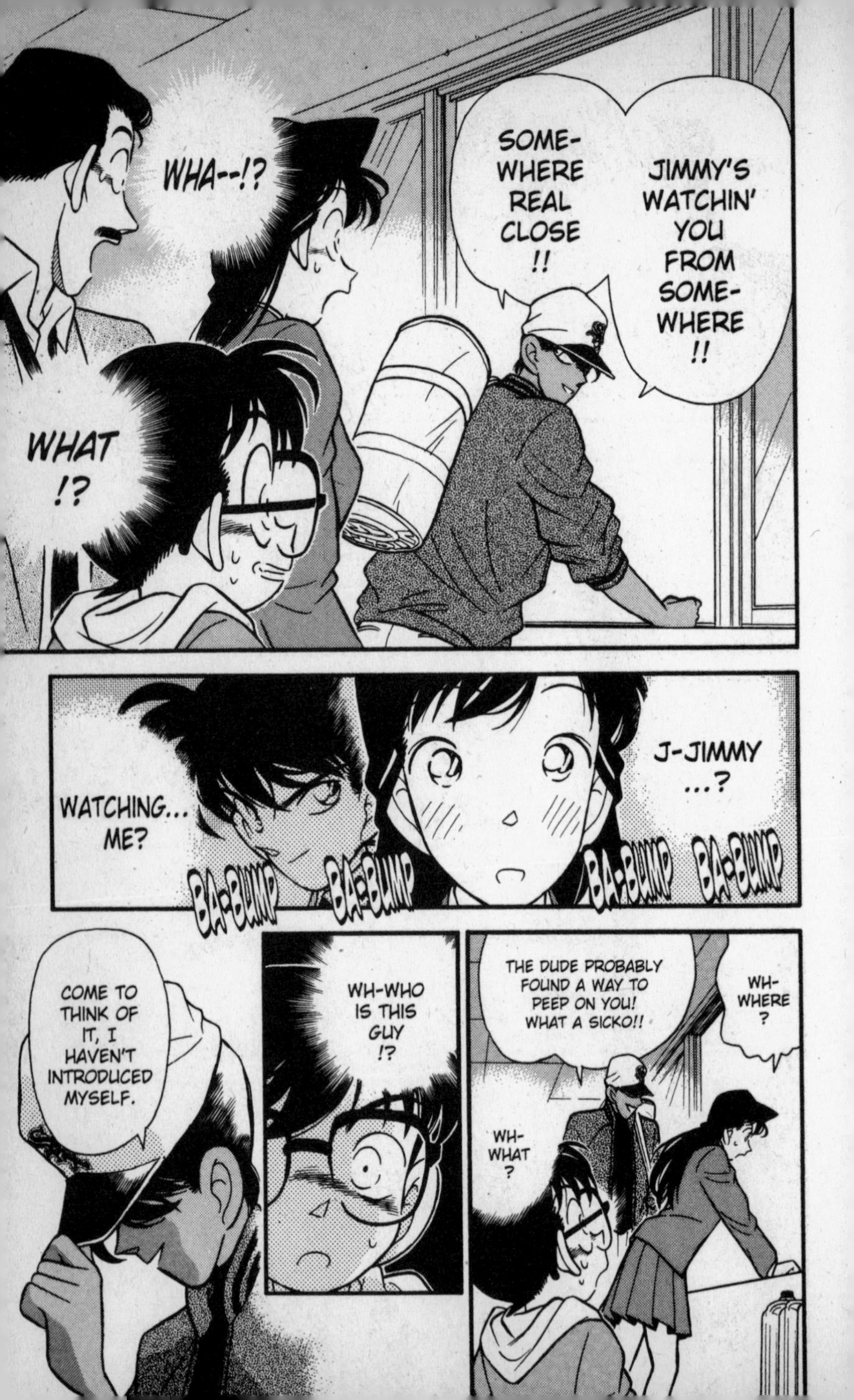
JIMMY'S WATCHIN' YOU FROM SOME-WHERE !!
SOME-WHERE REAL CLOSE !!
WHA--!?
WHAT !?
J-JIMMY ...?
BA-BUMP BA-BUMP
WATCHING... ME?
BA-BUMP BA-BUMP
WH-WHERE ?
THE DUDE PROBABLY FOUND A WAY TO PEEP ON YOU! WHAT A SICKO!!
WH-WHAT ?
WH-WHO IS THIS GUY !?
COME TO THINK OF IT, I HAVEN'T INTRODUCED MYSELF.

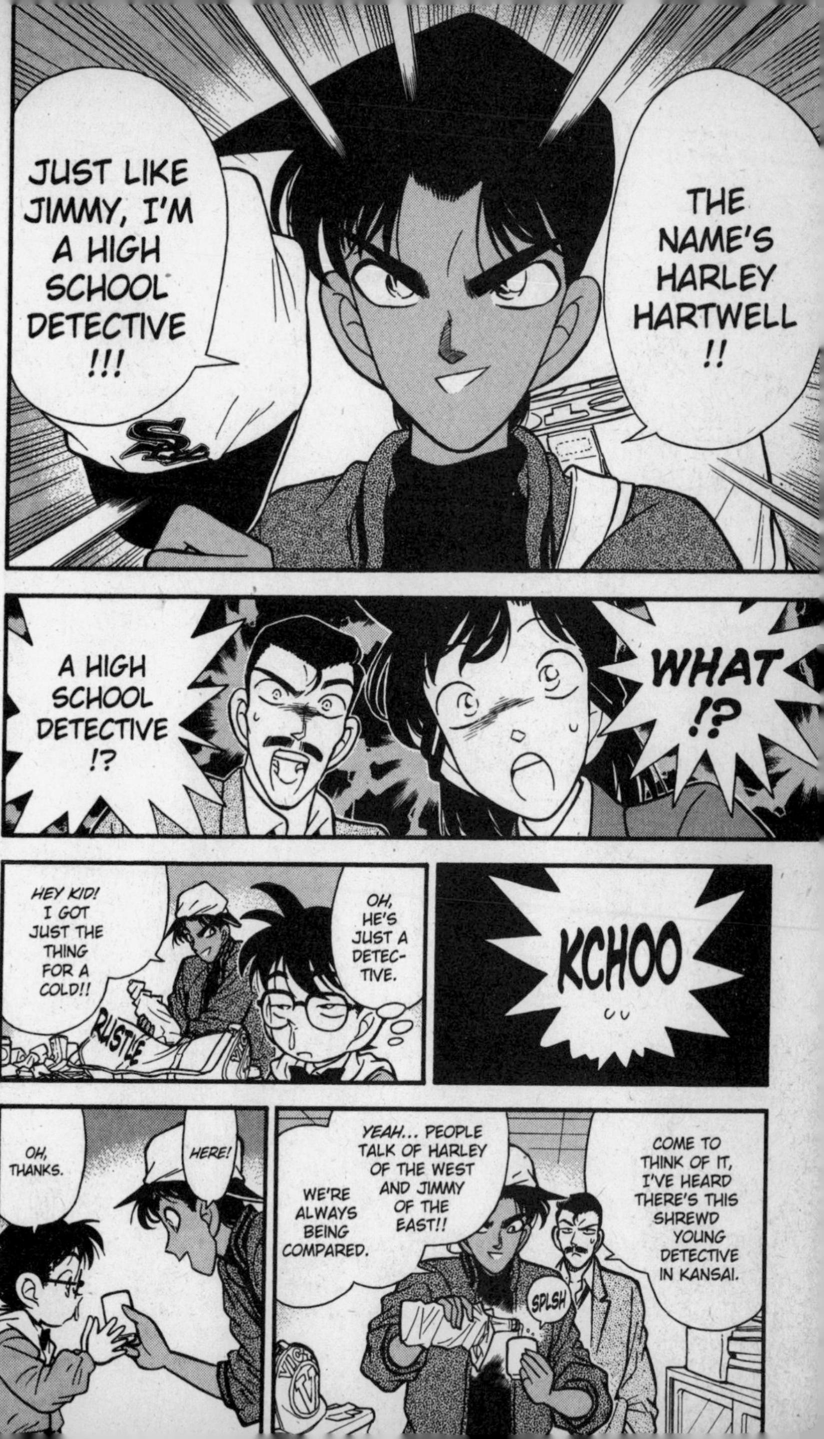
THE NAME'S HARLEY HARTWELL !!
JUST LIKE JIMMY, I'M A HIGH SCHOOL DETECTIVE !!!
WHAT !?
A HIGH SCHOOL DETECTIVE !?
KCHOO
OH, HE'S JUST A DETEC-TIVE.
HEY KID! I GOT JUST THE THING FOR A COLD!!
RUSTLE
COME TO THINK OF IT, I'VE HEARD THERE'S THIS SHREWD YOUNG DETECTIVE IN KANSAI.
YEAH... PEOPLE TALK OF HARLEY OF THE WEST AND JIMMY OF THE EAST!!
WE'RE ALWAYS BEING COMPARED.
SPLSH
HERE!
OH, THANKS.

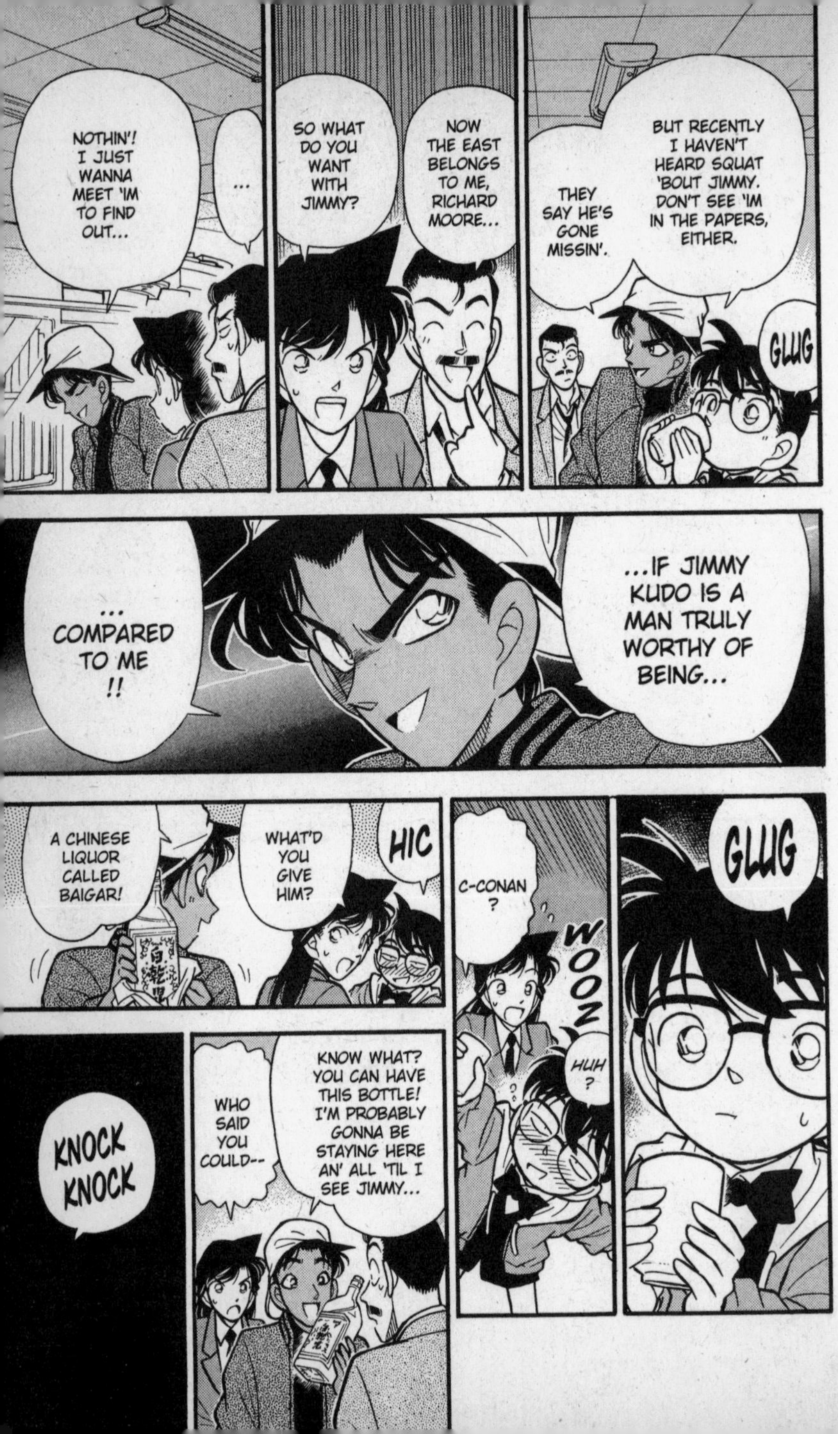
BUT RECENTLY I HAVEN'T HEARD SQUAT 'BOUT JIMMY. DON'T SEE 'IM IN THE PAPERS, EITHER.
THEY SAY HE'S GONE MISSIN'.
GLUG
NOW THE EAST BELONGS TO ME, RICHARD MOORE...
SO WHAT DO YOU WANT WITH JIMMY?
...
NOTHIN'! I JUST WANNA MEET 'IM TO FIND OUT...
...IF JIMMY KUDO IS A MAN TRULY WORTHY OF BEING...
... COMPARED TO ME !!
GLUG
C-CONAN ?
WOOZ
HUH ?
HIC
WHAT'D YOU GIVE HIM?
A CHINESE LIQUOR CALLED BAIGAR!
KNOW WHAT? YOU CAN HAVE THIS BOTTLE! I'M PROBABLY GONNA BE STAYING HERE AN' ALL 'TIL I SEE JIMMY...
WHO SAID YOU COULD--
KNOCK KNOCK

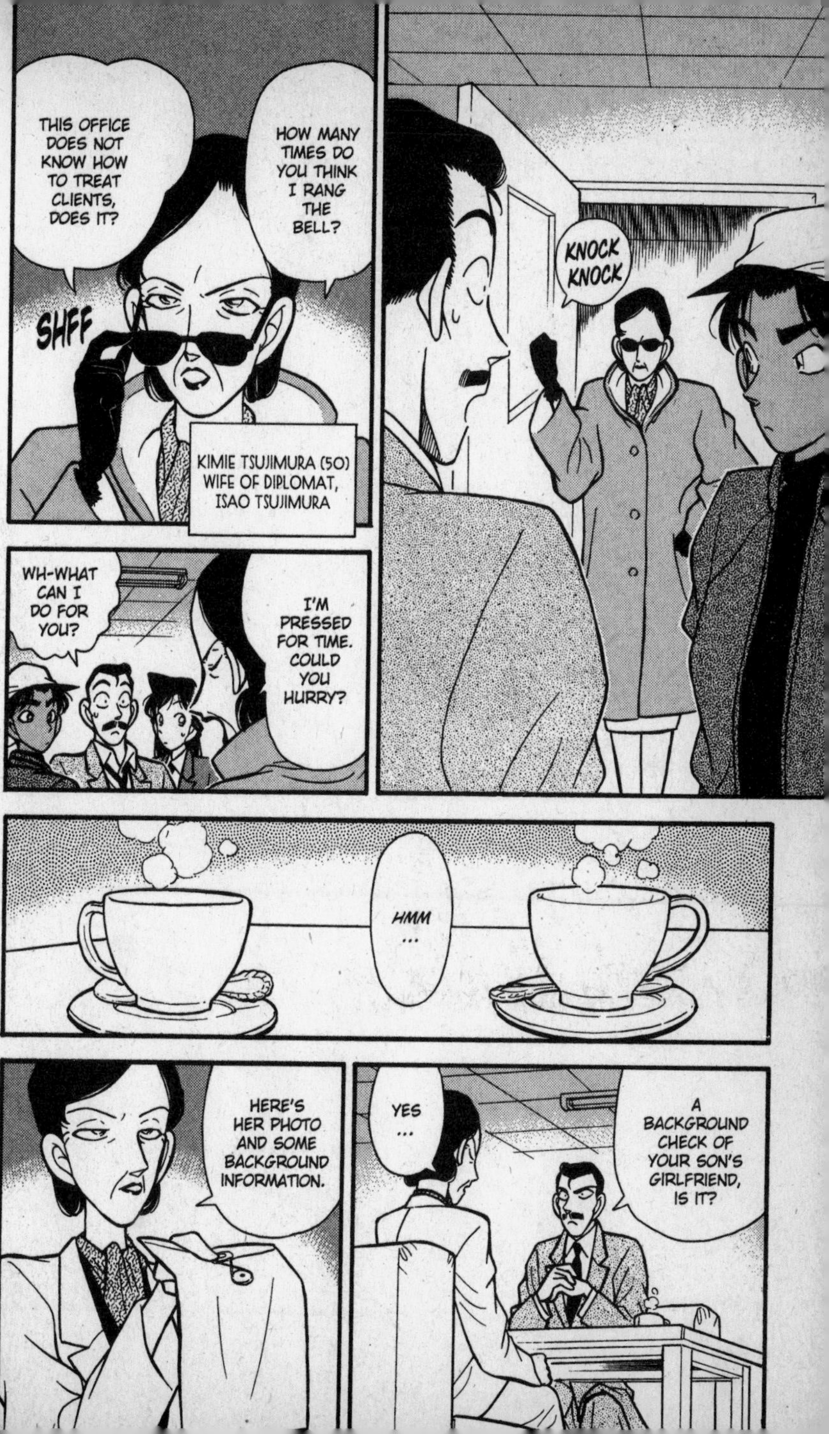
KNOCK KNOCK
HOW MANY TIMES DO YOU THINK I RANG THE BELL?
THIS OFFICE DOES NOT KNOW HOW TO TREAT CLIENTS, DOES IT?
SHFF
KIMIE TSUJIMURA (50) WIFE OF DIPLOMAT, ISAO TSUJIMURA
WH-WHAT CAN I DO FOR YOU?
I'M PRESSED FOR TIME. COULD YOU HURRY?
HMM ...
A BACKGROUND CHECK OF YOUR SON'S GIRLFRIEND, IS IT?
YES ...
HERE'S HER PHOTO AND SOME BACKGROUND INFORMATION.

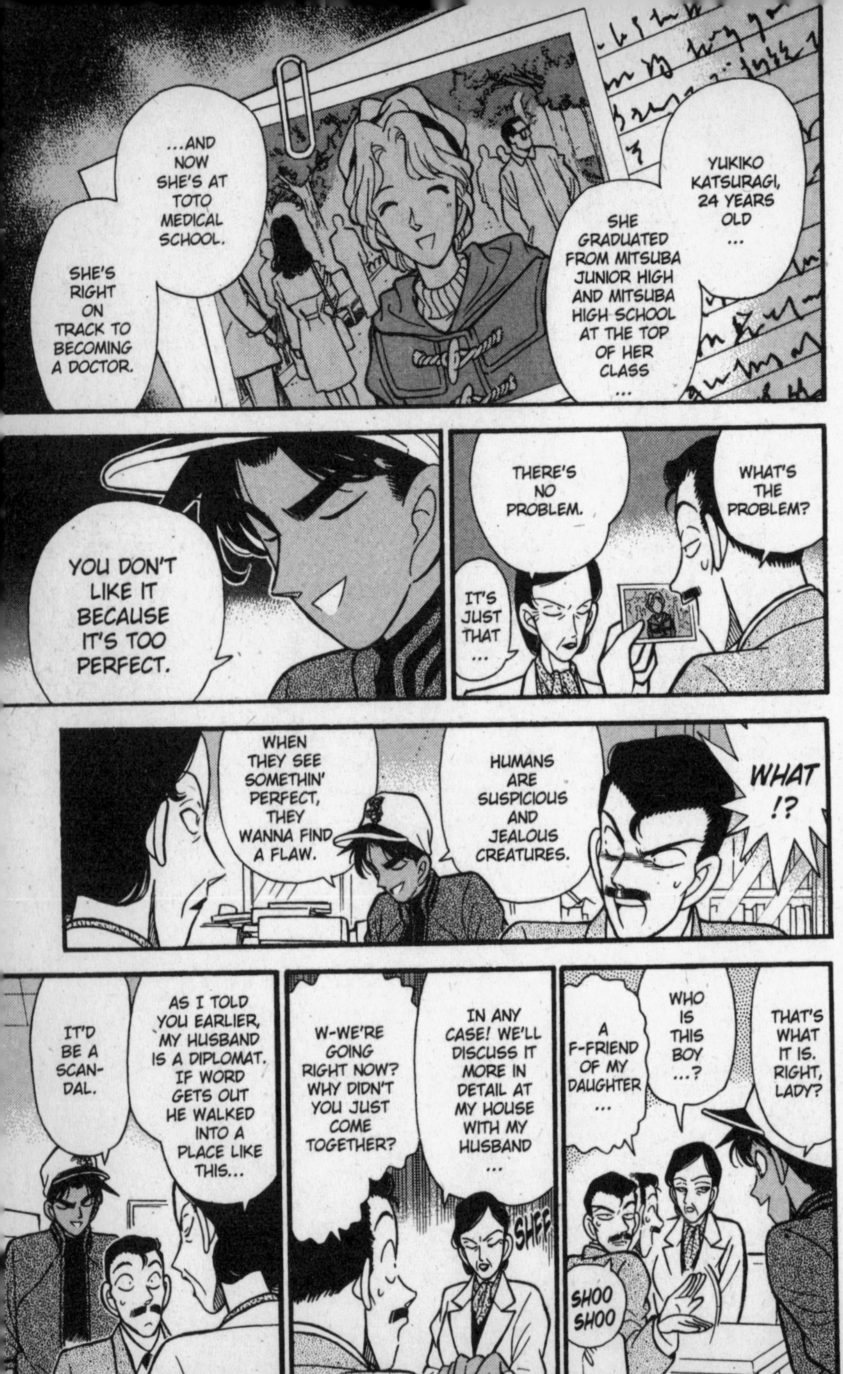
YUKIKO KATSURAGI, 24 YEARS OLD ...
SHE GRADUATED FROM MITSUBA JUNIOR HIGH AND MITSUBA HIGH SCHOOL AT THE TOP OF HER CLASS ...
...AND NOW SHE'S AT TOTO MEDICAL SCHOOL.
SHE'S RIGHT ON TRACK TO BECOMING A DOCTOR.
WHAT'S THE PROBLEM?
THERE'S NO PROBLEM.
IT'S JUST THAT ...
YOU DON'T LIKE IT BECAUSE IT'S TOO PERFECT.
WHAT !?
HUMANS ARE SUSPICIOUS AND JEALOUS CREATURES.
WHEN THEY SEE SOMETHIN' PERFECT, THEY WANNA FIND A FLAW.
THAT'S WHAT IT IS. RIGHT, LADY?
WHO IS THIS BOY ...?
A F-FRIEND OF MY DAUGHTER ...
SHOO SHOO
IN ANY CASE! WE'LL DISCUSS IT MORE IN DETAIL AT MY HOUSE WITH MY HUSBAND ...
SHFF
W-WE'RE GOING RIGHT NOW? WHY DIDN'T YOU JUST COME TOGETHER?
AS I TOLD YOU EARLIER, MY HUSBAND IS A DIPLOMAT. IF WORD GETS OUT HE WALKED INTO A PLACE LIKE THIS...
IT'D BE A SCAN-DAL.

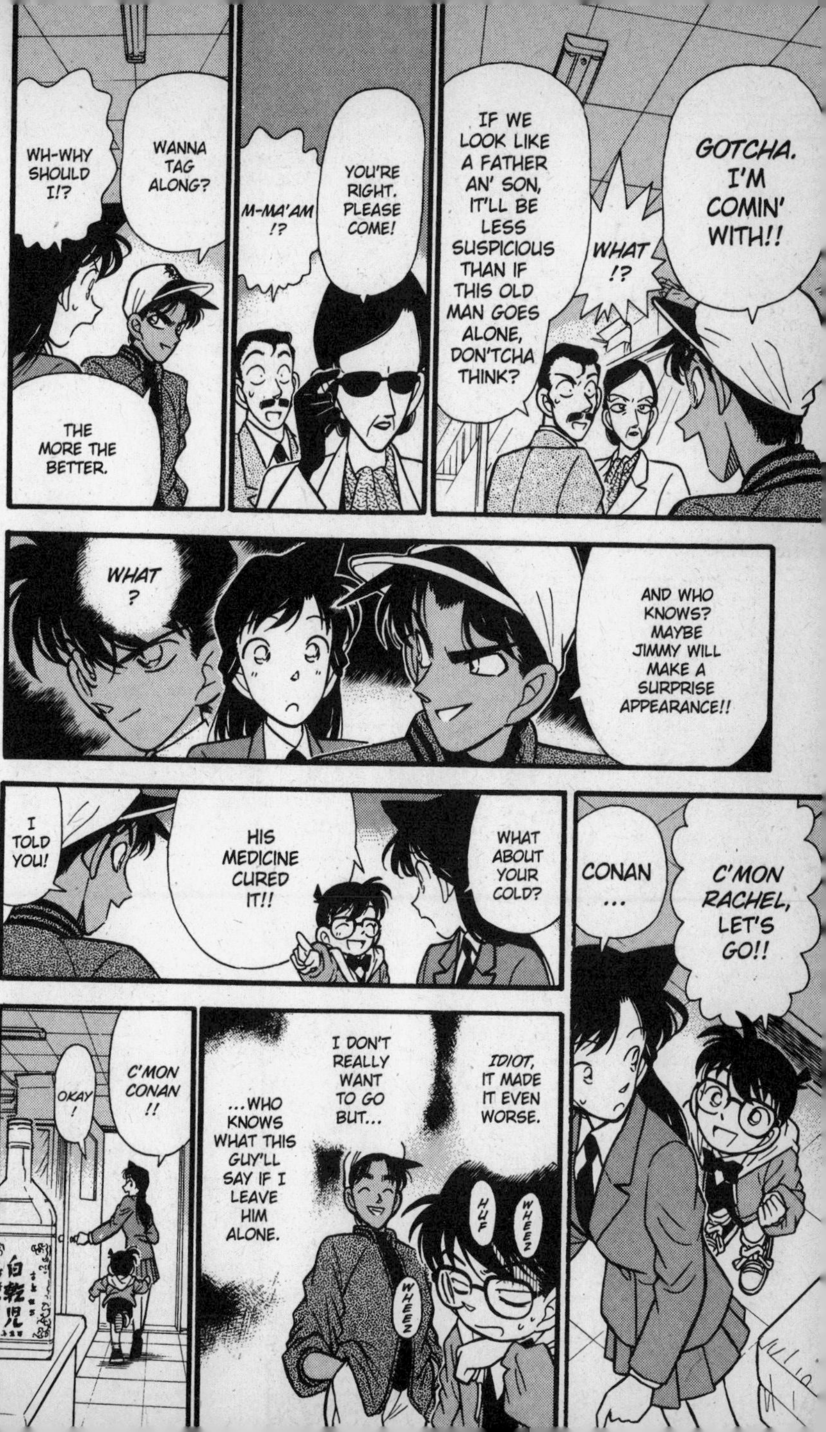
GOTCHA. I'M COMIN' WITH!!
WHAT !?
IF WE LOOK LIKE A FATHER AN' SON, IT'LL BE LESS SUSPICIOUS THAN IF THIS OLD MAN GOES ALONE, DON'TCHA THINK?
YOU'RE RIGHT. PLEASE COME!
M-MA'AM !?
WANNA TAG ALONG?
WH-WHY SHOULD I!?
THE MORE THE BETTER.
AND WHO KNOWS? MAYBE JIMMY WILL MAKE A SURPRISE APPEARANCE!!
WHAT ?
C'MON RACHEL, LET'S GO!!
CONAN ...
WHAT ABOUT YOUR COLD?
HIS MEDICINE CURED IT!!
I TOLD YOU!
IDIOT, IT MADE IT EVEN WORSE.
I DON'T REALLY WANT TO GO BUT...
...WHO KNOWS WHAT THIS GUY'LL SAY IF I LEAVE HIM ALONE.
WHEEZ
HUF
WHEEZ
C'MON CONAN !!
OKAY !
白乾児

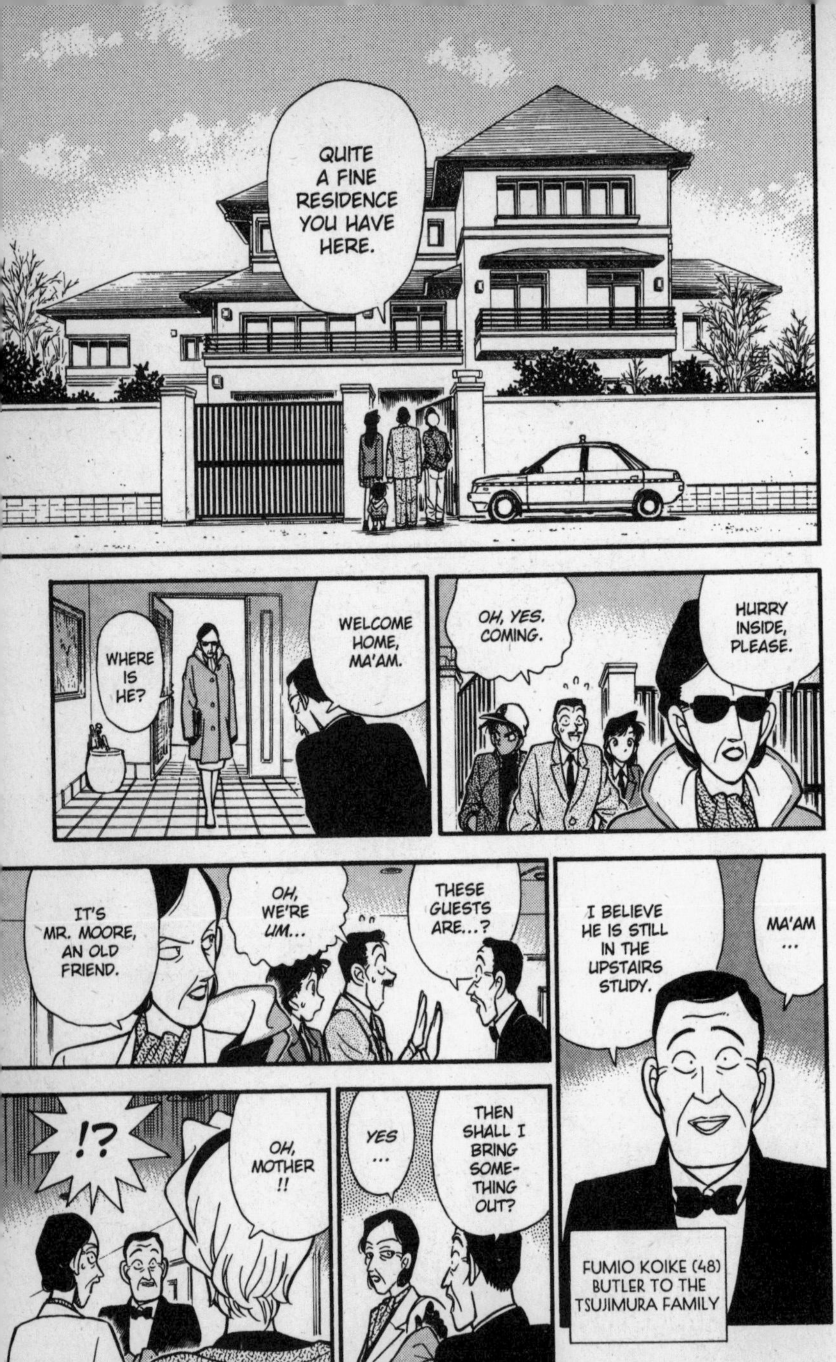
QUITE A FINE RESIDENCE YOU HAVE HERE.
HURRY INSIDE, PLEASE.
OH, YES. COMING.
WELCOME HOME, MA'AM.
WHERE IS HE?
MA'AM ...
I BELIEVE HE IS STILL IN THE UPSTAIRS STUDY.
FUMIO KOIKE (48) BUTLER TO THE TSUJIMURA FAMILY
THESE GUESTS ARE...?
OH, WE'RE UM...
IT'S MR. MOORE, AN OLD FRIEND.
THEN SHALL I BRING SOME-THING OUT?
YES ...
OH, MOTHER !!
!?

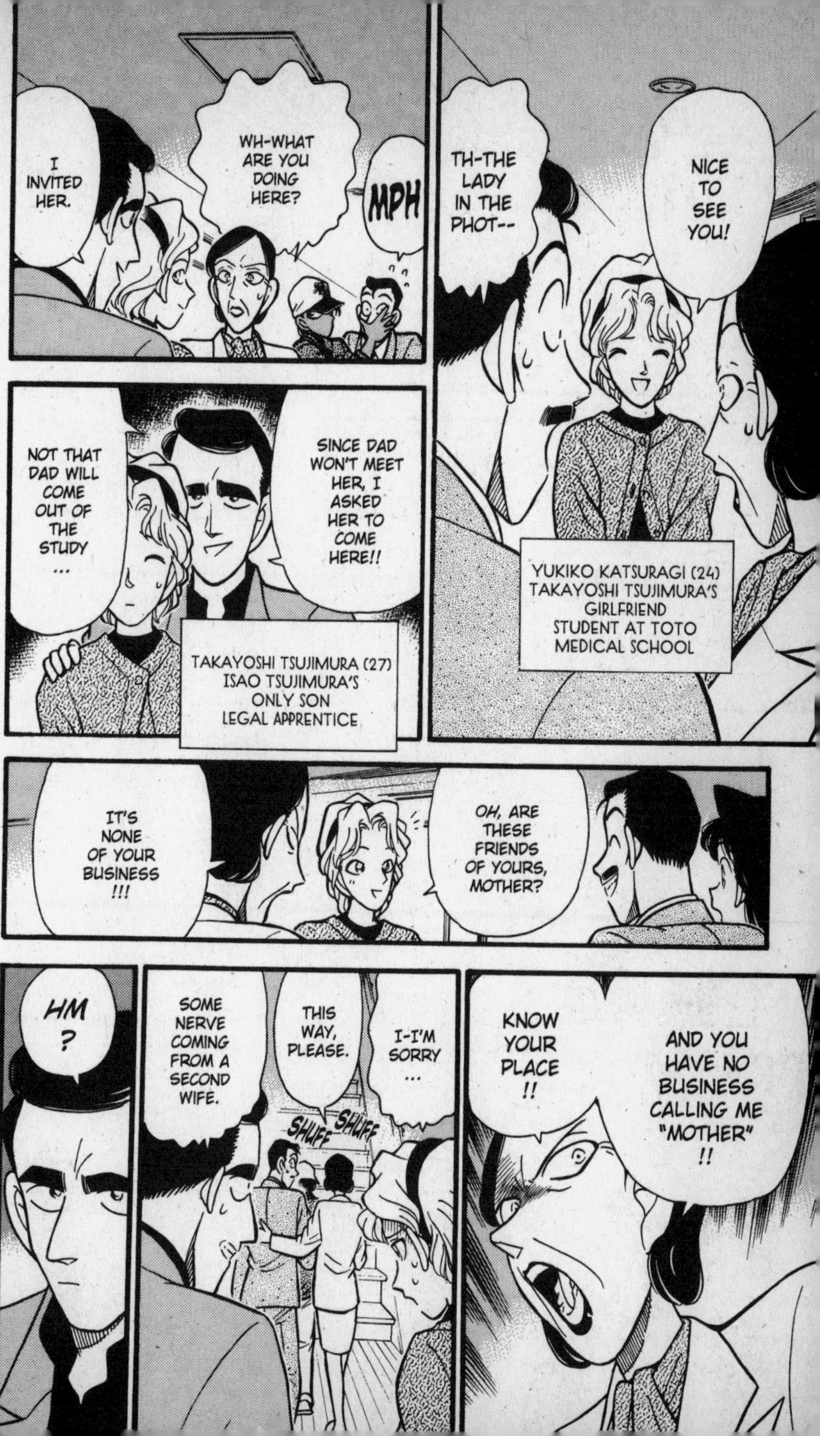
NICE TO SEE YOU!
TH-THE LADY IN THE PHOT--
YUKIKO KATSURAGI (24) TAKAYOSHI TSUJIMURA'S GIRLFRIEND STUDENT AT TOTO MEDICAL SCHOOL
MPH
WH-WHAT ARE YOU DOING HERE?
I INVITED HER.
SINCE DAD WON'T MEET HER, I ASKED HER TO COME HERE!!
NOT THAT DAD WILL COME OUT OF THE STUDY ...
TAKAYOSHI TSUJIMURA (27) ISAO TSUJIMURA'S ONLY SON LEGAL APPRENTICE
OH, ARE THESE FRIENDS OF YOURS, MOTHER?
IT'S NONE OF YOUR BUSINESS !!!
AND YOU HAVE NO BUSINESS CALLING ME "MOTHER" !!
KNOW YOUR PLACE !!
I-I'M SORRY ...
THIS WAY, PLEASE.
SHUFF SHUFF
SOME NERVE COMING FROM A SECOND WIFE.
HM ?

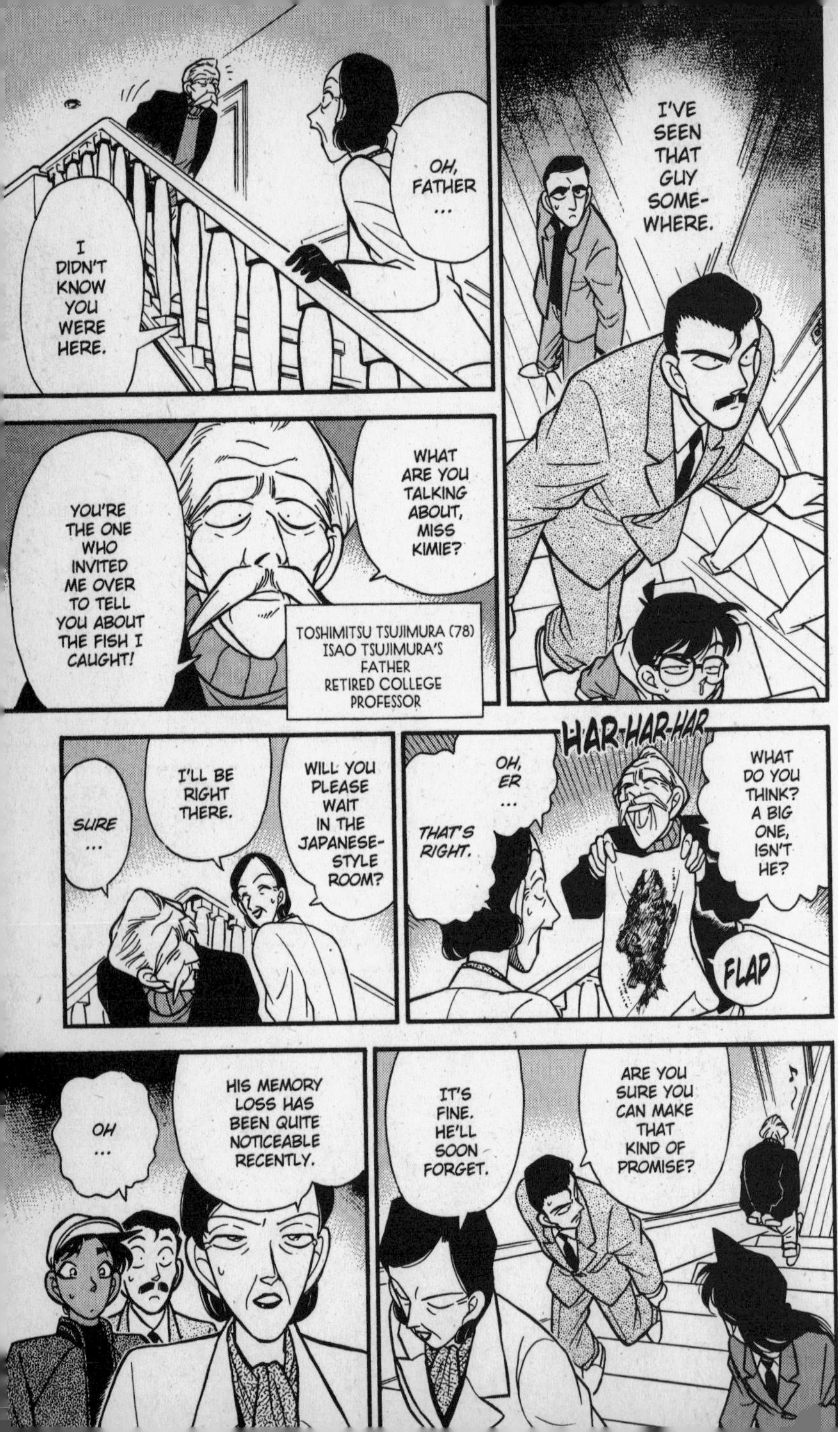
I'VE SEEN THAT GUY SOMEWHERE.
OH, FATHER ...
I DIDN'T KNOW YOU WERE HERE.
WHAT ARE YOU TALKING ABOUT, MISS KIMIE?
YOU'RE THE ONE WHO INVITED ME OVER TO TELL YOU ABOUT THE FISH I CAUGHT!
TOSHIMITSU TSUJIMURA (78)
ISAO TSUJIMURA'S FATHER
RETIRED COLLEGE PROFESSOR
HAR-HAR-HAR
WHAT DO YOU THINK? A BIG ONE, ISN'T HE?
FLAP
OH, ER ...
THAT'S RIGHT.
WILL YOU PLEASE WAIT IN THE JAPANESE-STYLE ROOM?
I'LL BE RIGHT THERE.
SURE ...
ARE YOU SURE YOU CAN MAKE THAT KIND OF PROMISE?
IT'S FINE. HE'LL SOON FORGET.
HIS MEMORY LOSS HAS BEEN QUITE NOTICEABLE RECENTLY.
OH ...

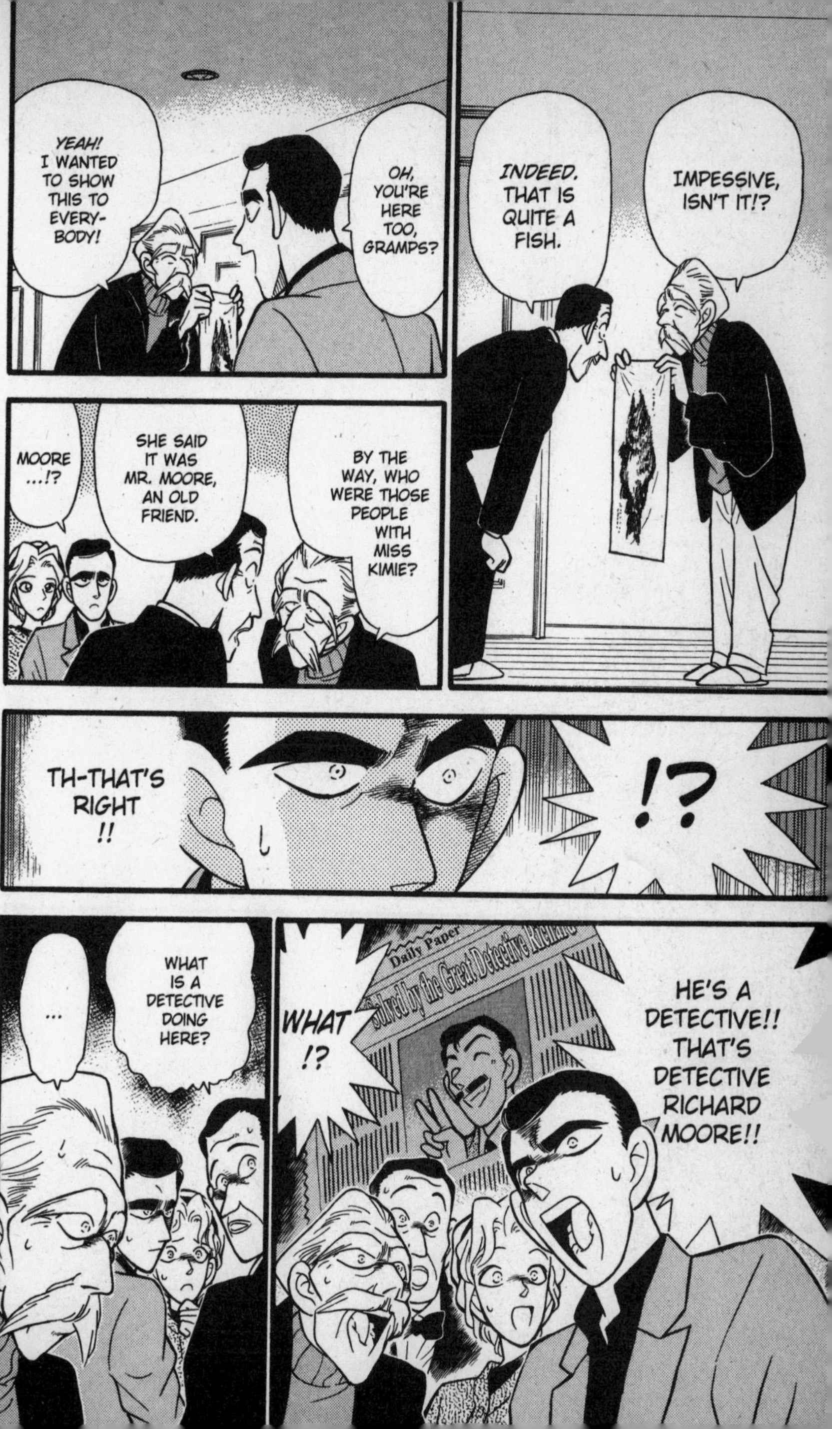
IMPESSIVE, ISN'T IT!?
INDEED. THAT IS QUITE A FISH.
OH, YOU'RE HERE TOO, GRAMPS?
YEAH! I WANTED TO SHOW THIS TO EVERY-BODY!
BY THE WAY, WHO WERE THOSE PEOPLE WITH MISS KIMIE?
SHE SAID IT WAS MR. MOORE, AN OLD FRIEND.
MOORE ...!?
!?
TH-THAT'S RIGHT !!
HE'S A DETECTIVE!! THAT'S DETECTIVE RICHARD MOORE!!
Daily Paper
Solved by the Great Detective
WHAT !?
WHAT IS A DETECTIVE DOING HERE?
...

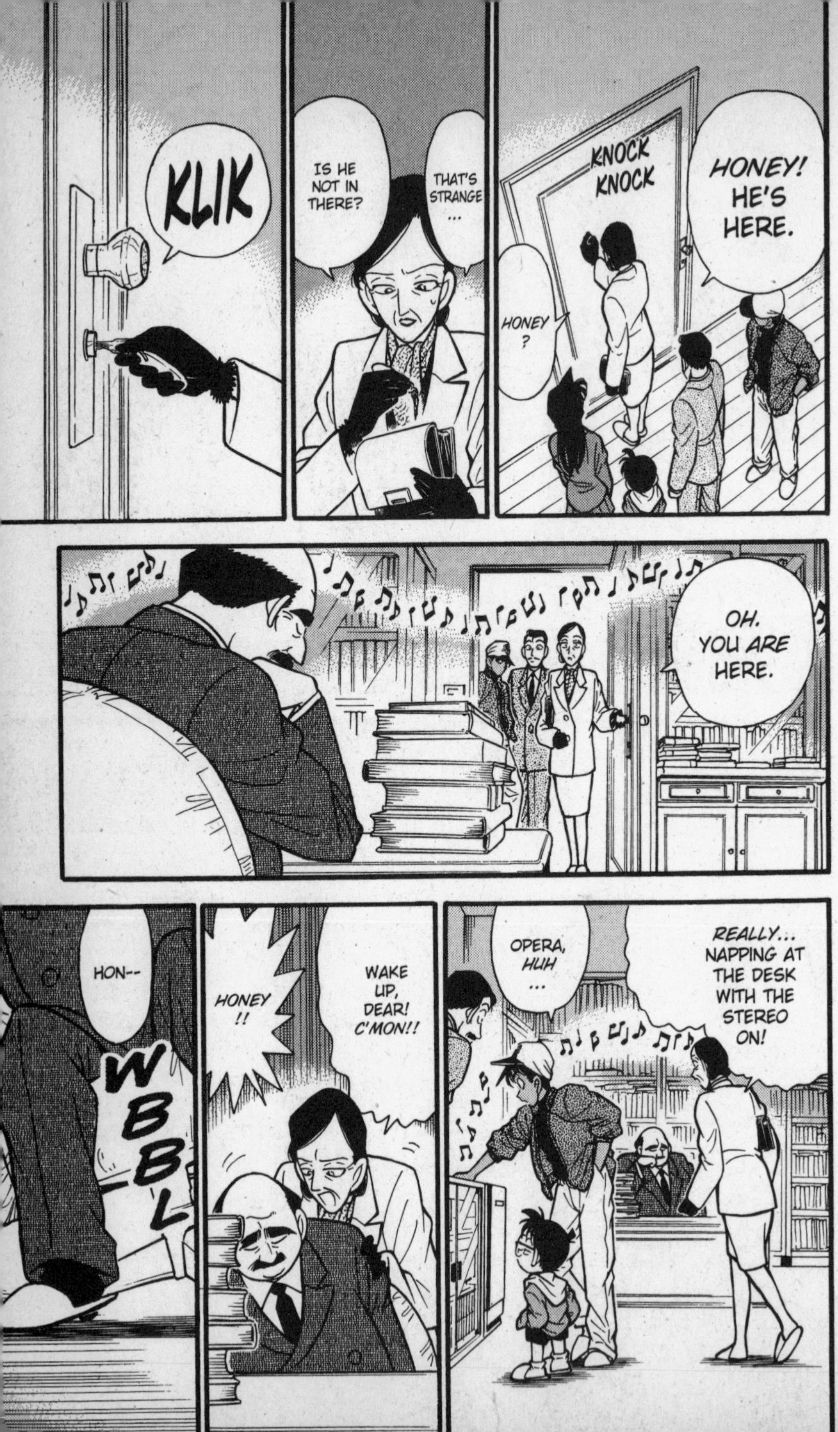
HONEY! HE'S HERE.
KNOCK KNOCK
HONEY ?
THAT'S STRANGE ...
IS HE NOT IN THERE?
KLIK
OH. YOU ARE HERE.
REALLY... NAPPING AT THE DESK WITH THE STEREO ON!
OPERA, HUH ...
WAKE UP, DEAR! C'MON!!
HONEY !!
HON--
WBBL

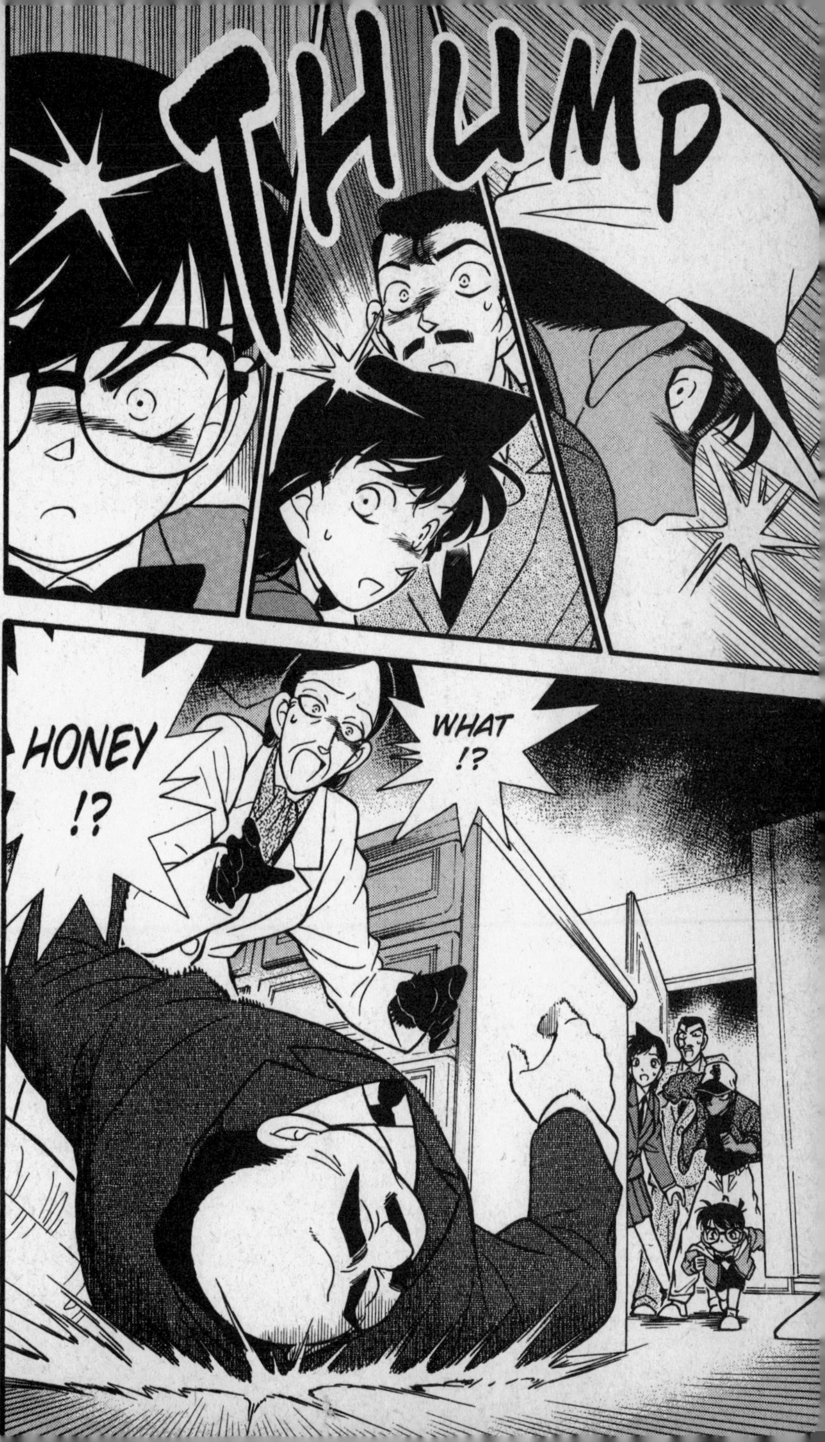
THUMP
WHAT !?
HONEY !?

FILE 3:

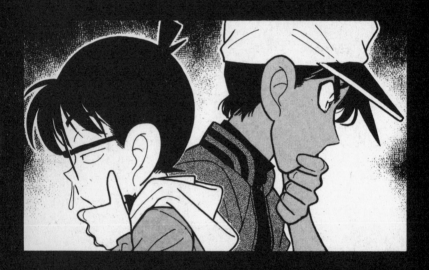

TWO THEORIES

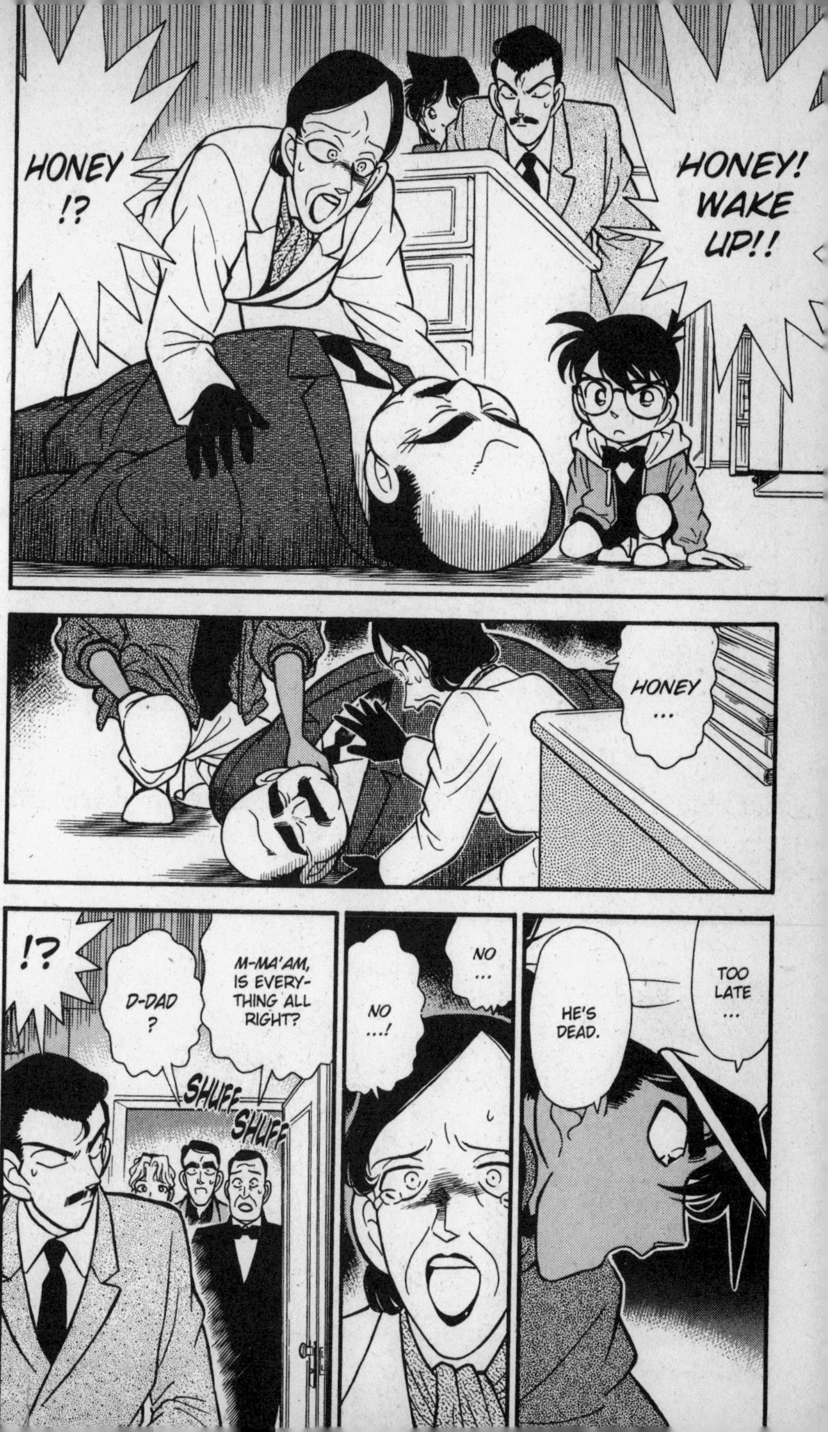
HONEY! WAKE UP!!
HONEY !?
HONEY ...
TOO LATE ...
HE'S DEAD.
NO ...
NO ...!
M-MA'AM, IS EVERY-THING ALL RIGHT?
D-DAD ?
SHUFF SHUFF
!?

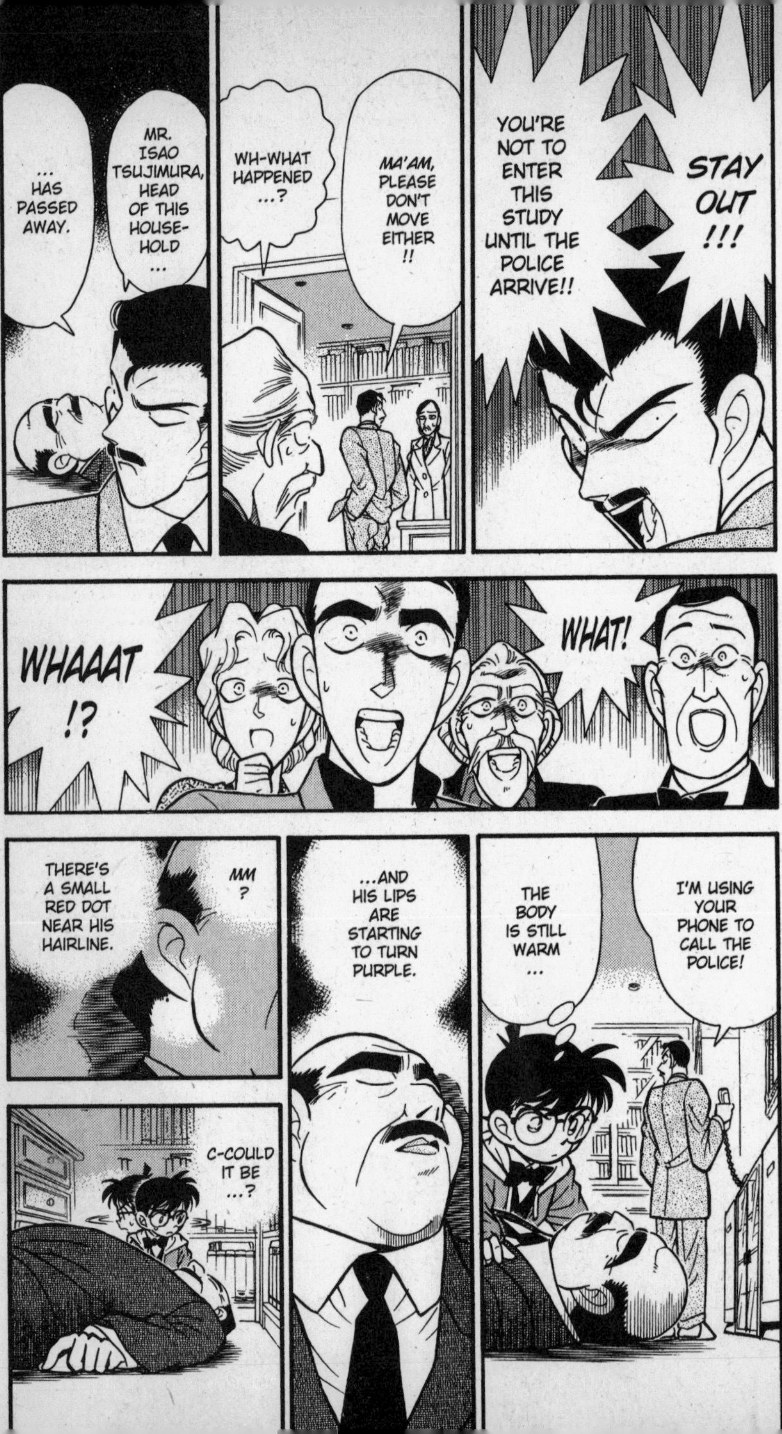
STAY OUT!!!
YOU'RE NOT TO ENTER THIS STUDY UNTIL THE POLICE ARRIVE!!
MA'AM, PLEASE DON'T MOVE EITHER!!
WH-WHAT HAPPENED...?
MR. ISAO TSUJIMURA, HEAD OF THIS HOUSE-HOLD...
...HAS PASSED AWAY.
WHAT!
WHAAAT!?
I'M USING YOUR PHONE TO CALL THE POLICE!
THE BODY IS STILL WARM...
...AND HIS LIPS ARE STARTING TO TURN PURPLE.
MM?
THERE'S A SMALL RED DOT NEAR HIS HAIRLINE.
C-COULD IT BE...?

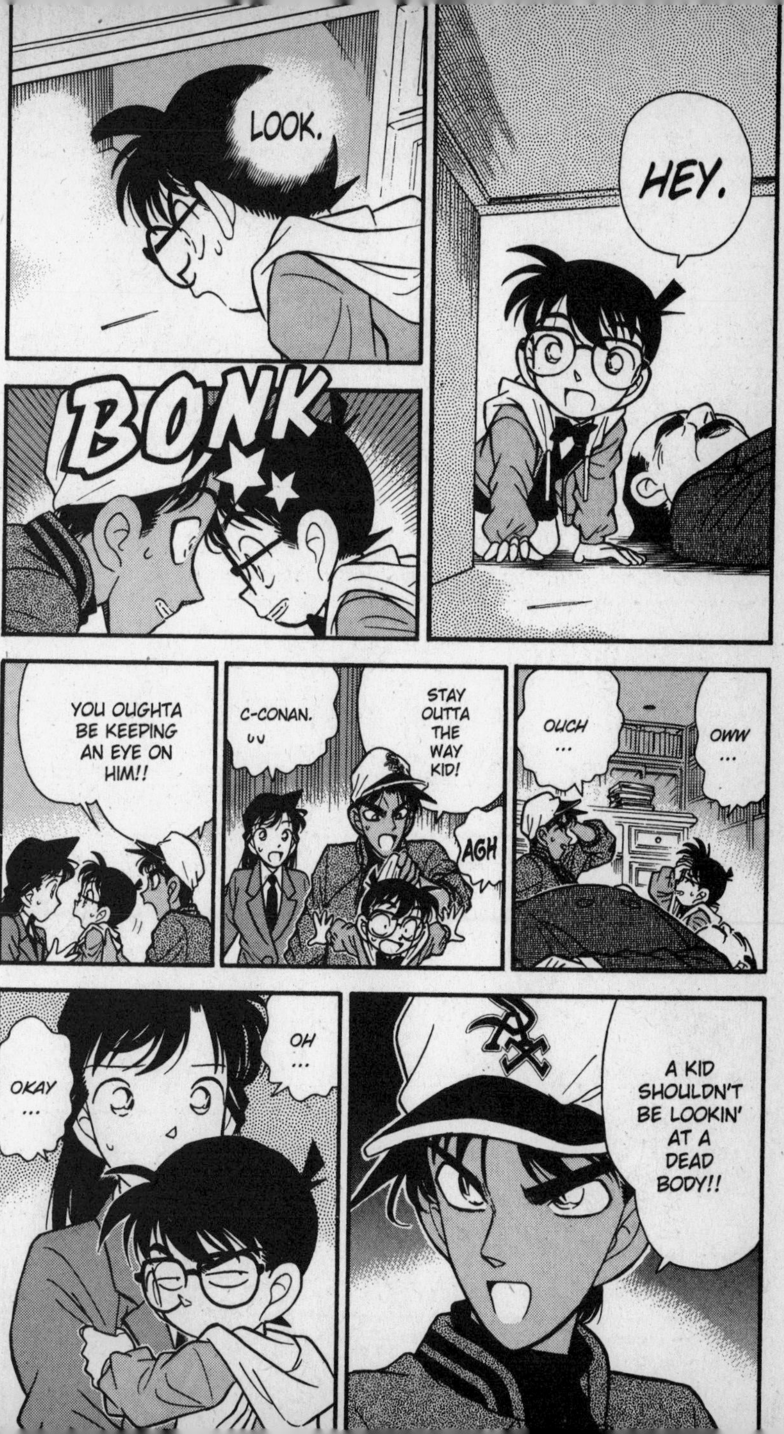
HEY.
LOOK.
BONK
OWW ...
OUCH ...
STAY OUTTA THE WAY KID!
AGH
C-CONAN.
YOU OUGHTA BE KEEPING AN EYE ON HIM!!
A KID SHOULDN'T BE LOOKIN' AT A DEAD BODY!!
OH ...
OKAY ...

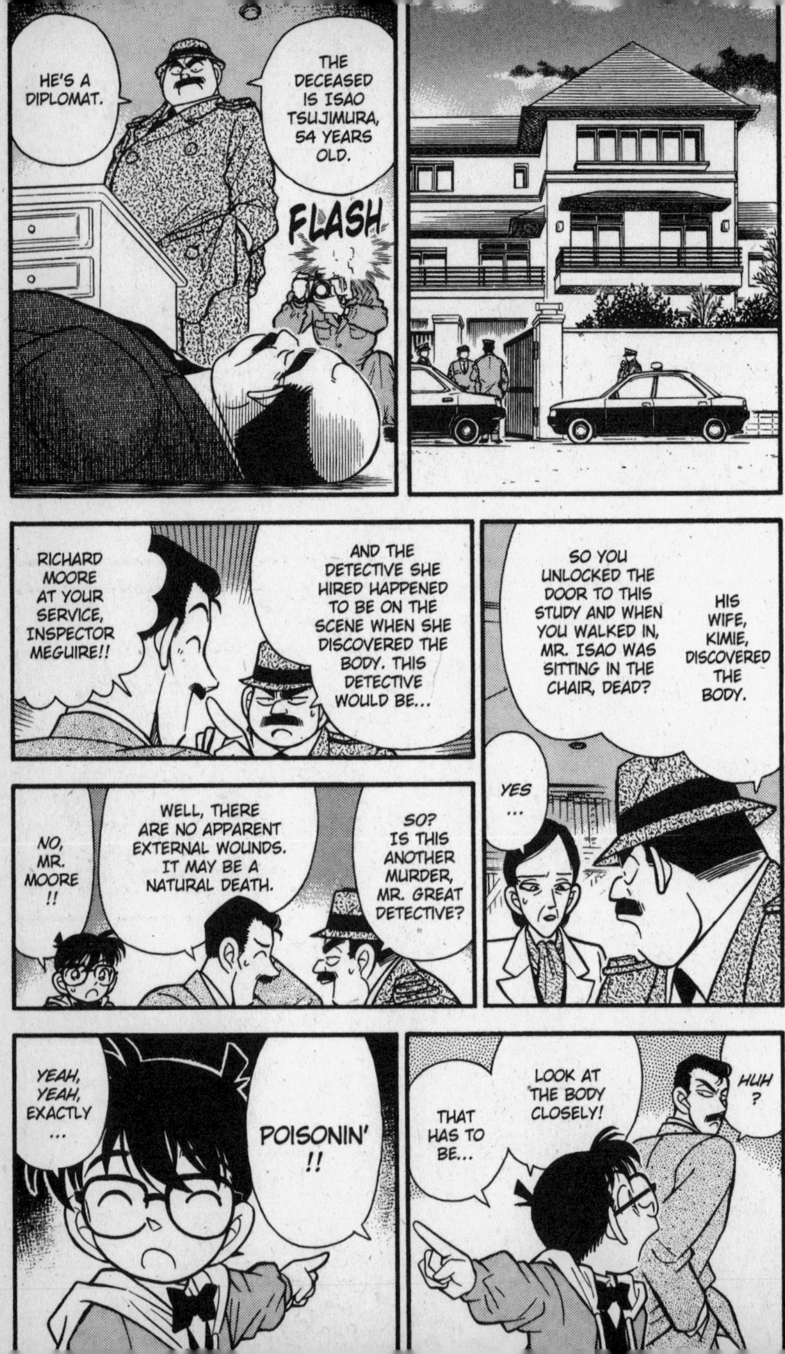
THE DECEASED IS ISAO TSUJIMURA, 54 YEARS OLD.
HE'S A DIPLOMAT.
FLASH
HIS WIFE, KIMIE, DISCOVERED THE BODY.
SO YOU UNLOCKED THE DOOR TO THIS STUDY AND WHEN YOU WALKED IN, MR. ISAO WAS SITTING IN THE CHAIR, DEAD?
YES...
AND THE DETECTIVE SHE HIRED HAPPENED TO BE ON THE SCENE WHEN SHE DISCOVERED THE BODY. THIS DETECTIVE WOULD BE...
RICHARD MOORE AT YOUR SERVICE, INSPECTOR MEGUIRE!!
SO? IS THIS ANOTHER MURDER, MR. GREAT DETECTIVE?
WELL, THERE ARE NO APPARENT EXTERNAL WOUNDS. IT MAY BE A NATURAL DEATH.
NO, MR. MOORE!!
HUH?
LOOK AT THE BODY CLOSELY!
THAT HAS TO BE...
POISONIN'!!
YEAH, YEAH, EXACTLY...

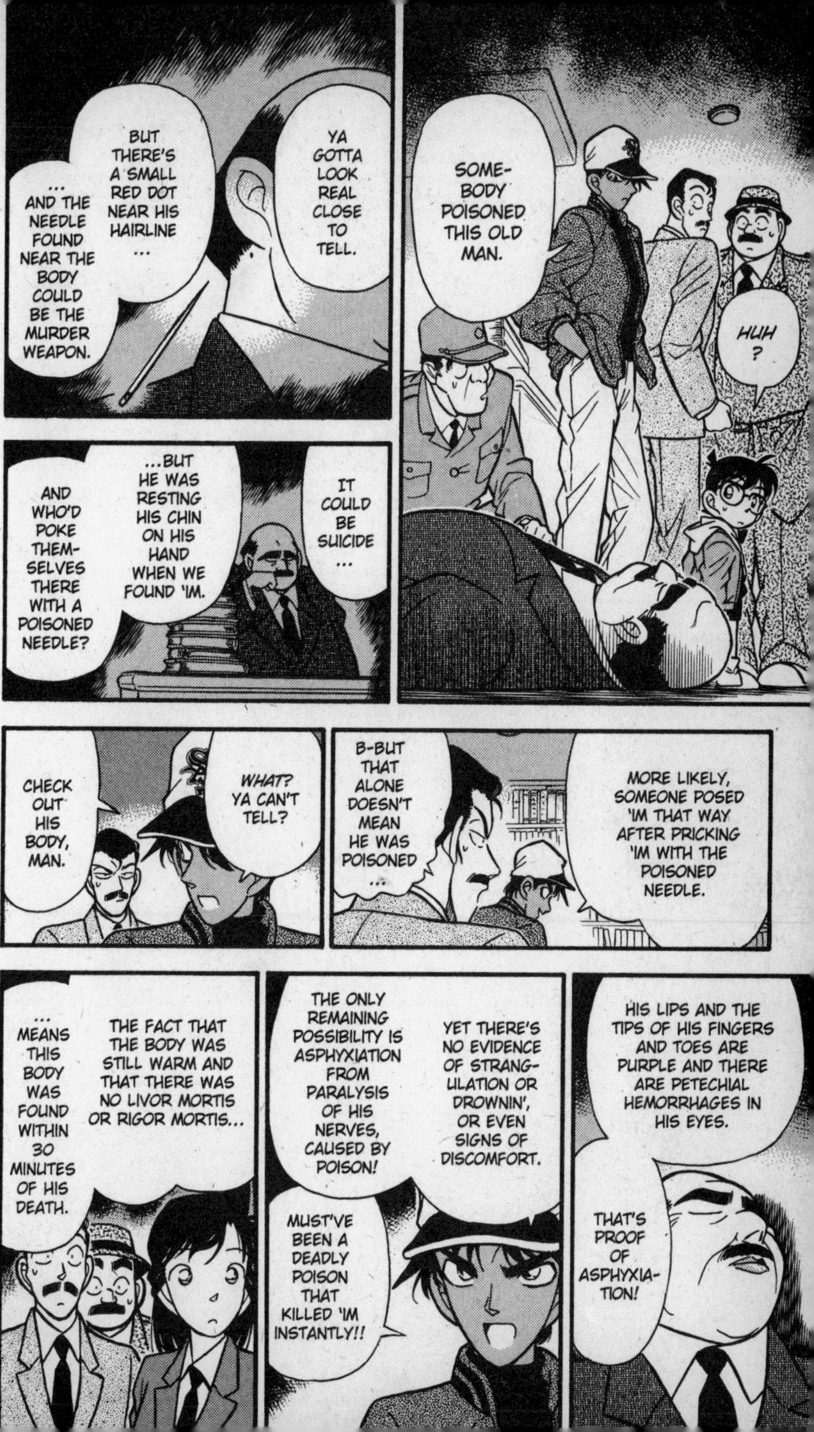
SOMEBODY POISONED THIS OLD MAN.
HUH?
YA GOTTA LOOK REAL CLOSE TO TELL.
BUT THERE'S A SMALL RED DOT NEAR HIS HAIRLINE ...
... AND THE NEEDLE FOUND NEAR THE BODY COULD BE THE MURDER WEAPON.
IT COULD BE SUICIDE ...
...BUT HE WAS RESTING HIS CHIN ON HIS HAND WHEN WE FOUND 'IM.
AND WHO'D POKE THEMSELVES THERE WITH A POISONED NEEDLE?
MORE LIKELY, SOMEONE POSED 'IM THAT WAY AFTER PRICKING 'IM WITH THE POISONED NEEDLE.
B-BUT THAT ALONE DOESN'T MEAN HE WAS POISONED ...
WHAT? YA CAN'T TELL?
CHECK OUT HIS BODY, MAN.
HIS LIPS AND THE TIPS OF HIS FINGERS AND TOES ARE PURPLE AND THERE ARE PETECHIAL HEMORRHAGES IN HIS EYES.
THAT'S PROOF OF ASPHYXIATION!
YET THERE'S NO EVIDENCE OF STRANGULATION OR DROWNIN', OR EVEN SIGNS OF DISCOMFORT.
THE ONLY REMAINING POSSIBILITY IS ASPHYXIATION FROM PARALYSIS OF HIS NERVES, CAUSED BY POISON!
MUST'VE BEEN A DEADLY POISON THAT KILLED 'IM INSTANTLY!!
THE FACT THAT THE BODY WAS STILL WARM AND THAT THERE WAS NO LIVOR MORTIS OR RIGOR MORTIS...
... MEANS THIS BODY WAS FOUND WITHIN 30 MINUTES OF HIS DEATH.

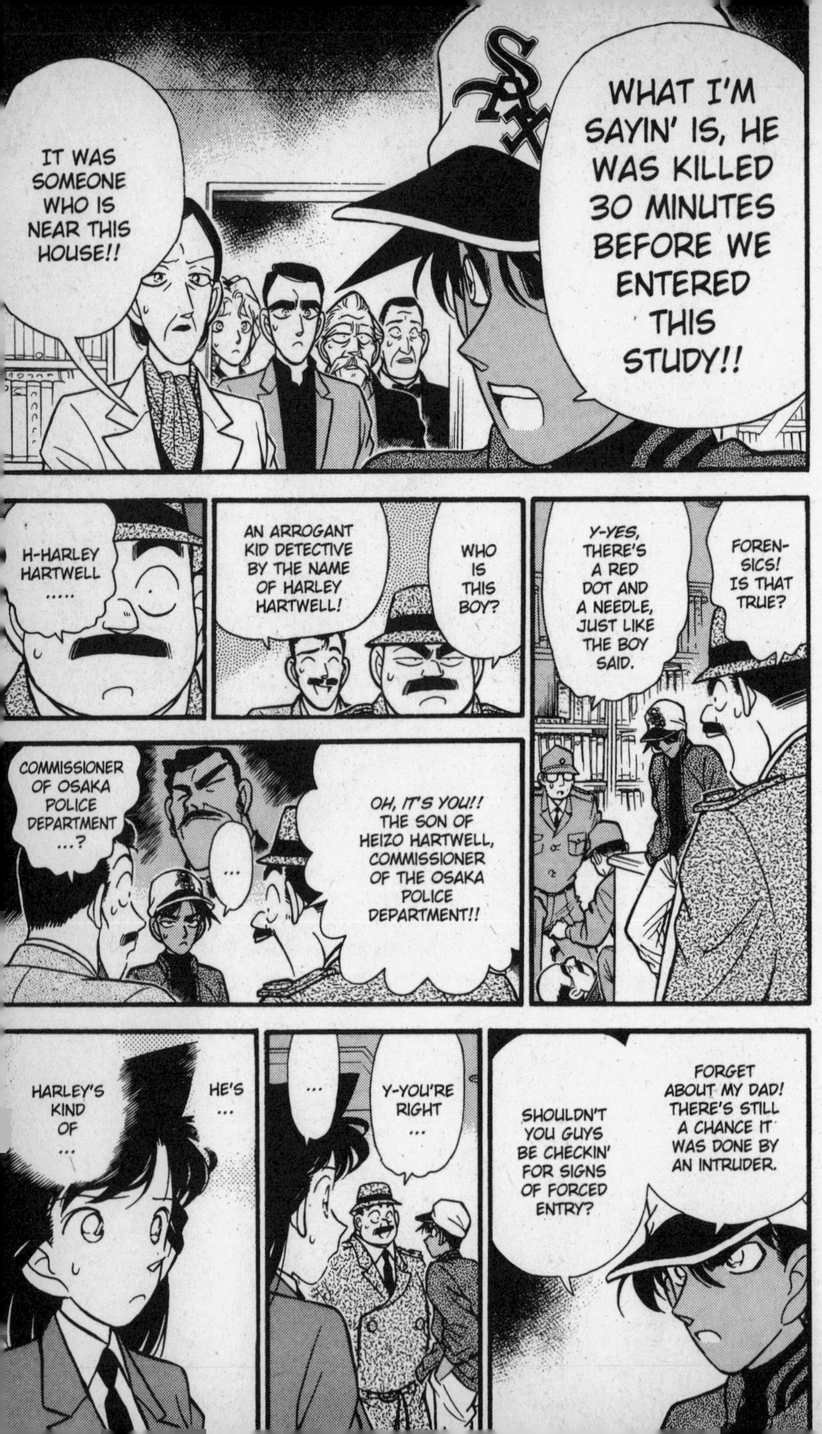
WHAT I'M SAYIN' IS, HE WAS KILLED 30 MINUTES BEFORE WE ENTERED THIS STUDY!!
IT WAS SOMEONE WHO IS NEAR THIS HOUSE!!
FOREN-SICS! IS THAT TRUE?
Y-YES, THERE'S A RED DOT AND A NEEDLE, JUST LIKE THE BOY SAID.
WHO IS THIS BOY?
AN ARROGANT KID DETECTIVE BY THE NAME OF HARLEY HARTWELL!
H-HARLEY HARTWELL .....
OH, IT'S YOU!! THE SON OF HEIZO HARTWELL, COMMISSIONER OF THE OSAKA POLICE DEPARTMENT!!
...
COMMISSIONER OF OSAKA POLICE DEPARTMENT ...?
FORGET ABOUT MY DAD! THERE'S STILL A CHANCE IT WAS DONE BY AN INTRUDER.
SHOULDN'T YOU GUYS BE CHECKIN' FOR SIGNS OF FORCED ENTRY?
Y-YOU'RE RIGHT ...
...
HE'S ...
HARLEY'S KIND OF ...

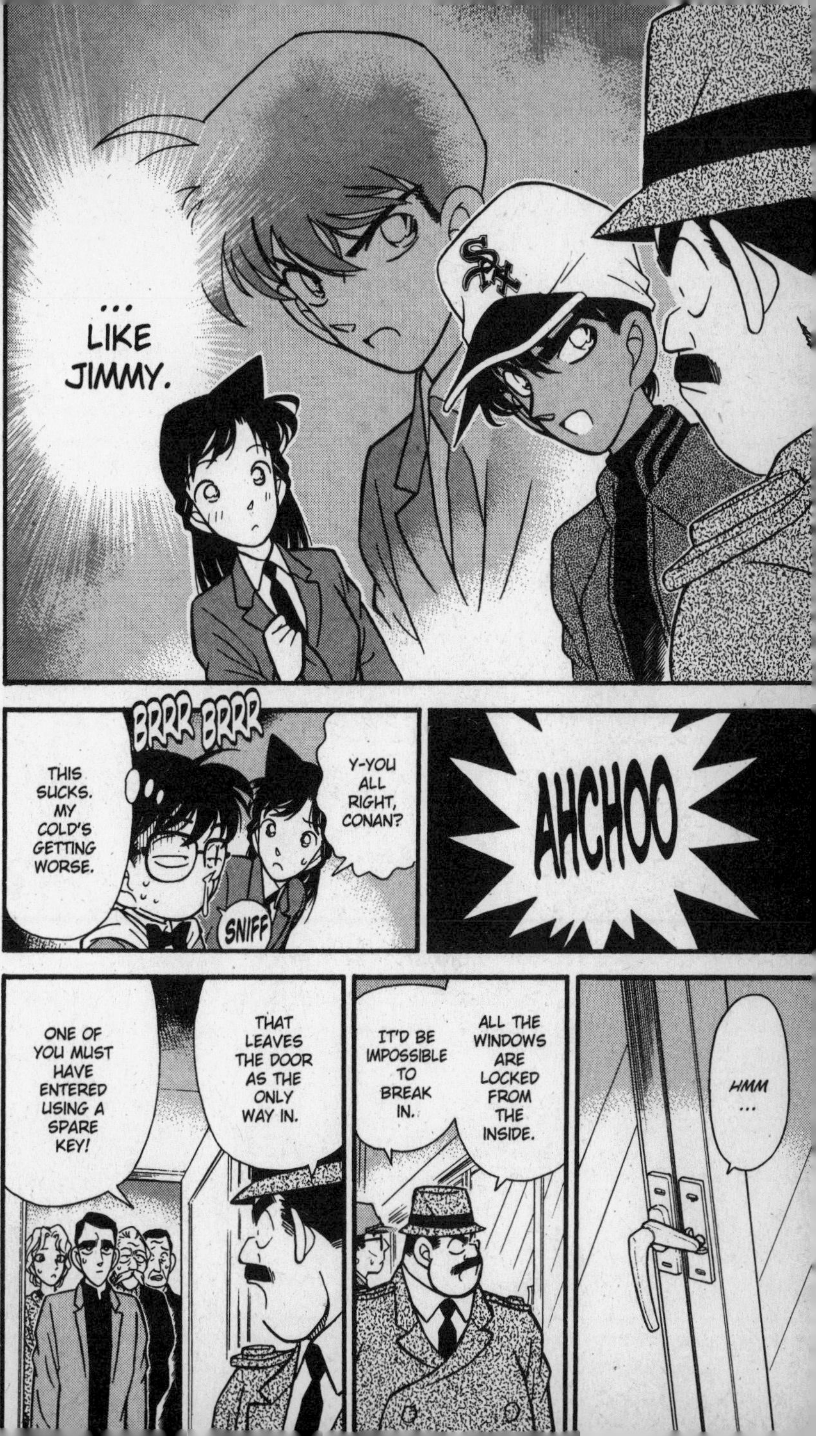
... LIKE JIMMY.
AHCHOO
Y-YOU ALL RIGHT, CONAN?
BRRR BRRR
THIS SUCKS. MY COLD'S GETTING WORSE.
SNIFF
HMM ...
ALL THE WINDOWS ARE LOCKED FROM THE INSIDE.
IT'D BE IMPOSSIBLE TO BREAK IN.
THAT LEAVES THE DOOR AS THE ONLY WAY IN.
ONE OF YOU MUST HAVE ENTERED USING A SPARE KEY!

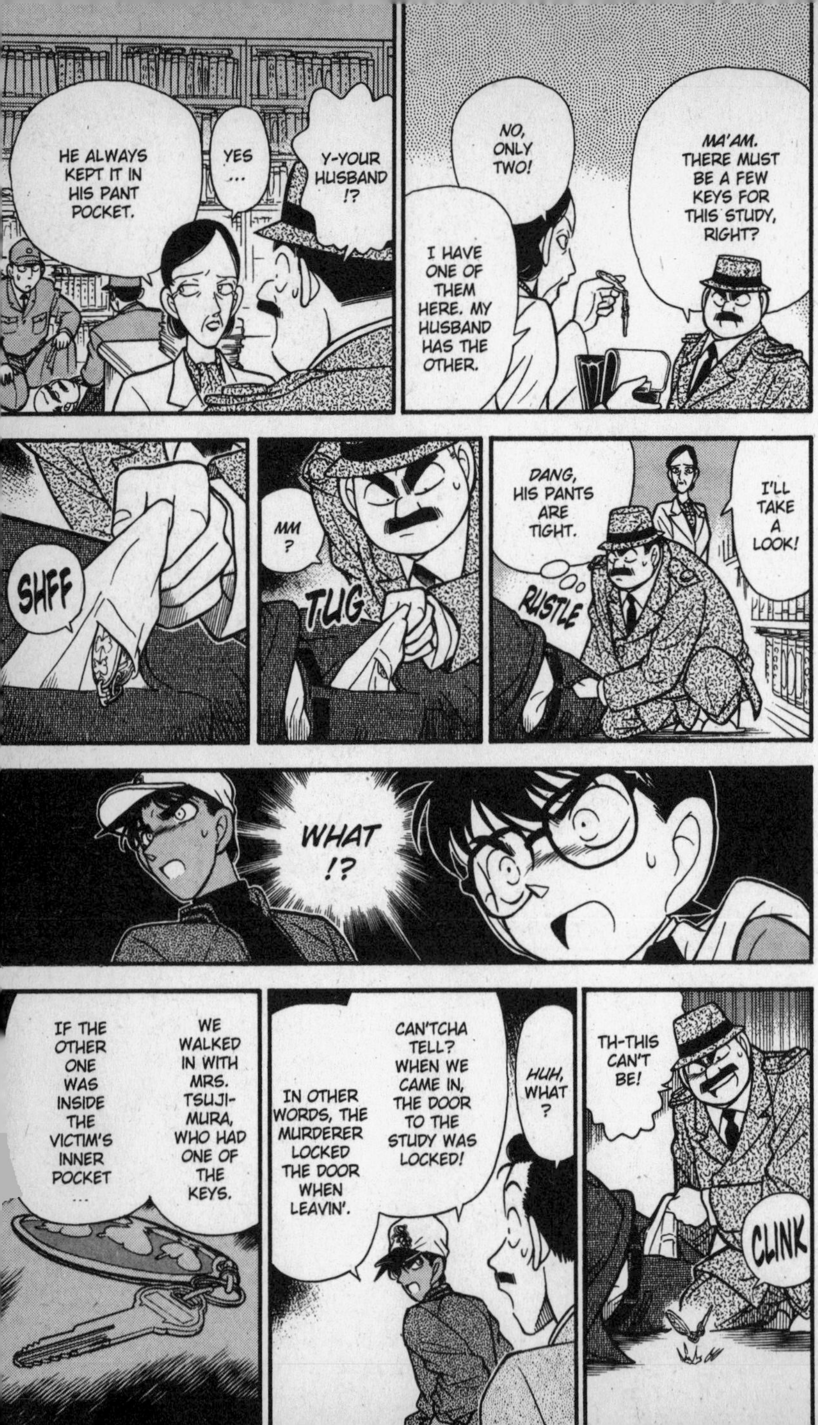
MA'AM. THERE MUST BE A FEW KEYS FOR THIS STUDY, RIGHT?
NO, ONLY TWO!
I HAVE ONE OF THEM HERE. MY HUSBAND HAS THE OTHER.
Y-YOUR HUSBAND !?
YES ...
HE ALWAYS KEPT IT IN HIS PANT POCKET.
I'LL TAKE A LOOK!
DANG, HIS PANTS ARE TIGHT.
RUSTLE
MM ?
TUG
SHFF
WHAT !?
TH-THIS CAN'T BE!
CLINK
HUH, WHAT ?
CAN'TCHA TELL? WHEN WE CAME IN, THE DOOR TO THE STUDY WAS LOCKED!
IN OTHER WORDS, THE MURDERER LOCKED THE DOOR WHEN LEAVIN'.
WE WALKED IN WITH MRS. TSUJI-MURA, WHO HAD ONE OF THE KEYS.
IF THE OTHER ONE WAS INSIDE THE VICTIM'S INNER POCKET ...

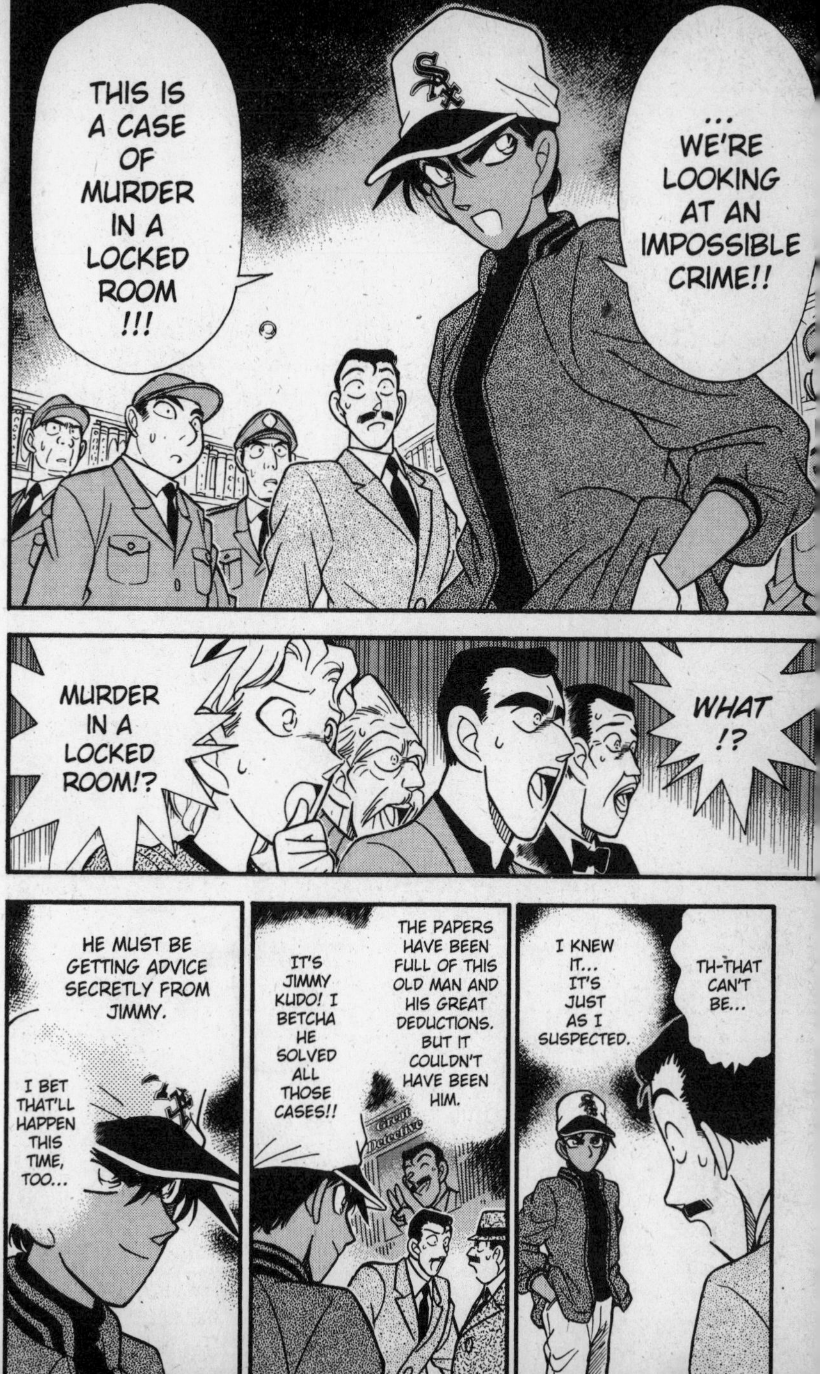
... WE'RE LOOKING AT AN IMPOSSIBLE CRIME!!
THIS IS A CASE OF MURDER IN A LOCKED ROOM!!!
WHAT!?
MURDER IN A LOCKED ROOM!?
TH-THAT CAN'T BE...
I KNEW IT... IT'S JUST AS I SUSPECTED.
THE PAPERS HAVE BEEN FULL OF THIS OLD MAN AND HIS GREAT DEDUCTIONS. BUT IT COULDN'T HAVE BEEN HIM.
IT'S JIMMY KUDO! I BETCHA HE SOLVED ALL THOSE CASES!!
Great Detective
HE MUST BE GETTING ADVICE SECRETLY FROM JIMMY.
I BET THAT'LL HAPPEN THIS TIME, TOO...

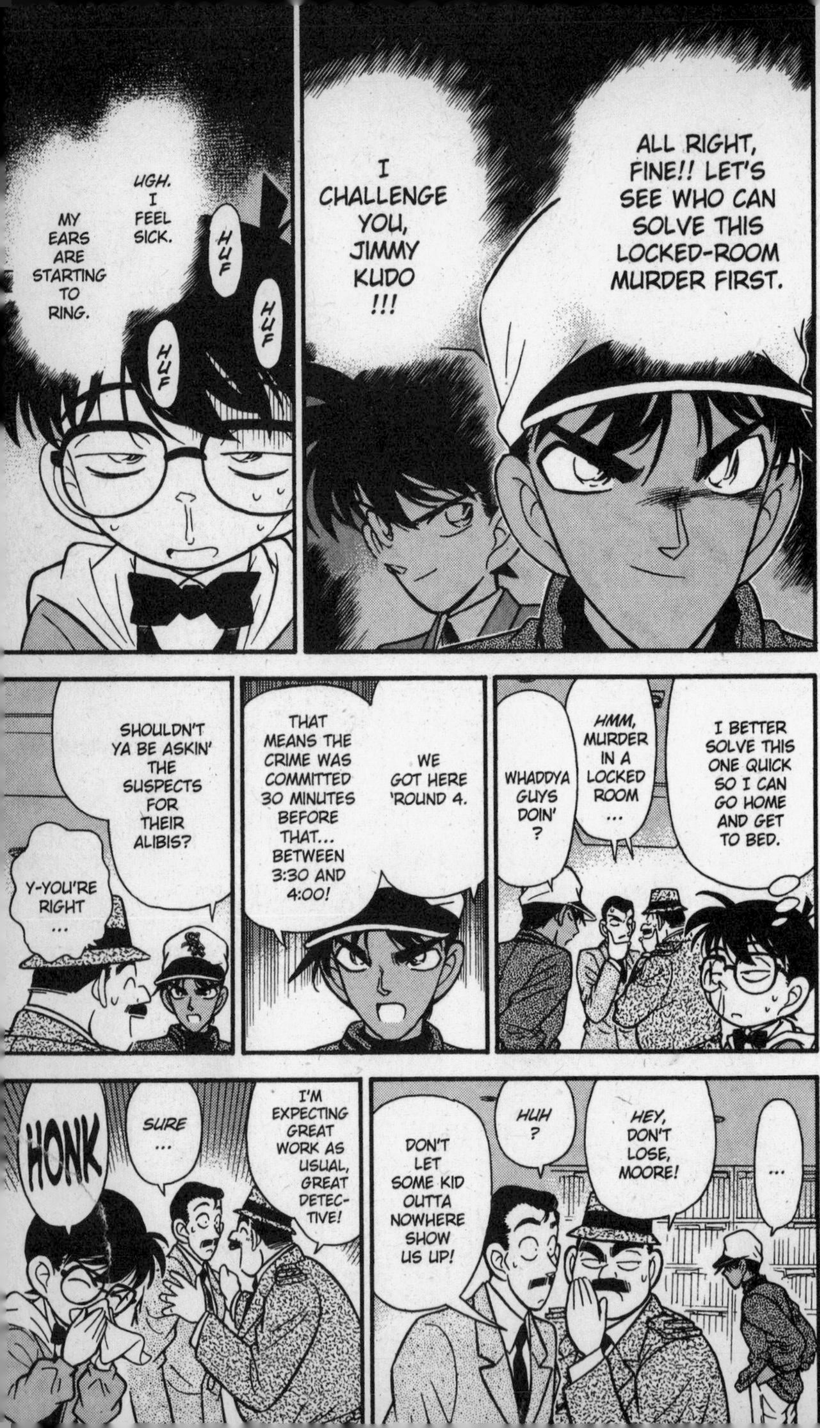
ALL RIGHT, FINE!! LET'S SEE WHO CAN SOLVE THIS LOCKED-ROOM MURDER FIRST.
I CHALLENGE YOU, JIMMY KUDO!!!
HUF
HUF
HUF
UGH. I FEEL SICK.
MY EARS ARE STARTING TO RING.
I BETTER SOLVE THIS ONE QUICK SO I CAN GO HOME AND GET TO BED.
HMM, MURDER IN A LOCKED ROOM...
WHADDYA GUYS DOIN'?
WE GOT HERE 'ROUND 4.
THAT MEANS THE CRIME WAS COMMITTED 30 MINUTES BEFORE THAT... BETWEEN 3:30 AND 4:00!
SHOULDN'T YA BE ASKIN' THE SUSPECTS FOR THEIR ALIBIS?
Y-YOU'RE RIGHT...
...
HEY, DON'T LOSE, MOORE!
HUH?
DON'T LET SOME KID OUTTA NOWHERE SHOW US UP!
I'M EXPECTING GREAT WORK AS USUAL, GREAT DETECTIVE!
SURE...
HONK

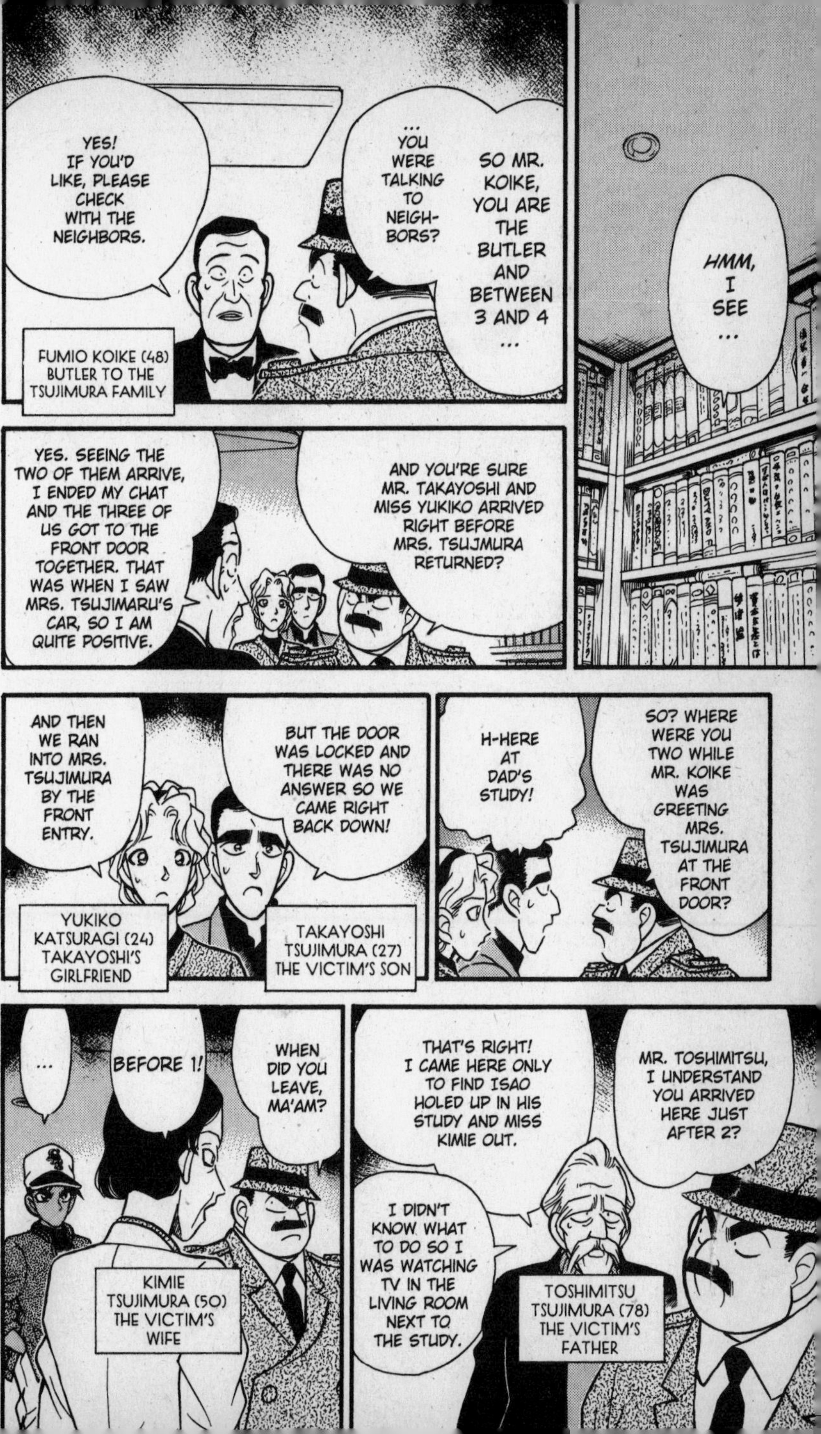
HMM, I SEE ...
SO MR. KOIKE, YOU ARE THE BUTLER AND BETWEEN 3 AND 4 ...
... YOU WERE TALKING TO NEIGH-BORS?
YES! IF YOU'D LIKE, PLEASE CHECK WITH THE NEIGHBORS.
FUMIO KOIKE (48) BUTLER TO THE TSUJIMURA FAMILY
AND YOU'RE SURE MR. TAKAYOSHI AND MISS YUKIKO ARRIVED RIGHT BEFORE MRS. TSUJMURA RETURNED?
YES. SEEING THE TWO OF THEM ARRIVE, I ENDED MY CHAT AND THE THREE OF US GOT TO THE FRONT DOOR TOGETHER. THAT WAS WHEN I SAW MRS. TSUJIMARU'S CAR, SO I AM QUITE POSITIVE.
SO? WHERE WERE YOU TWO WHILE MR. KOIKE WAS GREETING MRS. TSUJIMURA AT THE FRONT DOOR?
H-HERE AT DAD'S STUDY!
BUT THE DOOR WAS LOCKED AND THERE WAS NO ANSWER SO WE CAME RIGHT BACK DOWN!
AND THEN WE RAN INTO MRS. TSUJIMURA BY THE FRONT ENTRY.
TAKAYOSHI TSUJIMURA (27) THE VICTIM'S SON
YUKIKO KATSURAGI (24) TAKAYOSHI'S GIRLFRIEND
MR. TOSHIMITSU, I UNDERSTAND YOU ARRIVED HERE JUST AFTER 2?
THAT'S RIGHT! I CAME HERE ONLY TO FIND ISAO HOLED UP IN HIS STUDY AND MISS KIMIE OUT.
I DIDN'T KNOW WHAT TO DO SO I WAS WATCHING TV IN THE LIVING ROOM NEXT TO THE STUDY.
TOSHIMITSU TSUJIMURA (78) THE VICTIM'S FATHER
WHEN DID YOU LEAVE, MA'AM?
BEFORE 1!
...
KIMIE TSUJIMURA (50) THE VICTIM'S WIFE

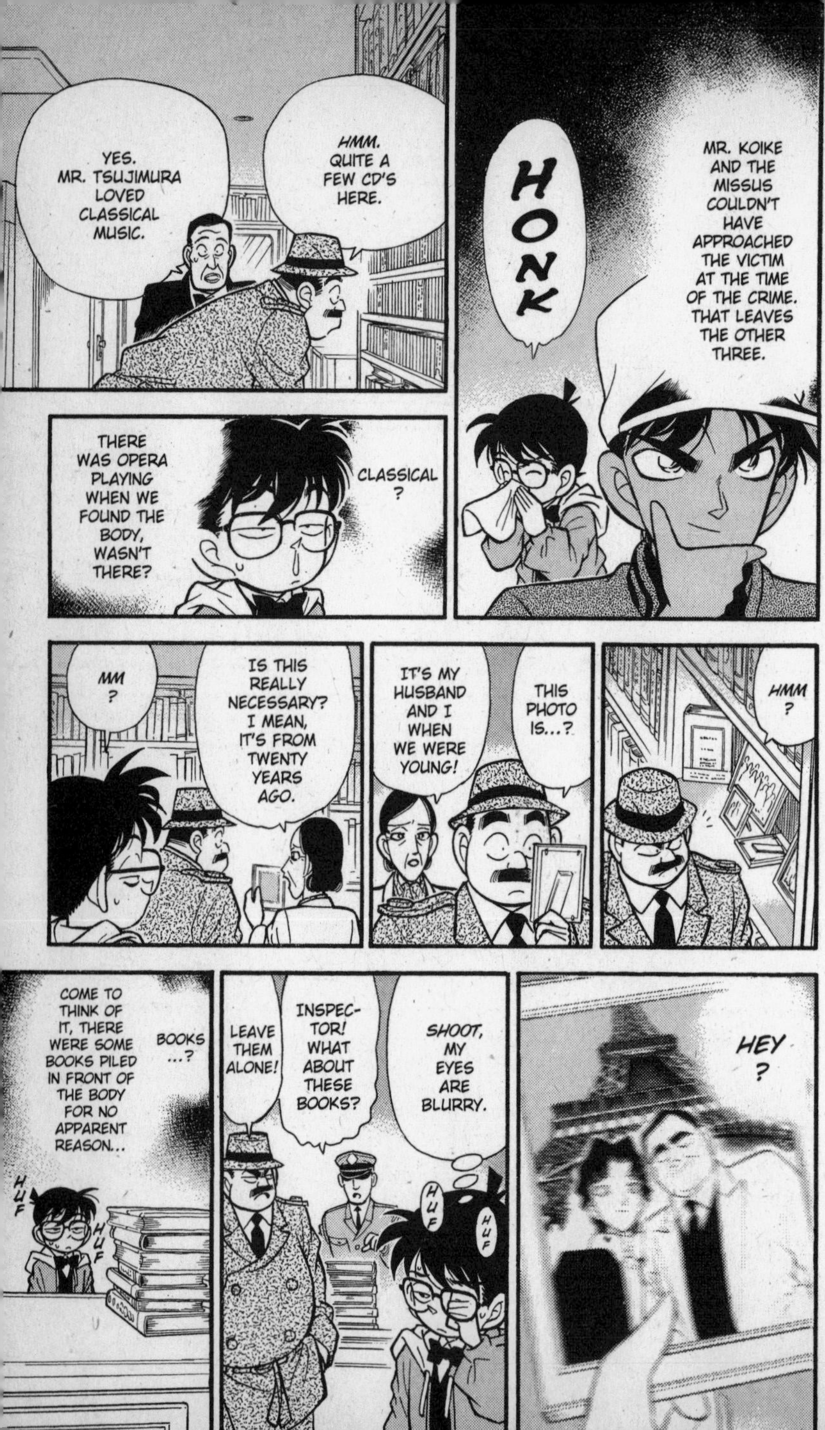
MR. KOIKE AND THE MISSUS COULDN'T HAVE APPROACHED THE VICTIM AT THE TIME OF THE CRIME. THAT LEAVES THE OTHER THREE.
HONK
HMM. QUITE A FEW CD'S HERE.
YES. MR. TSUJIMURA LOVED CLASSICAL MUSIC.
CLASSICAL?
THERE WAS OPERA PLAYING WHEN WE FOUND THE BODY, WASN'T THERE?
HMM?
THIS PHOTO IS...?
IT'S MY HUSBAND AND I WHEN WE WERE YOUNG!
IS THIS REALLY NECESSARY? I MEAN, IT'S FROM TWENTY YEARS AGO.
MM?
HEY?
SHOOT, MY EYES ARE BLURRY.
HUF
HUF
INSPECTOR! WHAT ABOUT THESE BOOKS?
LEAVE THEM ALONE!
BOOKS...?
COME TO THINK OF IT, THERE WERE SOME BOOKS PILED IN FRONT OF THE BODY FOR NO APPARENT REASON...
HUF
HUF

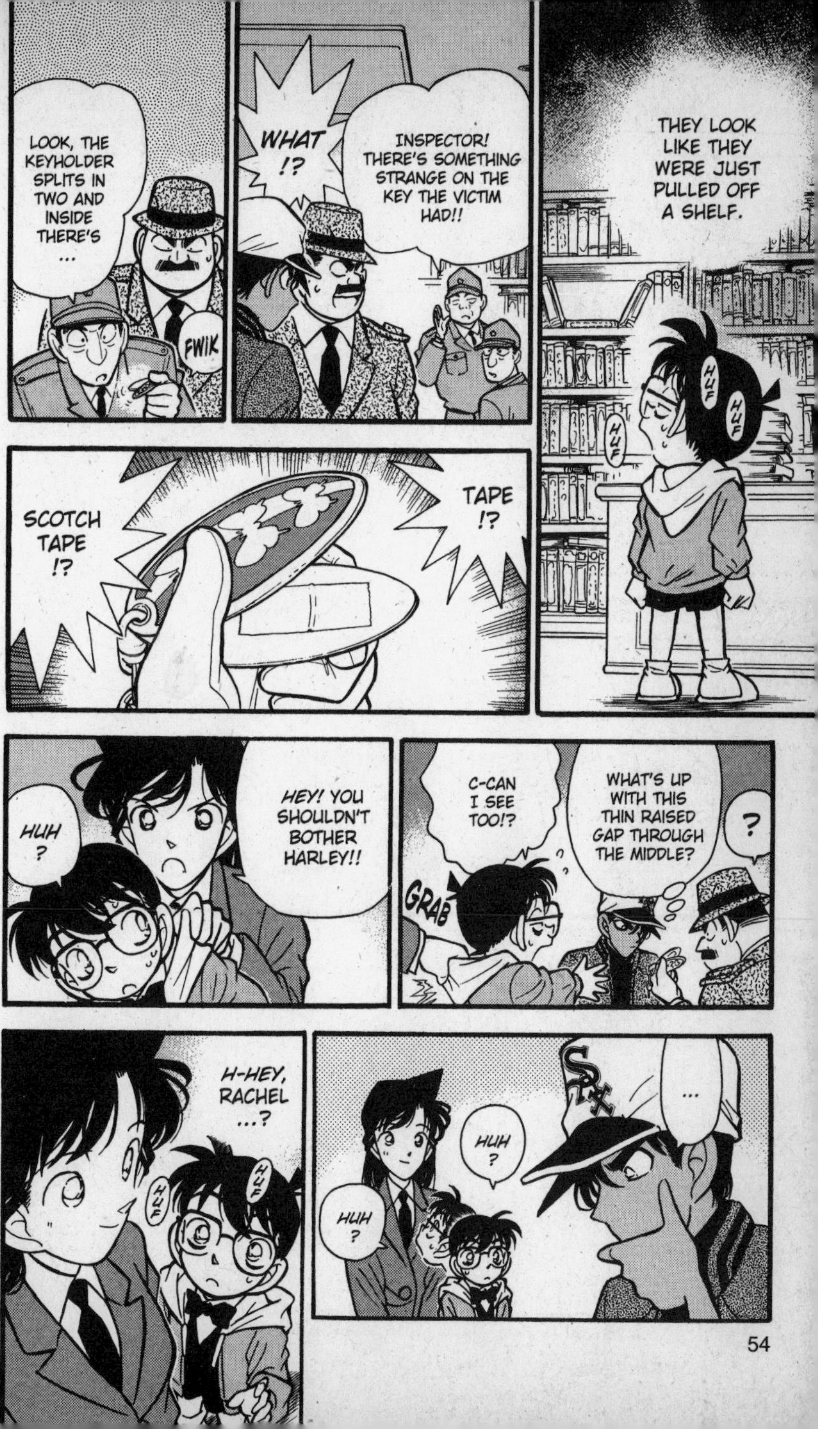
THEY LOOK LIKE THEY WERE JUST PULLED OFF A SHELF.
HUF
HUF
HUF
INSPECTOR! THERE'S SOMETHING STRANGE ON THE KEY THE VICTIM HAD!!
WHAT !?
LOOK, THE KEYHOLDER SPLITS IN TWO AND INSIDE THERE'S ...
FWIK
TAPE !?
SCOTCH TAPE !?
?
WHAT'S UP WITH THIS THIN RAISED GAP THROUGH THE MIDDLE?
C-CAN I SEE TOO!?
GRAB
HEY! YOU SHOULDN'T BOTHER HARLEY!!
HUH ?
...
HUH ?
HUH ?
H-HEY, RACHEL ...?
HUF
HUF

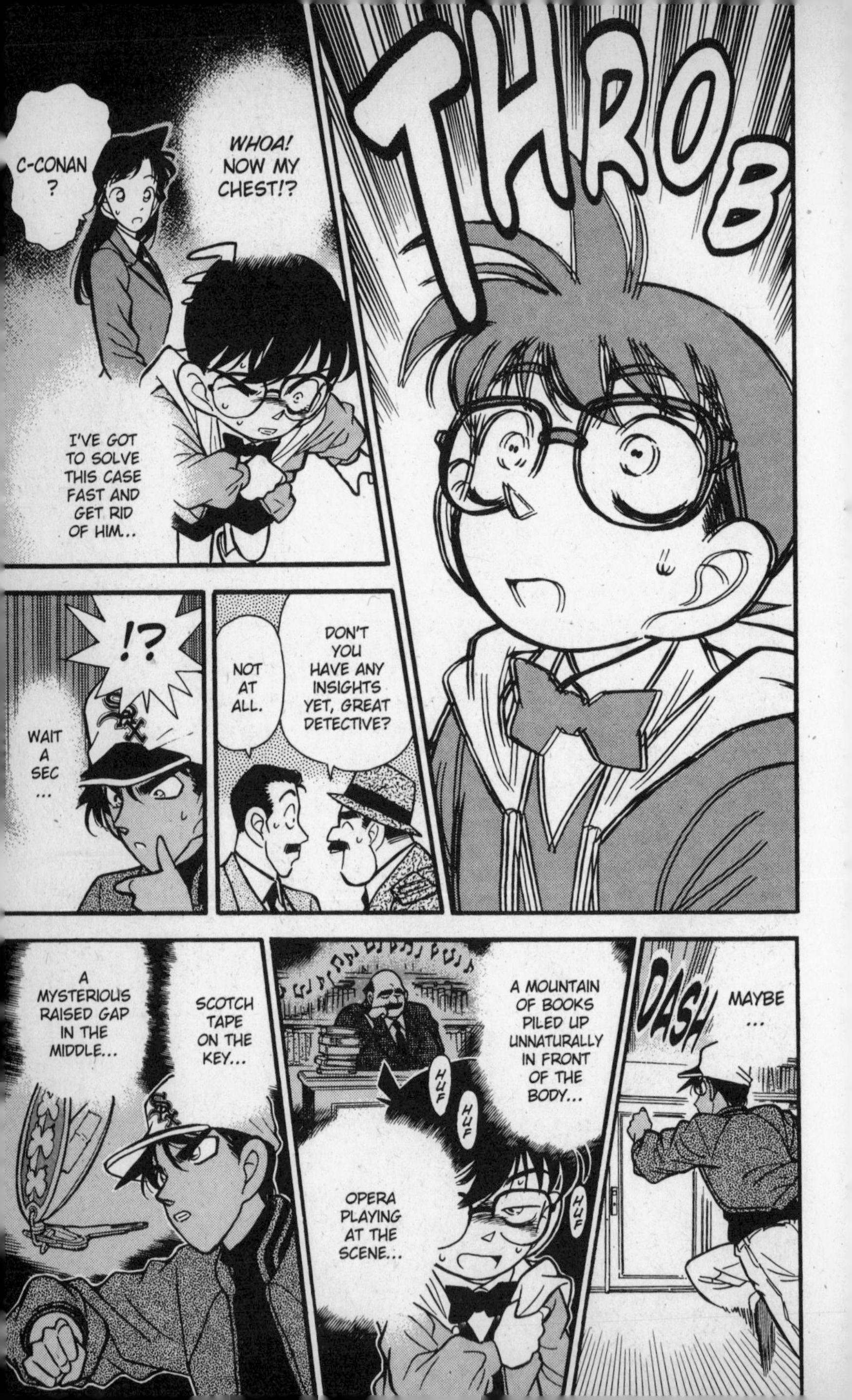
THROB
WHOA! NOW MY CHEST!?
C-CONAN ?
I'VE GOT TO SOLVE THIS CASE FAST AND GET RID OF HIM...
DON'T YOU HAVE ANY INSIGHTS YET, GREAT DETECTIVE?
NOT AT ALL.
!?
WAIT A SEC ...
MAYBE ...
DASH
A MOUNTAIN OF BOOKS PILED UP UNNATURALLY IN FRONT OF THE BODY...
HUF
HUF
HUF
OPERA PLAYING AT THE SCENE...
SCOTCH TAPE ON THE KEY...
A MYSTERIOUS RAISED GAP IN THE MIDDLE...

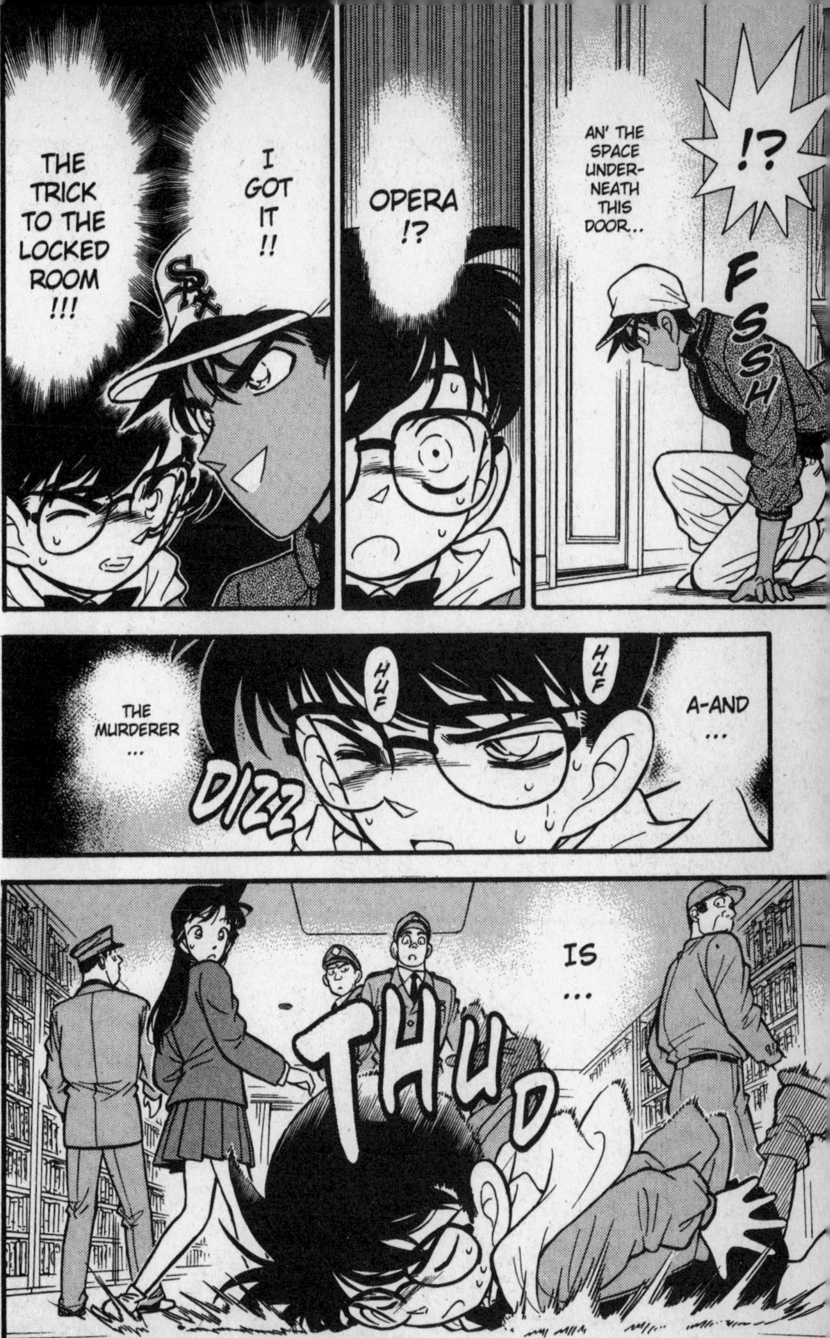
!?
AN' THE SPACE UNDER-NEATH THIS DOOR...
FSSH
OPERA !?
I GOT IT !!
THE TRICK TO THE LOCKED ROOM !!!
A-AND ...
HUF
HUF
THE MURDERER ...
DIZZ
IS ...
THUD

FILE 4: THE GREAT DETECTIVE OF THE EAST...!?

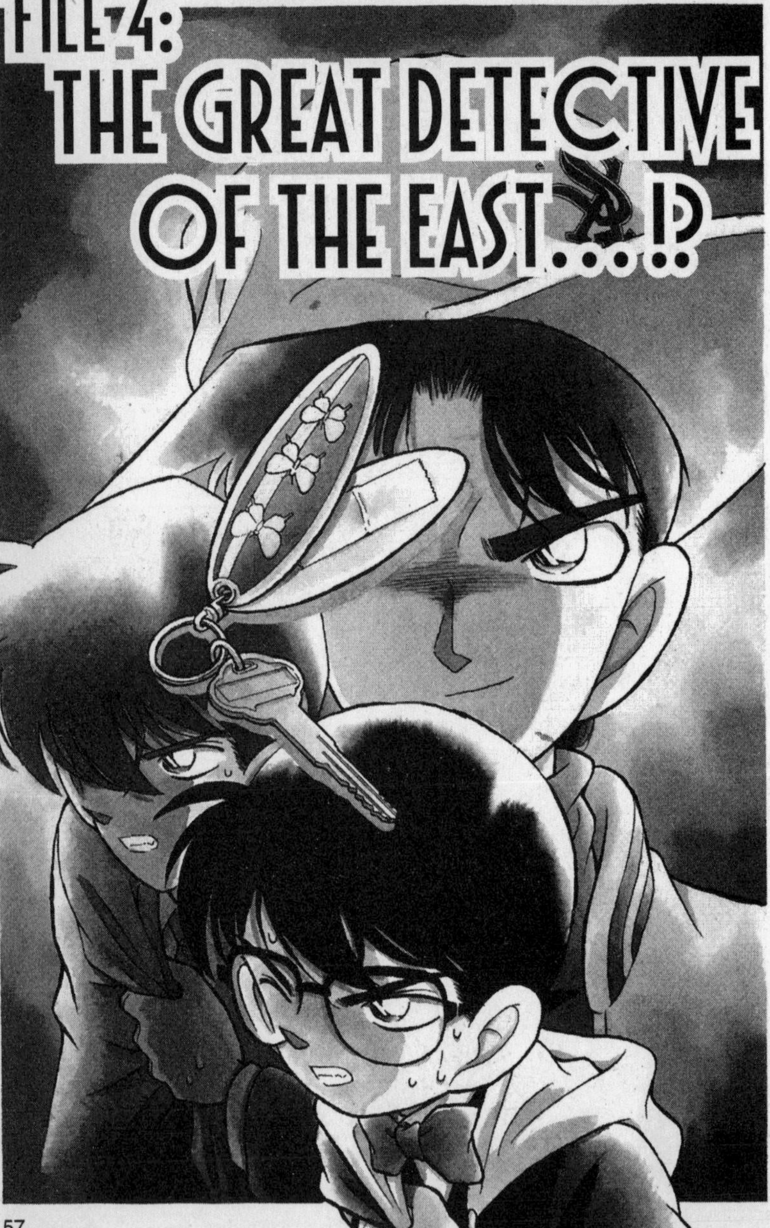

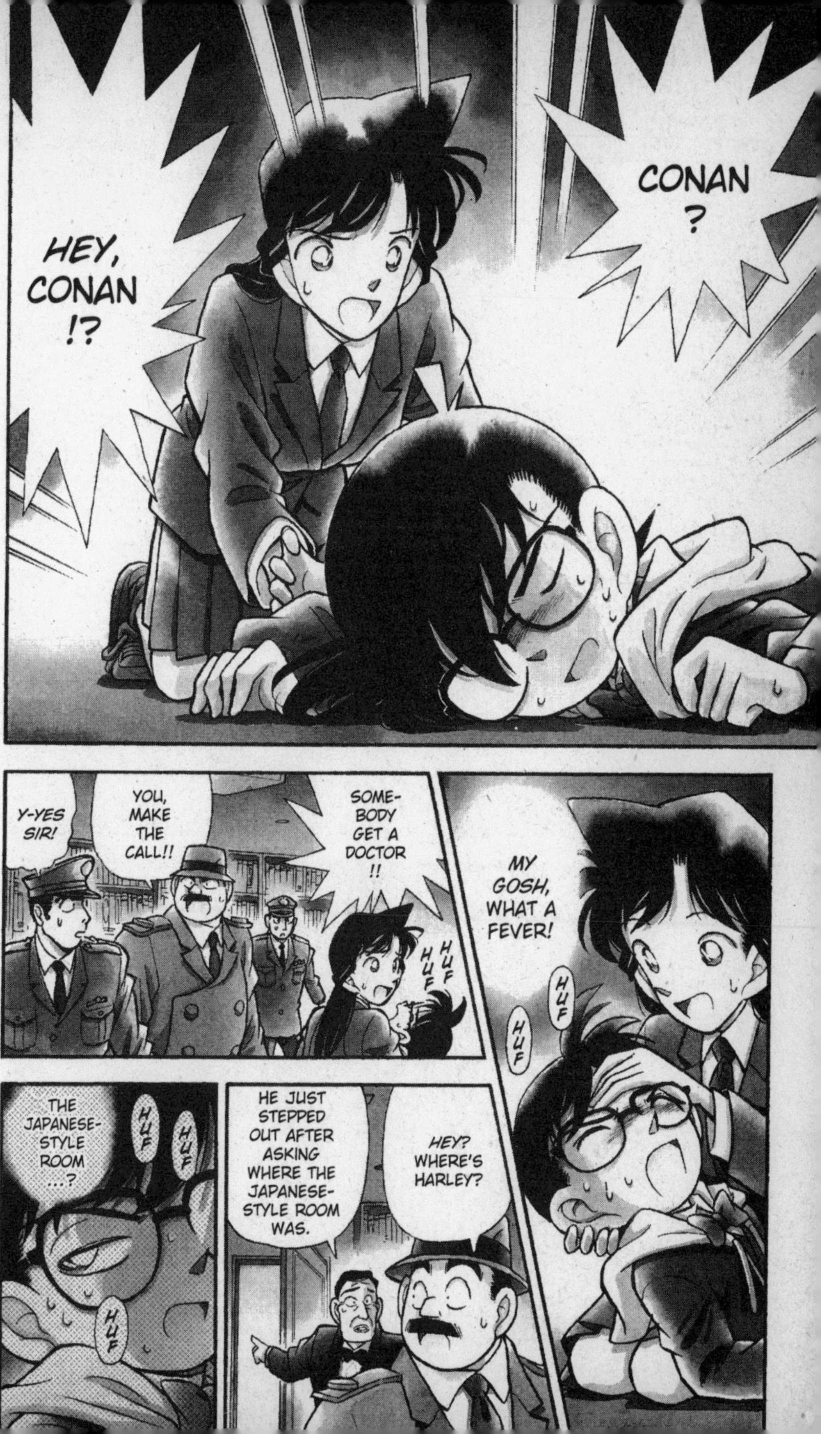
CONAN ?
HEY, CONAN !?
MY GOSH, WHAT A FEVER!
HUF HUF
SOME-BODY GET A DOCTOR !!
YOU, MAKE THE CALL!!
Y-YES SIR!
HUF HUF
HEY? WHERE'S HARLEY?
HE JUST STEPPED OUT AFTER ASKING WHERE THE JAPANESE-STYLE ROOM WAS.
HUF HUF
THE JAPANESE-STYLE ROOM ...?
HUF

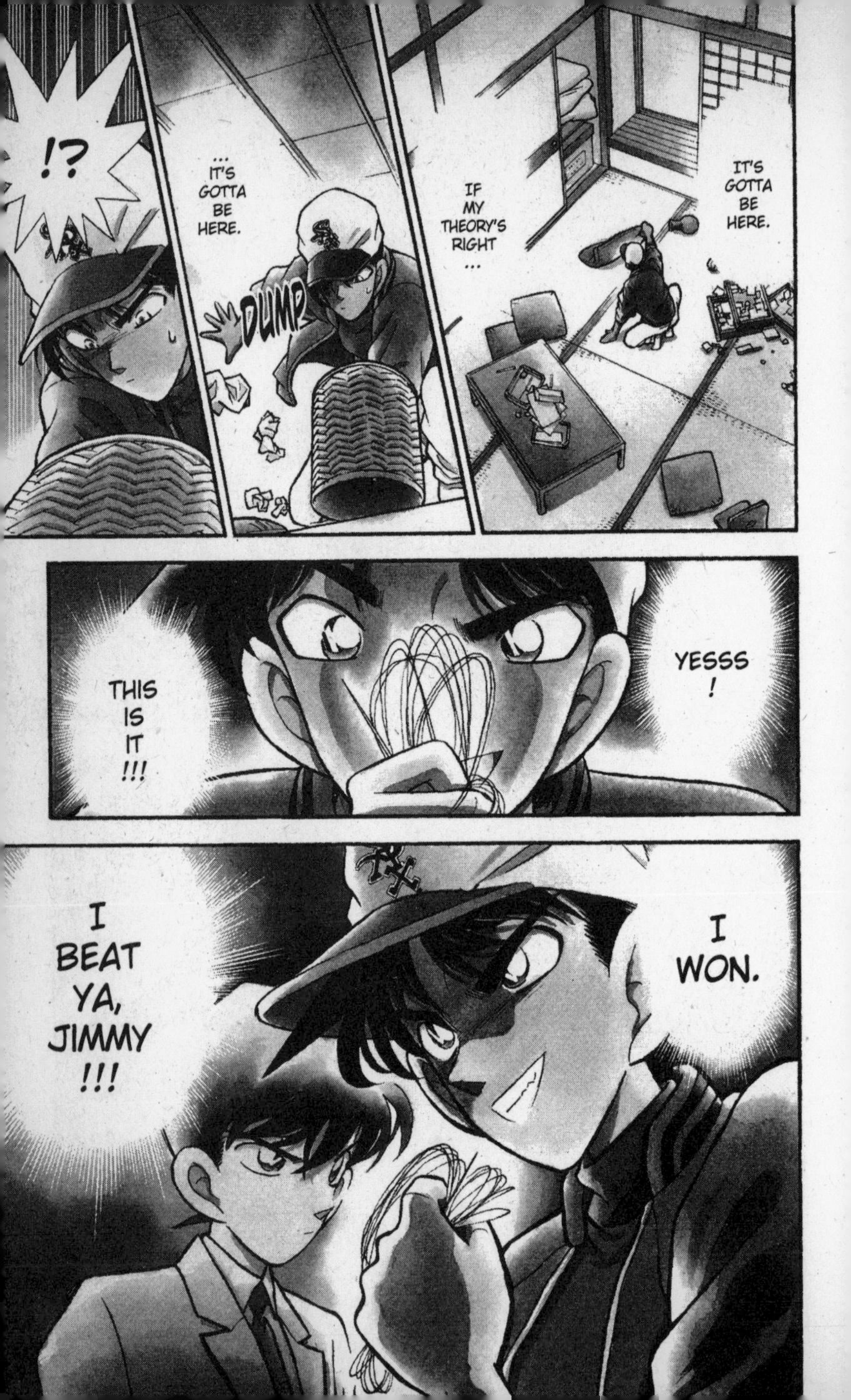

IT'S GOTTA BE HERE.
IF MY THEORY'S RIGHT...
... IT'S GOTTA BE HERE.
DUMP
!?
YESSS!
THIS IS IT!!!
I WON.
I BEAT YA, JIMMY!!!

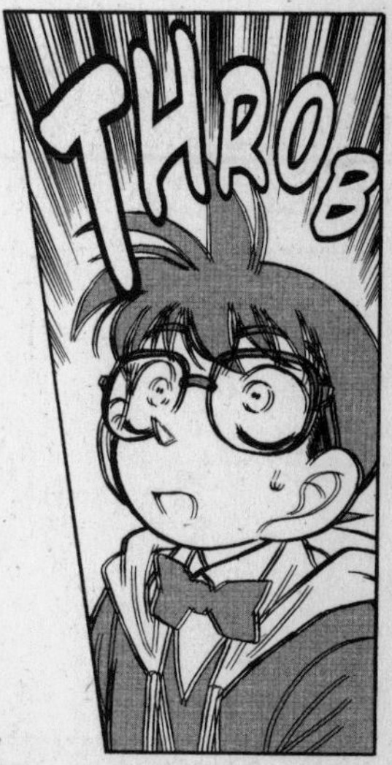
THROB

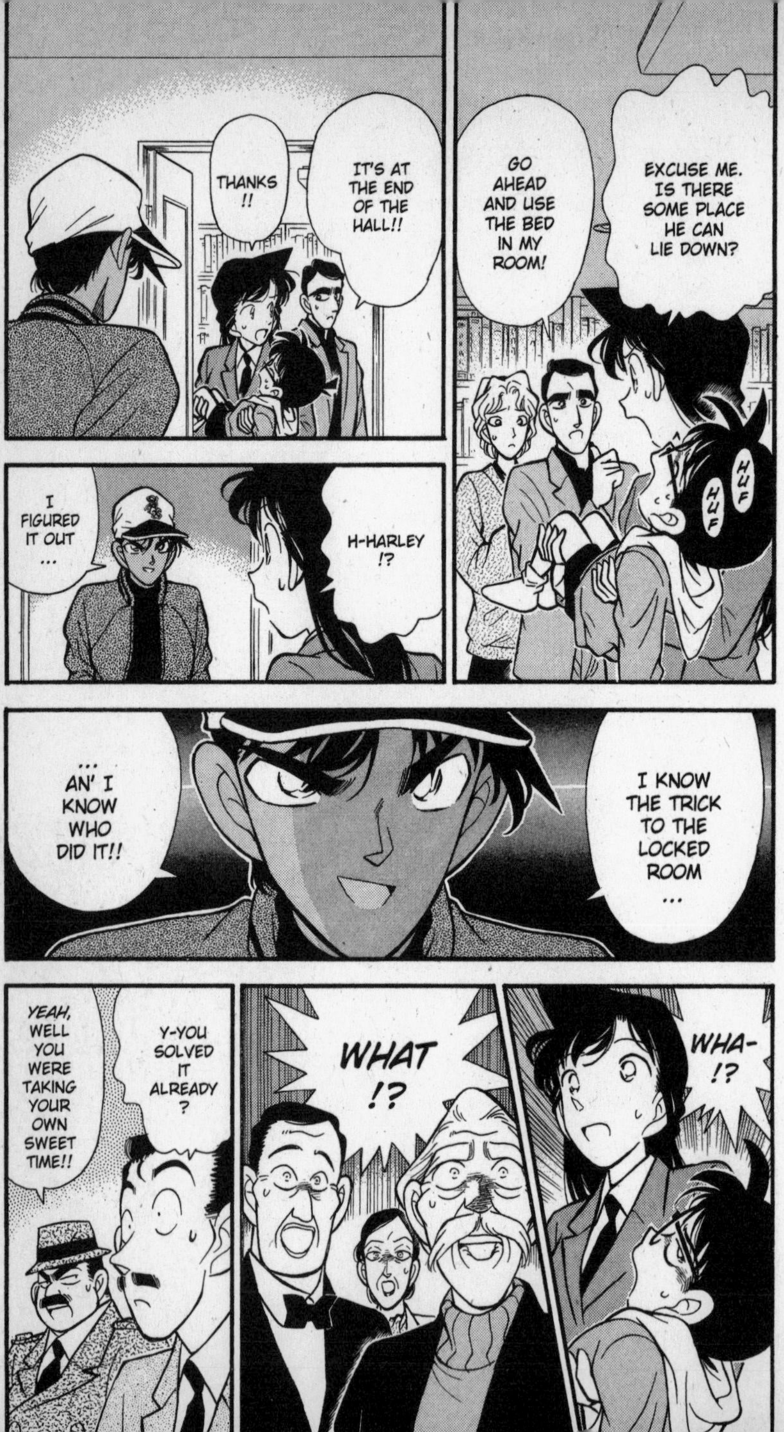
EXCUSE ME. IS THERE SOME PLACE HE CAN LIE DOWN?
GO AHEAD AND USE THE BED IN MY ROOM!
HUF HUF
IT'S AT THE END OF THE HALL!!
THANKS !!
H-HARLEY !?
I FIGURED IT OUT ...
I KNOW THE TRICK TO THE LOCKED ROOM ...
... AN' I KNOW WHO DID IT!!
WHA- !?
WHAT !?
Y-YOU SOLVED IT ALREADY ?
YEAH, WELL YOU WERE TAKING YOUR OWN SWEET TIME!!

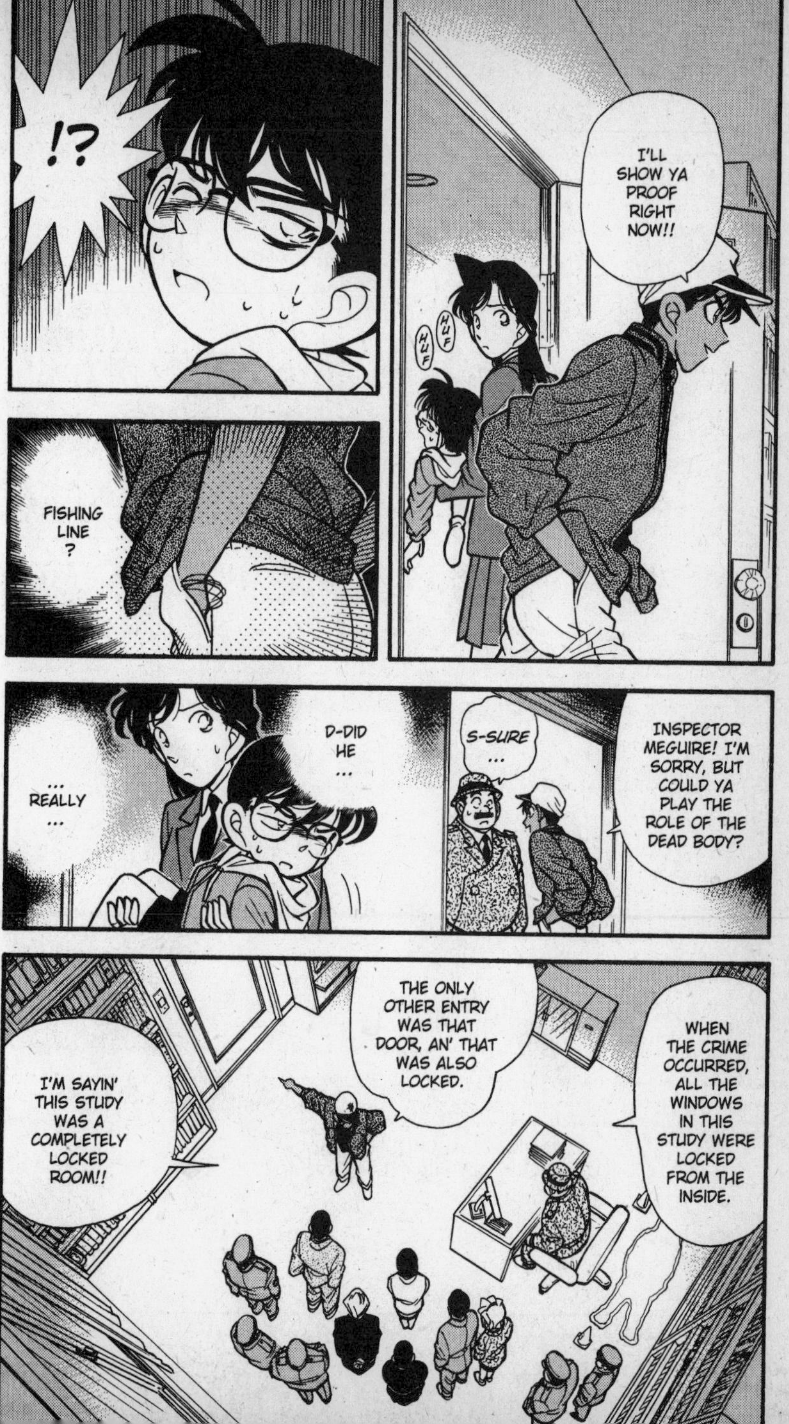
I'LL SHOW YA PROOF RIGHT NOW!!
HUF HUF
!?
FISHING LINE ?
INSPECTOR MEGUIRE! I'M SORRY, BUT COULD YA PLAY THE ROLE OF THE DEAD BODY?
S-SURE ...
D-DID HE ...
... REALLY ...
WHEN THE CRIME OCCURRED, ALL THE WINDOWS IN THIS STUDY WERE LOCKED FROM THE INSIDE.
THE ONLY OTHER ENTRY WAS THAT DOOR, AN' THAT WAS ALSO LOCKED.
I'M SAYIN' THIS STUDY WAS A COMPLETELY LOCKED ROOM!!

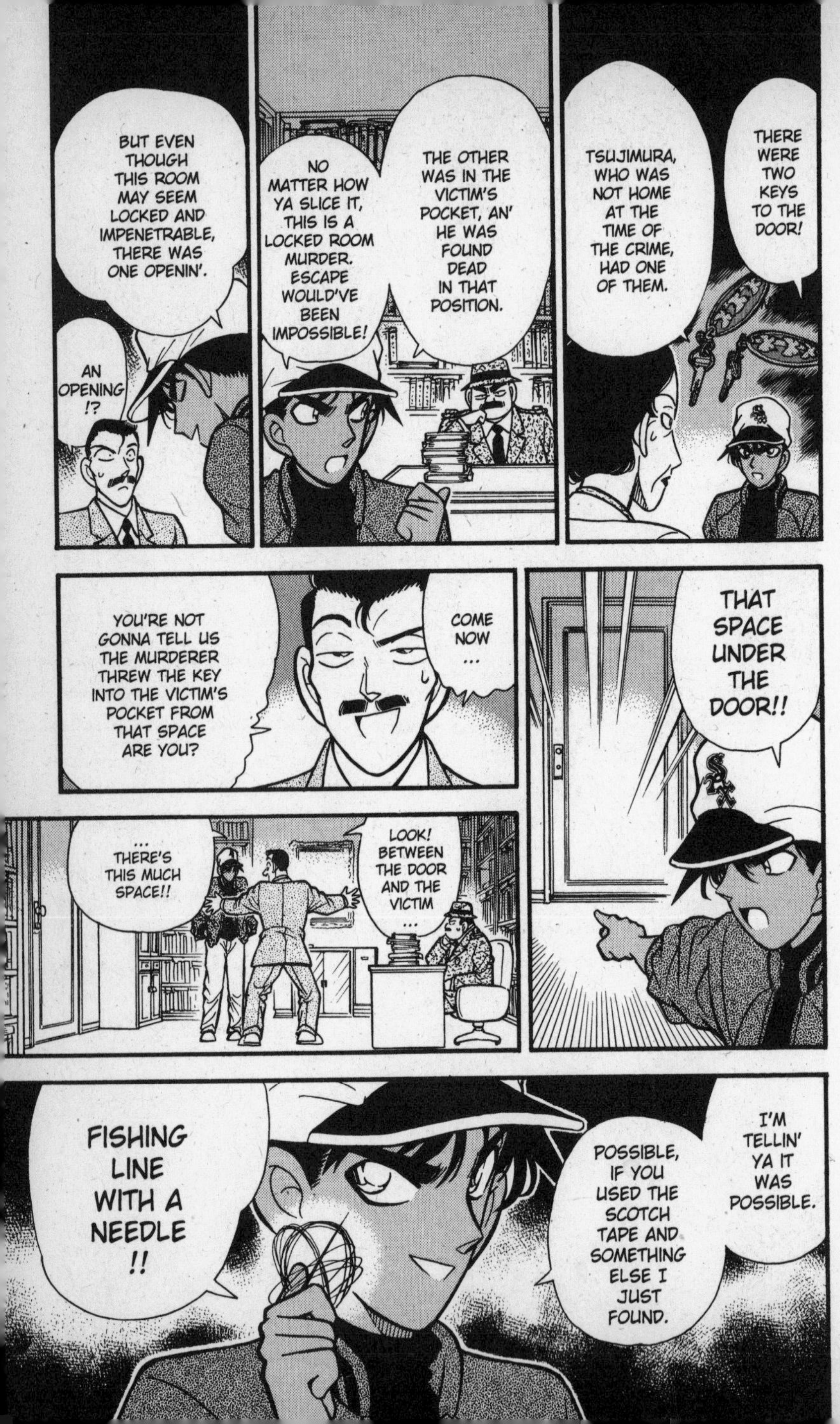
THERE WERE TWO KEYS TO THE DOOR!
TSUJIMURA, WHO WAS NOT HOME AT THE TIME OF THE CRIME, HAD ONE OF THEM.
THE OTHER WAS IN THE VICTIM'S POCKET, AN' HE WAS FOUND DEAD IN THAT POSITION.
NO MATTER HOW YA SLICE IT, THIS IS A LOCKED ROOM MURDER. ESCAPE WOULD'VE BEEN IMPOSSIBLE!
BUT EVEN THOUGH THIS ROOM MAY SEEM LOCKED AND IMPENETRABLE, THERE WAS ONE OPENIN'.
AN OPENING!?
THAT SPACE UNDER THE DOOR!!
COME NOW ...
YOU'RE NOT GONNA TELL US THE MURDERER THREW THE KEY INTO THE VICTIM'S POCKET FROM THAT SPACE ARE YOU?
LOOK! BETWEEN THE DOOR AND THE VICTIM ...
... THERE'S THIS MUCH SPACE!!
I'M TELLIN' YA IT WAS POSSIBLE.
POSSIBLE, IF YOU USED THE SCOTCH TAPE AND SOMETHING ELSE I JUST FOUND.
FISHING LINE WITH A NEEDLE !!

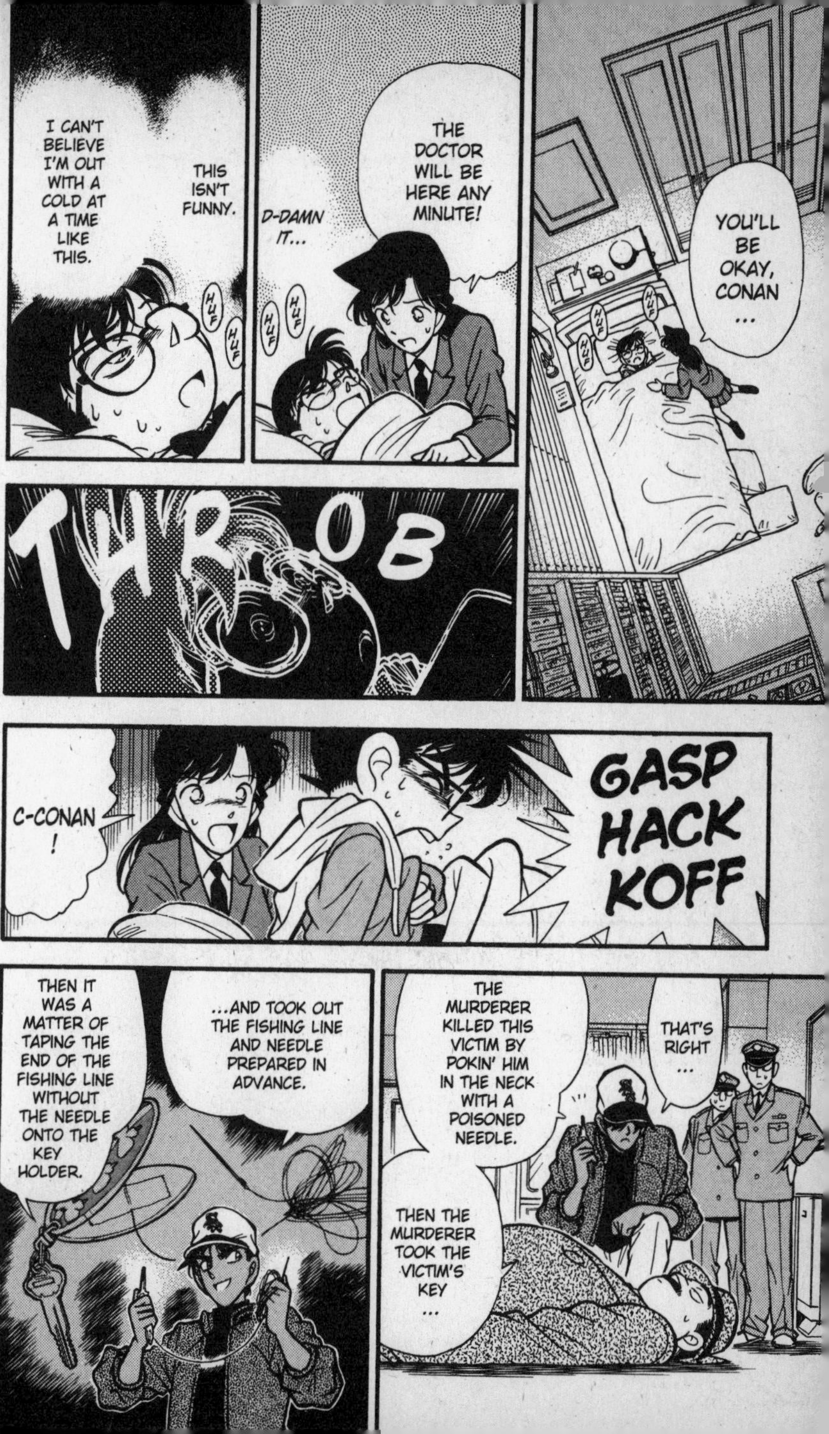

YOU'LL BE OKAY, CONAN ...
HUF
HUF
THE DOCTOR WILL BE HERE ANY MINUTE!
D-DAMN IT...
HUF
HUF
I CAN'T BELIEVE I'M OUT WITH A COLD AT A TIME LIKE THIS.
THIS ISN'T FUNNY.
HUF
HUF
THROB
GASP HACK KOFF
C-CONAN!
THAT'S RIGHT ...
THE MURDERER KILLED THIS VICTIM BY POKIN' HIM IN THE NECK WITH A POISONED NEEDLE.
THEN THE MURDERER TOOK THE VICTIM'S KEY ...
...AND TOOK OUT THE FISHING LINE AND NEEDLE PREPARED IN ADVANCE.
THEN IT WAS A MATTER OF TAPING THE END OF THE FISHING LINE WITHOUT THE NEEDLE ONTO THE KEY HOLDER.

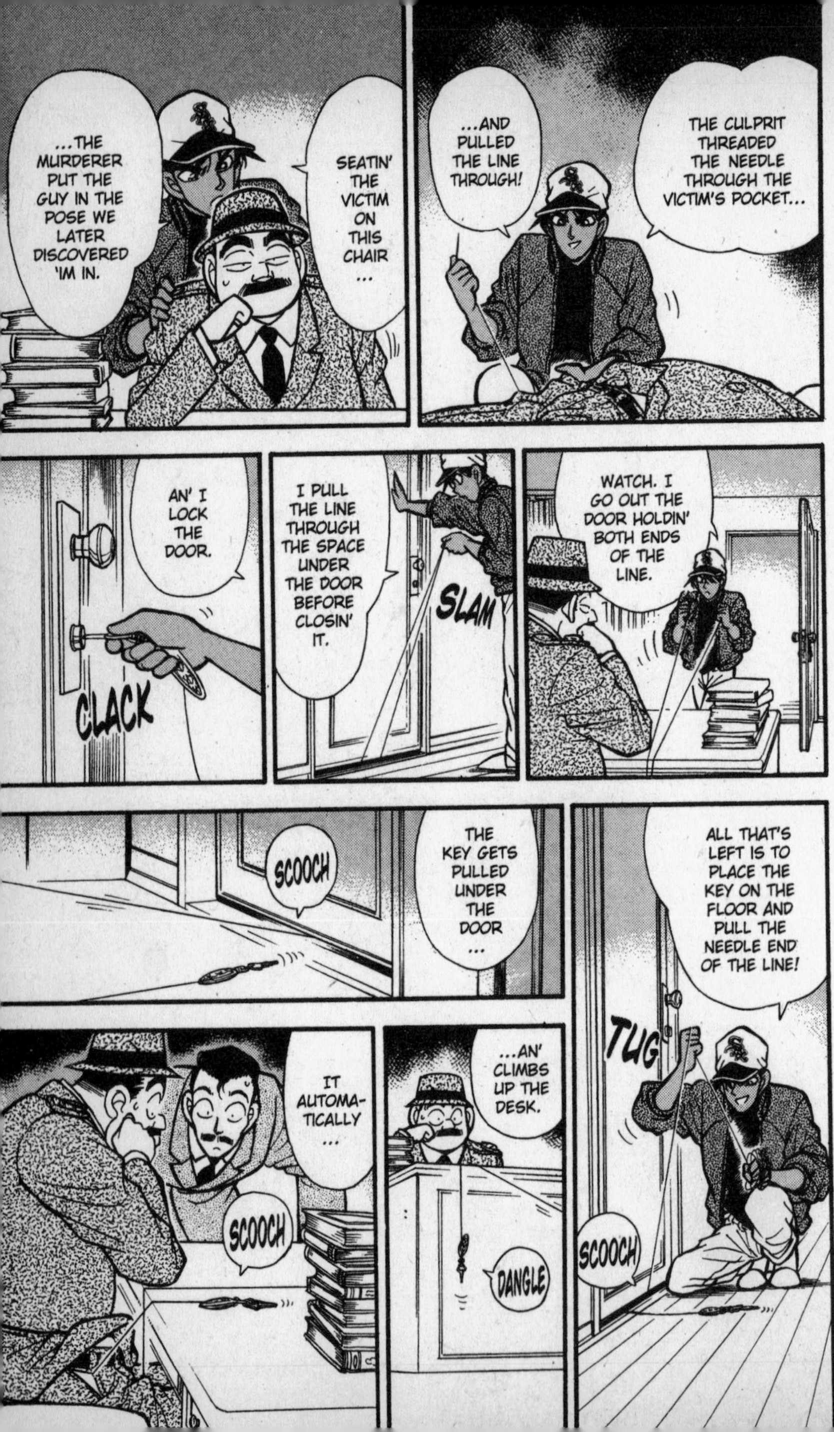
THE CULPRIT THREADED THE NEEDLE THROUGH THE VICTIM'S POCKET...
...AND PULLED THE LINE THROUGH!
SEATIN' THE VICTIM ON THIS CHAIR...
...THE MURDERER PUT THE GUY IN THE POSE WE LATER DISCOVERED 'IM IN.
WATCH. I GO OUT THE DOOR HOLDIN' BOTH ENDS OF THE LINE.
I PULL THE LINE THROUGH THE SPACE UNDER THE DOOR BEFORE CLOSIN' IT.
SLAM
AN' I LOCK THE DOOR.
CLACK
ALL THAT'S LEFT IS TO PLACE THE KEY ON THE FLOOR AND PULL THE NEEDLE END OF THE LINE!
TUG
SCOOCH
THE KEY GETS PULLED UNDER THE DOOR...
SCOOCH
...AN' CLIMBS UP THE DESK.
DANGLE
IT AUTOMATICALLY...
SCOOCH

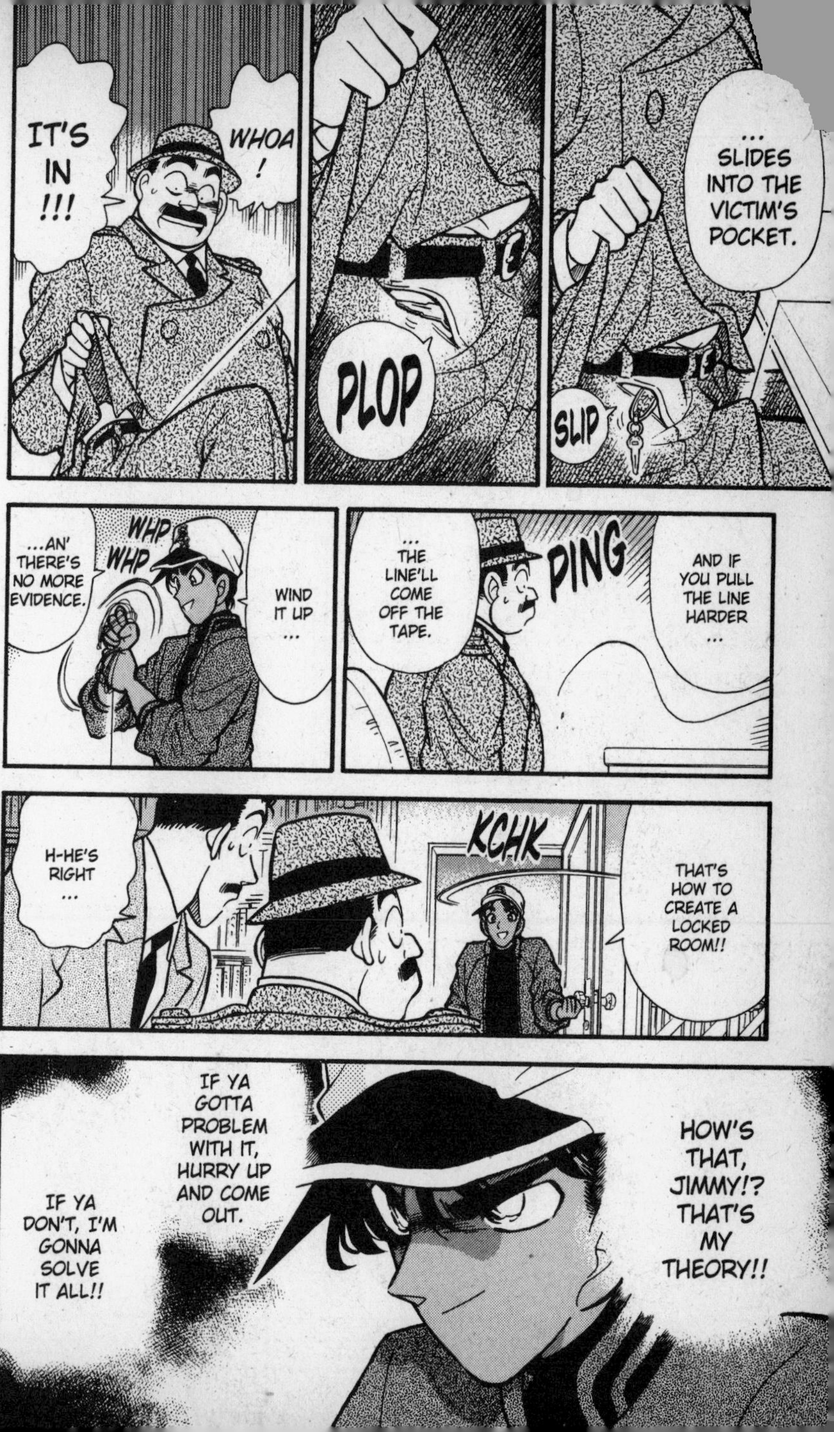

... SLIDES INTO THE VICTIM'S POCKET.
SLIP
PLOP
WHOA!
IT'S IN!!!
AND IF YOU PULL THE LINE HARDER ...
PING
... THE LINE'LL COME OFF THE TAPE.
WIND IT UP ...
WHP WHP
...AN' THERE'S NO MORE EVIDENCE.
THAT'S HOW TO CREATE A LOCKED ROOM!!
KCHK
H-HE'S RIGHT ...
HOW'S THAT, JIMMY!? THAT'S MY THEORY!!
IF YA GOTTA PROBLEM WITH IT, HURRY UP AND COME OUT.
IF YA DON'T, I'M GONNA SOLVE IT ALL!!

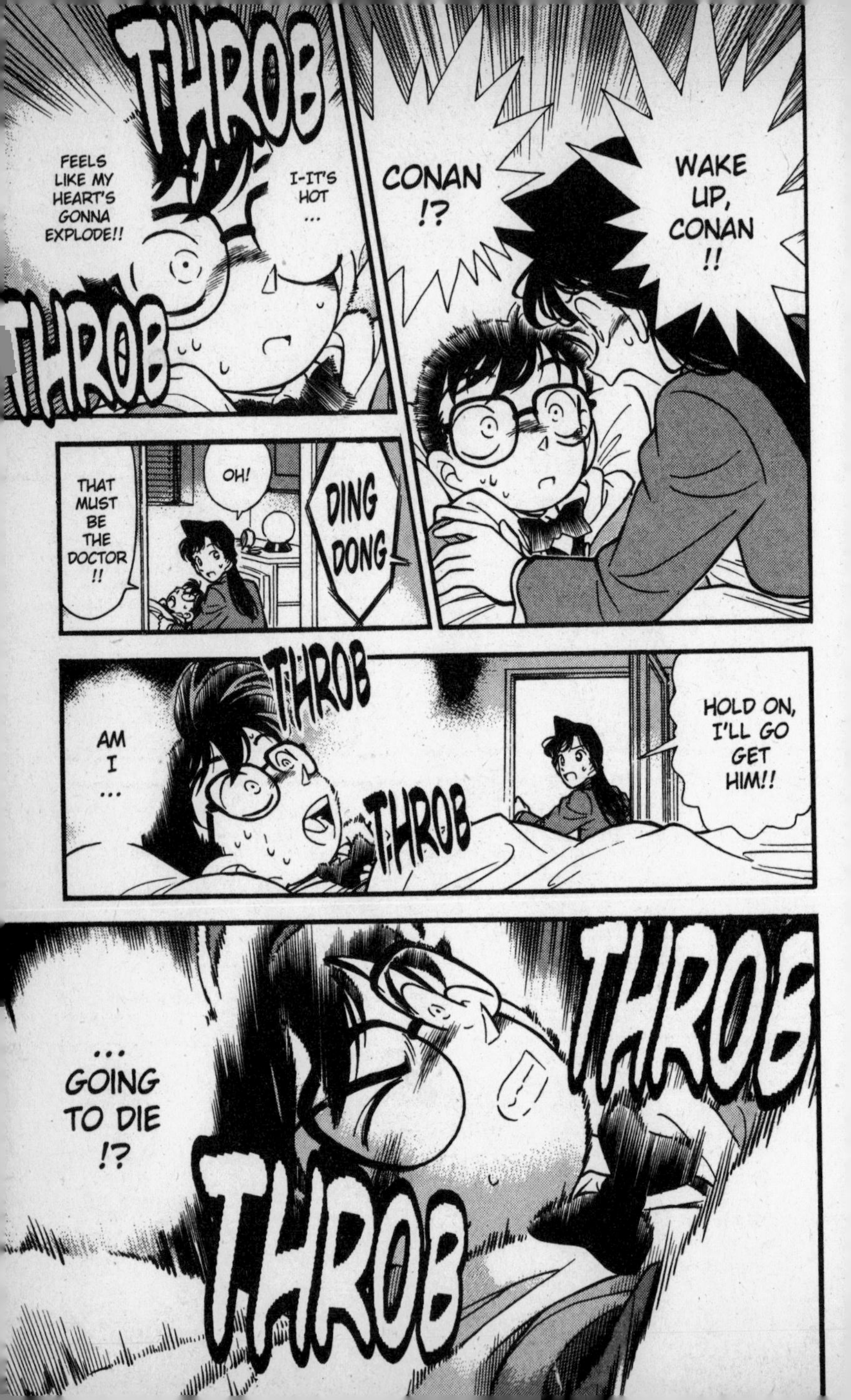
WAKE UP, CONAN!!
CONAN!?
THROB
I-IT'S HOT ...
FEELS LIKE MY HEART'S GONNA EXPLODE!!
THROB
DING DONG
OH!
THAT MUST BE THE DOCTOR!!
HOLD ON, I'LL GO GET HIM!!
THROB
THROB
AM I ...
THROB
... GOING TO DIE!?
THROB

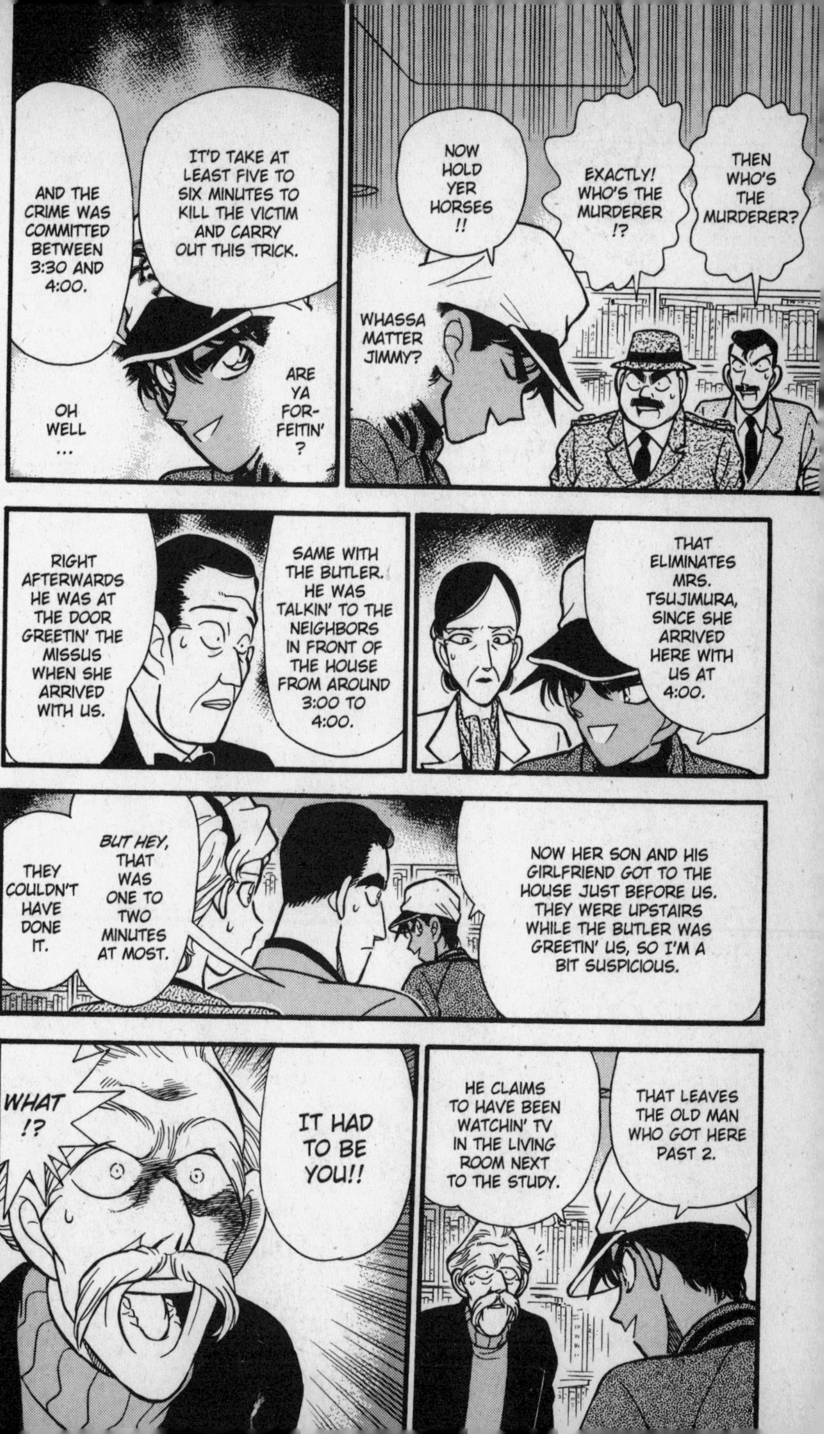
THEN WHO'S THE MURDERER?
EXACTLY! WHO'S THE MURDERER !?
NOW HOLD YER HORSES !!
WHASSA MATTER JIMMY?
IT'D TAKE AT LEAST FIVE TO SIX MINUTES TO KILL THE VICTIM AND CARRY OUT THIS TRICK.
AND THE CRIME WAS COMMITTED BETWEEN 3:30 AND 4:00.
ARE YA FOR-FEITIN' ?
OH WELL ...
THAT ELIMINATES MRS. TSUJIMURA, SINCE SHE ARRIVED HERE WITH US AT 4:00.
SAME WITH THE BUTLER. HE WAS TALKIN' TO THE NEIGHBORS IN FRONT OF THE HOUSE FROM AROUND 3:00 TO 4:00.
RIGHT AFTERWARDS HE WAS AT THE DOOR GREETIN' THE MISSUS WHEN SHE ARRIVED WITH US.
NOW HER SON AND HIS GIRLFRIEND GOT TO THE HOUSE JUST BEFORE US. THEY WERE UPSTAIRS WHILE THE BUTLER WAS GREETIN' US, SO I'M A BIT SUSPICIOUS.
BUT HEY, THAT WAS ONE TO TWO MINUTES AT MOST.
THEY COULDN'T HAVE DONE IT.
THAT LEAVES THE OLD MAN WHO GOT HERE PAST 2.
HE CLAIMS TO HAVE BEEN WATCHIN' TV IN THE LIVING ROOM NEXT TO THE STUDY.
IT HAD TO BE YOU!!
WHAT !?

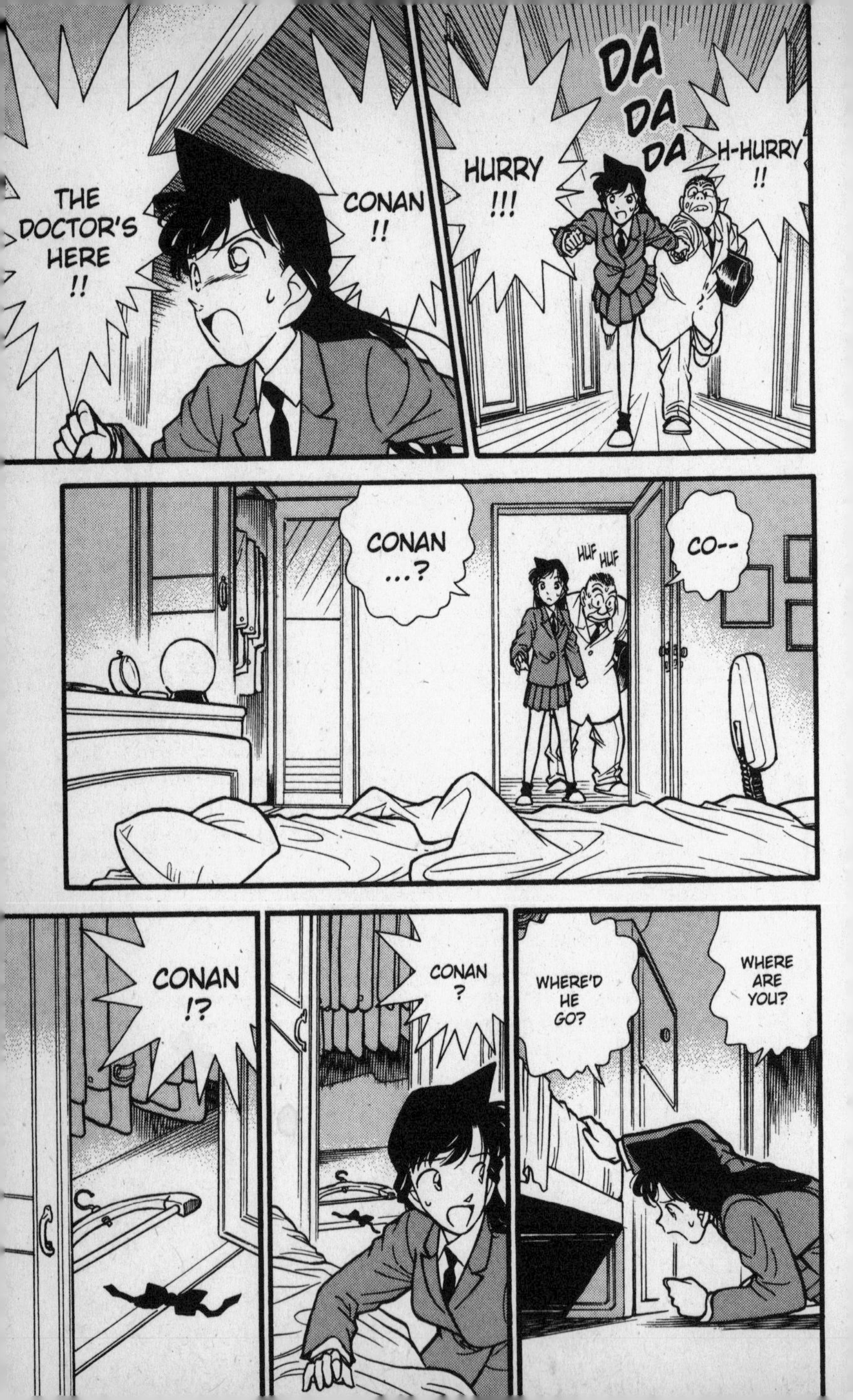
DA DA DA
H-HURRY !!
HURRY !!!
CONAN !!
THE DOCTOR'S HERE !!
CO--
HUF HUF
CONAN ...?
WHERE ARE YOU?
WHERE'D HE GO?
CONAN ?
CONAN !?

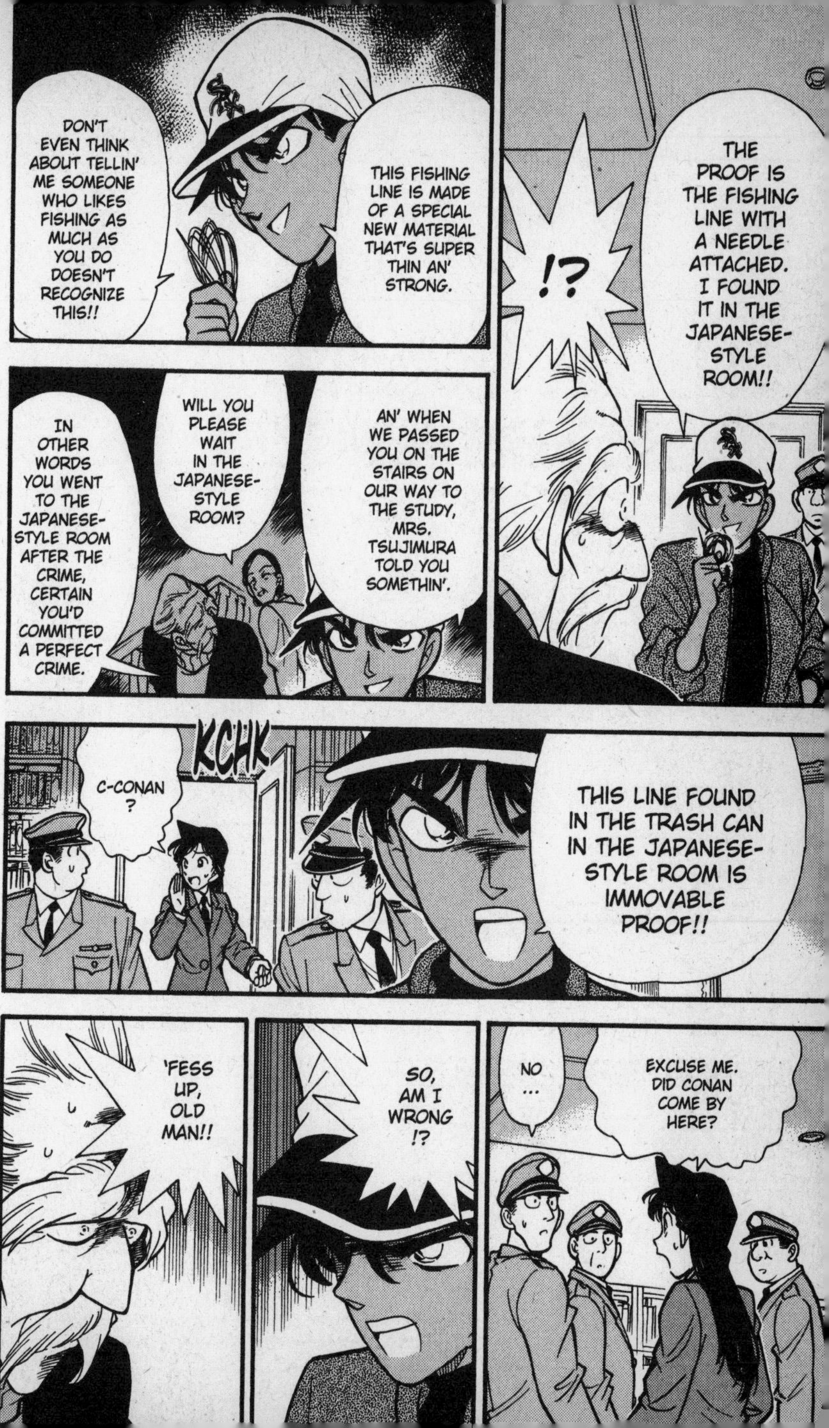
THE PROOF IS THE FISHING LINE WITH A NEEDLE ATTACHED. I FOUND IT IN THE JAPANESE-STYLE ROOM!!
!?
THIS FISHING LINE IS MADE OF A SPECIAL NEW MATERIAL THAT'S SUPER THIN AN' STRONG.
DON'T EVEN THINK ABOUT TELLIN' ME SOMEONE WHO LIKES FISHING AS MUCH AS YOU DO DOESN'T RECOGNIZE THIS!!
AN' WHEN WE PASSED YOU ON THE STAIRS ON OUR WAY TO THE STUDY, MRS. TSUJIMURA TOLD YOU SOMETHIN'.
WILL YOU PLEASE WAIT IN THE JAPANESE-STYLE ROOM?
IN OTHER WORDS YOU WENT TO THE JAPANESE-STYLE ROOM AFTER THE CRIME, CERTAIN YOU'D COMMITTED A PERFECT CRIME.
THIS LINE FOUND IN THE TRASH CAN IN THE JAPANESE-STYLE ROOM IS IMMOVABLE PROOF!!
KCHK
C-CONAN ?
EXCUSE ME. DID CONAN COME BY HERE?
NO ...
SO, AM I WRONG !?
'FESS UP, OLD MAN!!

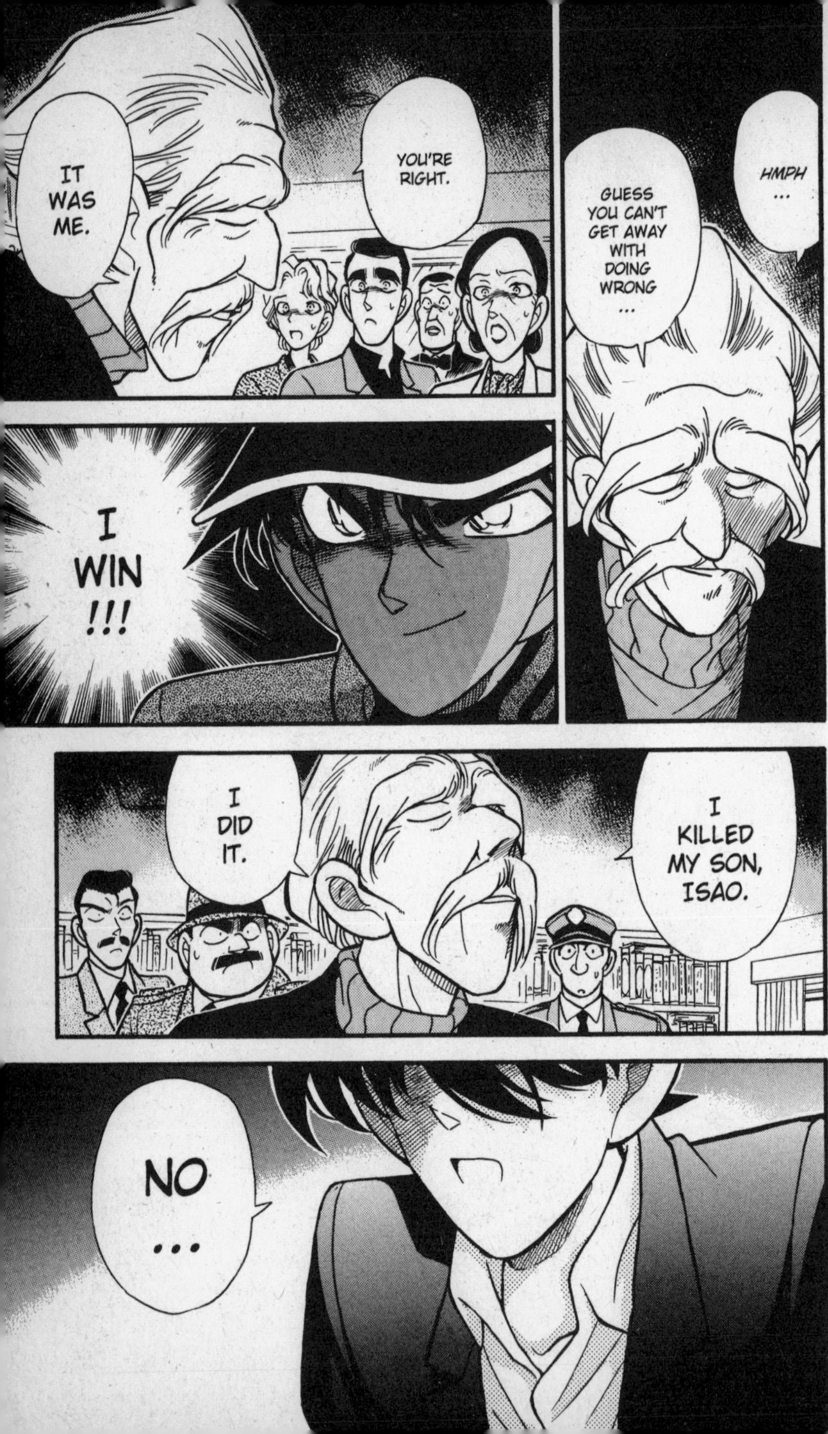
HMPH ...
GUESS YOU CAN'T GET AWAY WITH DOING WRONG ...
YOU'RE RIGHT.
IT WAS ME.
I WIN !!!
I KILLED MY SON, ISAO.
I DID IT.
NO ...

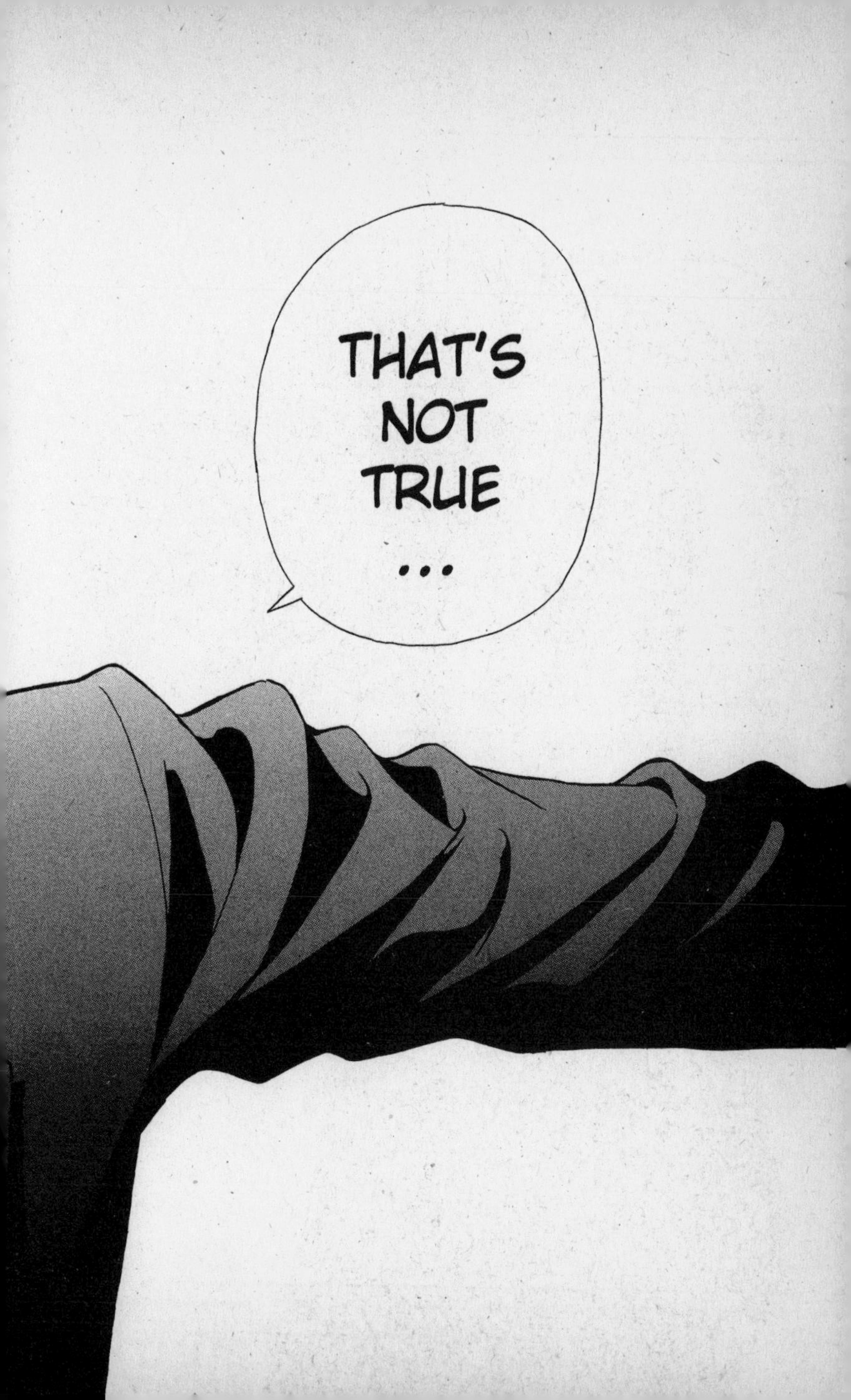
THAT'S NOT TRUE ...

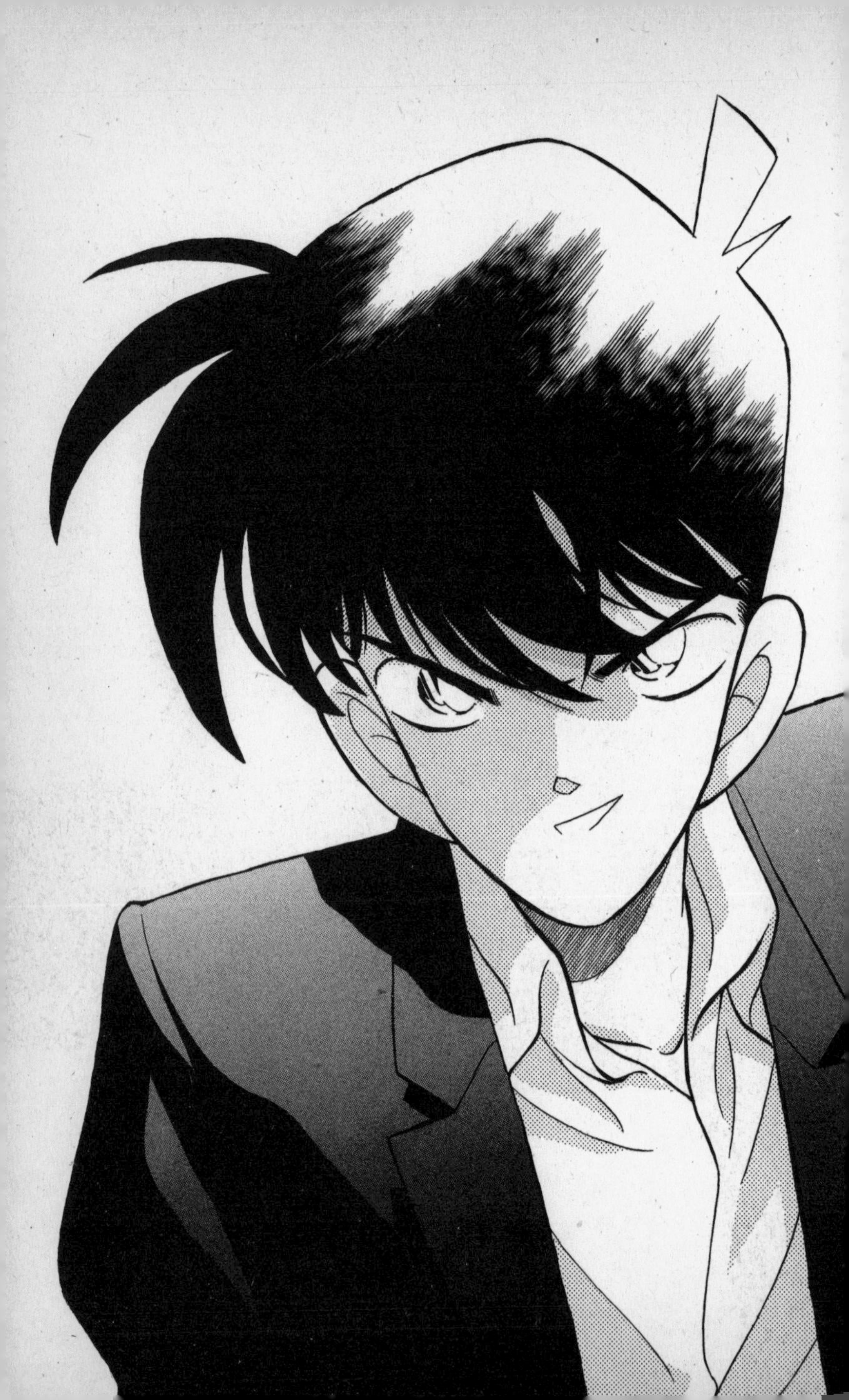

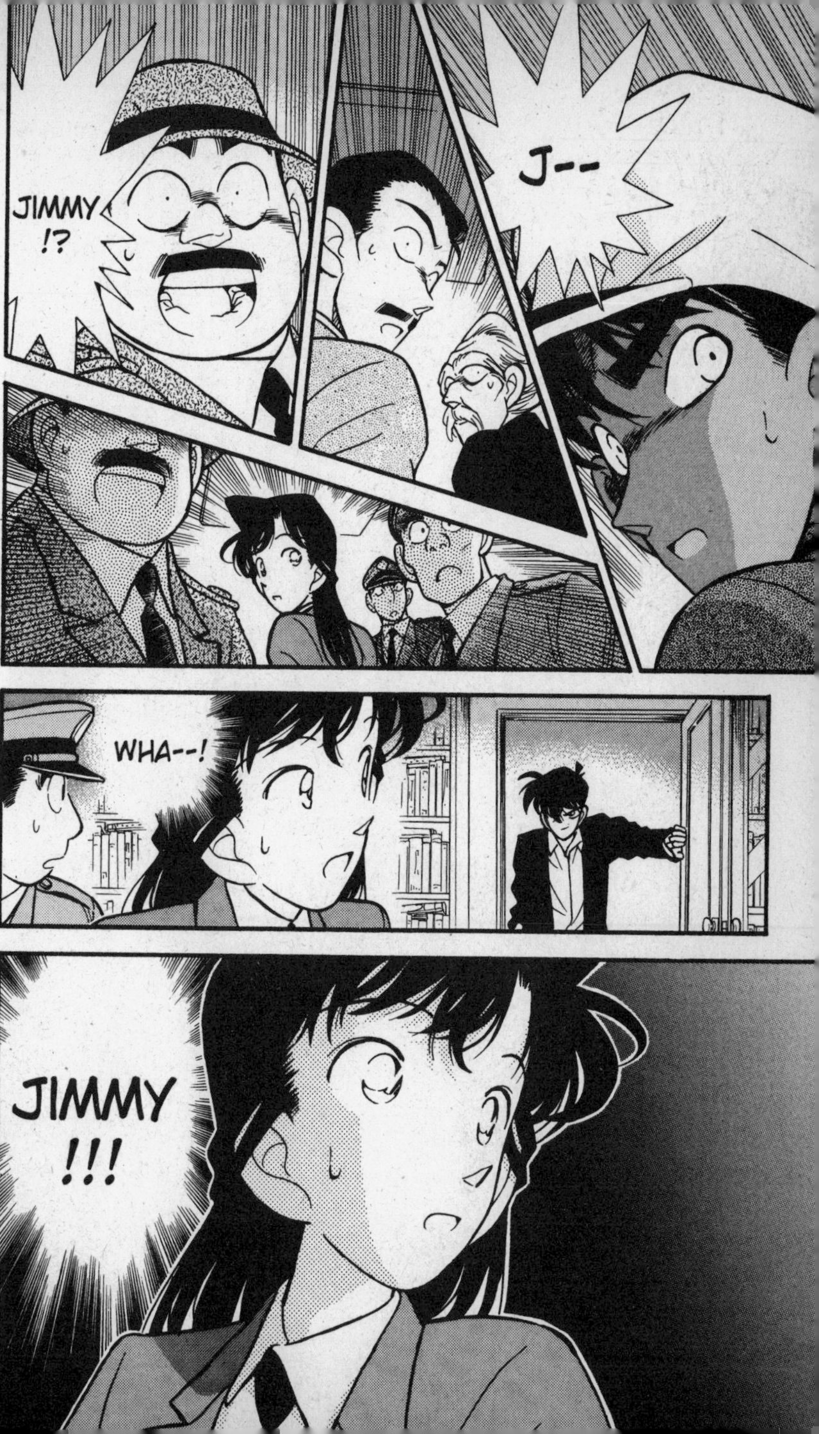
J--
JIMMY !?
WHA--!
JIMMY !!!

FILE 5: THE GREAT DETECTIVE OF THE EAST APPEARS!?

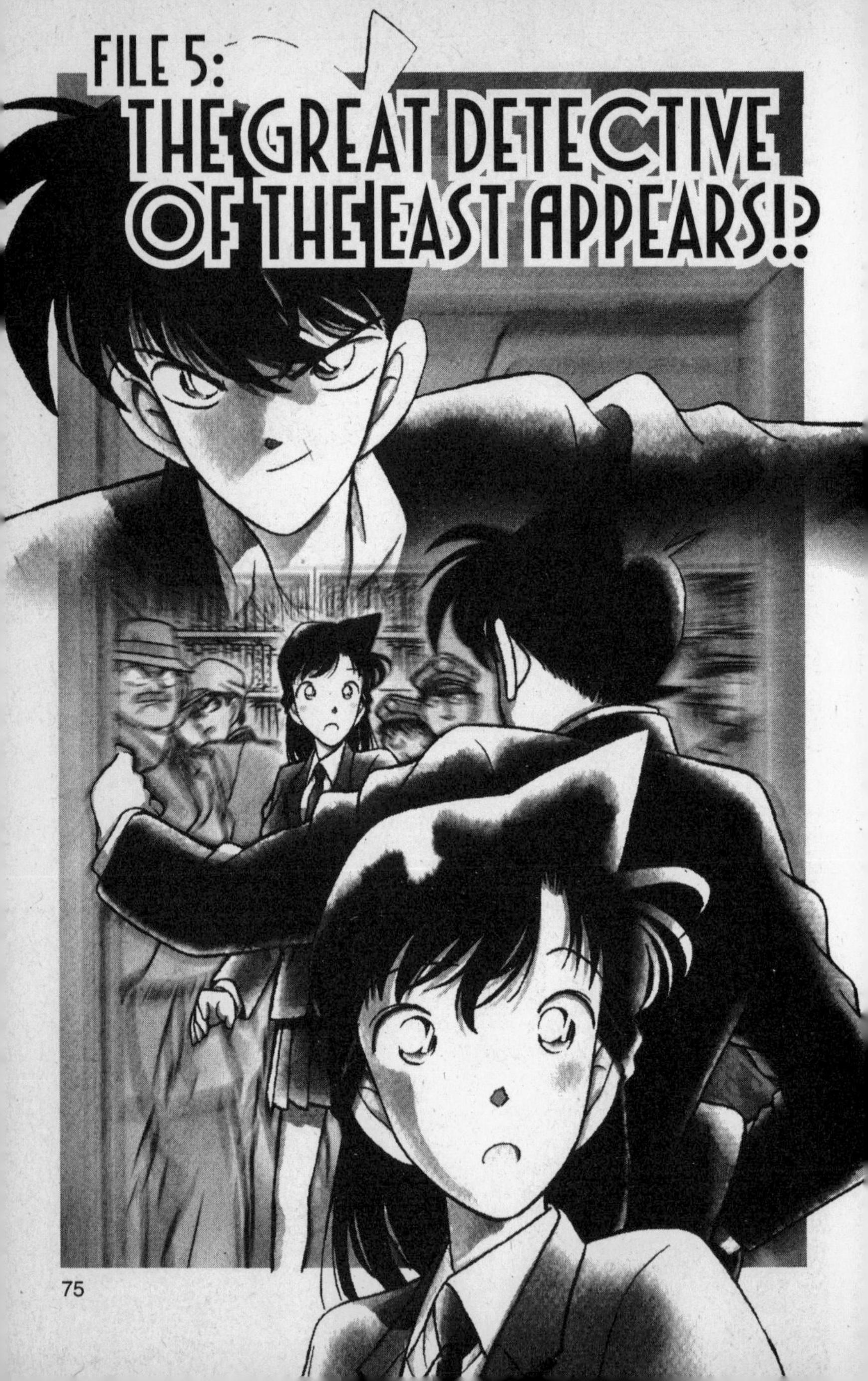

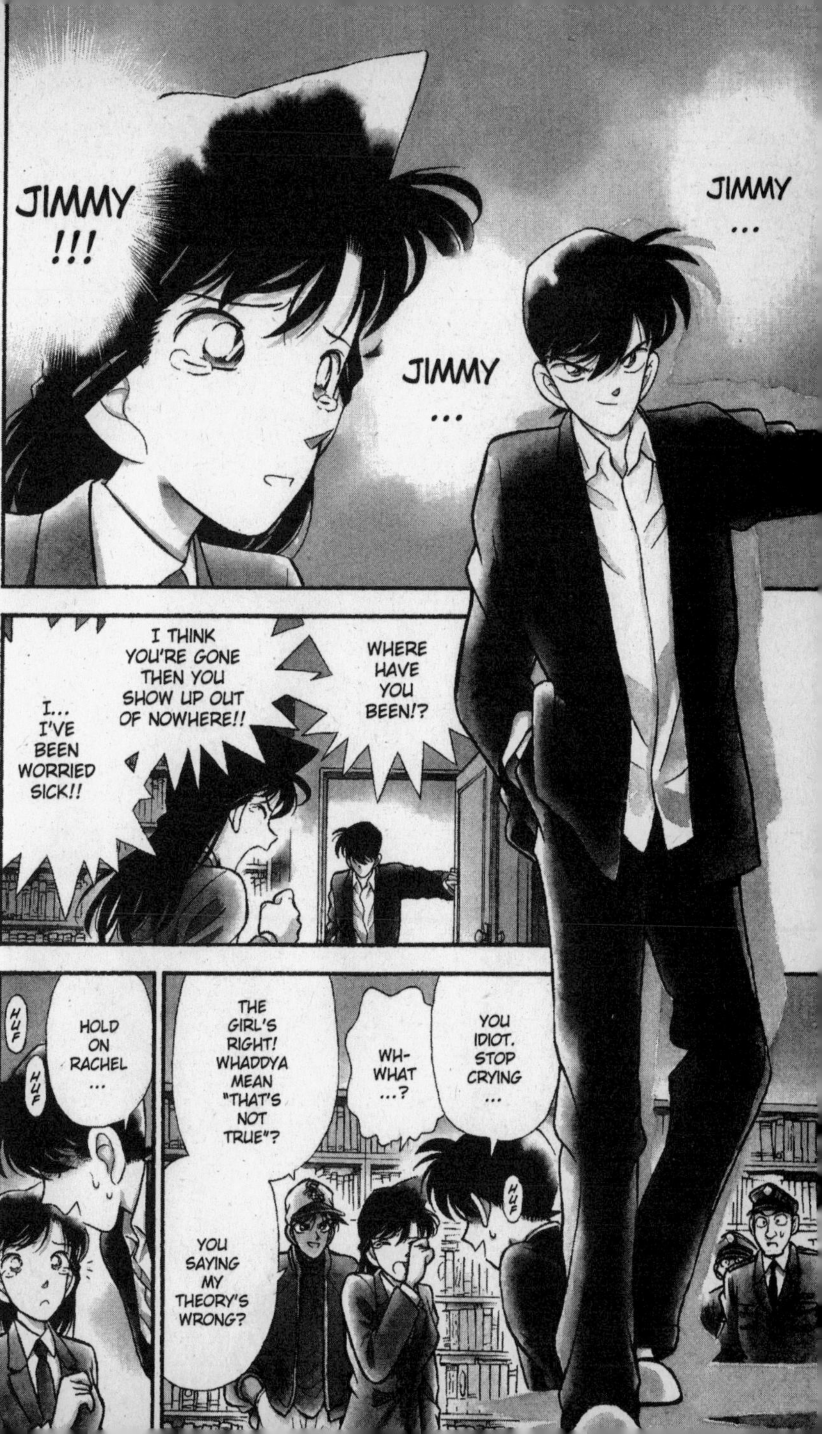
JIMMY ...
JIMMY ...
JIMMY !!!
WHERE HAVE YOU BEEN!?
I THINK YOU'RE GONE THEN YOU SHOW UP OUT OF NOWHERE!!
I... I'VE BEEN WORRIED SICK!!
YOU IDIOT. STOP CRYING ...
WH- WHAT ...?
HUF
THE GIRL'S RIGHT! WHADDYA MEAN "THAT'S NOT TRUE"?
YOU SAYING MY THEORY'S WRONG?
HUF
HUF
HOLD ON RACHEL ...

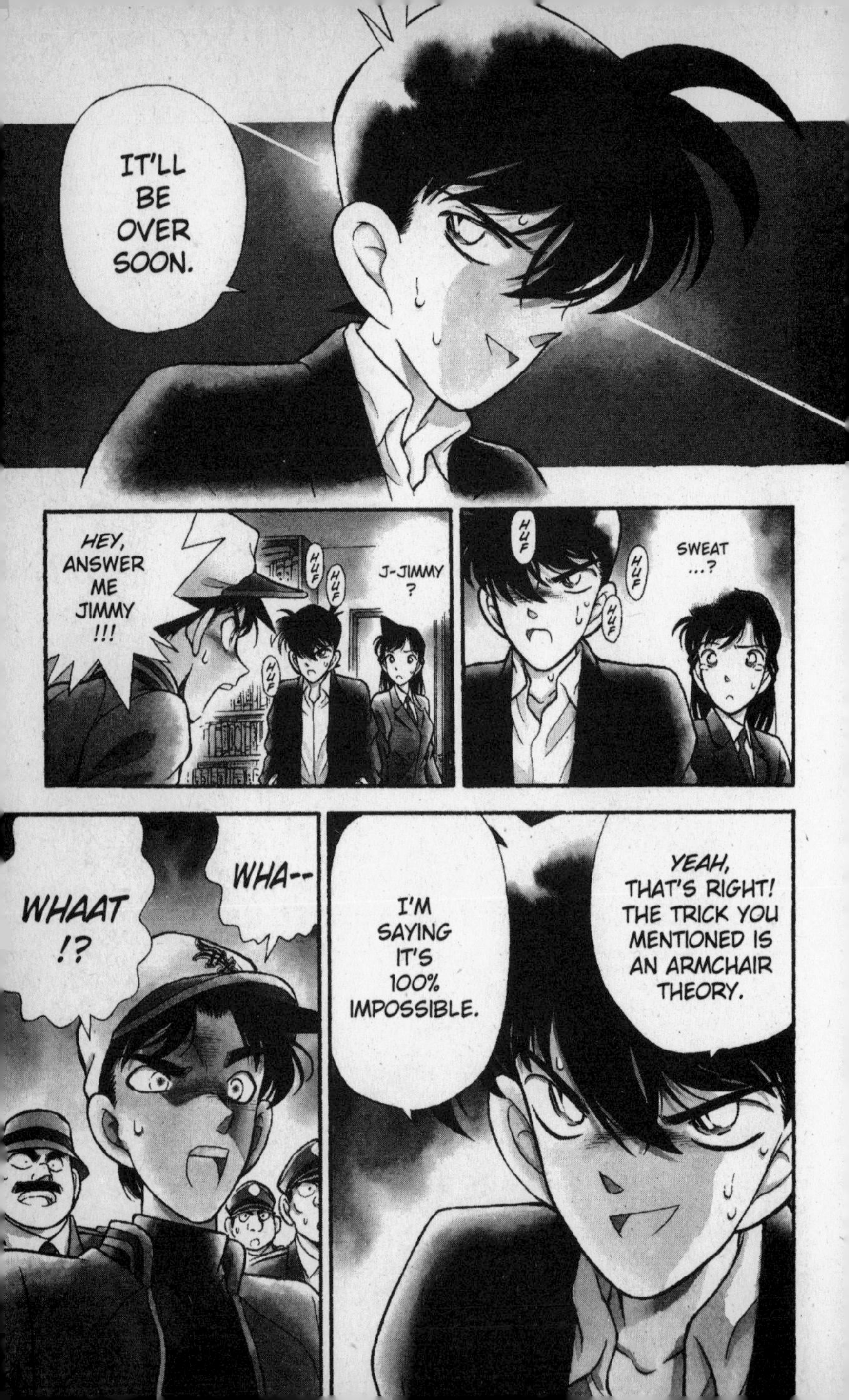
IT'LL BE OVER SOON.
SWEAT ...?
HUF
HUF
HUF
J-JIMMY ?
HUF
HUF
HUF
HEY, ANSWER ME JIMMY !!!
YEAH, THAT'S RIGHT! THE TRICK YOU MENTIONED IS AN ARMCHAIR THEORY.
I'M SAYING IT'S 100% IMPOSSIBLE.
WHA--
WHAAT !?

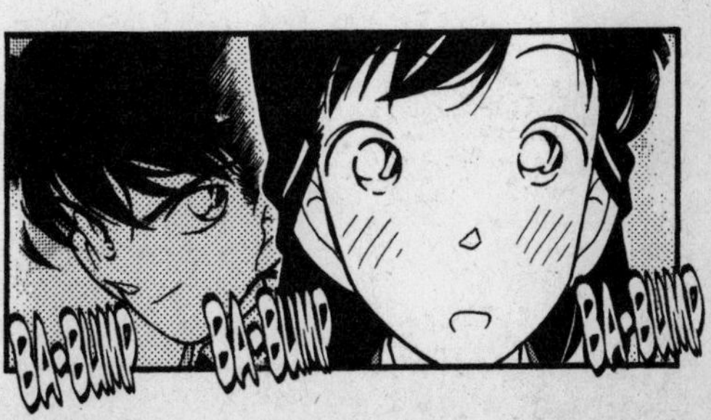
BA-BUMP
BA-BUMP
BA-BUMP

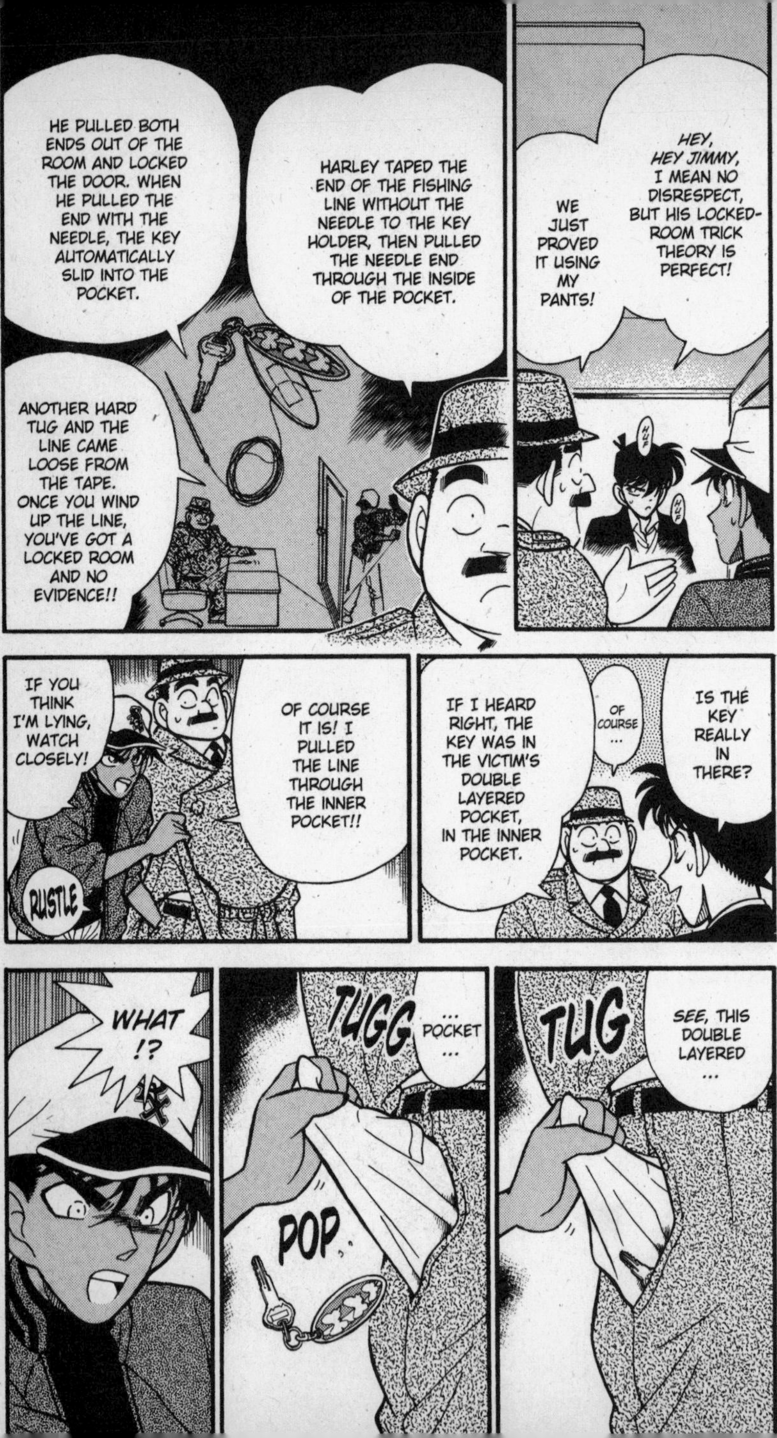
HEY, HEY JIMMY, I MEAN NO DISRESPECT, BUT HIS LOCKED-ROOM TRICK THEORY IS PERFECT!
WE JUST PROVED IT USING MY PANTS!
HUF
HUF
HARLEY TAPED THE END OF THE FISHING LINE WITHOUT THE NEEDLE TO THE KEY HOLDER, THEN PULLED THE NEEDLE END THROUGH THE INSIDE OF THE POCKET.
HE PULLED BOTH ENDS OUT OF THE ROOM AND LOCKED THE DOOR. WHEN HE PULLED THE END WITH THE NEEDLE, THE KEY AUTOMATICALLY SLID INTO THE POCKET.
ANOTHER HARD TUG AND THE LINE CAME LOOSE FROM THE TAPE. ONCE YOU WIND UP THE LINE, YOU'VE GOT A LOCKED ROOM AND NO EVIDENCE!!
IS THE KEY REALLY IN THERE?
OF COURSE ...
IF I HEARD RIGHT, THE KEY WAS IN THE VICTIM'S DOUBLE LAYERED POCKET, IN THE INNER POCKET.
OF COURSE IT IS! I PULLED THE LINE THROUGH THE INNER POCKET!!
IF YOU THINK I'M LYING, WATCH CLOSELY!
RUSTLE
SEE, THIS DOUBLE LAYERED ...
TUG
... POCKET ...
TUGG
POP
WHAT !?

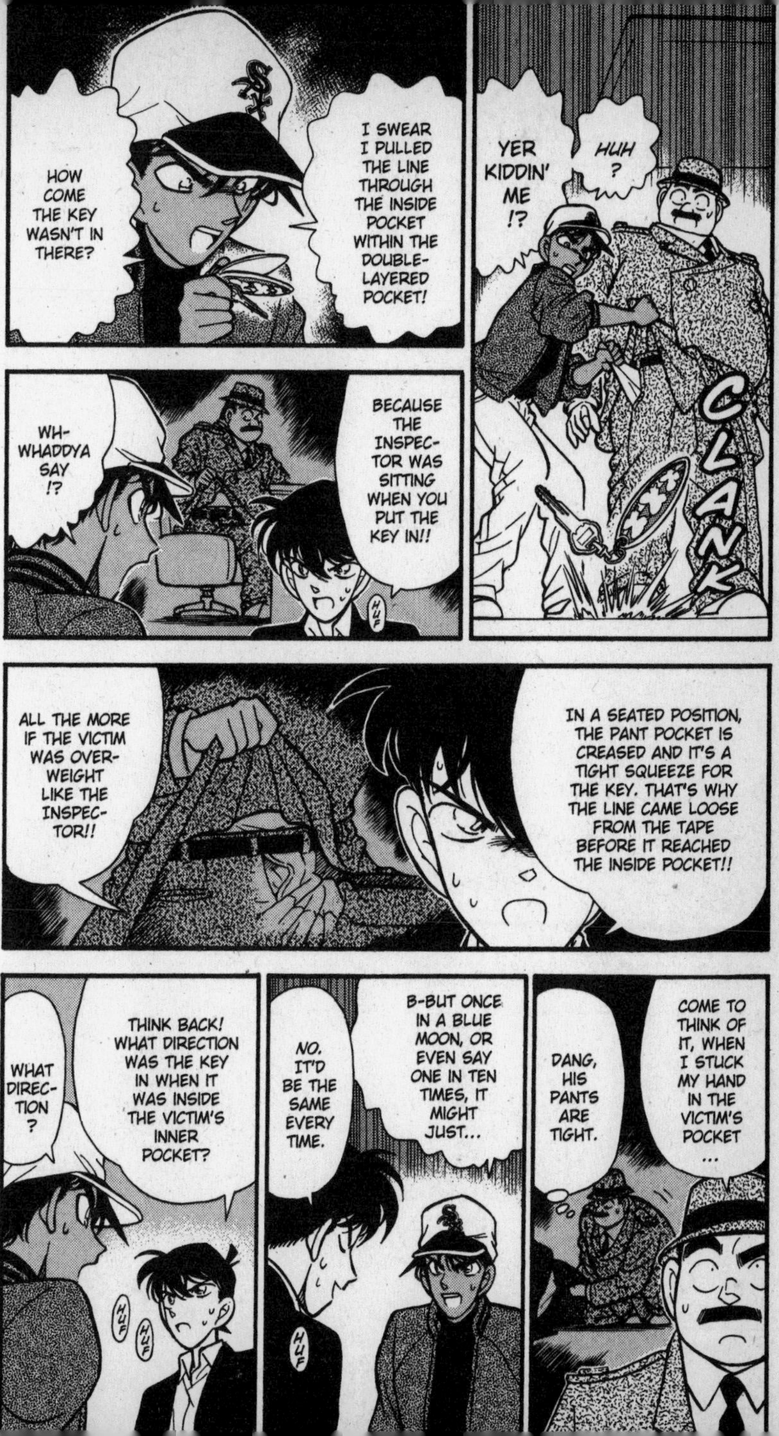
HUH ?
YER KIDDIN' ME !?
CLANK
I SWEAR I PULLED THE LINE THROUGH THE INSIDE POCKET WITHIN THE DOUBLE-LAYERED POCKET!
HOW COME THE KEY WASN'T IN THERE?
BECAUSE THE INSPECTOR WAS SITTING WHEN YOU PUT THE KEY IN!!
HUF
WH-WHADDYA SAY !?
IN A SEATED POSITION, THE PANT POCKET IS CREASED AND IT'S A TIGHT SQUEEZE FOR THE KEY. THAT'S WHY THE LINE CAME LOOSE FROM THE TAPE BEFORE IT REACHED THE INSIDE POCKET!!
ALL THE MORE IF THE VICTIM WAS OVERWEIGHT LIKE THE INSPECTOR!!
COME TO THINK OF IT, WHEN I STUCK MY HAND IN THE VICTIM'S POCKET ...
DANG, HIS PANTS ARE TIGHT.
B-BUT ONCE IN A BLUE MOON, OR EVEN SAY ONE IN TEN TIMES, IT MIGHT JUST...
NO. IT'D BE THE SAME EVERY TIME.
HUF
THINK BACK! WHAT DIRECTION WAS THE KEY IN WHEN IT WAS INSIDE THE VICTIM'S INNER POCKET?
WHAT DIRECTION ?
HUF
HUF

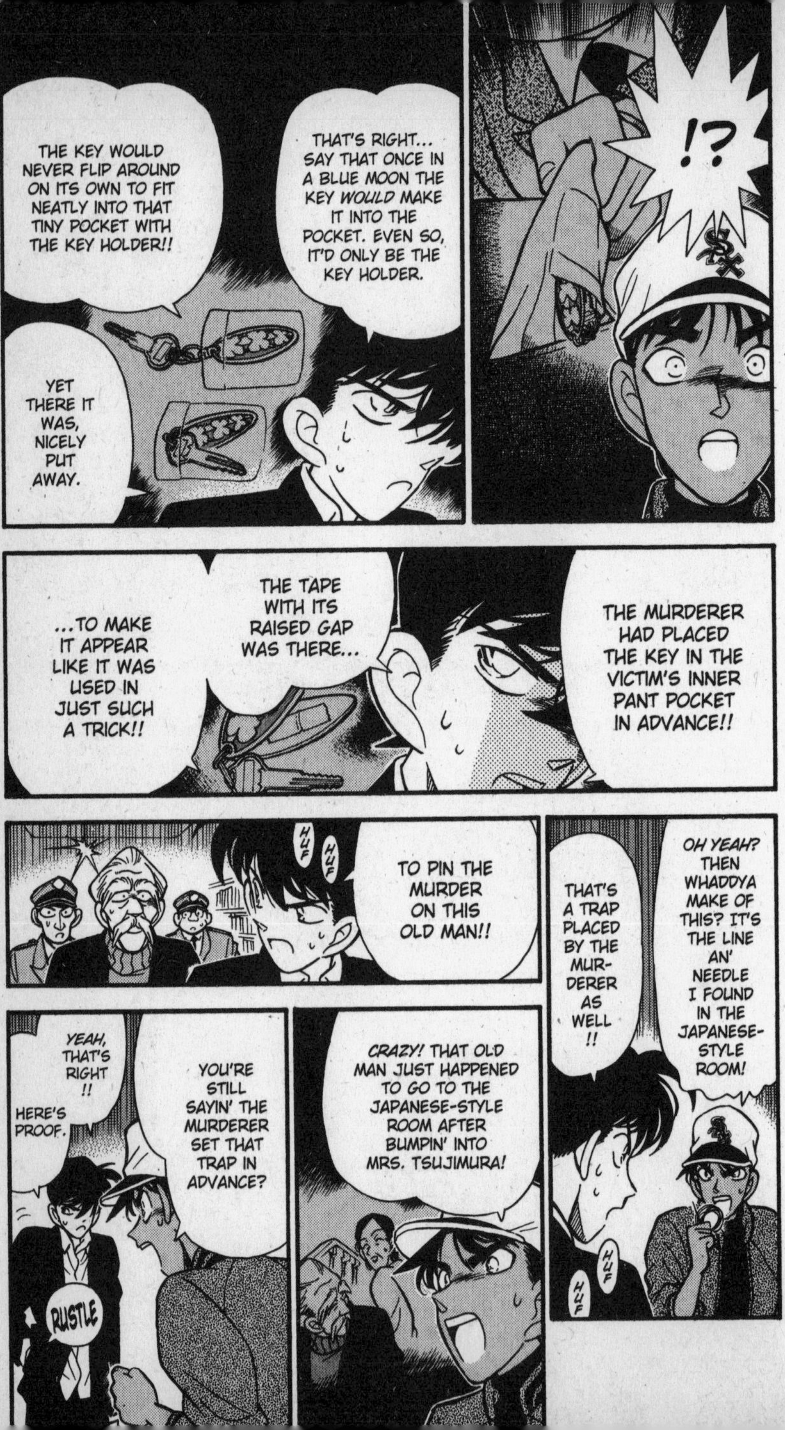
!?
THAT'S RIGHT... SAY THAT ONCE IN A BLUE MOON THE KEY *WOULD* MAKE IT INTO THE POCKET. EVEN SO, IT'D ONLY BE THE KEY HOLDER.
THE KEY WOULD NEVER FLIP AROUND ON ITS OWN TO FIT NEATLY INTO THAT TINY POCKET WITH THE KEY HOLDER!!
YET THERE IT WAS, NICELY PUT AWAY.
THE MURDERER HAD PLACED THE KEY IN THE VICTIM'S INNER PANT POCKET IN ADVANCE!!
THE TAPE WITH ITS RAISED GAP WAS THERE...
...TO MAKE IT APPEAR LIKE IT WAS USED IN JUST SUCH A TRICK!!
OH YEAH? THEN WHADDYA MAKE OF THIS? IT'S THE LINE AN' NEEDLE I FOUND IN THE JAPANESE-STYLE ROOM!
THAT'S A TRAP PLACED BY THE MURDERER AS WELL!!
HUF HUF
HUF HUF
TO PIN THE MURDER ON THIS OLD MAN!!
CRAZY! THAT OLD MAN JUST HAPPENED TO GO TO THE JAPANESE-STYLE ROOM AFTER BUMPIN' INTO MRS. TSUJIMURA!
YOU'RE STILL SAYIN' THE MURDERER SET THAT TRAP IN ADVANCE?
YEAH, THAT'S RIGHT!!
HERE'S PROOF.
RUSTLE

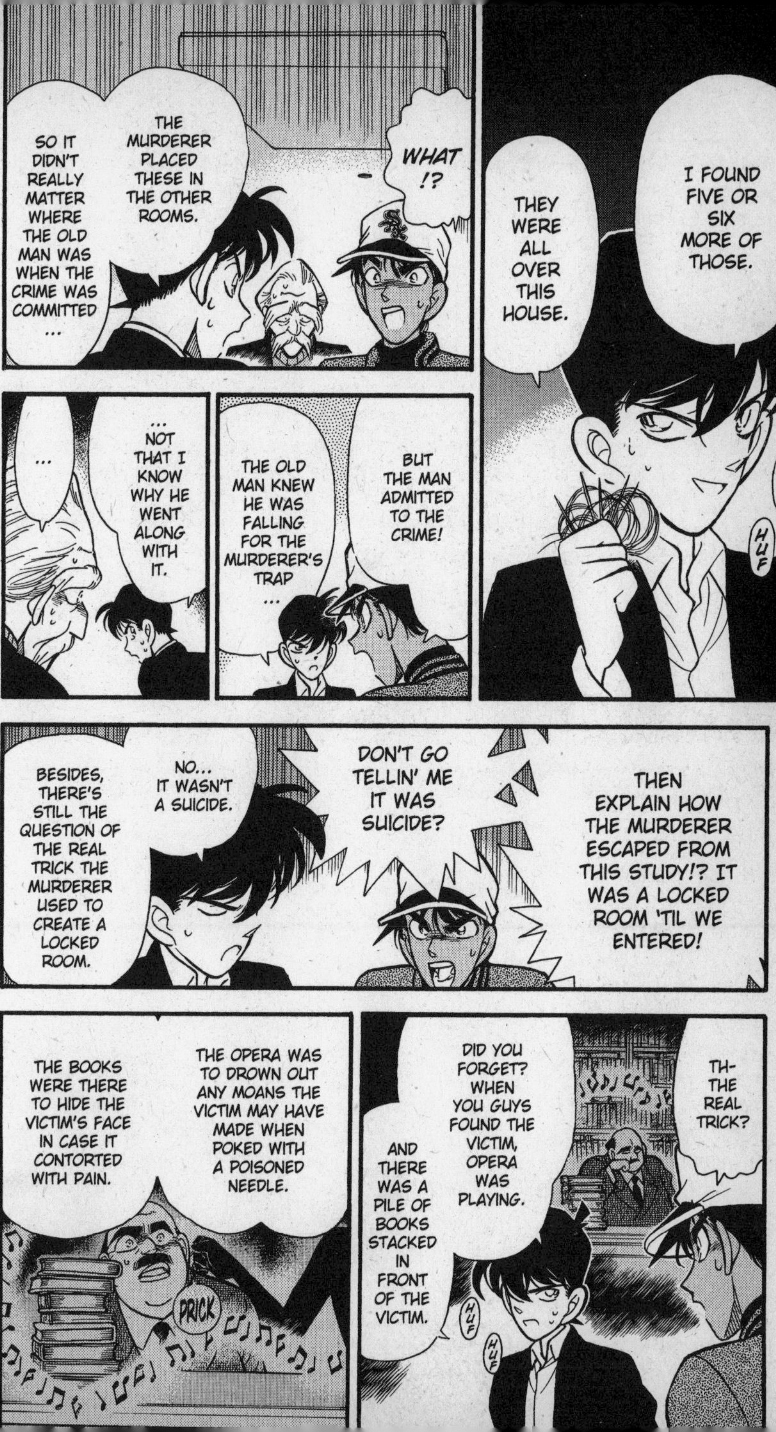

I FOUND FIVE OR SIX MORE OF THOSE.
THEY WERE ALL OVER THIS HOUSE.
HUF
HUF
WHAT!?
THE MURDERER PLACED THESE IN THE OTHER ROOMS.
SO IT DIDN'T REALLY MATTER WHERE THE OLD MAN WAS WHEN THE CRIME WAS COMMITTED...
BUT THE MAN ADMITTED TO THE CRIME!
THE OLD MAN KNEW HE WAS FALLING FOR THE MURDERER'S TRAP...
...NOT THAT I KNOW WHY HE WENT ALONG WITH IT.
...
THEN EXPLAIN HOW THE MURDERER ESCAPED FROM THIS STUDY!? IT WAS A LOCKED ROOM 'TIL WE ENTERED!
DON'T GO TELLIN' ME IT WAS SUICIDE?
NO... IT WASN'T A SUICIDE.
BESIDES, THERE'S STILL THE QUESTION OF THE REAL TRICK THE MURDERER USED TO CREATE A LOCKED ROOM.
TH-THE REAL TRICK?
DID YOU FORGET? WHEN YOU GUYS FOUND THE VICTIM, OPERA WAS PLAYING.
AND THERE WAS A PILE OF BOOKS STACKED IN FRONT OF THE VICTIM.
HUF
HUF
THE OPERA WAS TO DROWN OUT ANY MOANS THE VICTIM MAY HAVE MADE WHEN POKED WITH A POISONED NEEDLE.
THE BOOKS WERE THERE TO HIDE THE VICTIM'S FACE IN CASE IT CONTORTED WITH PAIN.
PRICK

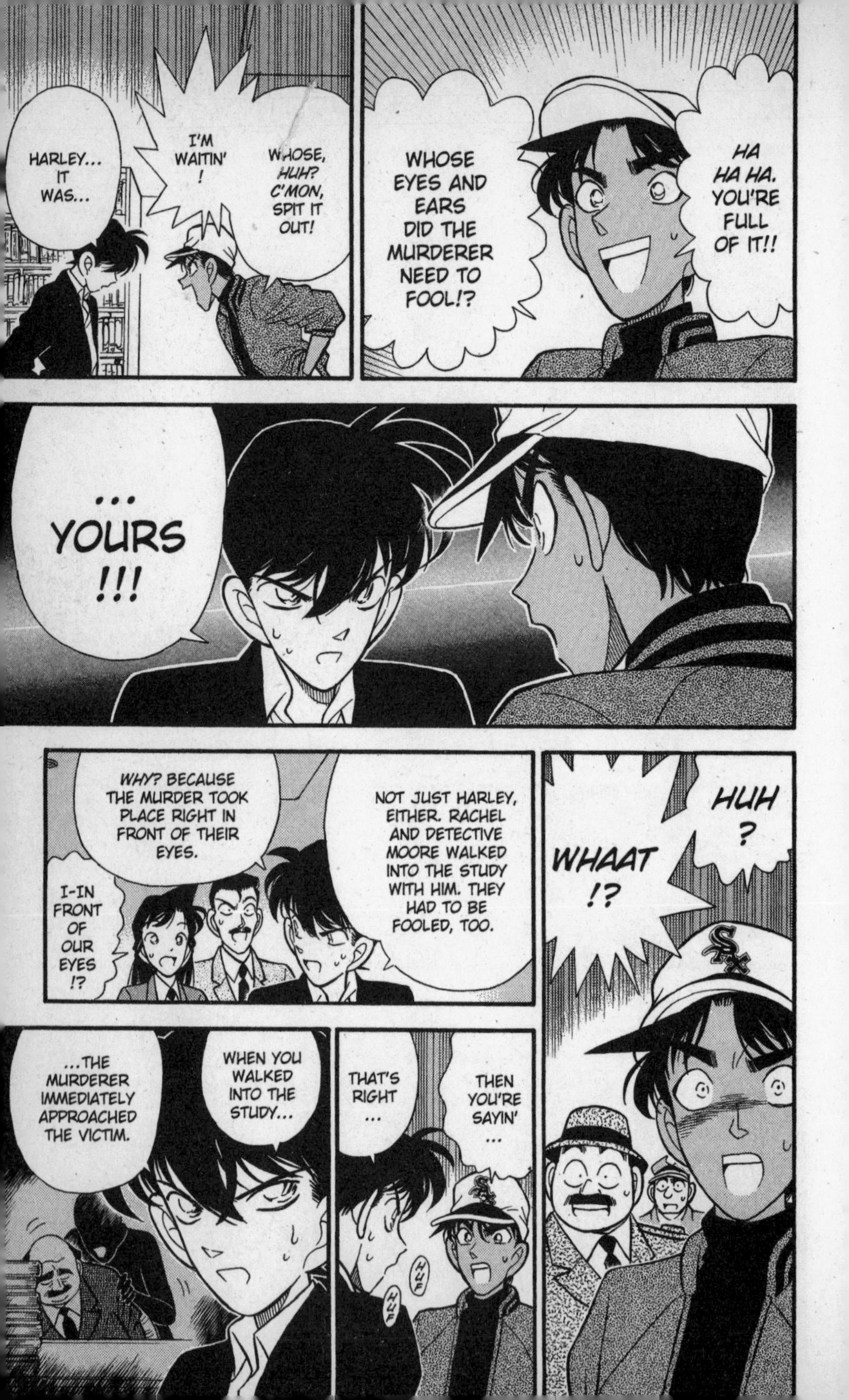
HA HA HA. YOU'RE FULL OF IT!!
WHOSE EYES AND EARS DID THE MURDERER NEED TO FOOL!?
WHOSE, HUH? C'MON, SPIT IT OUT!
I'M WAITIN'!
HARLEY... IT WAS...
... YOURS !!!
HUH?
WHAAT!?
NOT JUST HARLEY, EITHER. RACHEL AND DETECTIVE MOORE WALKED INTO THE STUDY WITH HIM. THEY HAD TO BE FOOLED, TOO.
WHY? BECAUSE THE MURDER TOOK PLACE RIGHT IN FRONT OF THEIR EYES.
I-IN FRONT OF OUR EYES!?
THEN YOU'RE SAYIN'...
THAT'S RIGHT...
HUF
HUF
WHEN YOU WALKED INTO THE STUDY...
...THE MURDERER IMMEDIATELY APPROACHED THE VICTIM.

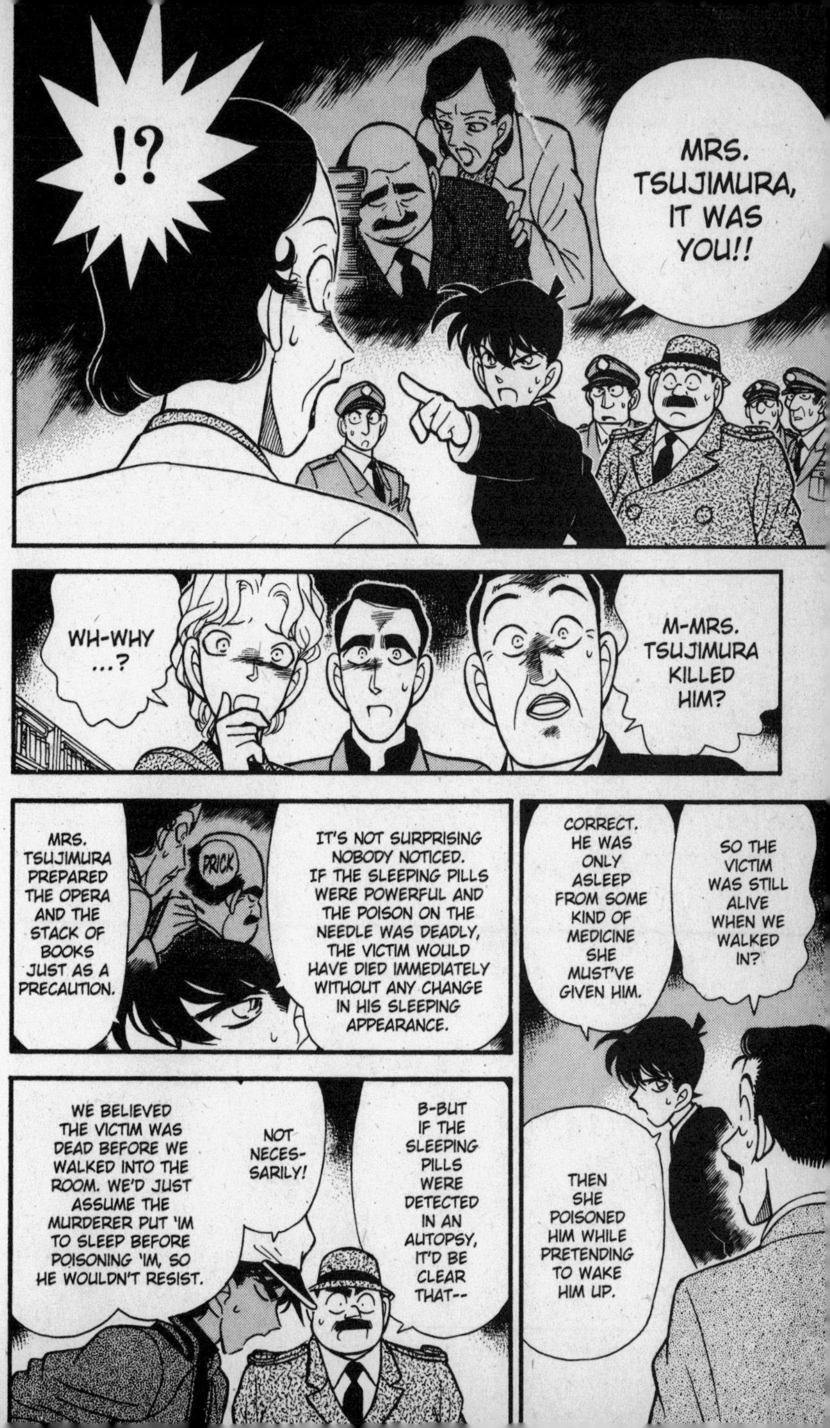
MRS. TSUJIMURA, IT WAS YOU!!
!?
M-MRS. TSUJIMURA KILLED HIM?
WH-WHY ...?
SO THE VICTIM WAS STILL ALIVE WHEN WE WALKED IN?
CORRECT. HE WAS ONLY ASLEEP FROM SOME KIND OF MEDICINE SHE MUST'VE GIVEN HIM.
THEN SHE POISONED HIM WHILE PRETENDING TO WAKE HIM UP.
IT'S NOT SURPRISING NOBODY NOTICED. IF THE SLEEPING PILLS WERE POWERFUL AND THE POISON ON THE NEEDLE WAS DEADLY, THE VICTIM WOULD HAVE DIED IMMEDIATELY WITHOUT ANY CHANGE IN HIS SLEEPING APPEARANCE.
PRICK
MRS. TSUJIMURA PREPARED THE OPERA AND THE STACK OF BOOKS JUST AS A PRECAUTION.
B-BUT IF THE SLEEPING PILLS WERE DETECTED IN AN AUTOPSY, IT'D BE CLEAR THAT--
NOT NECES-SARILY!
WE BELIEVED THE VICTIM WAS DEAD BEFORE WE WALKED INTO THE ROOM. WE'D JUST ASSUME THE MURDERER PUT 'IM TO SLEEP BEFORE POISONING 'IM, SO HE WOULDN'T RESIST.

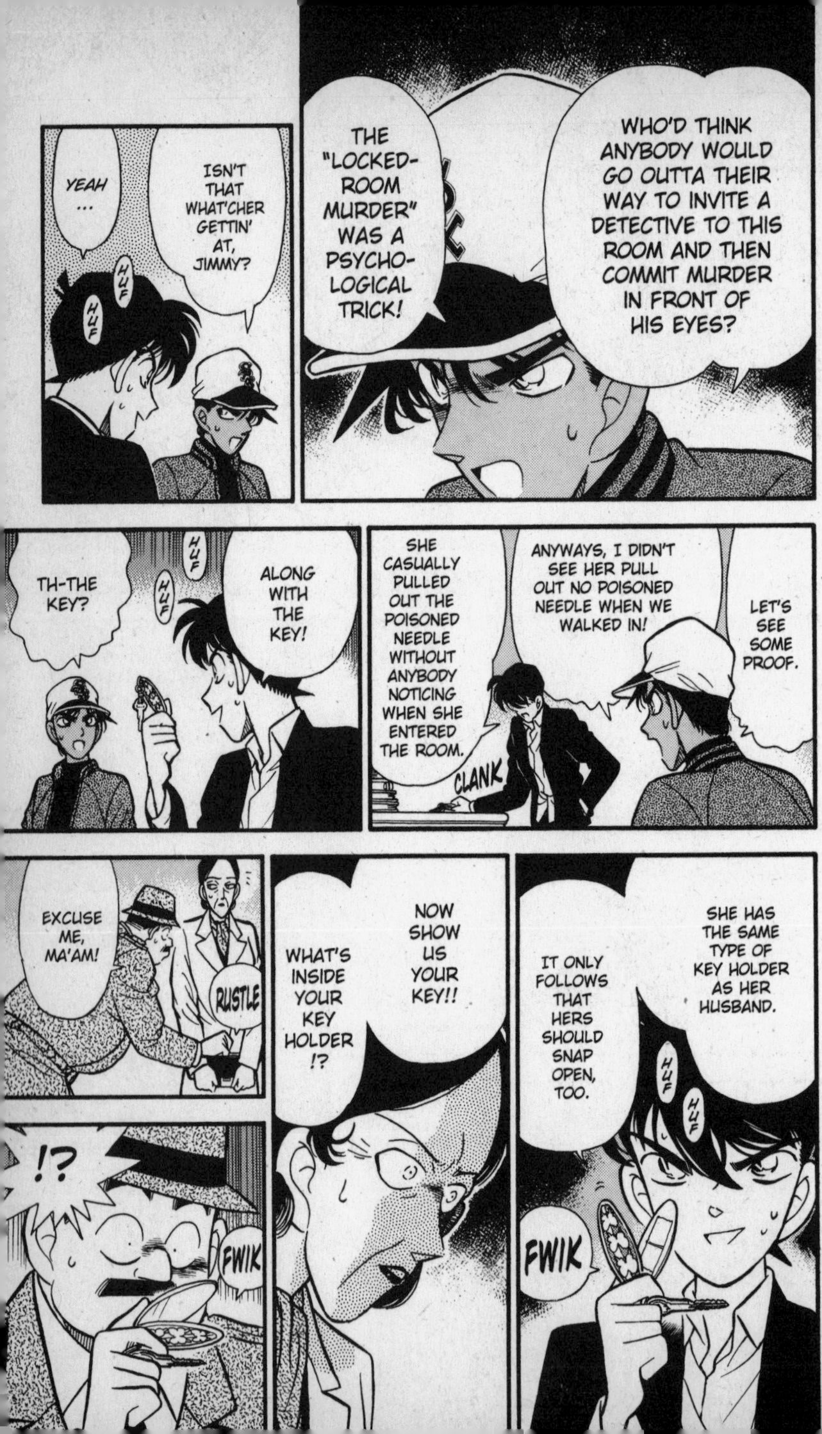
WHO'D THINK ANYBODY WOULD GO OUTTA THEIR WAY TO INVITE A DETECTIVE TO THIS ROOM AND THEN COMMIT MURDER IN FRONT OF HIS EYES?
THE "LOCKED-ROOM MURDER" WAS A PSYCHOLOGICAL TRICK!
ISN'T THAT WHAT'CHER GETTIN' AT, JIMMY?
HUF
HUF
YEAH...
ANYWAYS, I DIDN'T SEE HER PULL OUT NO POISONED NEEDLE WHEN WE WALKED IN!
LET'S SEE SOME PROOF.
SHE CASUALLY PULLED OUT THE POISONED NEEDLE WITHOUT ANYBODY NOTICING WHEN SHE ENTERED THE ROOM.
CLANK
HUF
HUF
ALONG WITH THE KEY!
TH-THE KEY?
SHE HAS THE SAME TYPE OF KEY HOLDER AS HER HUSBAND.
IT ONLY FOLLOWS THAT HERS SHOULD SNAP OPEN, TOO.
HUF
HUF
FWIK
NOW SHOW US YOUR KEY!!
WHAT'S INSIDE YOUR KEY HOLDER!?
EXCUSE ME, MA'AM!
RUSTLE
!?
FWIK

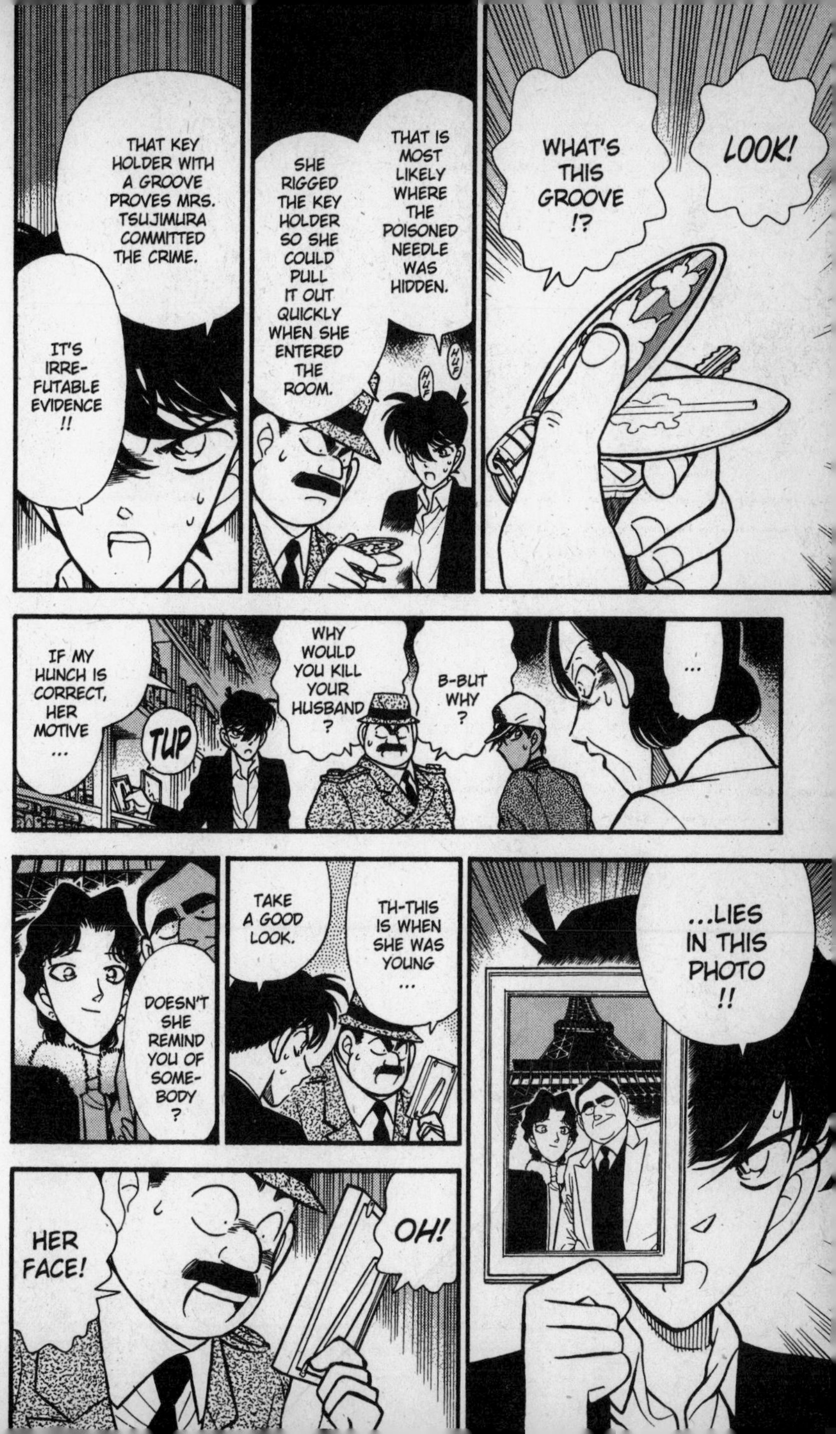
LOOK!
WHAT'S THIS GROOVE !?
THAT IS MOST LIKELY WHERE THE POISONED NEEDLE WAS HIDDEN.
SHE RIGGED THE KEY HOLDER SO SHE COULD PULL IT OUT QUICKLY WHEN SHE ENTERED THE ROOM.
HUF HUF
THAT KEY HOLDER WITH A GROOVE PROVES MRS. TSUJIMURA COMMITTED THE CRIME.
IT'S IRREFUTABLE EVIDENCE !!
...
B-BUT WHY ?
WHY WOULD YOU KILL YOUR HUSBAND ?
TUP
IF MY HUNCH IS CORRECT, HER MOTIVE ...
...LIES IN THIS PHOTO !!
TH-THIS IS WHEN SHE WAS YOUNG ...
TAKE A GOOD LOOK.
DOESN'T SHE REMIND YOU OF SOMEBODY ?
OH!
HER FACE!

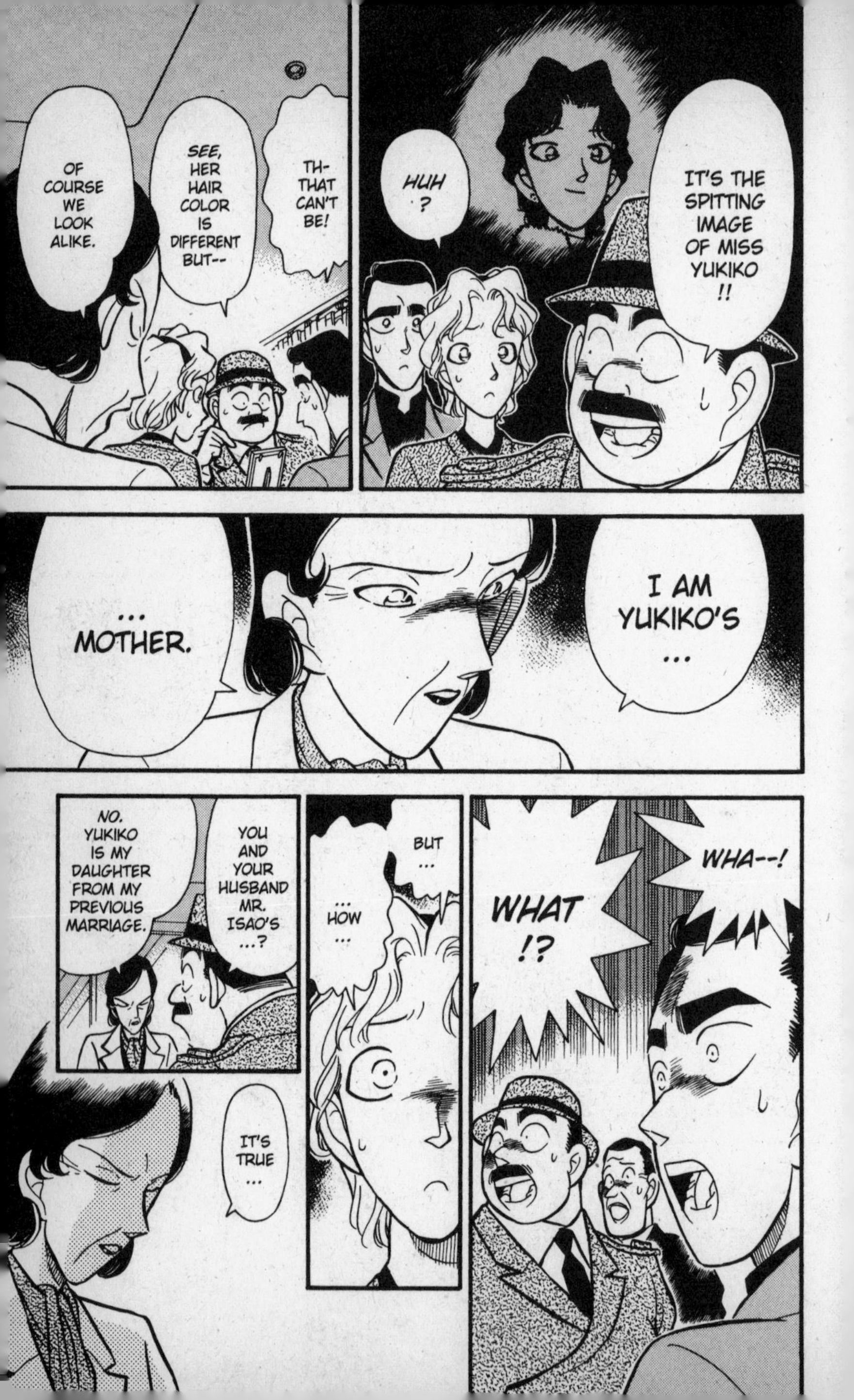
IT'S THE SPITTING IMAGE OF MISS YUKIKO !!
HUH ?
TH-THAT CAN'T BE!
SEE, HER HAIR COLOR IS DIFFERENT BUT--
OF COURSE WE LOOK ALIKE.
I AM YUKIKO'S ...
... MOTHER.
WHA--!
WHAT !?
BUT ...
... HOW ...
YOU AND YOUR HUSBAND MR. ISAO'S ...?
NO. YUKIKO IS MY DAUGHTER FROM MY PREVIOUS MARRIAGE.
IT'S TRUE ...

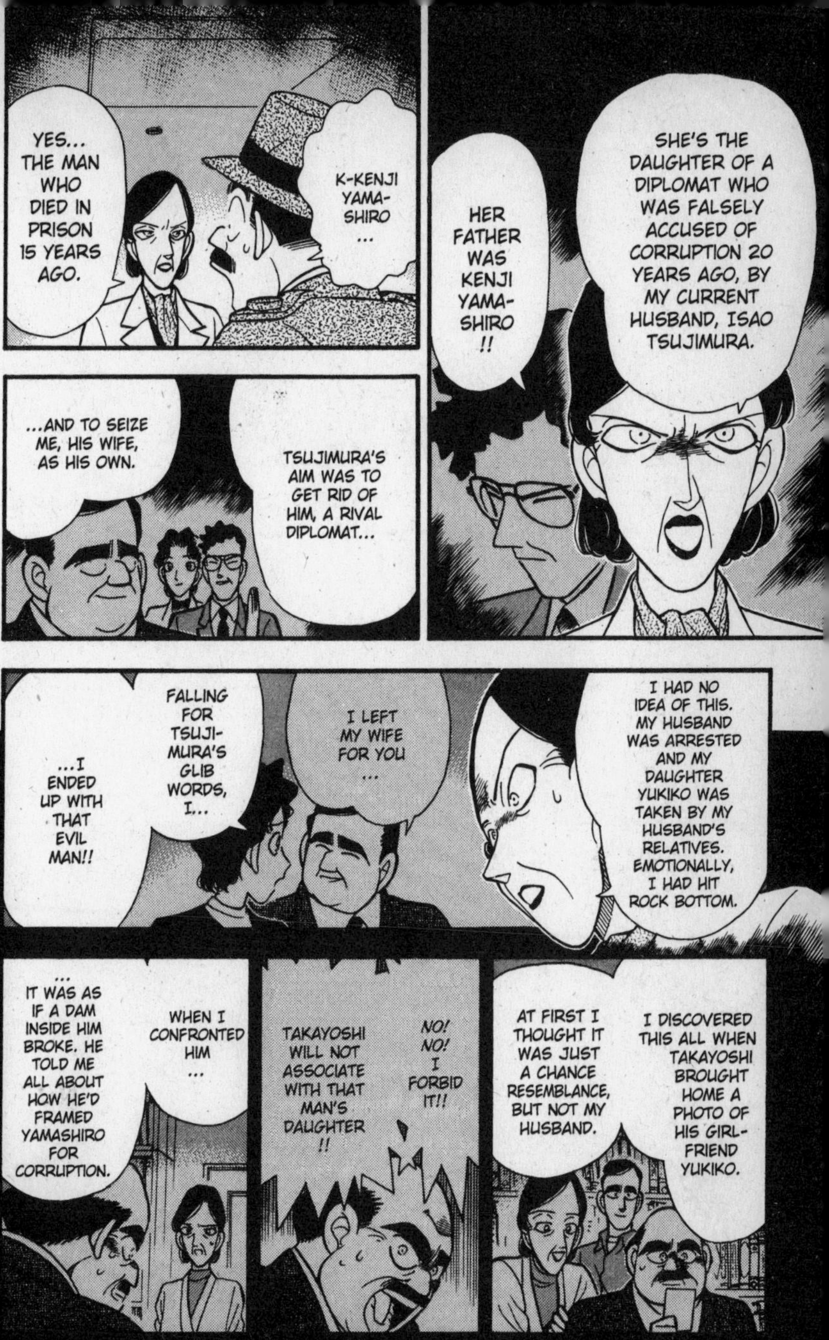
SHE'S THE DAUGHTER OF A DIPLOMAT WHO WAS FALSELY ACCUSED OF CORRUPTION 20 YEARS AGO, BY MY CURRENT HUSBAND, ISAO TSUJIMURA.
HER FATHER WAS KENJI YAMA-SHIRO !!
K-KENJI YAMA-SHIRO ...
YES... THE MAN WHO DIED IN PRISON 15 YEARS AGO.
TSUJIMURA'S AIM WAS TO GET RID OF HIM, A RIVAL DIPLOMAT...
...AND TO SEIZE ME, HIS WIFE, AS HIS OWN.
I HAD NO IDEA OF THIS. MY HUSBAND WAS ARRESTED AND MY DAUGHTER YUKIKO WAS TAKEN BY MY HUSBAND'S RELATIVES. EMOTIONALLY, I HAD HIT ROCK BOTTOM.
I LEFT MY WIFE FOR YOU ...
FALLING FOR TSUJI-MURA'S GLIB WORDS, I...
...I ENDED UP WITH THAT EVIL MAN!!
I DISCOVERED THIS ALL WHEN TAKAYOSHI BROUGHT HOME A PHOTO OF HIS GIRL-FRIEND YUKIKO.
AT FIRST I THOUGHT IT WAS JUST A CHANCE RESEMBLANCE, BUT NOT MY HUSBAND.
NO! NO! I FORBID IT!!
TAKAYOSHI WILL NOT ASSOCIATE WITH THAT MAN'S DAUGHTER !!
WHEN I CONFRONTED HIM ...
... IT WAS AS IF A DAM INSIDE HIM BROKE. HE TOLD ME ALL ABOUT HOW HE'D FRAMED YAMASHIRO FOR CORRUPTION.

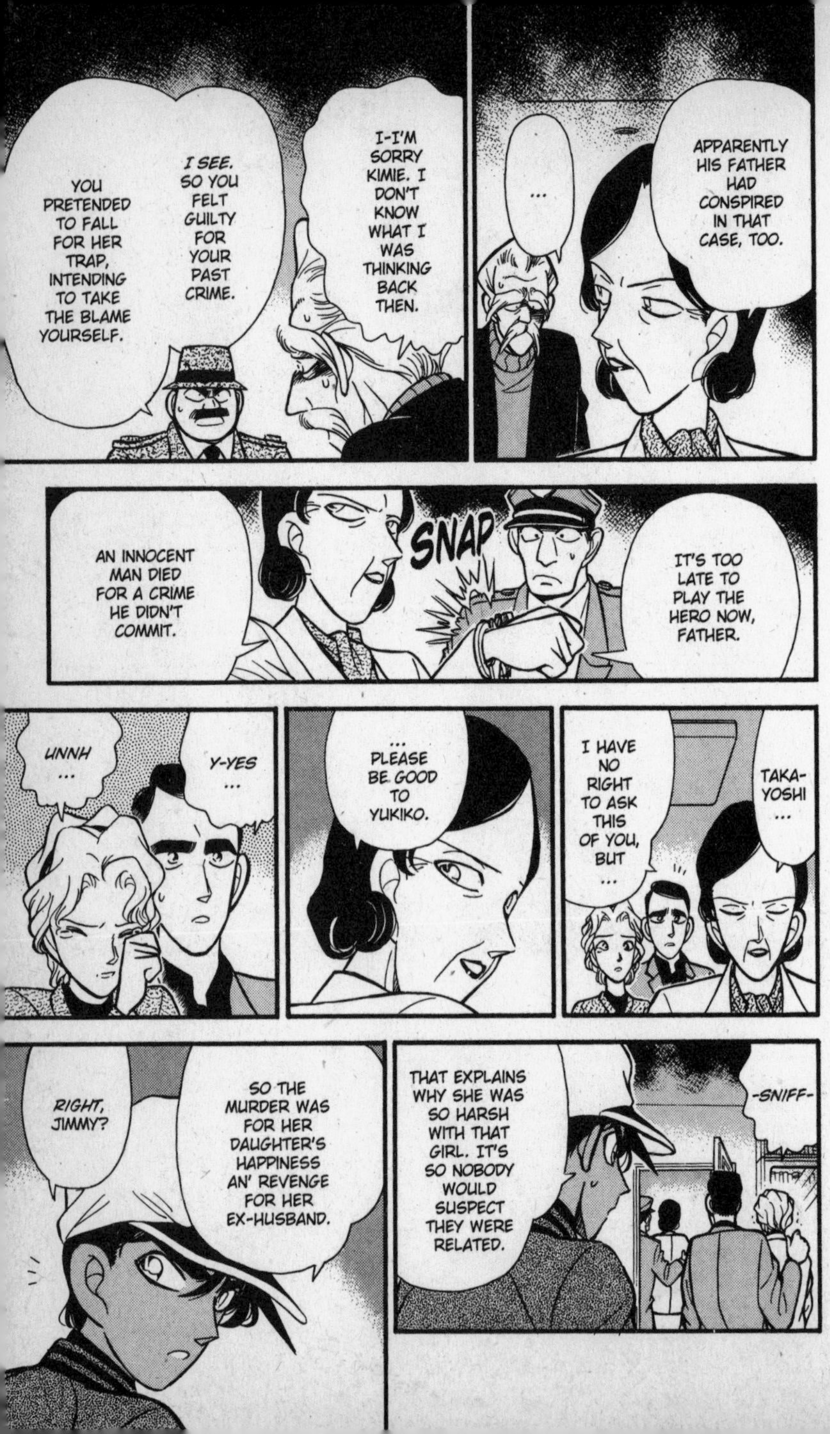
APPARENTLY HIS FATHER HAD CONSPIRED IN THAT CASE, TOO.
...
I-I'M SORRY KIMIE. I DON'T KNOW WHAT I WAS THINKING BACK THEN.
I SEE. SO YOU FELT GUILTY FOR YOUR PAST CRIME.
YOU PRETENDED TO FALL FOR HER TRAP, INTENDING TO TAKE THE BLAME YOURSELF.
IT'S TOO LATE TO PLAY THE HERO NOW, FATHER.
SNAP
AN INNOCENT MAN DIED FOR A CRIME HE DIDN'T COMMIT.
TAKA-YOSHI ...
I HAVE NO RIGHT TO ASK THIS OF YOU, BUT ...
... PLEASE BE GOOD TO YUKIKO.
Y-YES ...
UNNH ...
-SNIFF-
THAT EXPLAINS WHY SHE WAS SO HARSH WITH THAT GIRL. IT'S SO NOBODY WOULD SUSPECT THEY WERE RELATED.
SO THE MURDER WAS FOR HER DAUGHTER'S HAPPINESS AN' REVENGE FOR HER EX-HUSBAND.
RIGHT, JIMMY?

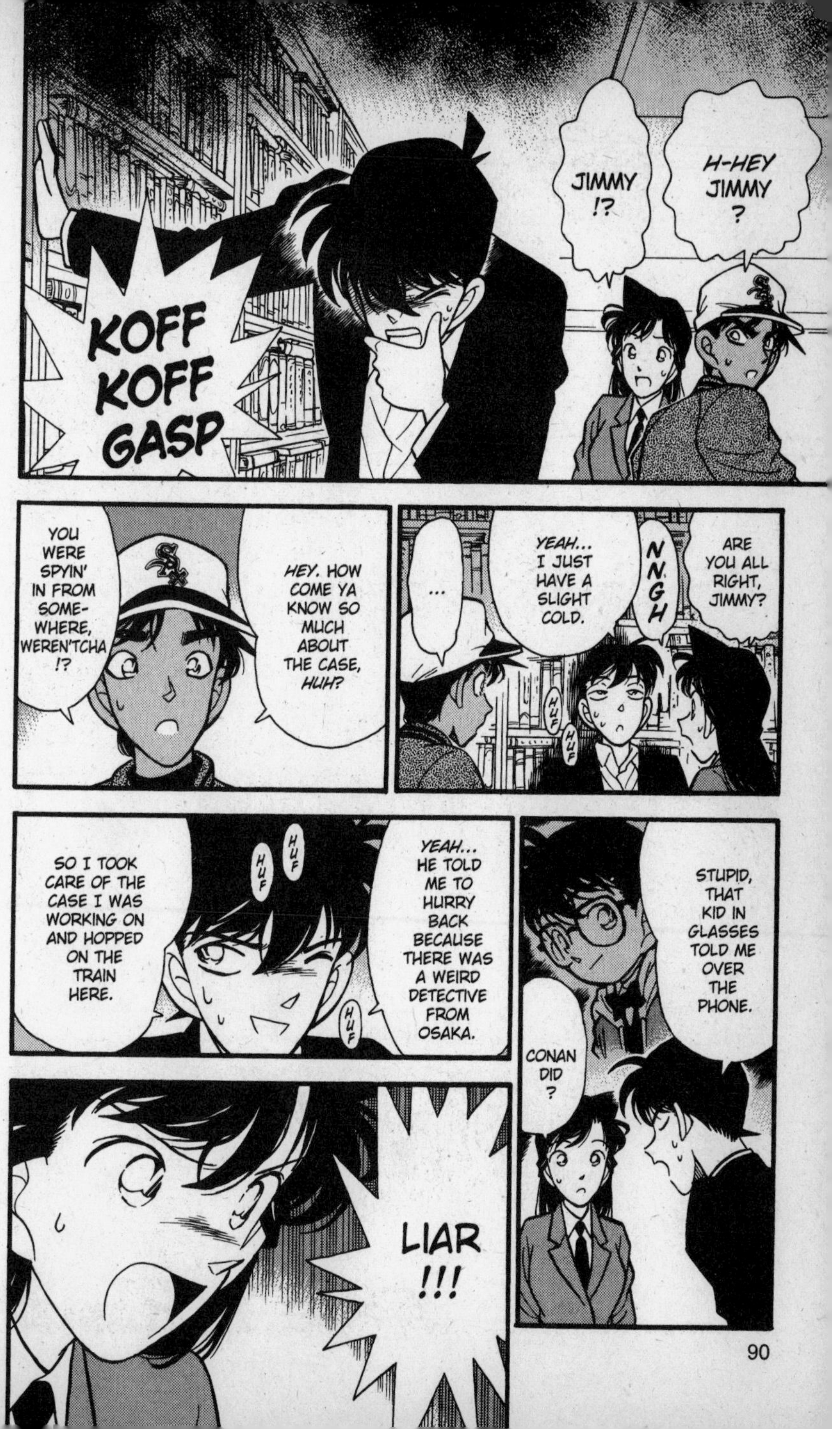
H-HEY JIMMY ?
JIMMY !?
KOFF KOFF GASP
ARE YOU ALL RIGHT, JIMMY?
NNGH
YEAH... I JUST HAVE A SLIGHT COLD.
HUF HUF
...
HEY. HOW COME YA KNOW SO MUCH ABOUT THE CASE, HUH?
YOU WERE SPYIN' IN FROM SOME-WHERE, WEREN'TCHA !?
STUPID, THAT KID IN GLASSES TOLD ME OVER THE PHONE.
CONAN DID ?
YEAH... HE TOLD ME TO HURRY BACK BECAUSE THERE WAS A WEIRD DETECTIVE FROM OSAKA.
HUF HUF
HUF
SO I TOOK CARE OF THE CASE I WAS WORKING ON AND HOPPED ON THE TRAIN HERE.
LIAR !!!

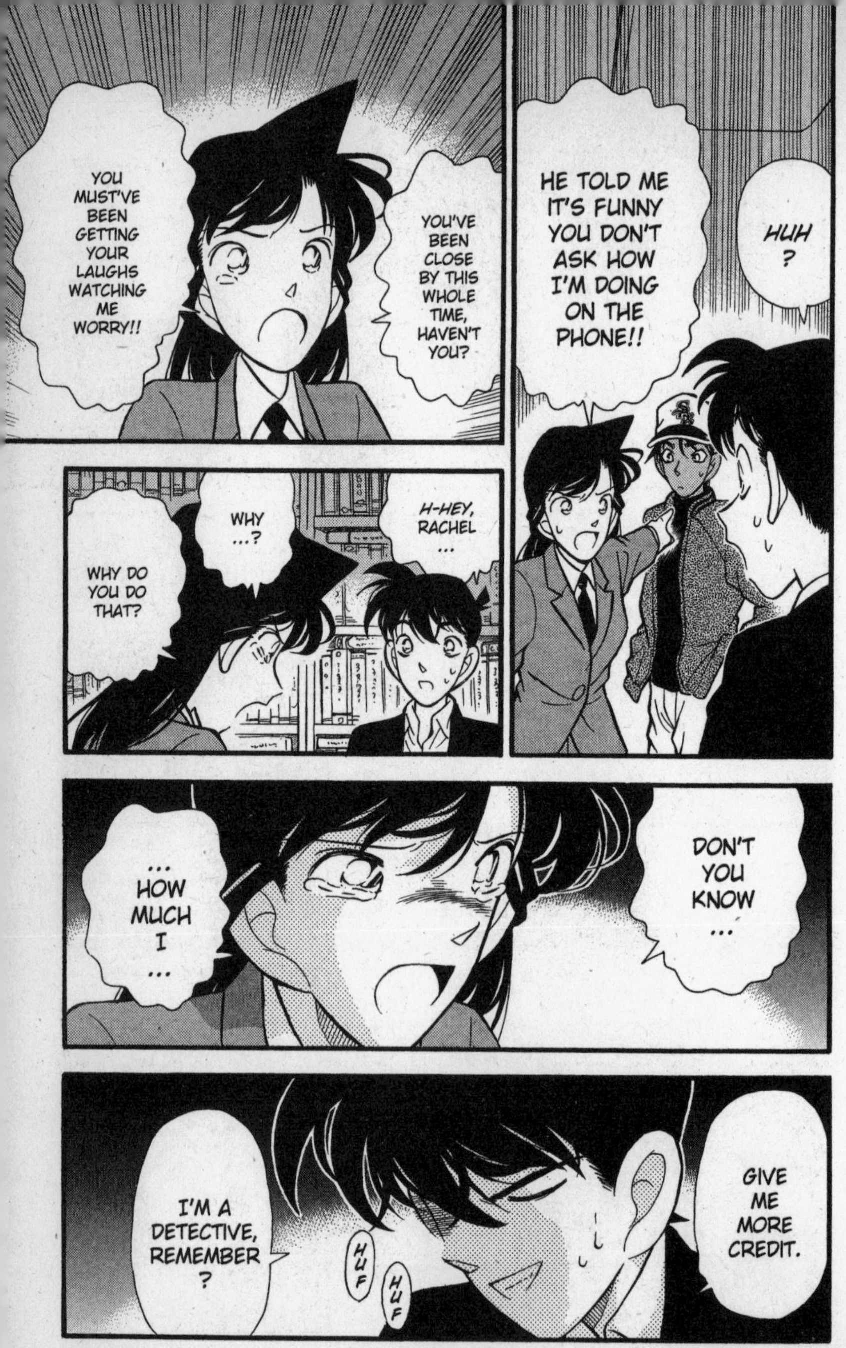
HUH?
HE TOLD ME IT'S FUNNY YOU DON'T ASK HOW I'M DOING ON THE PHONE!!
YOU'VE BEEN CLOSE BY THIS WHOLE TIME, HAVEN'T YOU?
YOU MUST'VE BEEN GETTING YOUR LAUGHS WATCHING ME WORRY!!
H-HEY, RACHEL...
WHY...?
WHY DO YOU DO THAT?
DON'T YOU KNOW...
...HOW MUCH I...
GIVE ME MORE CREDIT.
HUF
HUF
I'M A DETECTIVE, REMEMBER?

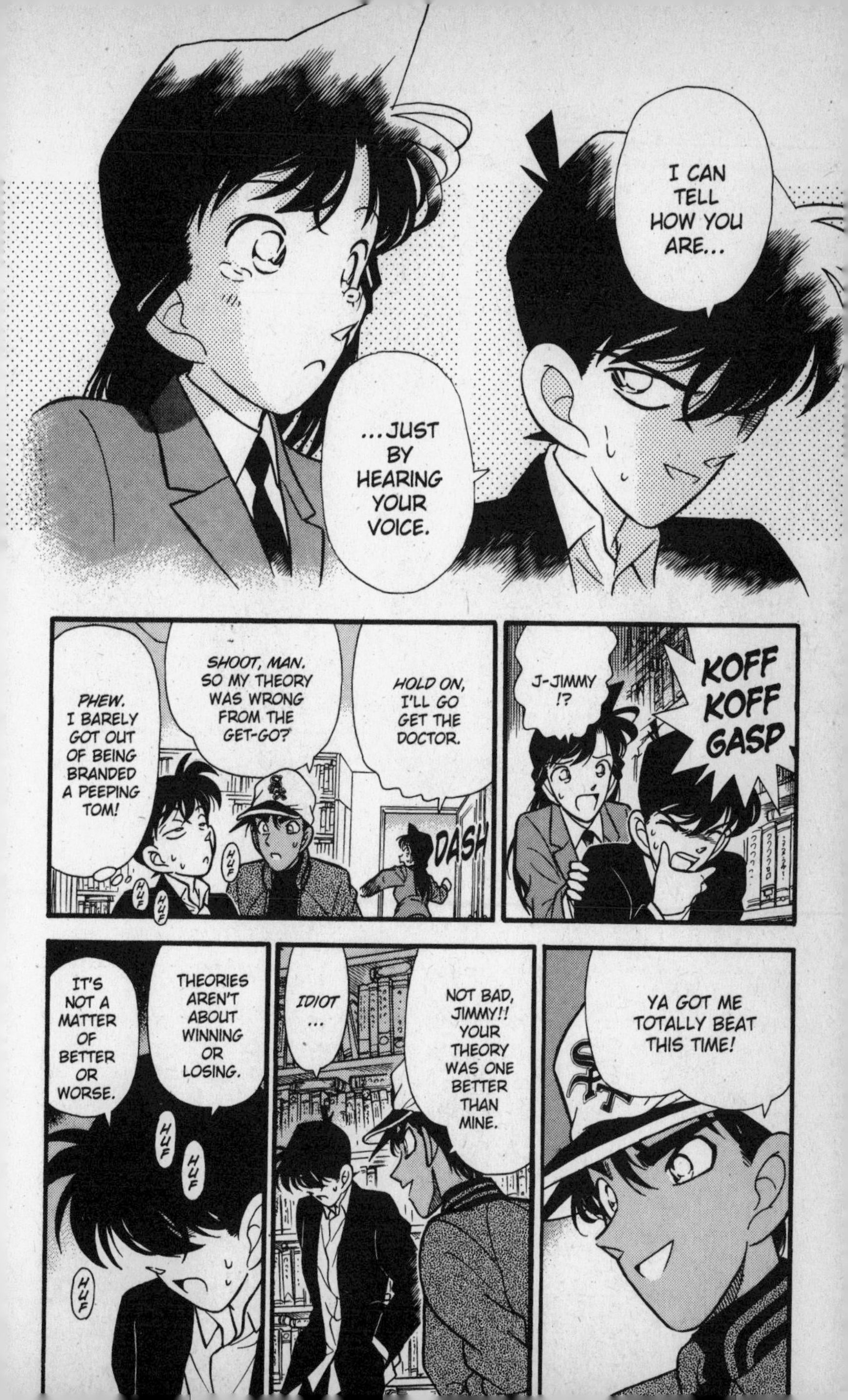
I CAN TELL HOW YOU ARE...
...JUST BY HEARING YOUR VOICE.
KOFF KOFF GASP
J-JIMMY !?
HOLD ON, I'LL GO GET THE DOCTOR.
DASH
SHOOT, MAN. SO MY THEORY WAS WRONG FROM THE GET-GO?
PHEW. I BARELY GOT OUT OF BEING BRANDED A PEEPING TOM!
HUF HUF HUF
YA GOT ME TOTALLY BEAT THIS TIME!
NOT BAD, JIMMY!! YOUR THEORY WAS ONE BETTER THAN MINE.
IDIOT ...
THEORIES AREN'T ABOUT WINNING OR LOSING.
IT'S NOT A MATTER OF BETTER OR WORSE.
HUF HUF HUF

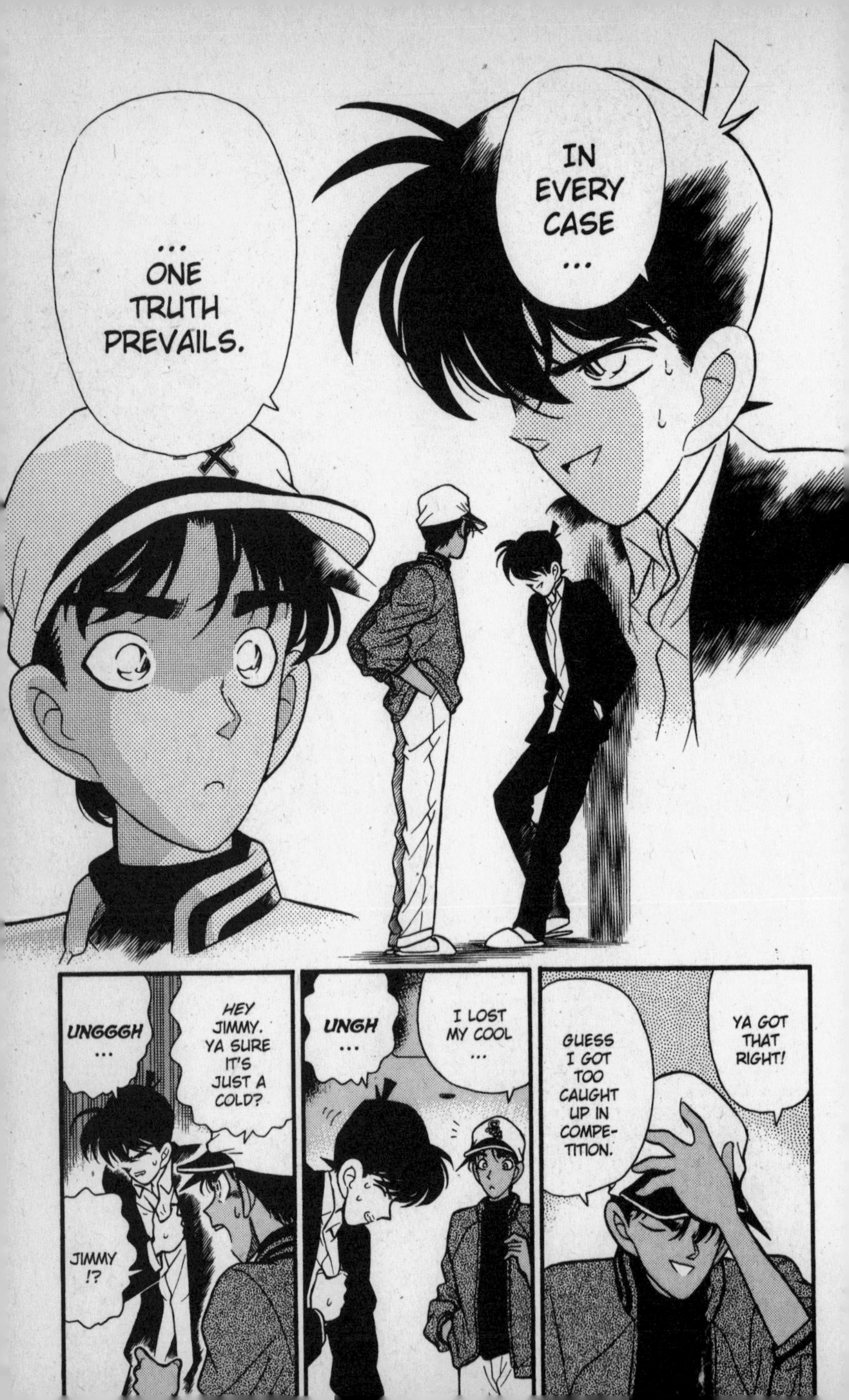
IN EVERY CASE ...
... ONE TRUTH PREVAILS.
GUESS I GOT TOO CAUGHT UP IN COMPETITION.
YA GOT THAT RIGHT!
I LOST MY COOL ...
UNGH ...
HEY JIMMY. YA SURE IT'S JUST A COLD?
UNGGGH ...
JIMMY !?

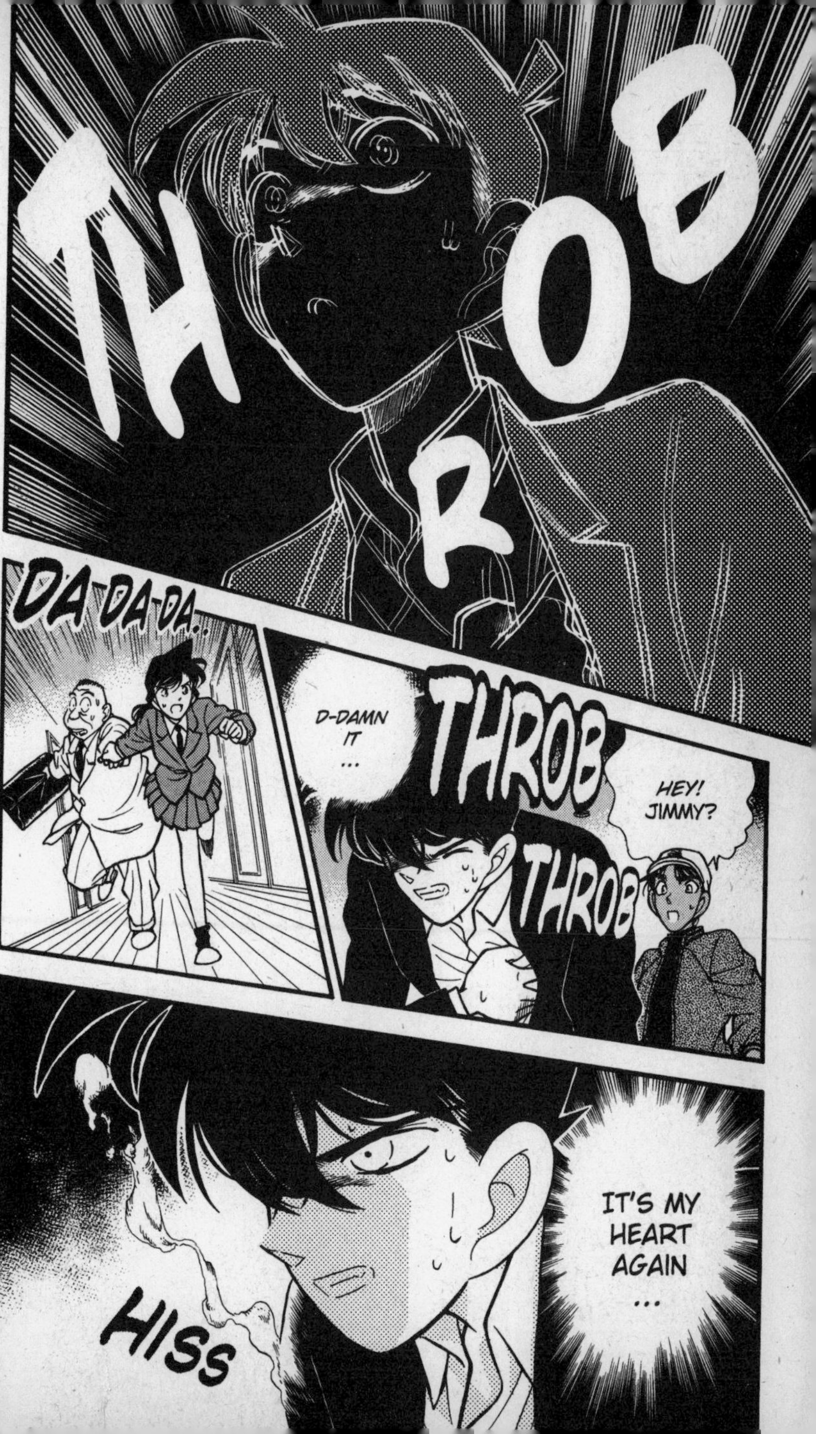
THROB
THROB
HEY! JIMMY?
D-DAMN IT ...
THROB
DA DA DA..
IT'S MY HEART AGAIN ...
HISS

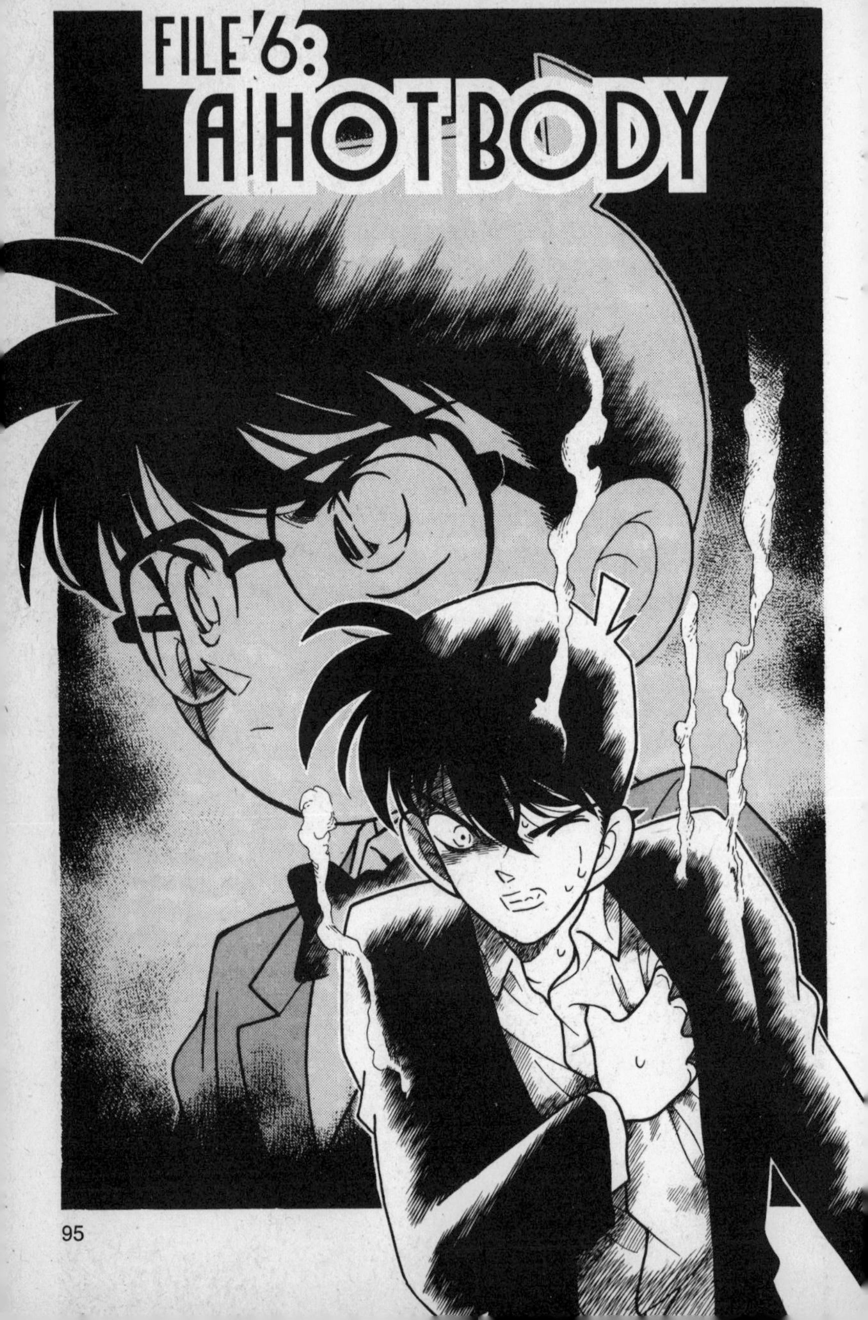
FILE 6:
A HOT BODY

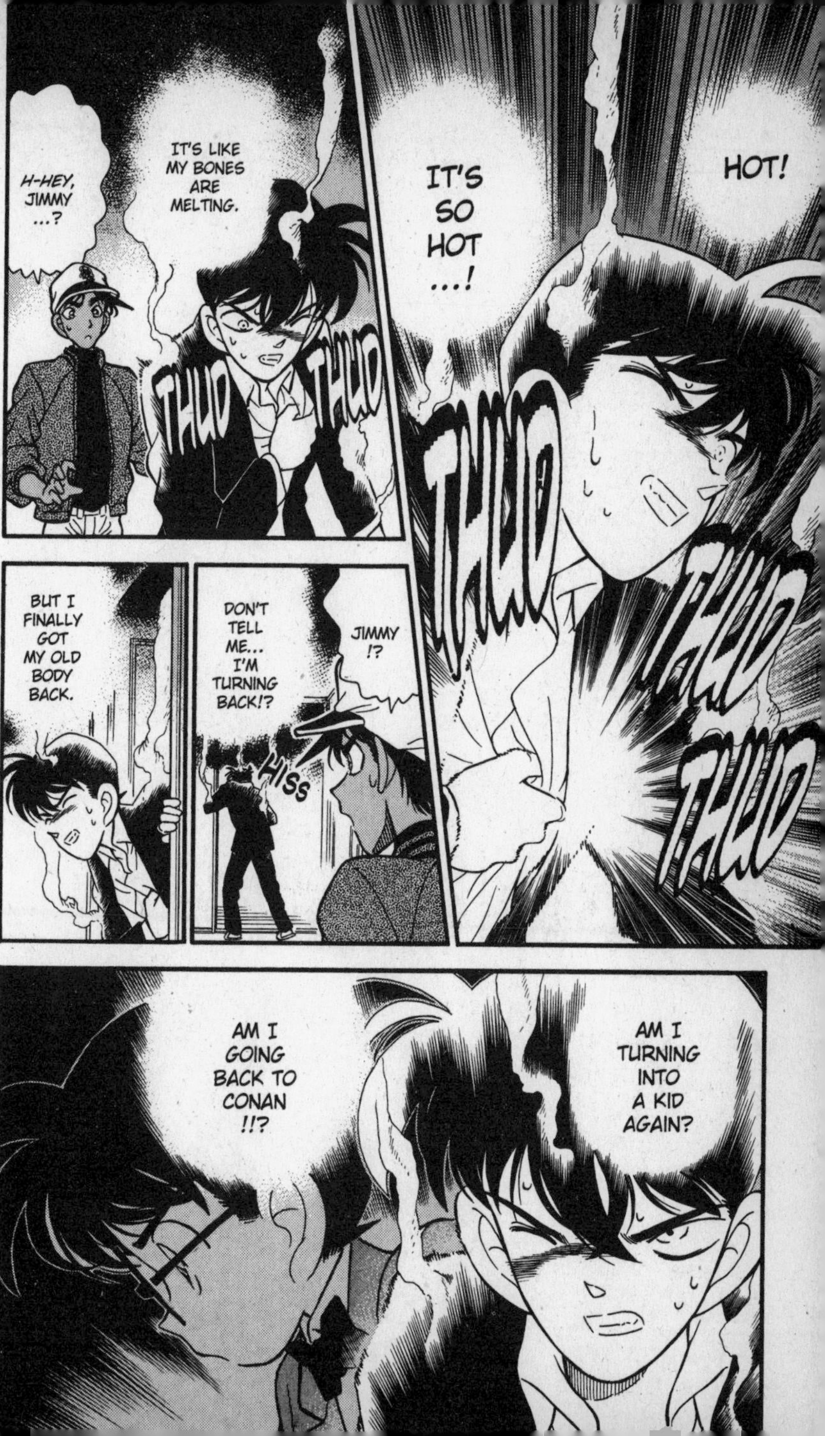
HOT!
IT'S SO HOT ...!
THUD
THUD
THUD
IT'S LIKE MY BONES ARE MELTING.
H-HEY, JIMMY ...?
THUD
THUD
DON'T TELL ME... I'M TURNING BACK!?
JIMMY !?
HISS
BUT I FINALLY GOT MY OLD BODY BACK.
AM I TURNING INTO A KID AGAIN?
AM I GOING BACK TO CONAN !!?

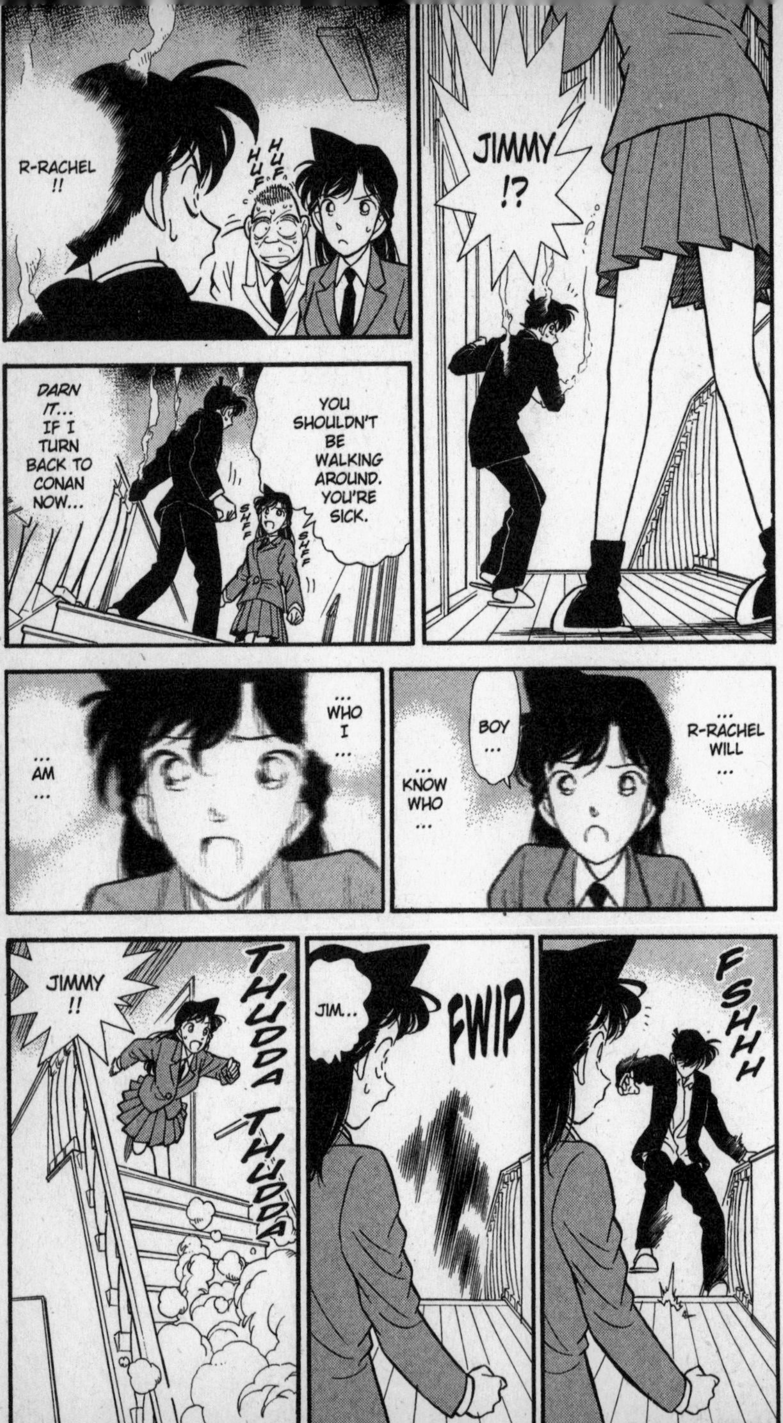
JIMMY !?
HUF HUF
R-RACHEL !!
YOU SHOULDN'T BE WALKING AROUND. YOU'RE SICK.
SHFF SHFF
DARN IT... IF I TURN BACK TO CONAN NOW...
... R-RACHEL WILL ...
BOY ...
... KNOW WHO ...
... WHO I ...
... AM ...
FSHHH
FWIP
JIM...
THUDDA THUDDA
JIMMY !!

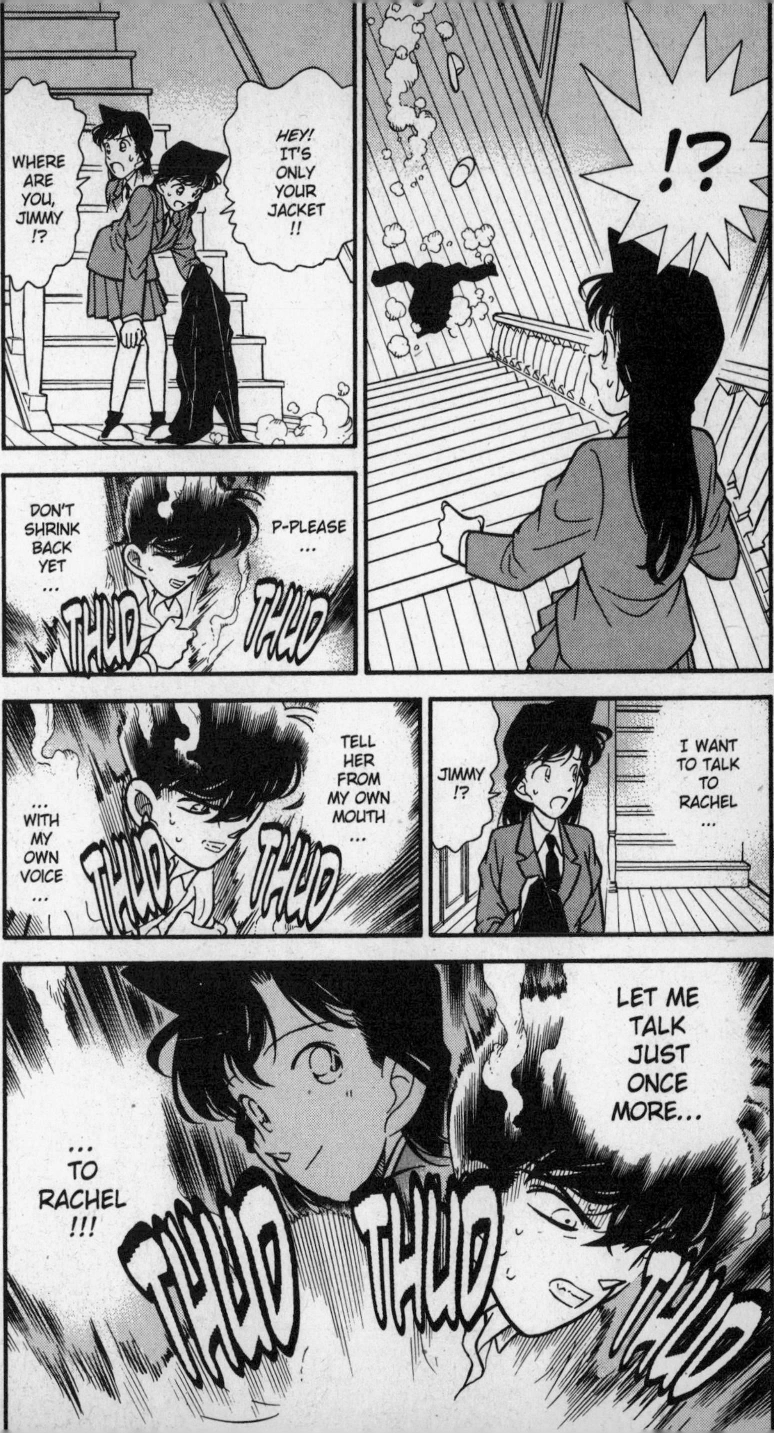
!?
HEY! IT'S ONLY YOUR JACKET !!
WHERE ARE YOU, JIMMY !?
P-PLEASE ...
DON'T SHRINK BACK YET ...
THUD
THUD
I WANT TO TALK TO RACHEL ...
JIMMY !?
TELL HER FROM MY OWN MOUTH ...
... WITH MY OWN VOICE ...
THUD
THUD
LET ME TALK JUST ONCE MORE...
... TO RACHEL !!!
THUD
THUD
THUD

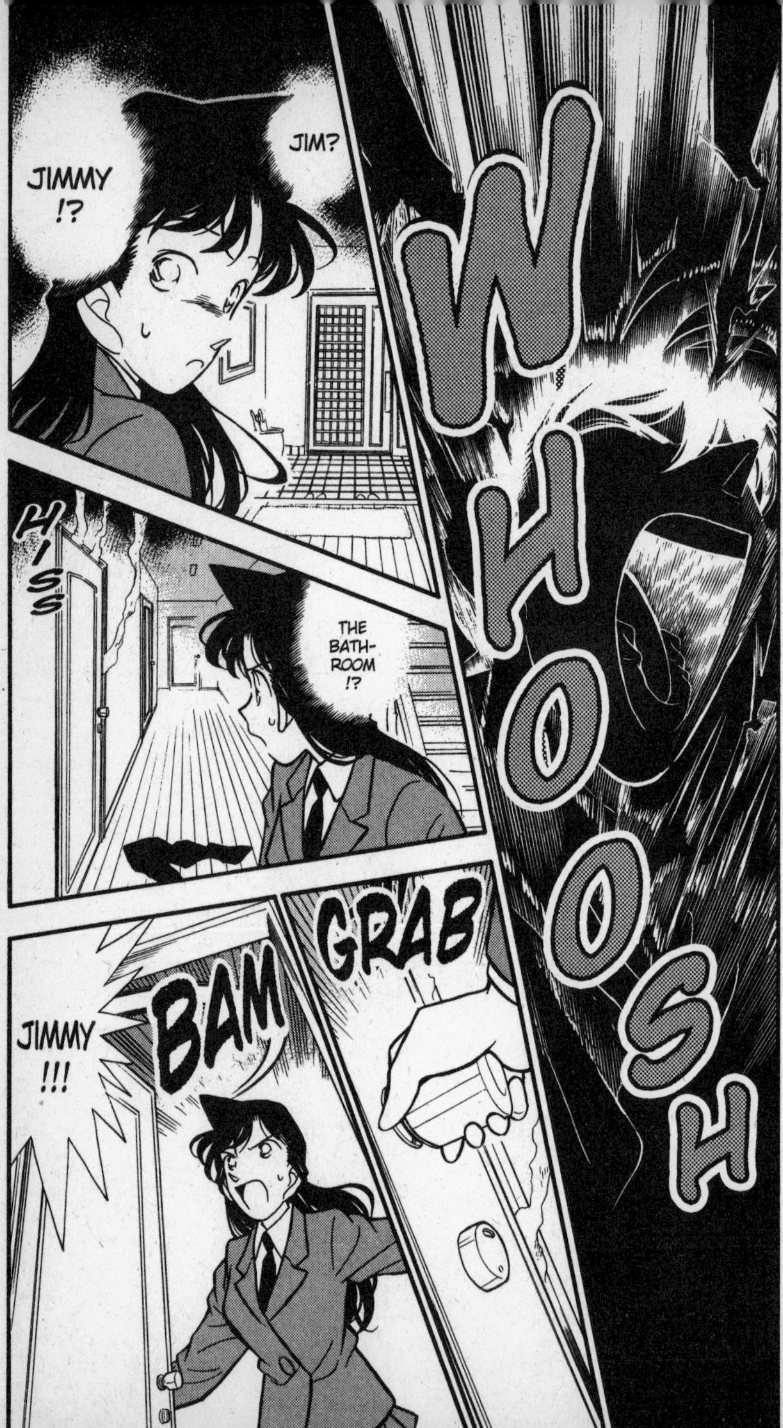
WHOOOSH
JIM?
JIMMY !?
THE BATH-ROOM !?
HISS
GRAB
BAM
JIMMY !!!

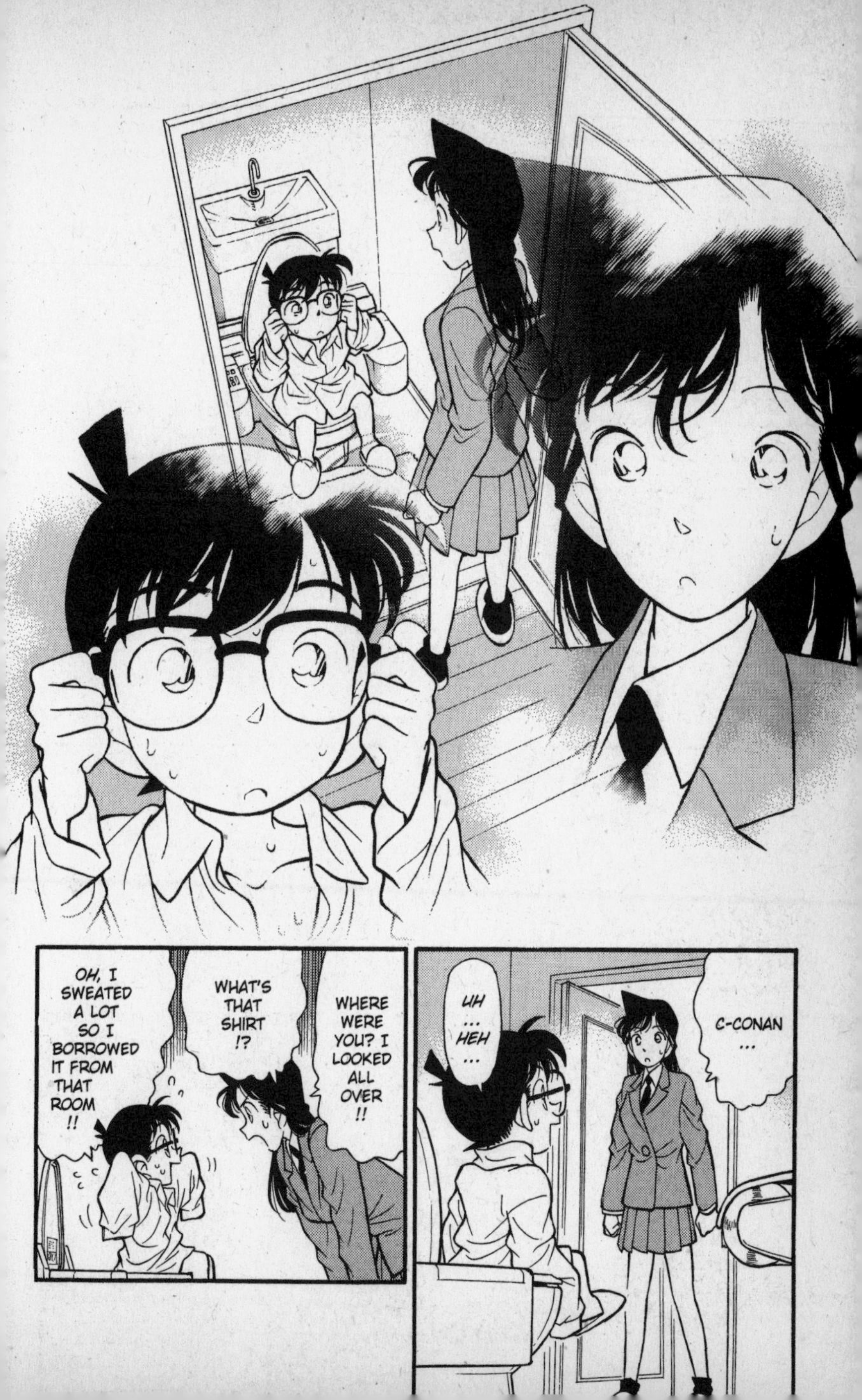
C-CONAN ...
UH ... HEH ...
WHERE WERE YOU? I LOOKED ALL OVER!!
WHAT'S THAT SHIRT!?
OH, I SWEATED A LOT SO I BORROWED IT FROM THAT ROOM!!

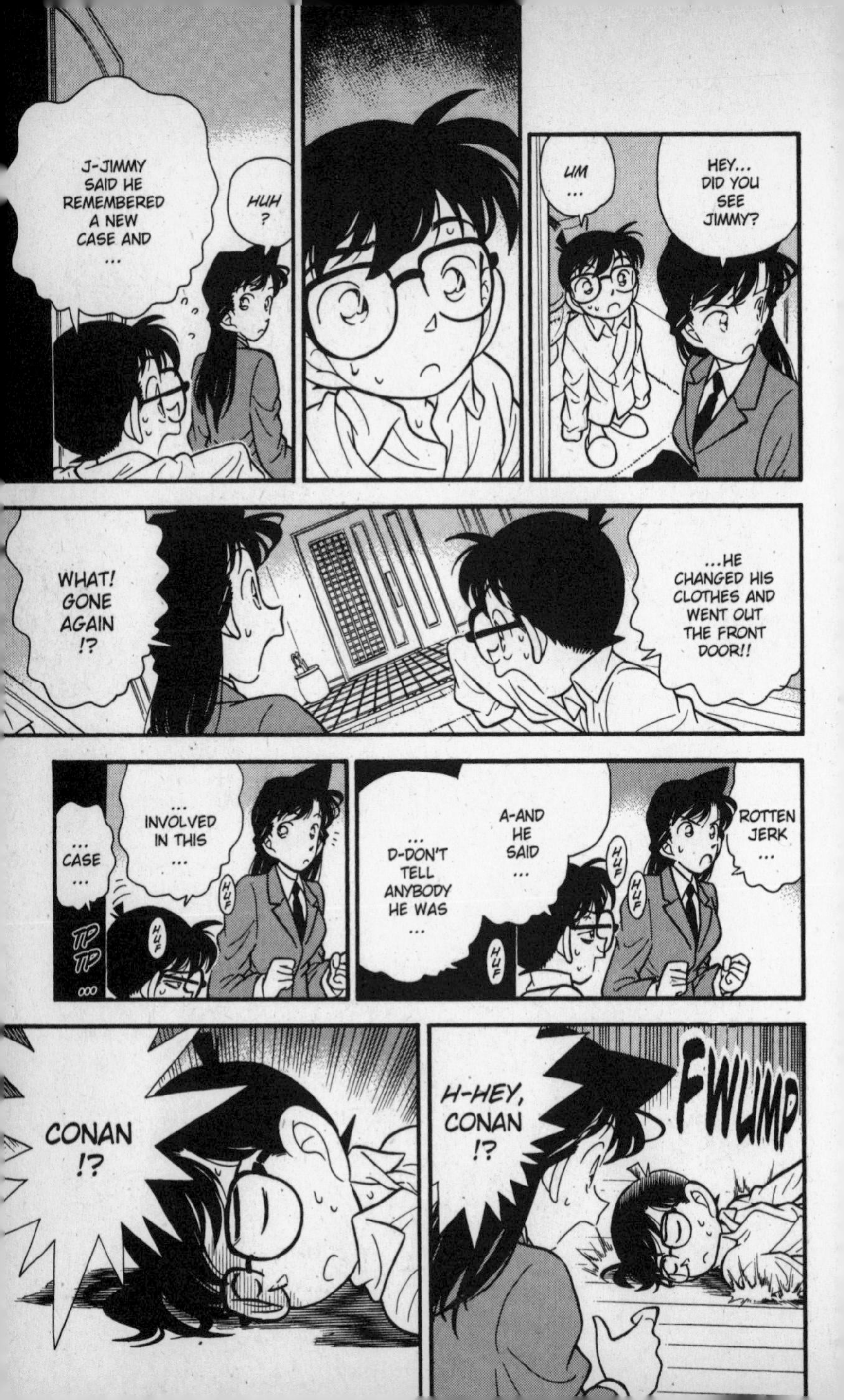
HEY... DID YOU SEE JIMMY?
UM ...
HUH ?
J-JIMMY SAID HE REMEMBERED A NEW CASE AND ...
...HE CHANGED HIS CLOTHES AND WENT OUT THE FRONT DOOR!!
WHAT! GONE AGAIN !?
ROTTEN JERK ...
HUF
HUF
A-AND HE SAID ...
... D-DON'T TELL ANYBODY HE WAS ...
HUF
... INVOLVED IN THIS ...
... CASE ...
HUF
TP TP ...
FWUMP
H-HEY, CONAN !?
CONAN !?

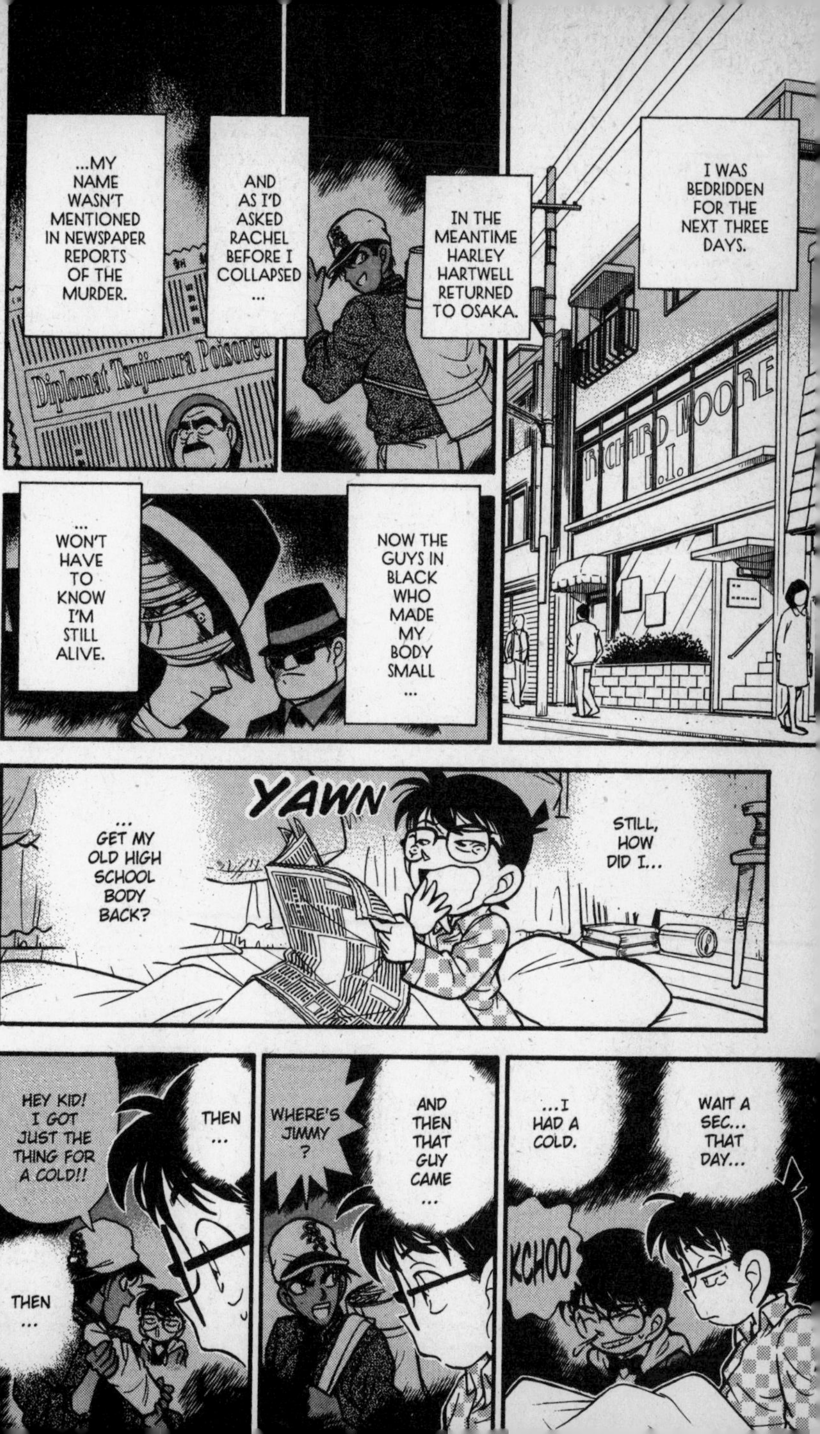

I WAS BEDRIDDEN FOR THE NEXT THREE DAYS.
RICHARD MOORE P.I.
IN THE MEANTIME HARLEY HARTWELL RETURNED TO OSAKA.
AND AS I'D ASKED RACHEL BEFORE I COLLAPSED ...
...MY NAME WASN'T MENTIONED IN NEWSPAPER REPORTS OF THE MURDER.
Diplomat Tsujimura Poisoned
NOW THE GUYS IN BLACK WHO MADE MY BODY SMALL ...
... WON'T HAVE TO KNOW I'M STILL ALIVE.
YAWN
STILL, HOW DID I...
... GET MY OLD HIGH SCHOOL BODY BACK?
WAIT A SEC... THAT DAY...
...I HAD A COLD.
KCHOO
AND THEN THAT GUY CAME ...
WHERE'S JIMMY?
THEN ...
HEY KID! I GOT JUST THE THING FOR A COLD!!
THEN ...

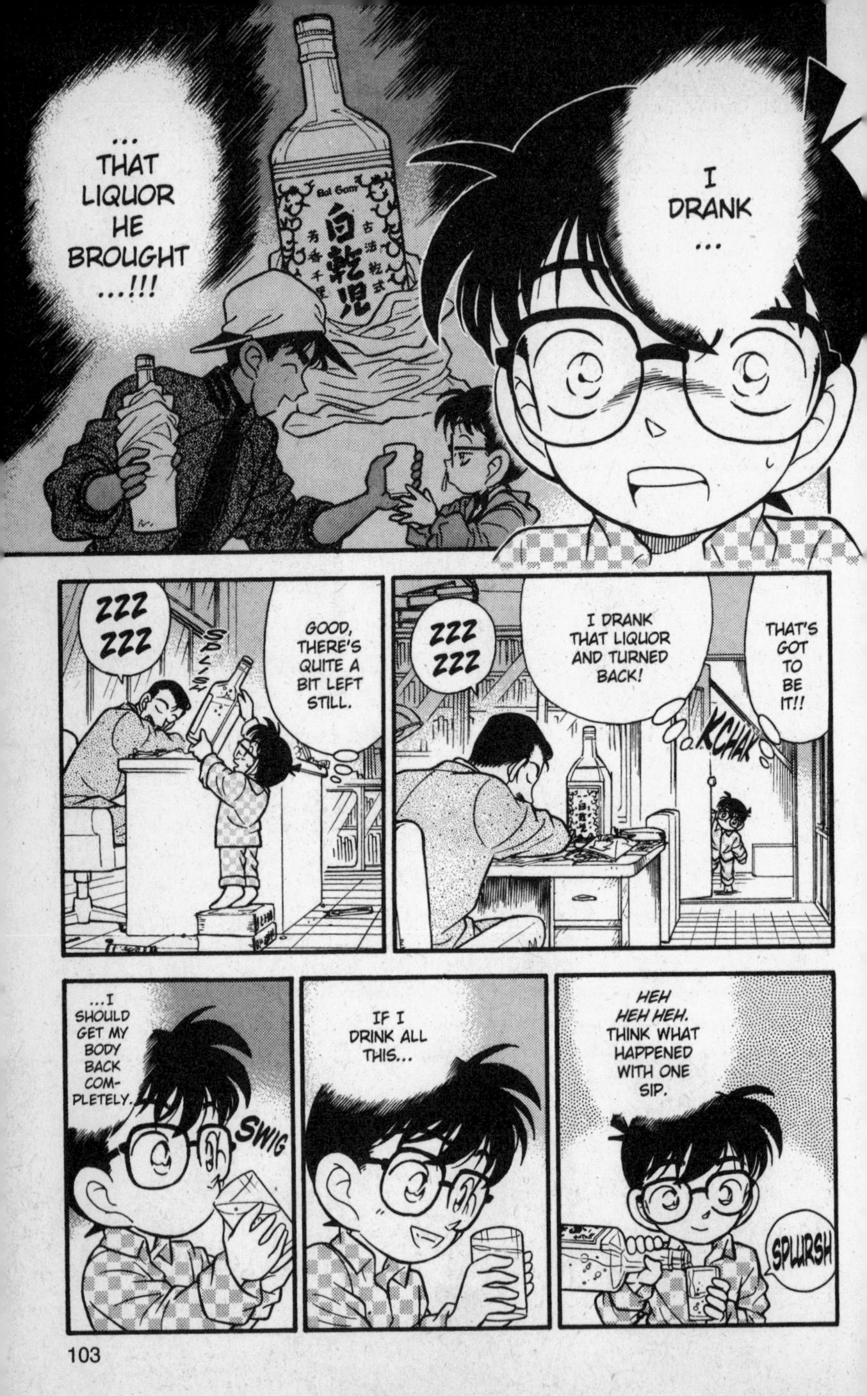
I DRANK ...
... THAT LIQUOR HE BROUGHT ...!!!
I DRANK THAT LIQUOR AND TURNED BACK!
THAT'S GOT TO BE IT!!
ZZZ ZZZ
KCHAK
GOOD, THERE'S QUITE A BIT LEFT STILL.
ZZZ ZZZ
SPLISH
HEH HEH HEH. THINK WHAT HAPPENED WITH ONE SIP.
SPLURSH
IF I DRINK ALL THIS...
...I SHOULD GET MY BODY BACK COMPLETELY.
SWIG

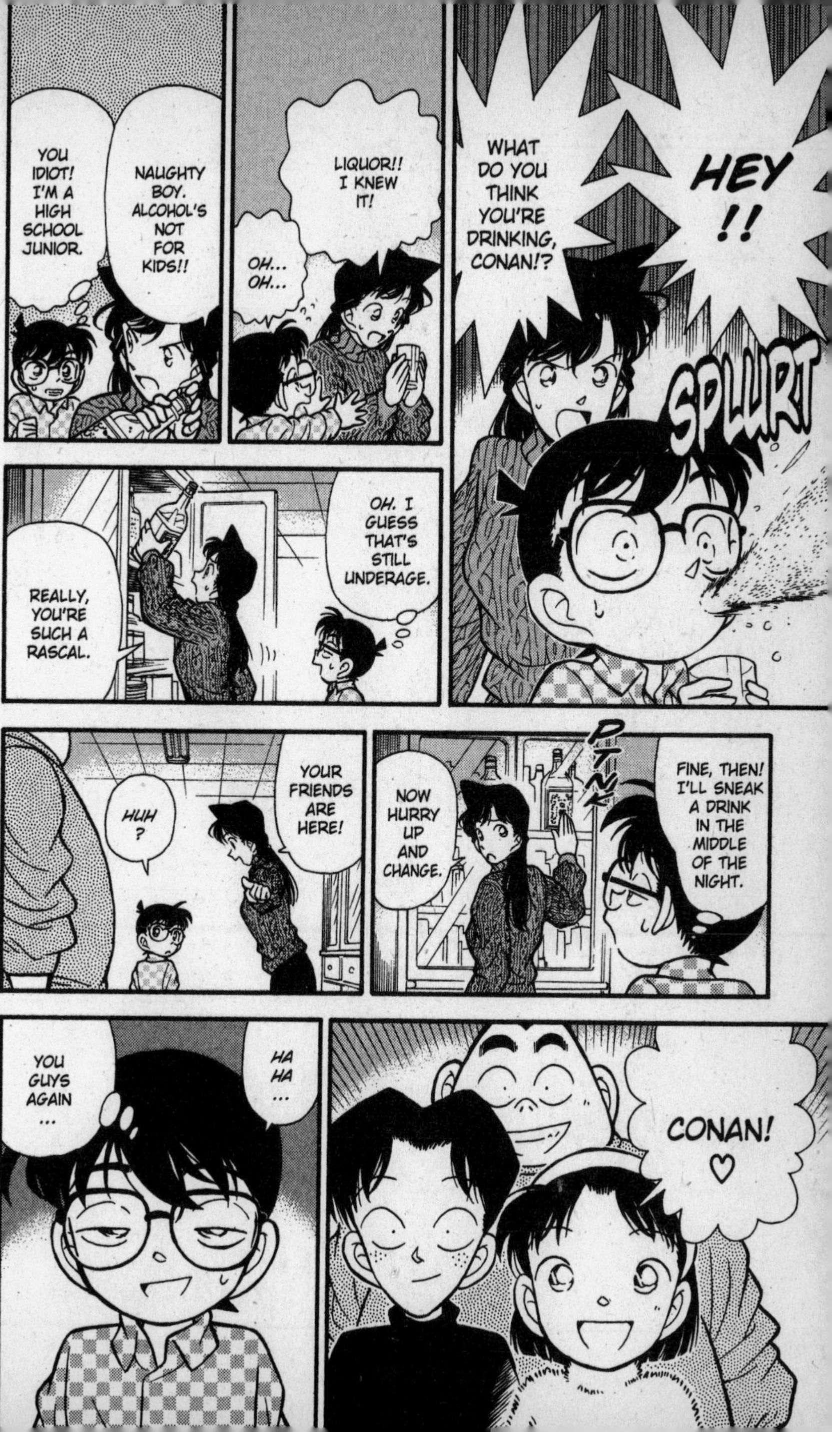
HEY!!
WHAT DO YOU THINK YOU'RE DRINKING, CONAN!?
SPLURT
LIQUOR!! I KNEW IT!
OH... OH...
NAUGHTY BOY. ALCOHOL'S NOT FOR KIDS!!
YOU IDIOT! I'M A HIGH SCHOOL JUNIOR.
OH. I GUESS THAT'S STILL UNDERAGE.
REALLY, YOU'RE SUCH A RASCAL.
FINE, THEN! I'LL SNEAK A DRINK IN THE MIDDLE OF THE NIGHT.
PTNK
NOW HURRY UP AND CHANGE.
YOUR FRIENDS ARE HERE!
HUH?
CONAN! ♡
HA HA ...
YOU GUYS AGAIN ...

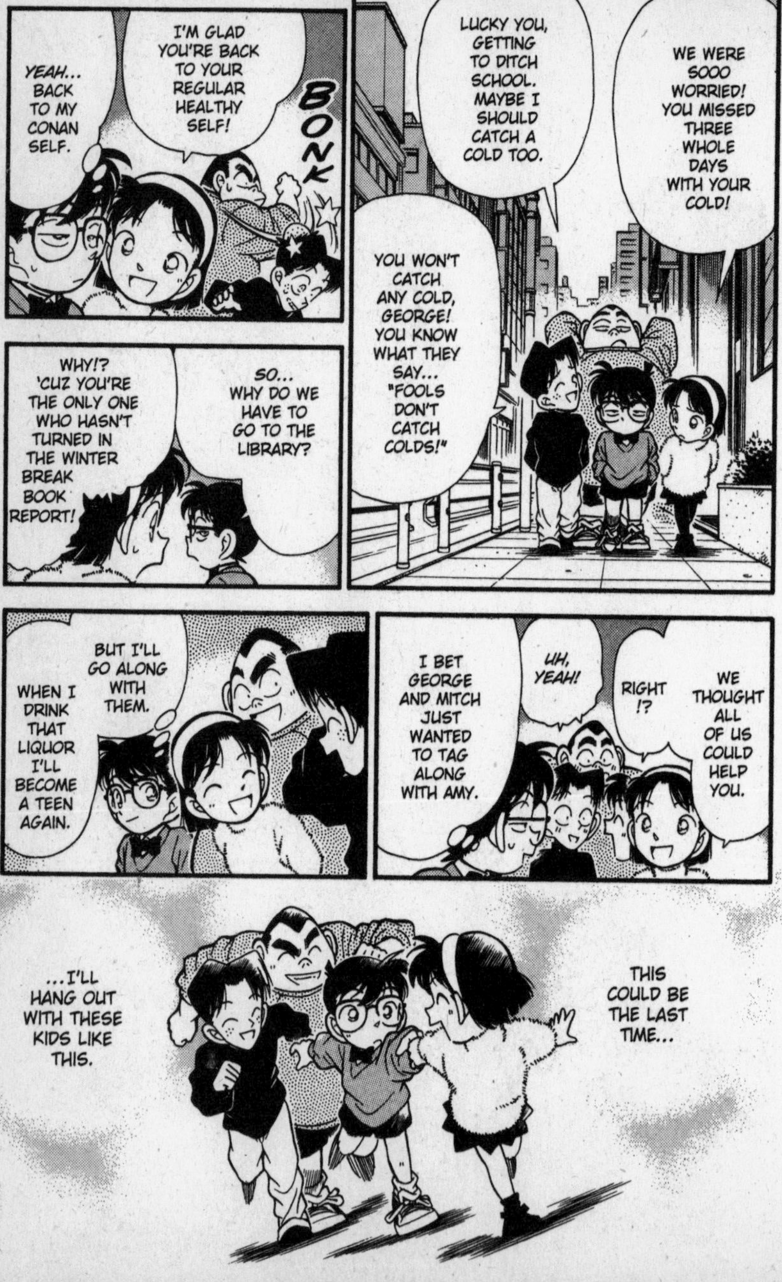
WE WERE SOOO WORRIED! YOU MISSED THREE WHOLE DAYS WITH YOUR COLD!
LUCKY YOU, GETTING TO DITCH SCHOOL. MAYBE I SHOULD CATCH A COLD TOO.
YOU WON'T CATCH ANY COLD, GEORGE! YOU KNOW WHAT THEY SAY... "FOOLS DON'T CATCH COLDS!"
I'M GLAD YOU'RE BACK TO YOUR REGULAR HEALTHY SELF!
BONK
YEAH... BACK TO MY CONAN SELF.
SO... WHY DO WE HAVE TO GO TO THE LIBRARY?
WHY!? 'CUZ YOU'RE THE ONLY ONE WHO HASN'T TURNED IN THE WINTER BREAK BOOK REPORT!
WE THOUGHT ALL OF US COULD HELP YOU.
RIGHT !?
UH, YEAH!
I BET GEORGE AND MITCH JUST WANTED TO TAG ALONG WITH AMY.
WHEN I DRINK THAT LIQUOR I'LL BECOME A TEEN AGAIN.
BUT I'LL GO ALONG WITH THEM.
THIS COULD BE THE LAST TIME...
...I'LL HANG OUT WITH THESE KIDS LIKE THIS.

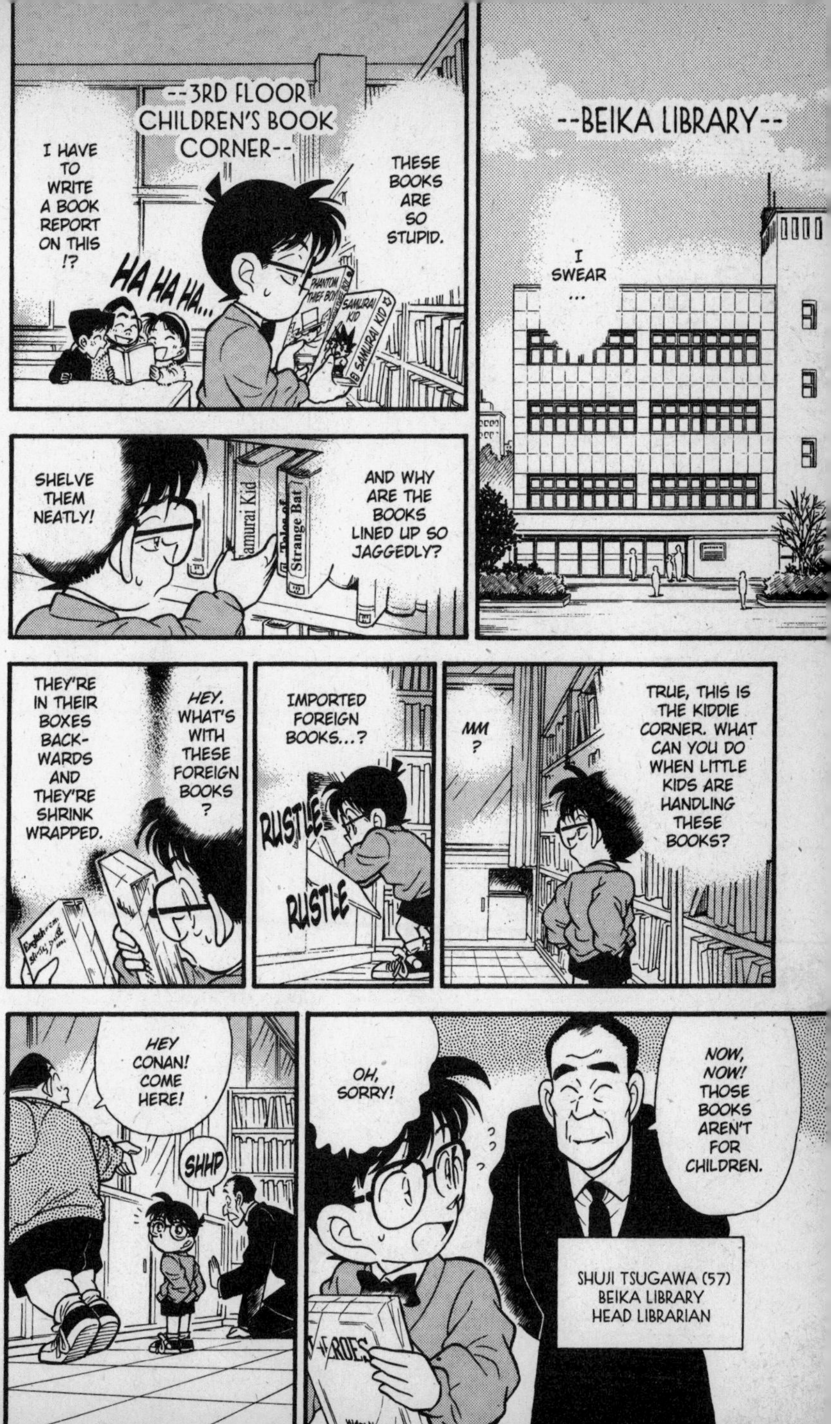

--BEIKA LIBRARY--
I SWEAR ...
--3RD FLOOR CHILDREN'S BOOK CORNER--
THESE BOOKS ARE SO STUPID.
I HAVE TO WRITE A BOOK REPORT ON THIS !?
HA HA HA...
PHANTOM THIEF BOY
SAMURAI KID
AND WHY ARE THE BOOKS LINED UP SO JAGGEDLY?
SHELVE THEM NEATLY!
Samurai Kid
Tales of Strange Bat
TRUE, THIS IS THE KIDDIE CORNER. WHAT CAN YOU DO WHEN LITTLE KIDS ARE HANDLING THESE BOOKS?
MM ?
IMPORTED FOREIGN BOOKS...?
RUSTLE
RUSTLE
HEY. WHAT'S WITH THESE FOREIGN BOOKS ?
THEY'RE IN THEIR BOXES BACK-WARDS AND THEY'RE SHRINK WRAPPED.
NOW, NOW! THOSE BOOKS AREN'T FOR CHILDREN.
OH, SORRY!
SHUJI TSUGAWA (57) BEIKA LIBRARY HEAD LIBRARIAN
HEY CONAN! COME HERE!
SHHP

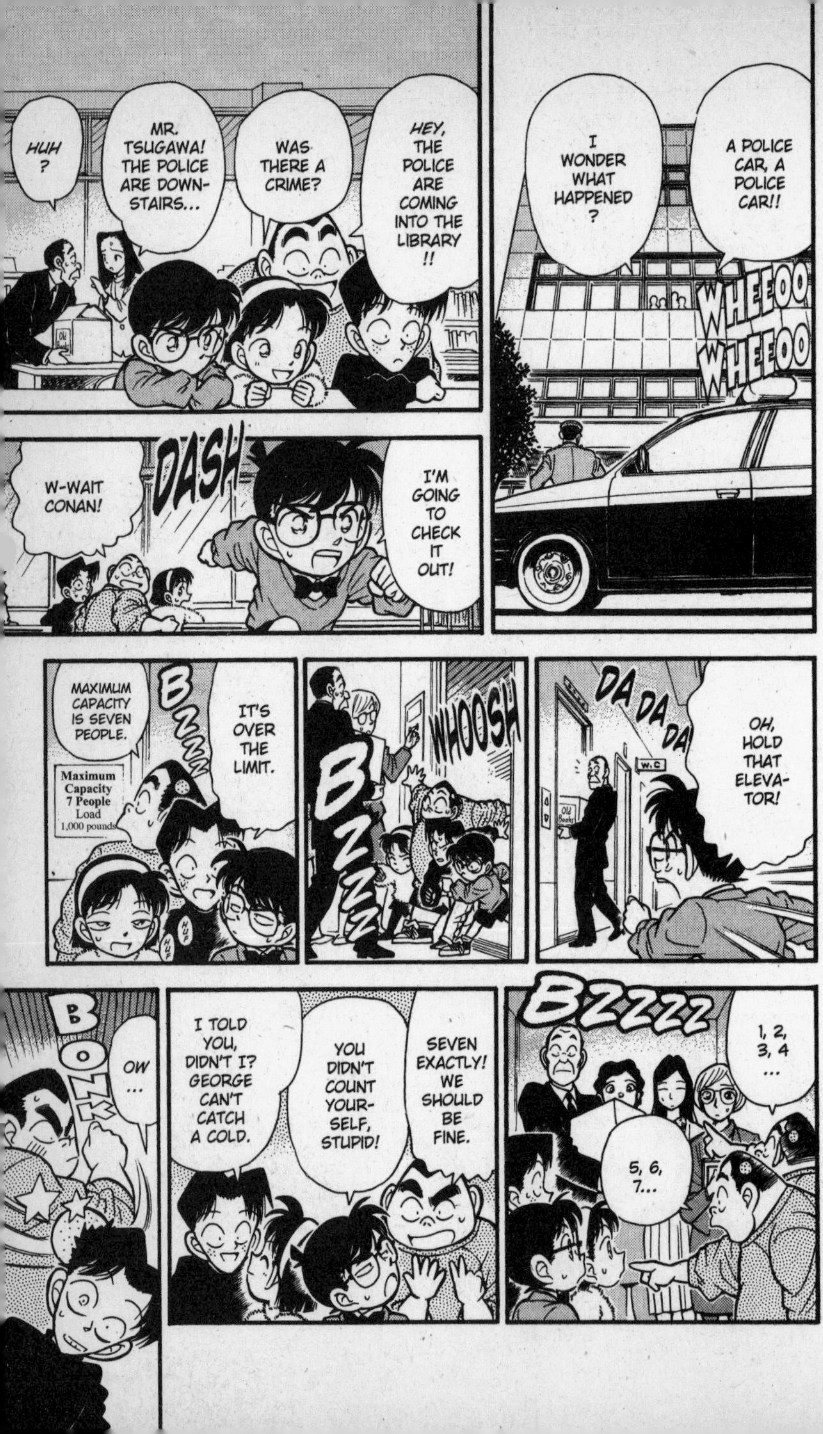
A POLICE CAR, A POLICE CAR!!
I WONDER WHAT HAPPENED?
WHEEOO
WHEEOO
HEY, THE POLICE ARE COMING INTO THE LIBRARY!!
WAS THERE A CRIME?
MR. TSUGAWA! THE POLICE ARE DOWN-STAIRS...
HUH?
I'M GOING TO CHECK IT OUT!
DASH
W-WAIT CONAN!
OH, HOLD THAT ELEVA-TOR!
DA DA DA
W.C
Old Books
WHOOSH
BZZZ
IT'S OVER THE LIMIT.
BZZZ
MAXIMUM CAPACITY IS SEVEN PEOPLE.
Maximum Capacity 7 People Load 1,000 pounds
HUF HUF
BZZZZZ
1, 2, 3, 4 ...
5, 6, 7...
SEVEN EXACTLY! WE SHOULD BE FINE.
YOU DIDN'T COUNT YOUR-SELF, STUPID!
I TOLD YOU, DIDN'T I? GEORGE CAN'T CATCH A COLD.
BONK
OW ...

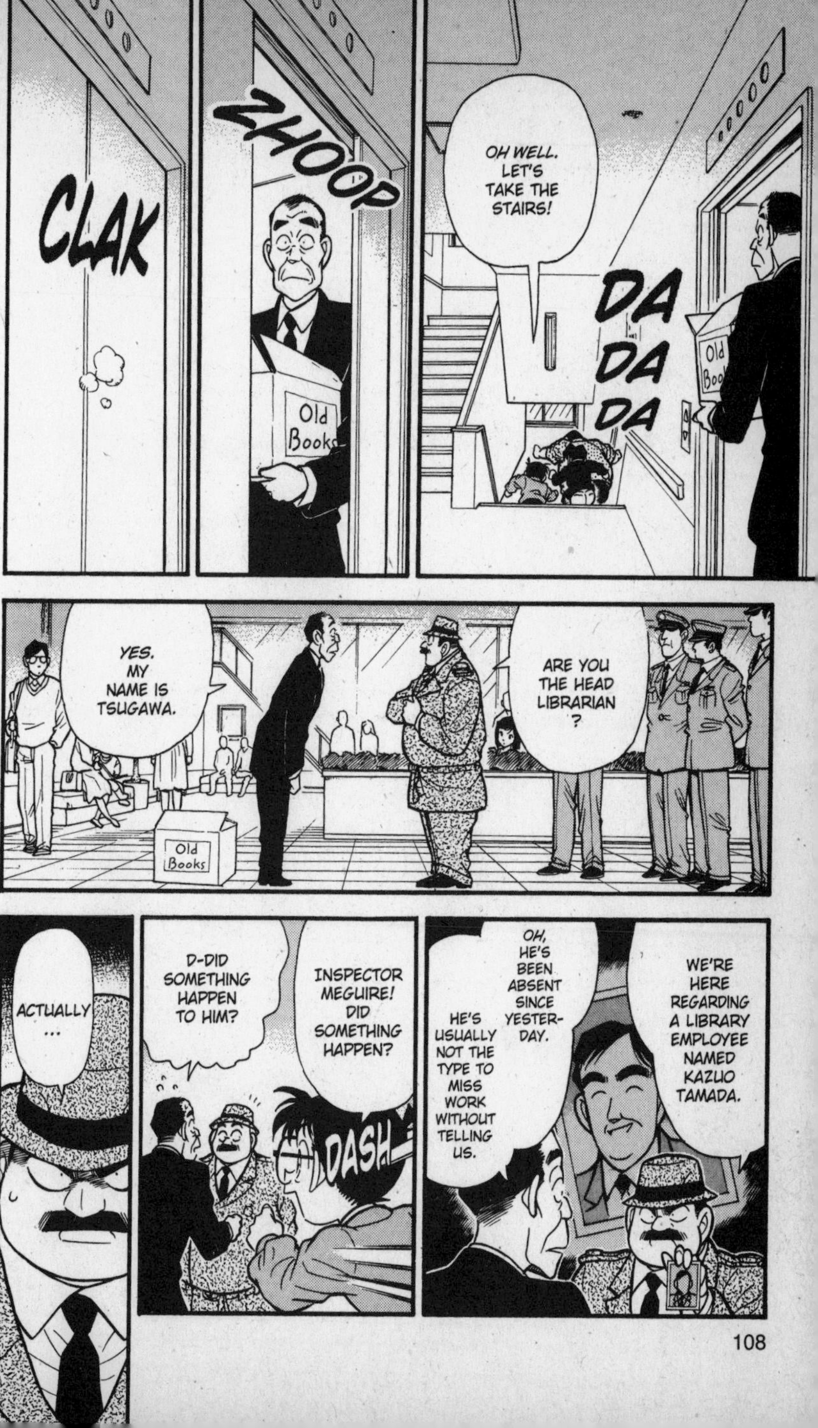
OH WELL. LET'S TAKE THE STAIRS!
DA DA DA
ZHOOP
CLAK
ARE YOU THE HEAD LIBRARIAN ?
YES. MY NAME IS TSUGAWA.
WE'RE HERE REGARDING A LIBRARY EMPLOYEE NAMED KAZUO TAMADA.
OH, HE'S BEEN ABSENT SINCE YESTER-DAY.
HE'S USUALLY NOT THE TYPE TO MISS WORK WITHOUT TELLING US.
INSPECTOR MEGUIRE! DID SOMETHING HAPPEN?
D-DID SOMETHING HAPPEN TO HIM?
DASH
ACTUALLY ...

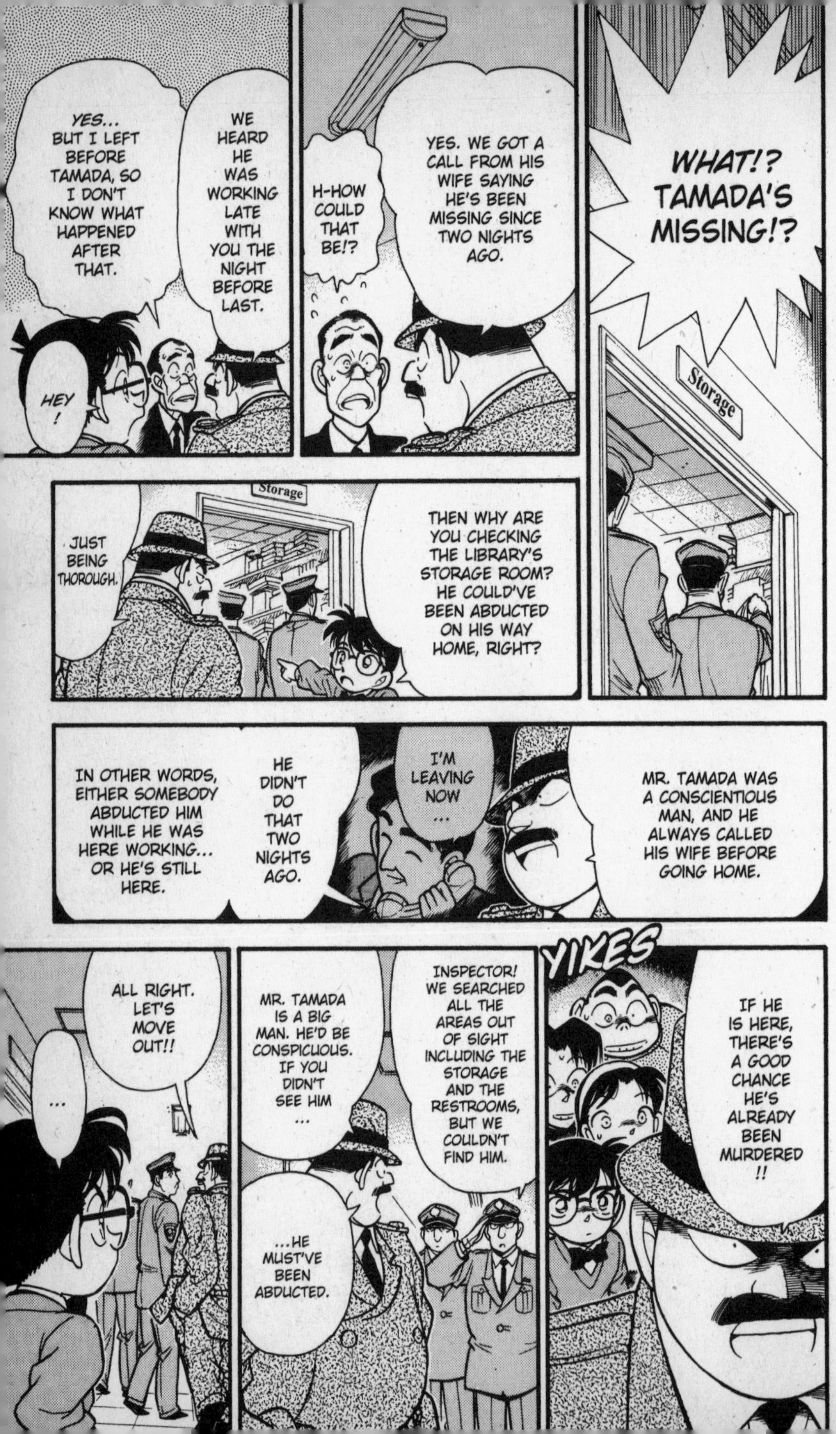
WHAT!? TAMADA'S MISSING!?
Storage
YES. WE GOT A CALL FROM HIS WIFE SAYING HE'S BEEN MISSING SINCE TWO NIGHTS AGO.
H-HOW COULD THAT BE!?
WE HEARD HE WAS WORKING LATE WITH YOU THE NIGHT BEFORE LAST.
YES... BUT I LEFT BEFORE TAMADA, SO I DON'T KNOW WHAT HAPPENED AFTER THAT.
HEY!
THEN WHY ARE YOU CHECKING THE LIBRARY'S STORAGE ROOM? HE COULD'VE BEEN ABDUCTED ON HIS WAY HOME, RIGHT?
Storage
JUST BEING THOROUGH.
MR. TAMADA WAS A CONSCIENTIOUS MAN, AND HE ALWAYS CALLED HIS WIFE BEFORE GOING HOME.
I'M LEAVING NOW...
HE DIDN'T DO THAT TWO NIGHTS AGO.
IN OTHER WORDS, EITHER SOMEBODY ABDUCTED HIM WHILE HE WAS HERE WORKING... OR HE'S STILL HERE.
YIKES
IF HE IS HERE, THERE'S A GOOD CHANCE HE'S ALREADY BEEN MURDERED!!
INSPECTOR! WE SEARCHED ALL THE AREAS OUT OF SIGHT INCLUDING THE STORAGE AND THE RESTROOMS, BUT WE COULDN'T FIND HIM.
MR. TAMADA IS A BIG MAN. HE'D BE CONSPICUOUS. IF YOU DIDN'T SEE HIM...
...HE MUST'VE BEEN ABDUCTED.
ALL RIGHT. LET'S MOVE OUT!!
...

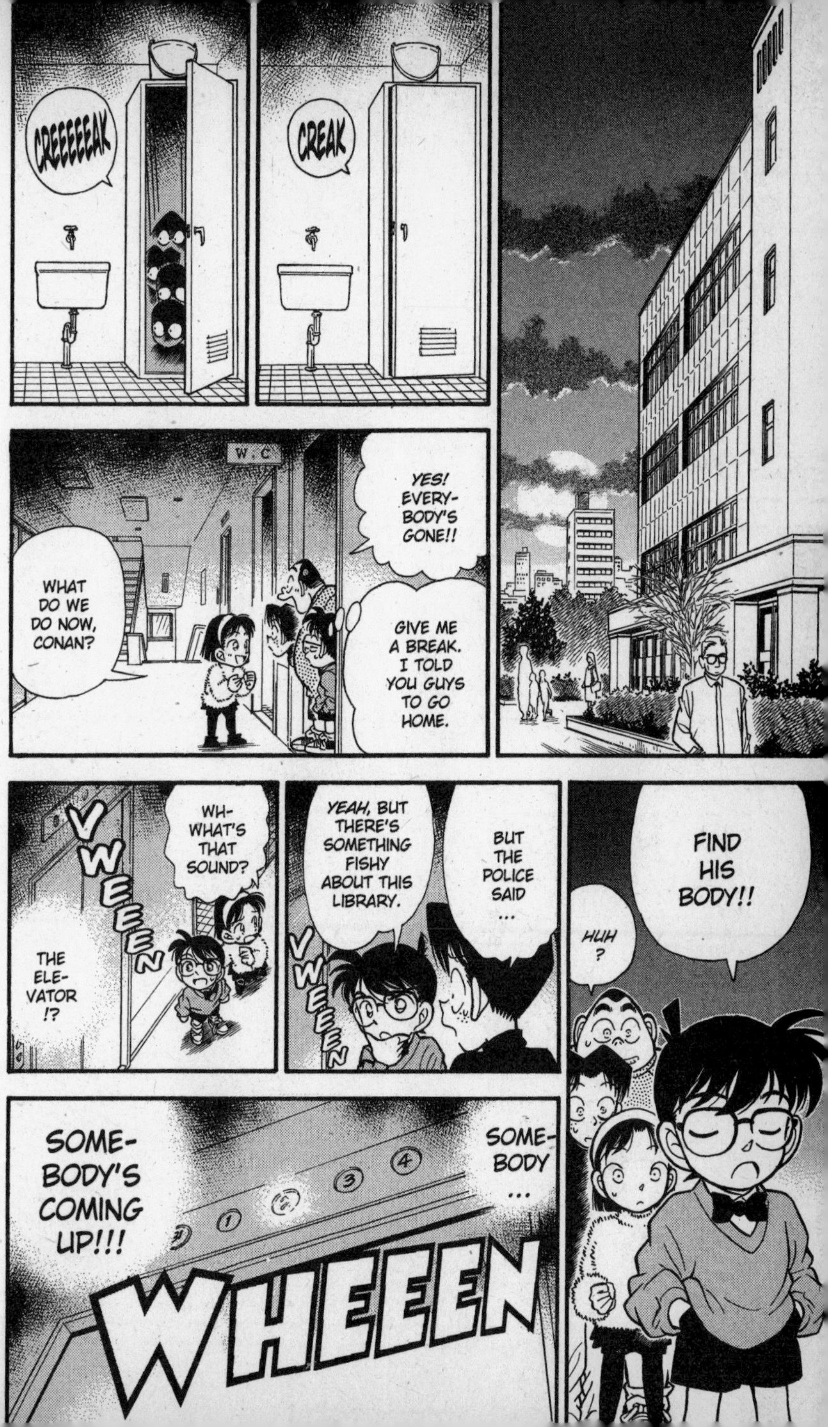
CREAK
CREEEEEAK
YES! EVERY-BODY'S GONE!!
GIVE ME A BREAK. I TOLD YOU GUYS TO GO HOME.
WHAT DO WE DO NOW, CONAN?
FIND HIS BODY!!
HUH?
BUT THE POLICE SAID ...
YEAH, BUT THERE'S SOMETHING FISHY ABOUT THIS LIBRARY.
VWEEEN
WH-WHAT'S THAT SOUND?
VWEEEN
THE ELE-VATOR !?
SOME-BODY ...
SOME-BODY'S COMING UP!!!
WHEEEN

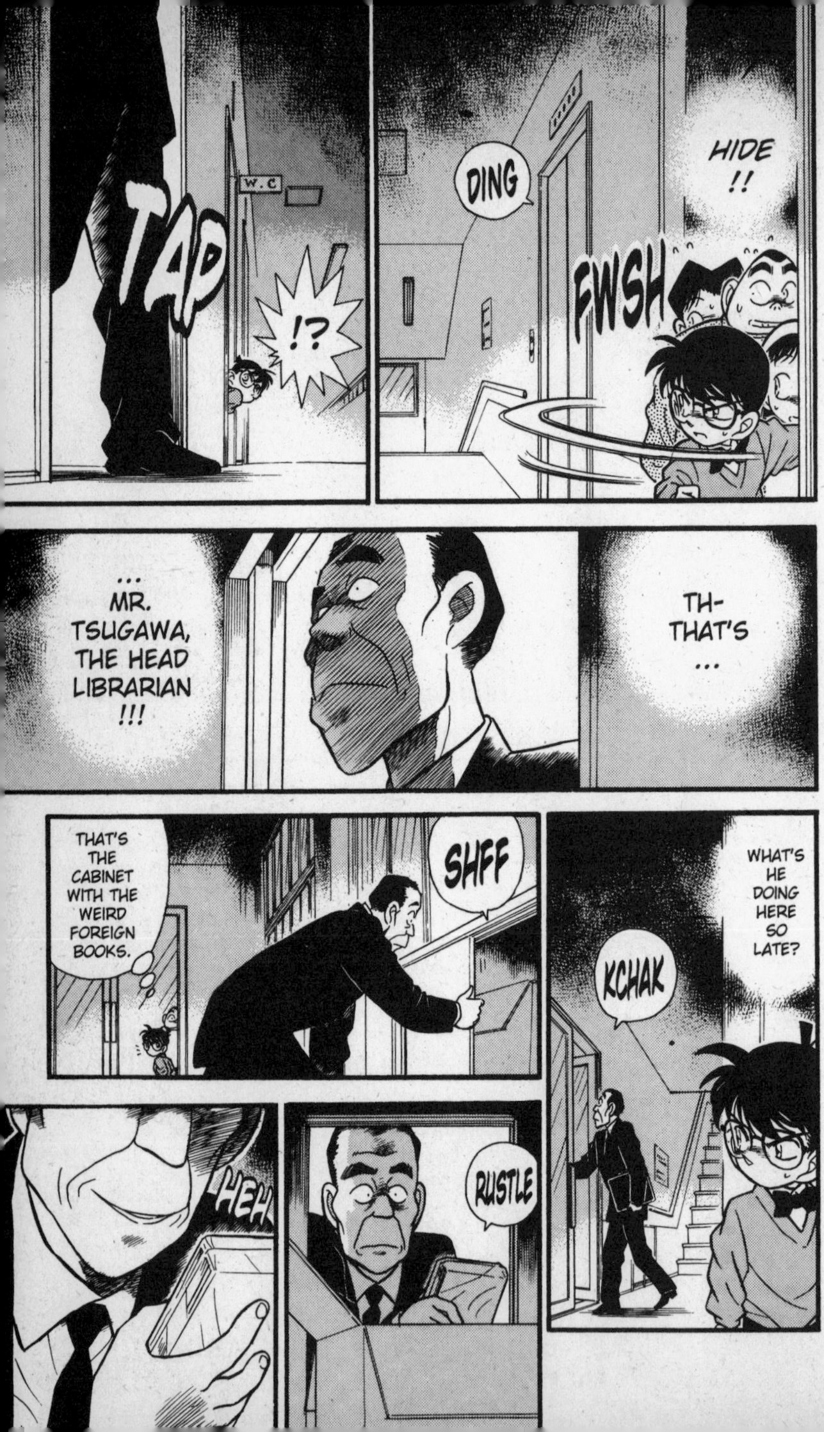
HIDE !!
DING
FWSH
!?
TAP
TH- THAT'S ...
... MR. TSUGAWA, THE HEAD LIBRARIAN !!!
WHAT'S HE DOING HERE SO LATE?
KCHAK
SHFF
THAT'S THE CABINET WITH THE WEIRD FOREIGN BOOKS.
RUSTLE
HEH

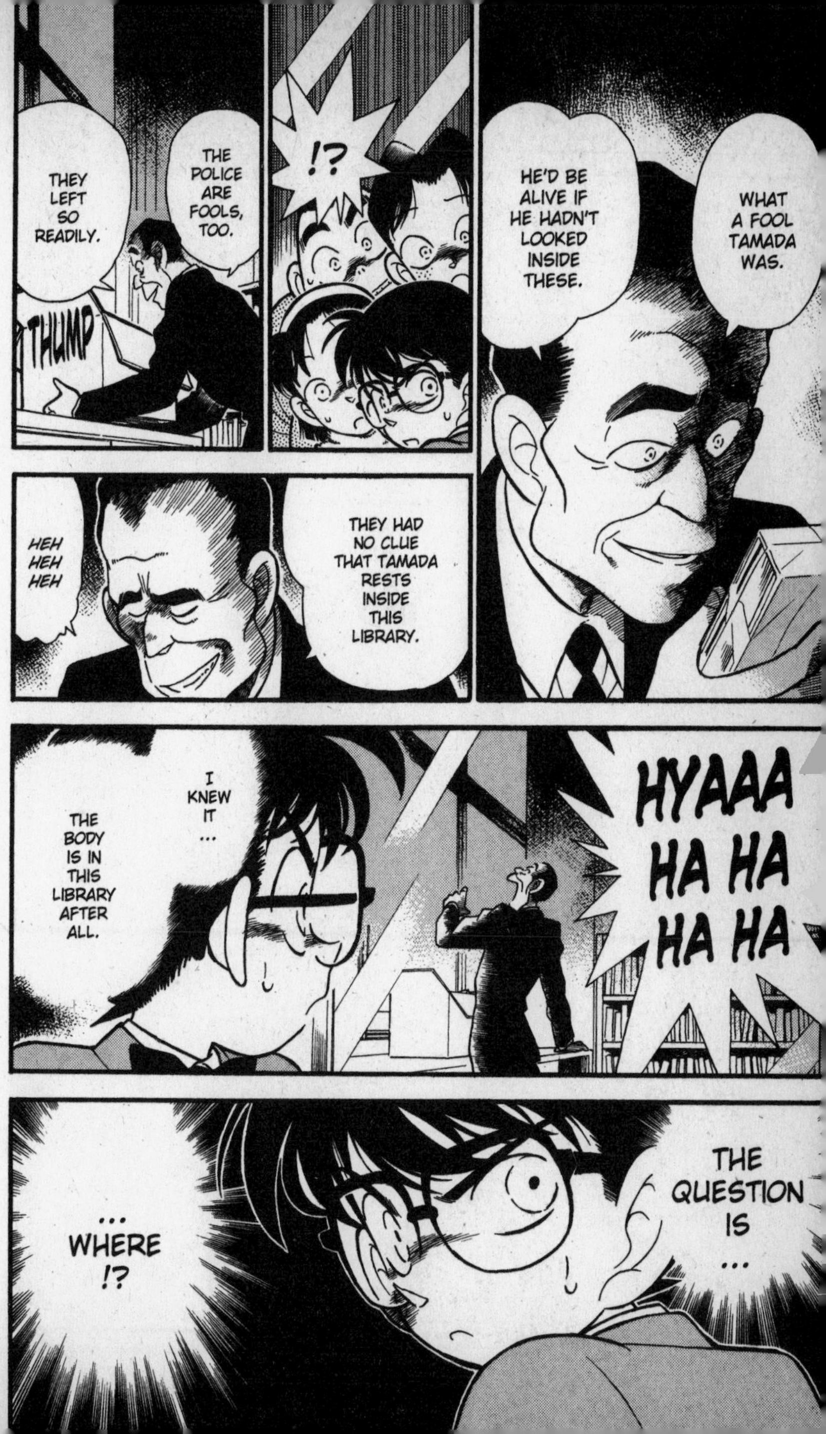
WHAT A FOOL TAMADA WAS.
HE'D BE ALIVE IF HE HADN'T LOOKED INSIDE THESE.
!?
THE POLICE ARE FOOLS, TOO.
THEY LEFT SO READILY.
THUMP
THEY HAD NO CLUE THAT TAMADA RESTS INSIDE THIS LIBRARY.
HEH HEH HEH
HYAAA HA HA HA HA
I KNEW IT ...
THE BODY IS IN THIS LIBRARY AFTER ALL.
THE QUESTION IS ...
... WHERE !?

THE KILLER CREEPS UP

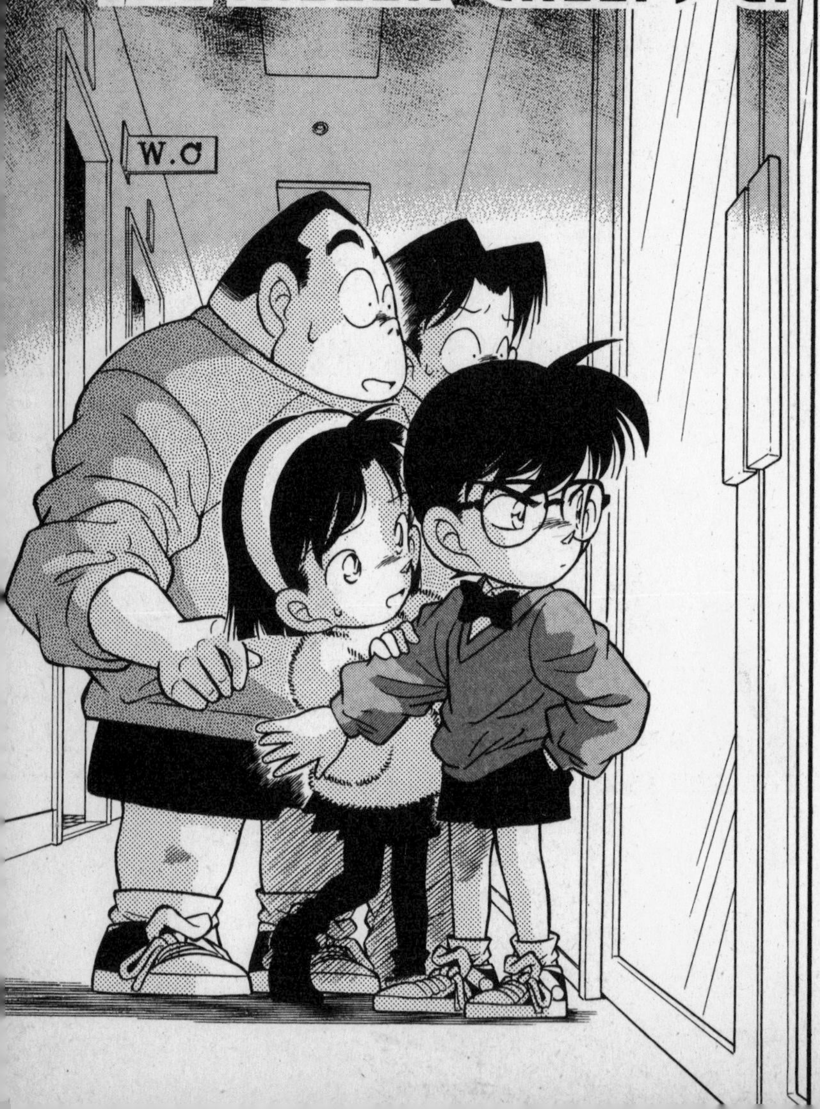
W.C

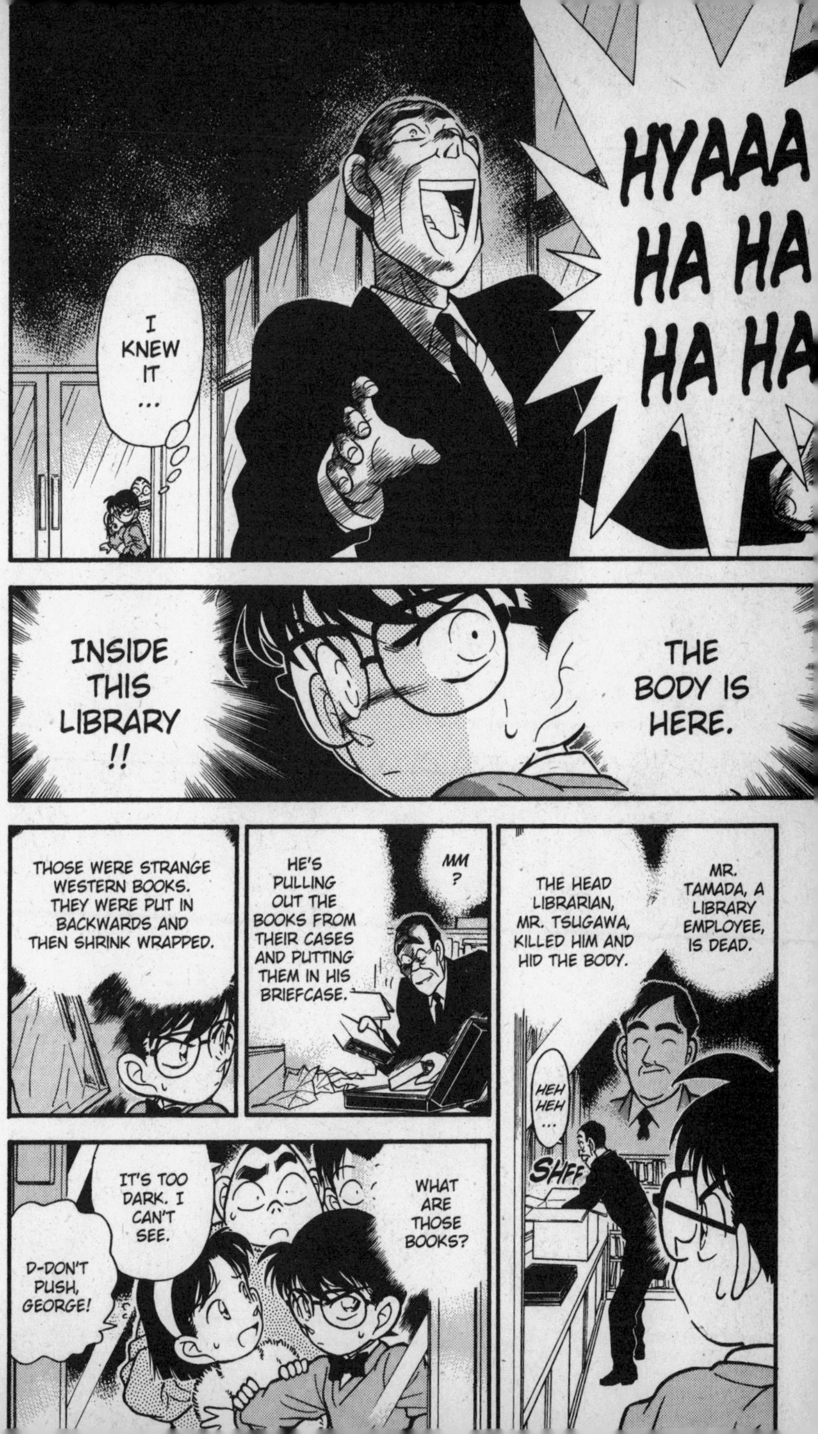
HYAAA HA HA HA HA
I KNEW IT ...
THE BODY IS HERE.
INSIDE THIS LIBRARY !!
MR. TAMADA, A LIBRARY EMPLOYEE, IS DEAD.
THE HEAD LIBRARIAN, MR. TSUGAWA, KILLED HIM AND HID THE BODY.
HEH HEH ...
SHFF
MM ?
HE'S PULLING OUT THE BOOKS FROM THEIR CASES AND PUTTING THEM IN HIS BRIEFCASE.
THOSE WERE STRANGE WESTERN BOOKS. THEY WERE PUT IN BACKWARDS AND THEN SHRINK WRAPPED.
WHAT ARE THOSE BOOKS?
IT'S TOO DARK. I CAN'T SEE.
D-DON'T PUSH, GEORGE!

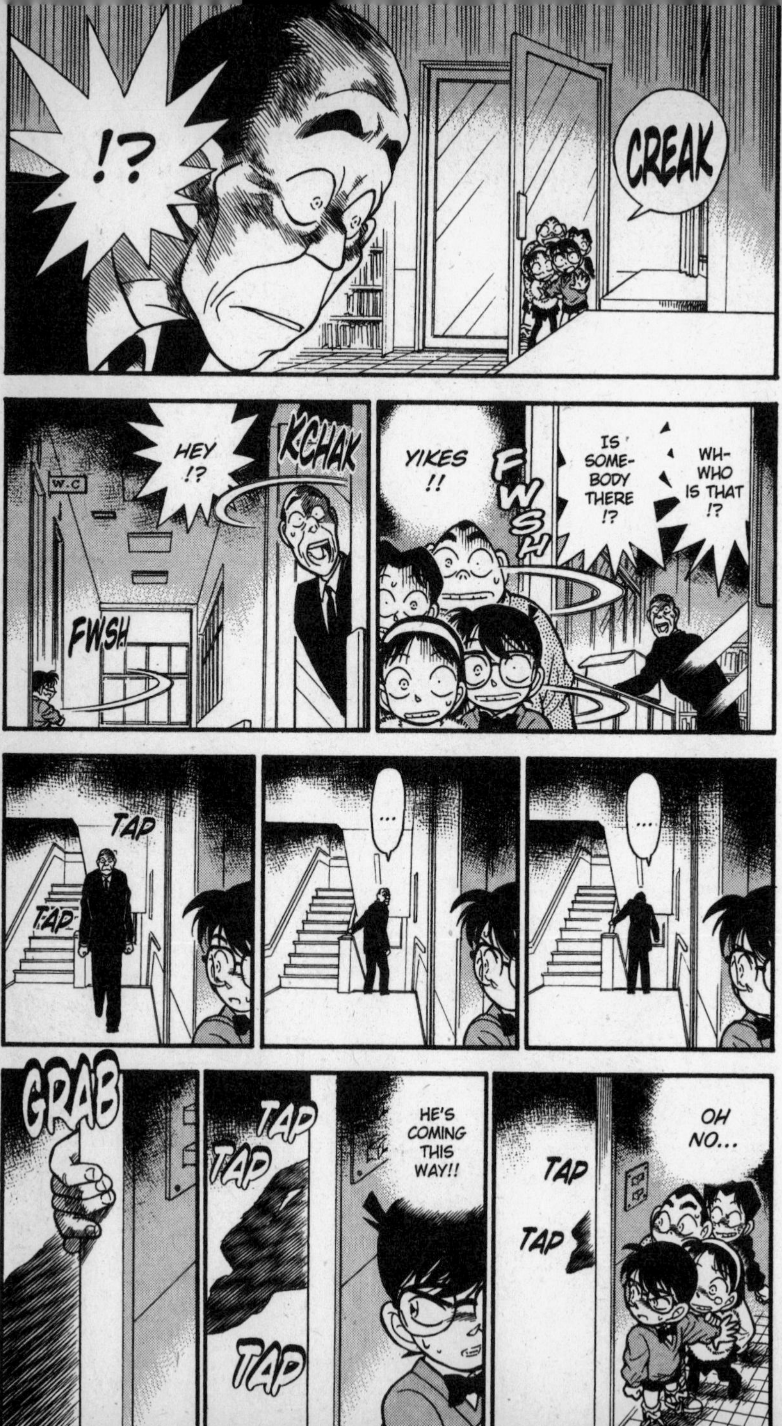
CREAK
!?
WH- WHO IS THAT !?
IS SOME-BODY THERE !?
FWSH
YIKES !!
KCHAK
HEY !?
FWSH
...
...
TAP
TAP
OH NO...
TAP
TAP
HE'S COMING THIS WAY!!
TAP
TAP
TAP
GRAB

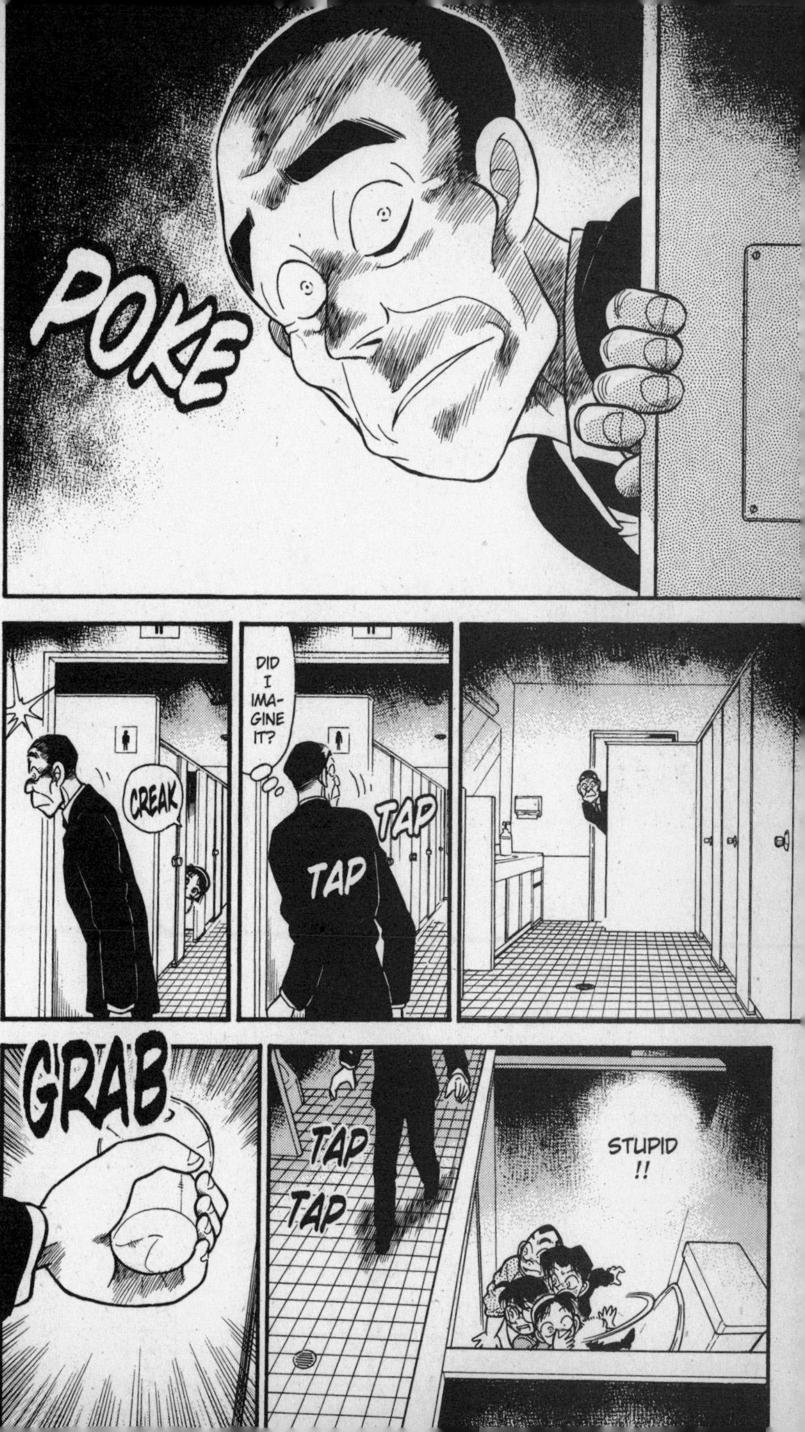
POKE
DID I IMAGINE IT?
TAP
TAP
CREAK
STUPID !!
TAP
TAP
GRAB

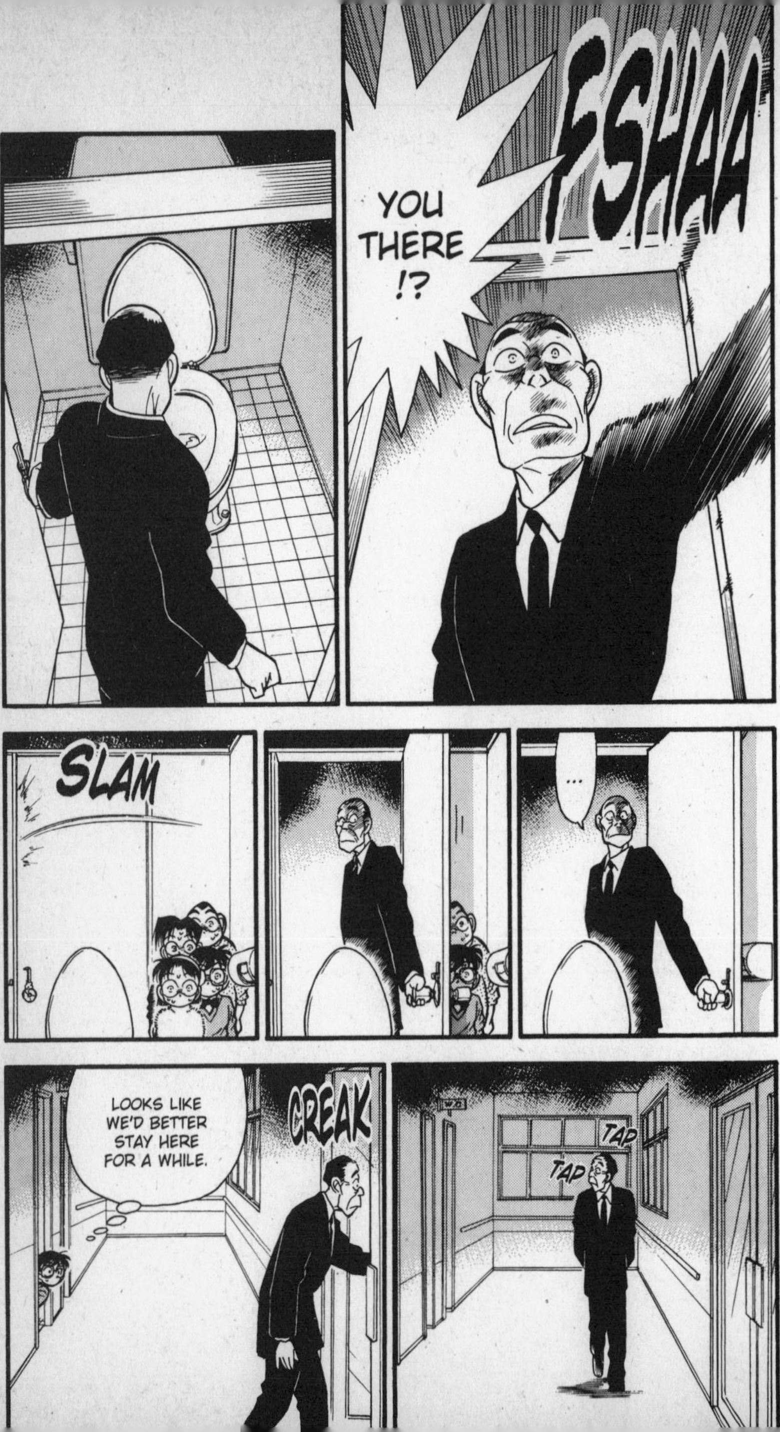
FSHAA
YOU THERE !?
...
SLAM
TAP
TAP
CREAK
LOOKS LIKE WE'D BETTER STAY HERE FOR A WHILE.

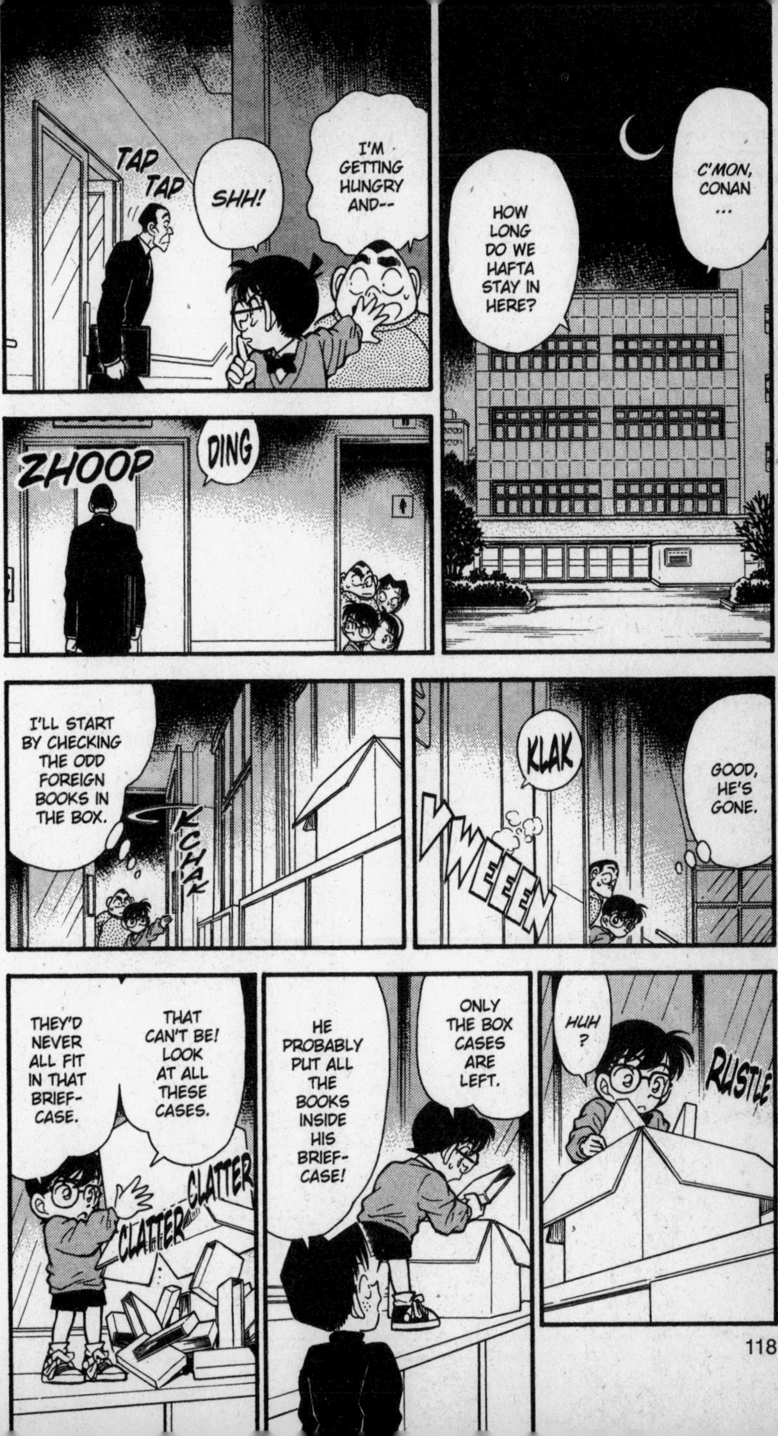
C'MON, CONAN ...
HOW LONG DO WE HAFTA STAY IN HERE?
I'M GETTING HUNGRY AND--
SHH!
TAP TAP
DING
ZHOOP
GOOD, HE'S GONE.
KLAK
VWEEEN
I'LL START BY CHECKING THE ODD FOREIGN BOOKS IN THE BOX.
KCHAK
RUSTLE
HUH?
ONLY THE BOX CASES ARE LEFT.
HE PROBABLY PUT ALL THE BOOKS INSIDE HIS BRIEF-CASE!
THAT CAN'T BE! LOOK AT ALL THESE CASES.
THEY'D NEVER ALL FIT IN THAT BRIEF-CASE.
CLATTER
CLATTER

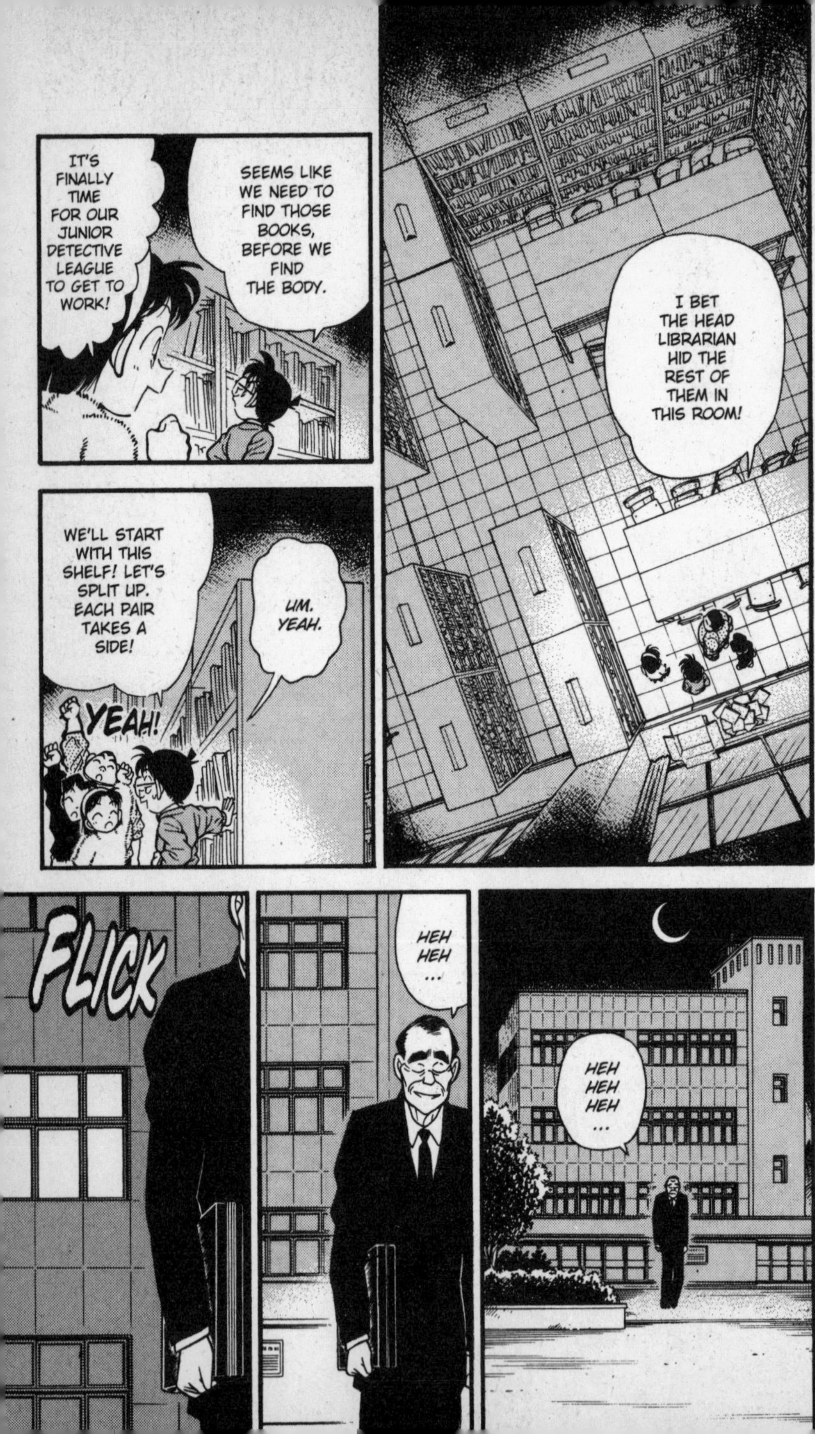
I BET THE HEAD LIBRARIAN HID THE REST OF THEM IN THIS ROOM!
SEEMS LIKE WE NEED TO FIND THOSE BOOKS, BEFORE WE FIND THE BODY.
IT'S FINALLY TIME FOR OUR JUNIOR DETECTIVE LEAGUE TO GET TO WORK!
UM. YEAH.
WE'LL START WITH THIS SHELF! LET'S SPLIT UP. EACH PAIR TAKES A SIDE!
YEAH!
HEH HEH HEH ...
HEH HEH ...
FLICK

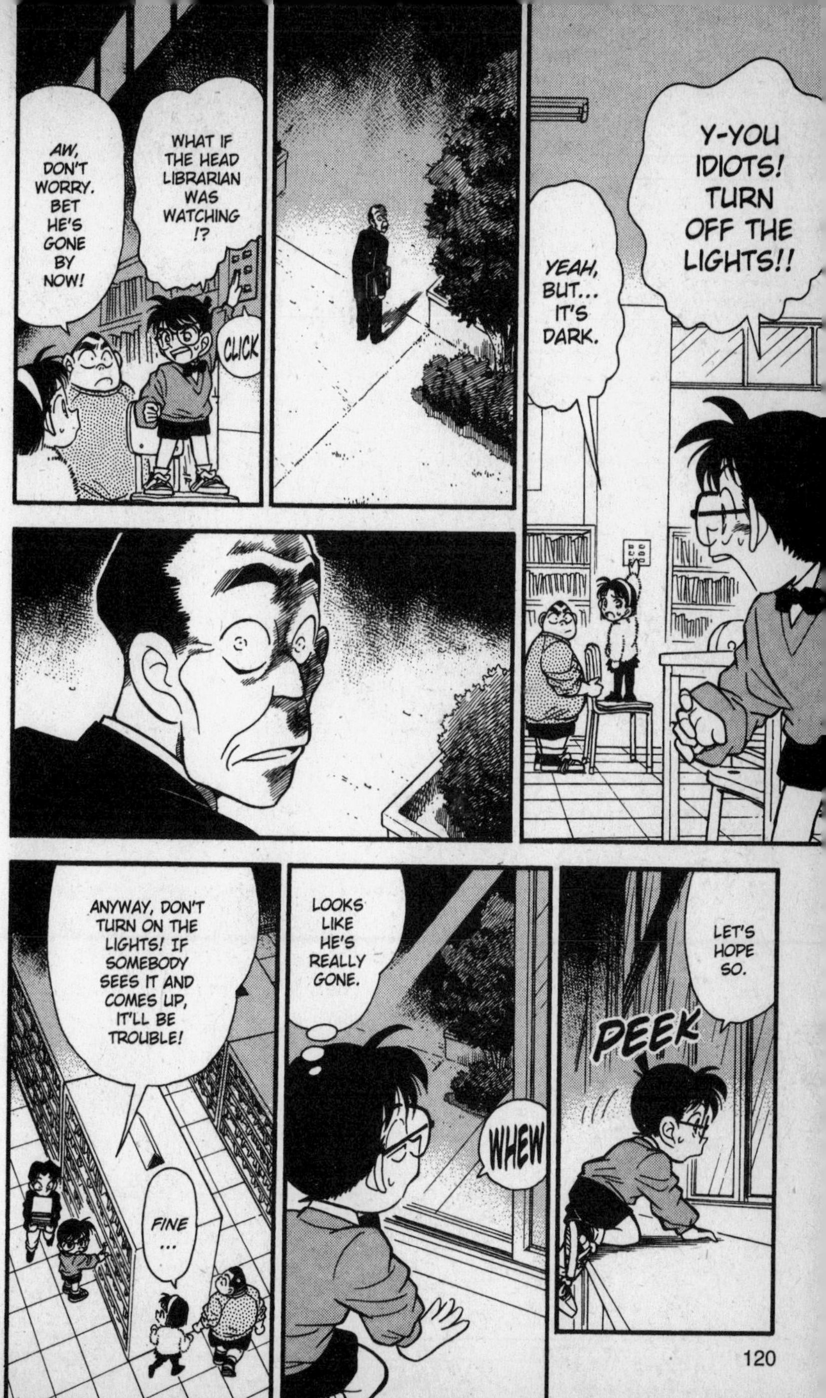
Y-YOU IDIOTS! TURN OFF THE LIGHTS!!
YEAH, BUT... IT'S DARK.
WHAT IF THE HEAD LIBRARIAN WAS WATCHING !?
AW, DON'T WORRY. BET HE'S GONE BY NOW!
CLICK
LET'S HOPE SO.
PEEK
LOOKS LIKE HE'S REALLY GONE.
WHEW
ANYWAY, DON'T TURN ON THE LIGHTS! IF SOMEBODY SEES IT AND COMES UP, IT'LL BE TROUBLE!
FINE ...

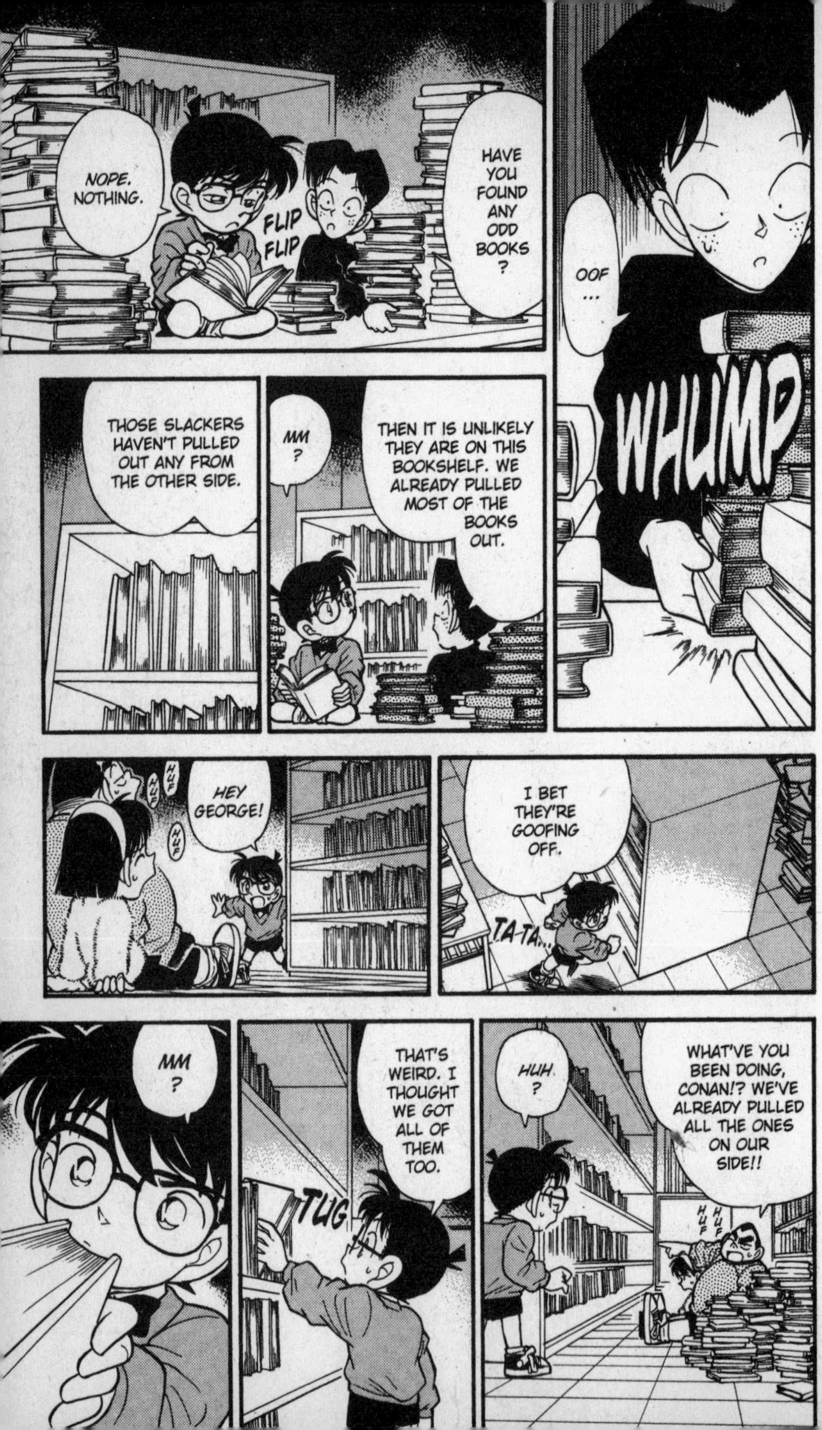
OOF ...
WHUMP
HAVE YOU FOUND ANY ODD BOOKS ?
NOPE. NOTHING.
FLIP FLIP
MM ?
THEN IT IS UNLIKELY THEY ARE ON THIS BOOKSHELF. WE ALREADY PULLED MOST OF THE BOOKS OUT.
THOSE SLACKERS HAVEN'T PULLED OUT ANY FROM THE OTHER SIDE.
I BET THEY'RE GOOFING OFF.
TA-TA...
HEY GEORGE!
HUF HUF HUF
WHAT'VE YOU BEEN DOING, CONAN!? WE'VE ALREADY PULLED ALL THE ONES ON OUR SIDE!!
HUF HUF
HUH ?
THAT'S WEIRD. I THOUGHT WE GOT ALL OF THEM TOO.
TUG
MM ?

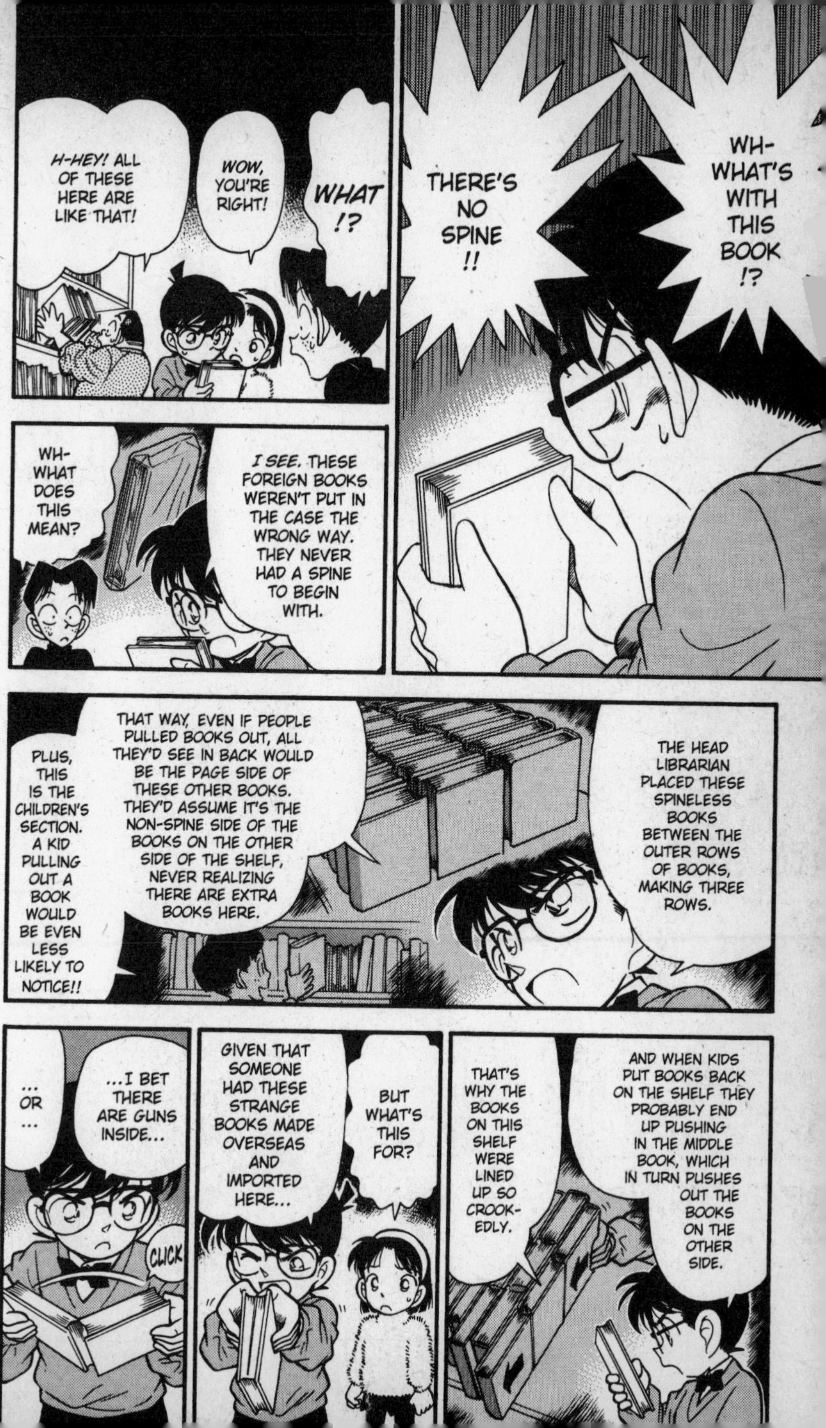
WH- WHAT'S WITH THIS BOOK !?
THERE'S NO SPINE !!
WHAT !?
WOW, YOU'RE RIGHT!
H-HEY! ALL OF THESE HERE ARE LIKE THAT!
I SEE. THESE FOREIGN BOOKS WEREN'T PUT IN THE CASE THE WRONG WAY. THEY NEVER HAD A SPINE TO BEGIN WITH.
WH- WHAT DOES THIS MEAN?
THE HEAD LIBRARIAN PLACED THESE SPINELESS BOOKS BETWEEN THE OUTER ROWS OF BOOKS, MAKING THREE ROWS.
THAT WAY, EVEN IF PEOPLE PULLED BOOKS OUT, ALL THEY'D SEE IN BACK WOULD BE THE PAGE SIDE OF THESE OTHER BOOKS. THEY'D ASSUME IT'S THE NON-SPINE SIDE OF THE BOOKS ON THE OTHER SIDE OF THE SHELF, NEVER REALIZING THERE ARE EXTRA BOOKS HERE.
PLUS, THIS IS THE CHILDREN'S SECTION. A KID PULLING OUT A BOOK WOULD BE EVEN LESS LIKELY TO NOTICE!!
AND WHEN KIDS PUT BOOKS BACK ON THE SHELF THEY PROBABLY END UP PUSHING IN THE MIDDLE BOOK, WHICH IN TURN PUSHES OUT THE BOOKS ON THE OTHER SIDE.
THAT'S WHY THE BOOKS ON THIS SHELF WERE LINED UP SO CROOK-EDLY.
BUT WHAT'S THIS FOR?
GIVEN THAT SOMEONE HAD THESE STRANGE BOOKS MADE OVERSEAS AND IMPORTED HERE...
...I BET THERE ARE GUNS INSIDE...
... OR ...
CLICK

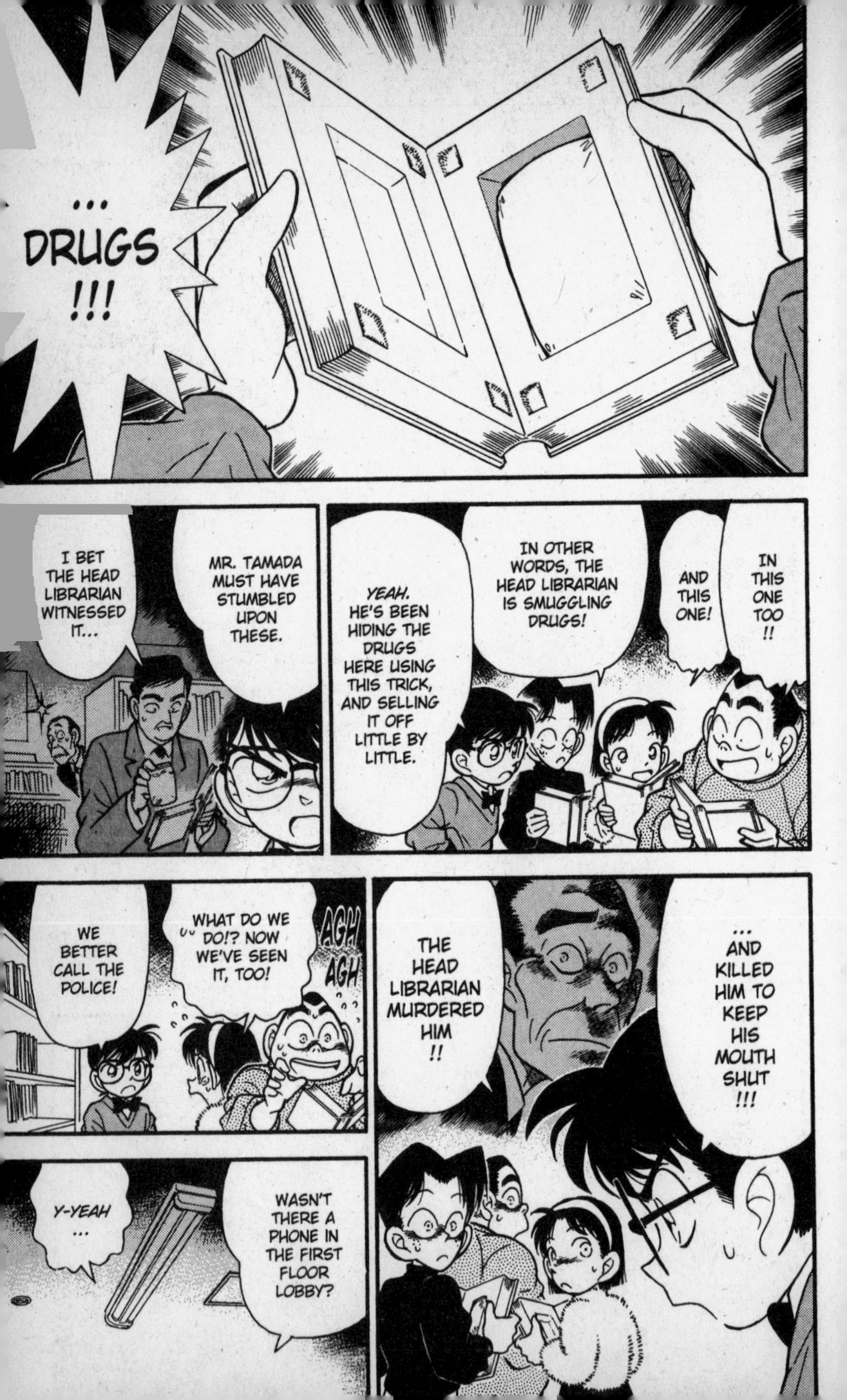
... DRUGS !!!
IN THIS ONE TOO !!
AND THIS ONE!
IN OTHER WORDS, THE HEAD LIBRARIAN IS SMUGGLING DRUGS!
YEAH. HE'S BEEN HIDING THE DRUGS HERE USING THIS TRICK, AND SELLING IT OFF LITTLE BY LITTLE.
MR. TAMADA MUST HAVE STUMBLED UPON THESE.
I BET THE HEAD LIBRARIAN WITNESSED IT...
... AND KILLED HIM TO KEEP HIS MOUTH SHUT !!!
THE HEAD LIBRARIAN MURDERED HIM !!
AGH AGH
WHAT DO WE DO!? NOW WE'VE SEEN IT, TOO!
WE BETTER CALL THE POLICE!
WASN'T THERE A PHONE IN THE FIRST FLOOR LOBBY?
Y-YEAH ...

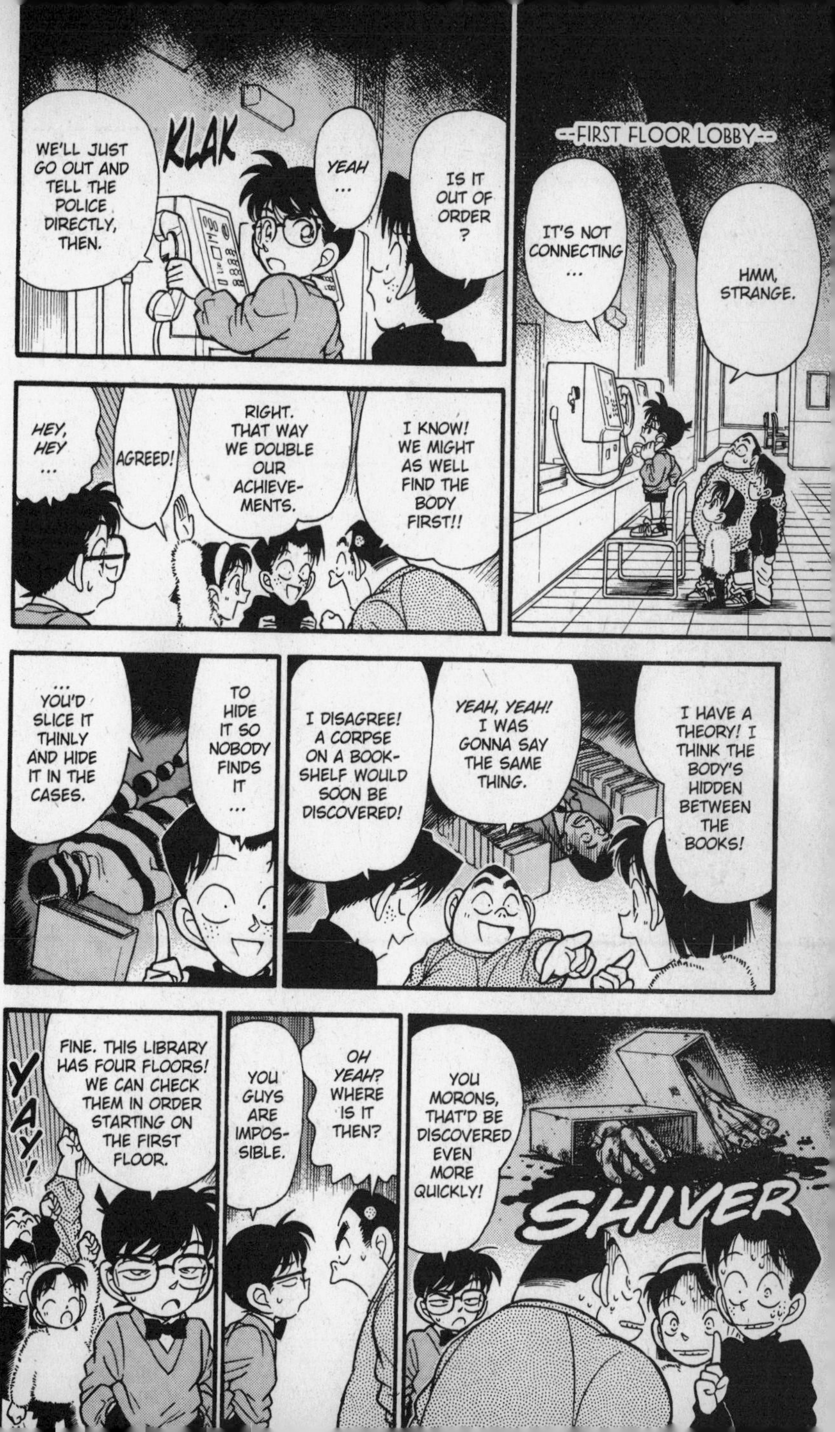
--FIRST FLOOR LOBBY--
HMM, STRANGE.
IT'S NOT CONNECTING ...
IS IT OUT OF ORDER ?
YEAH ...
KLAK
WE'LL JUST GO OUT AND TELL THE POLICE DIRECTLY, THEN.
I KNOW! WE MIGHT AS WELL FIND THE BODY FIRST!!
RIGHT. THAT WAY WE DOUBLE OUR ACHIEVE-MENTS.
AGREED!
HEY, HEY ...
I HAVE A THEORY! I THINK THE BODY'S HIDDEN BETWEEN THE BOOKS!
YEAH, YEAH! I WAS GONNA SAY THE SAME THING.
I DISAGREE! A CORPSE ON A BOOK-SHELF WOULD SOON BE DISCOVERED!
TO HIDE IT SO NOBODY FINDS IT ...
... YOU'D SLICE IT THINLY AND HIDE IT IN THE CASES.
YOU MORONS, THAT'D BE DISCOVERED EVEN MORE QUICKLY!
SHIVER
OH YEAH? WHERE IS IT THEN?
YOU GUYS ARE IMPOS-SIBLE.
FINE. THIS LIBRARY HAS FOUR FLOORS! WE CAN CHECK THEM IN ORDER STARTING ON THE FIRST FLOOR.
YAY!

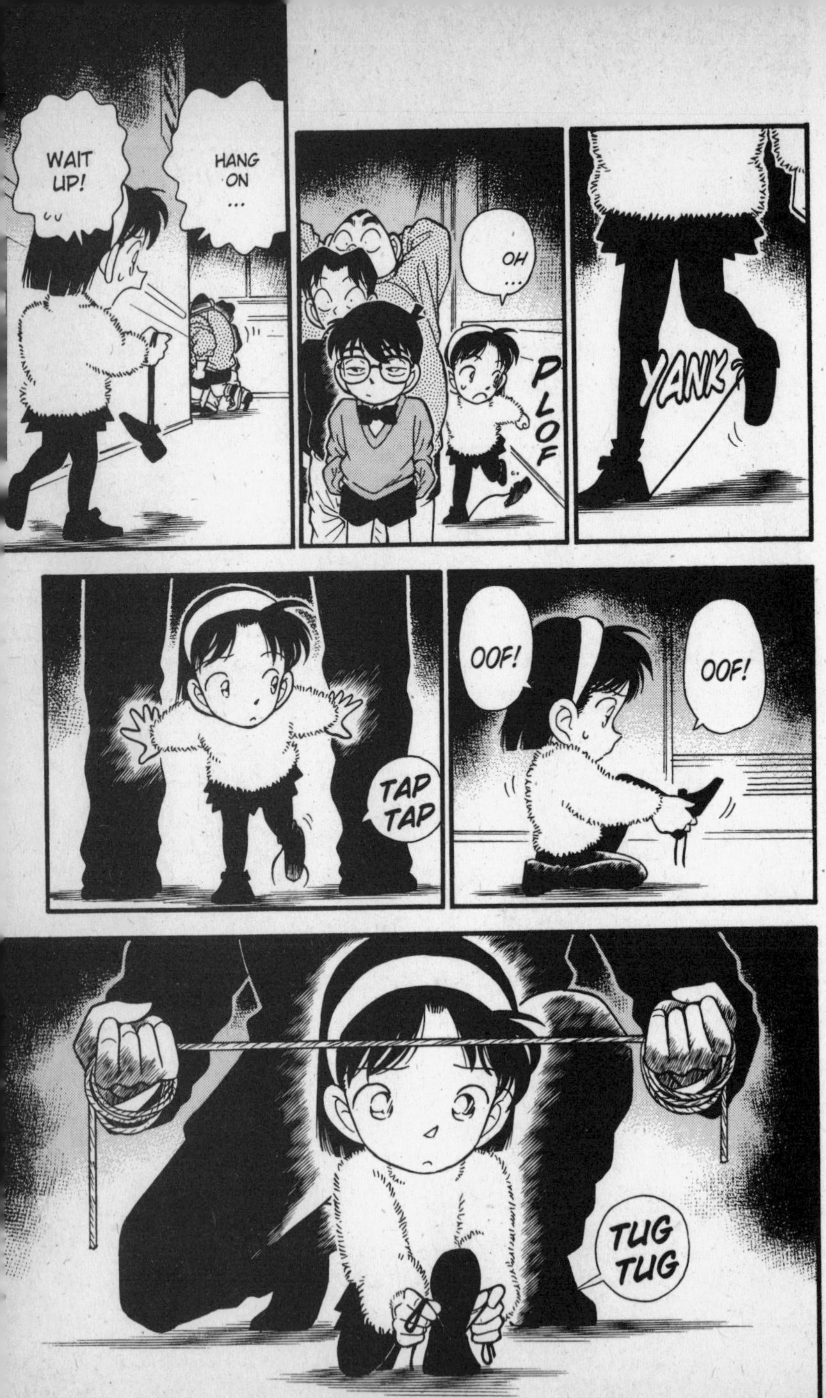
YANK
OH ...
PLOF
HANG ON ...
WAIT UP!
OOF!
OOF!
TAP TAP
TUG TUG

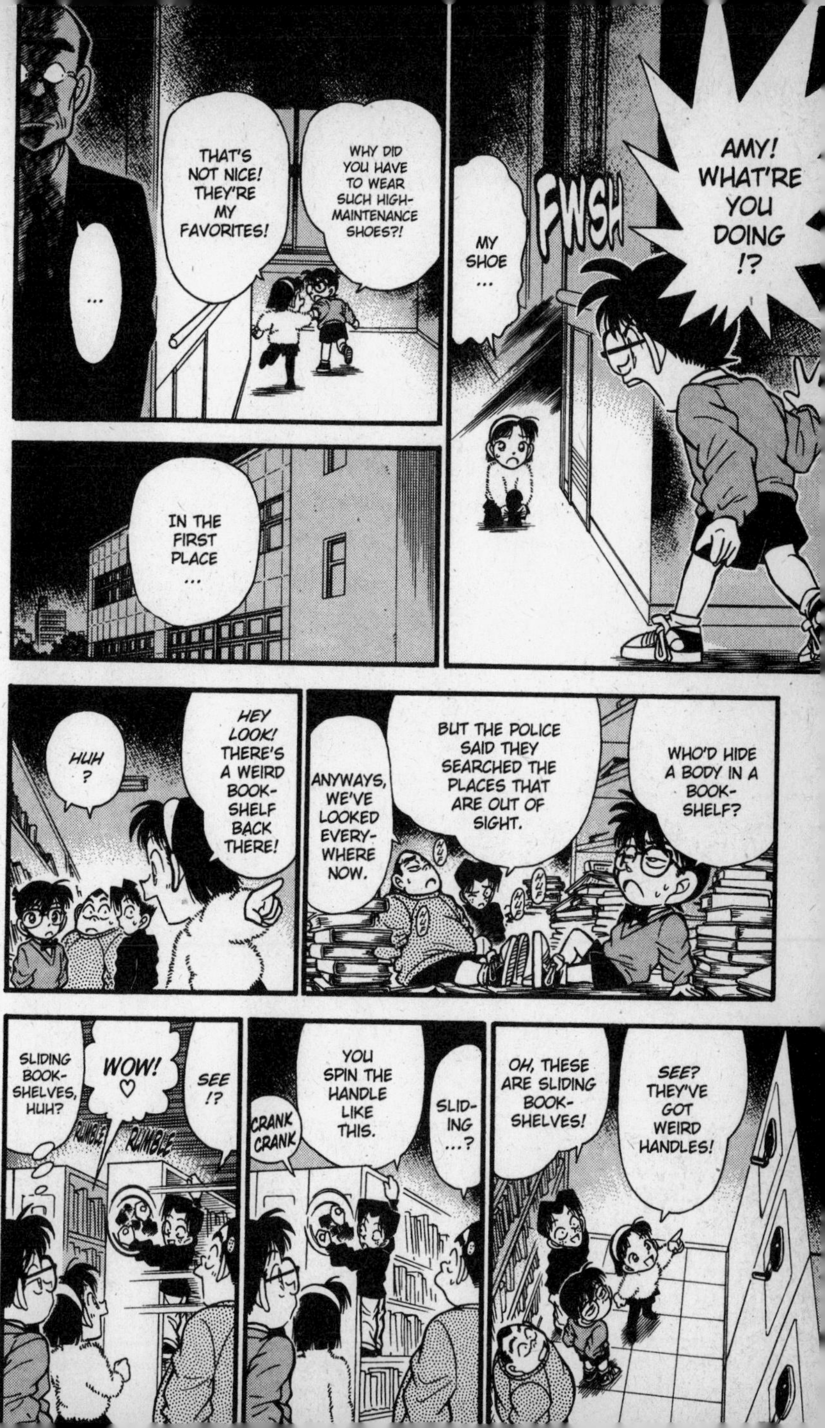
AMY! WHAT'RE YOU DOING !?
FWSH
MY SHOE ...
WHY DID YOU HAVE TO WEAR SUCH HIGH-MAINTENANCE SHOES?!
THAT'S NOT NICE! THEY'RE MY FAVORITES!
...
IN THE FIRST PLACE ...
WHO'D HIDE A BODY IN A BOOK-SHELF?
BUT THE POLICE SAID THEY SEARCHED THE PLACES THAT ARE OUT OF SIGHT.
ANYWAYS, WE'VE LOOKED EVERY-WHERE NOW.
HEY LOOK! THERE'S A WEIRD BOOK-SHELF BACK THERE!
HUH ?
SEE? THEY'VE GOT WEIRD HANDLES!
OH, THESE ARE SLIDING BOOK-SHELVES!
SLID-ING ...?
YOU SPIN THE HANDLE LIKE THIS.
CRANK CRANK
SEE !?
WOW! ♡
SLIDING BOOK-SHELVES, HUH?
RUMBLE
RUMBLE

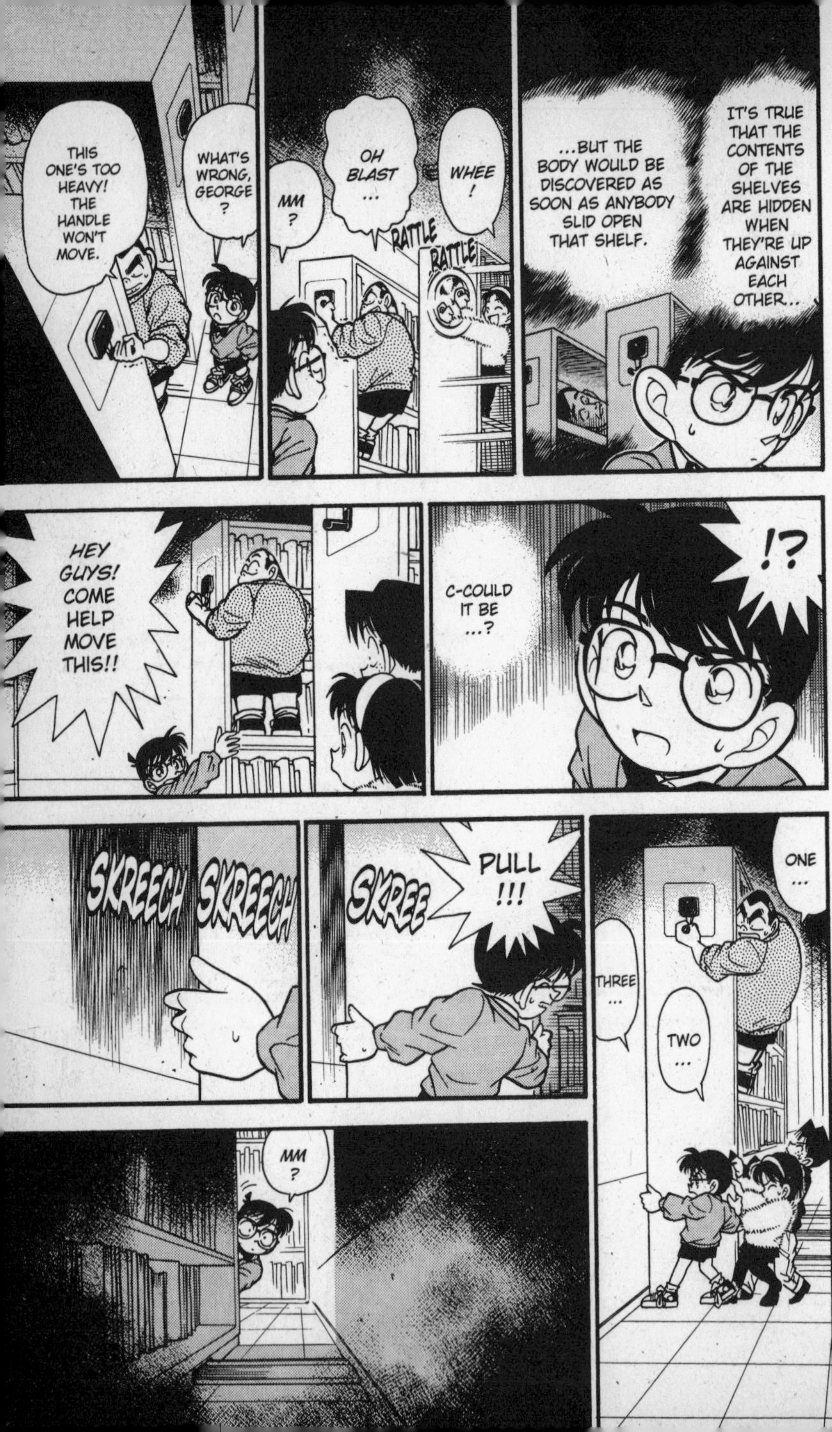
IT'S TRUE THAT THE CONTENTS OF THE SHELVES ARE HIDDEN WHEN THEY'RE UP AGAINST EACH OTHER...
...BUT THE BODY WOULD BE DISCOVERED AS SOON AS ANYBODY SLID OPEN THAT SHELF.
WHEE!
OH BLAST...
MM?
RATTLE
RATTLE
WHAT'S WRONG, GEORGE?
THIS ONE'S TOO HEAVY! THE HANDLE WON'T MOVE.
!?
C-COULD IT BE...?
HEY GUYS! COME HELP MOVE THIS!!
ONE...
TWO...
THREE...
PULL!!!
SKREE
SKREECH
SKREECH
MM?

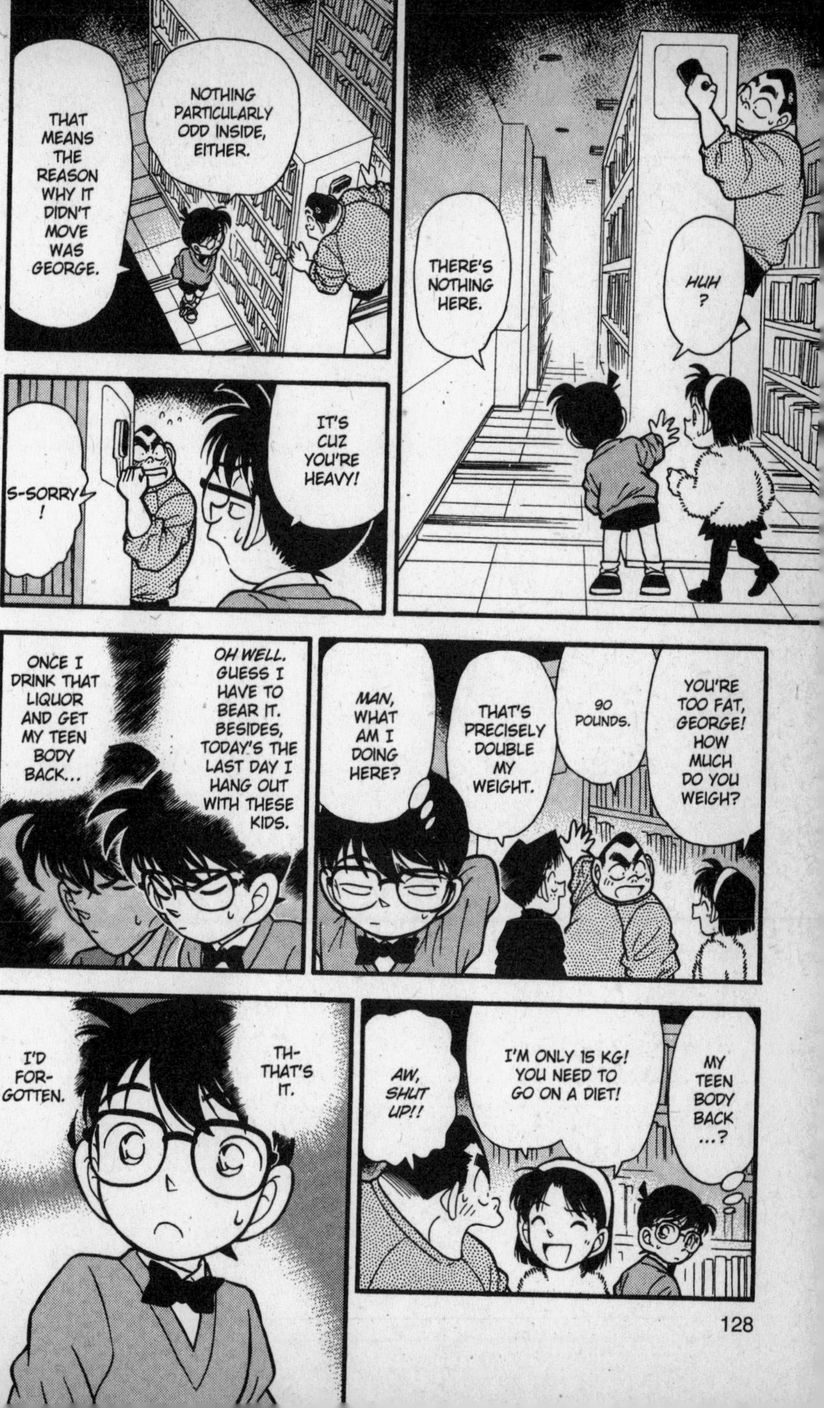
HUH ?
THERE'S NOTHING HERE.
NOTHING PARTICULARLY ODD INSIDE, EITHER.
THAT MEANS THE REASON WHY IT DIDN'T MOVE WAS GEORGE.
IT'S CUZ YOU'RE HEAVY!
S-SORRY !
YOU'RE TOO FAT, GEORGE! HOW MUCH DO YOU WEIGH?
90 POUNDS.
THAT'S PRECISELY DOUBLE MY WEIGHT.
MAN, WHAT AM I DOING HERE?
OH WELL. GUESS I HAVE TO BEAR IT. BESIDES, TODAY'S THE LAST DAY I HANG OUT WITH THESE KIDS.
ONCE I DRINK THAT LIQUOR AND GET MY TEEN BODY BACK...
MY TEEN BODY BACK ...?
I'M ONLY 15 KG! YOU NEED TO GO ON A DIET!
AW, SHUT UP!!
TH-THAT'S IT.
I'D FOR-GOTTEN.

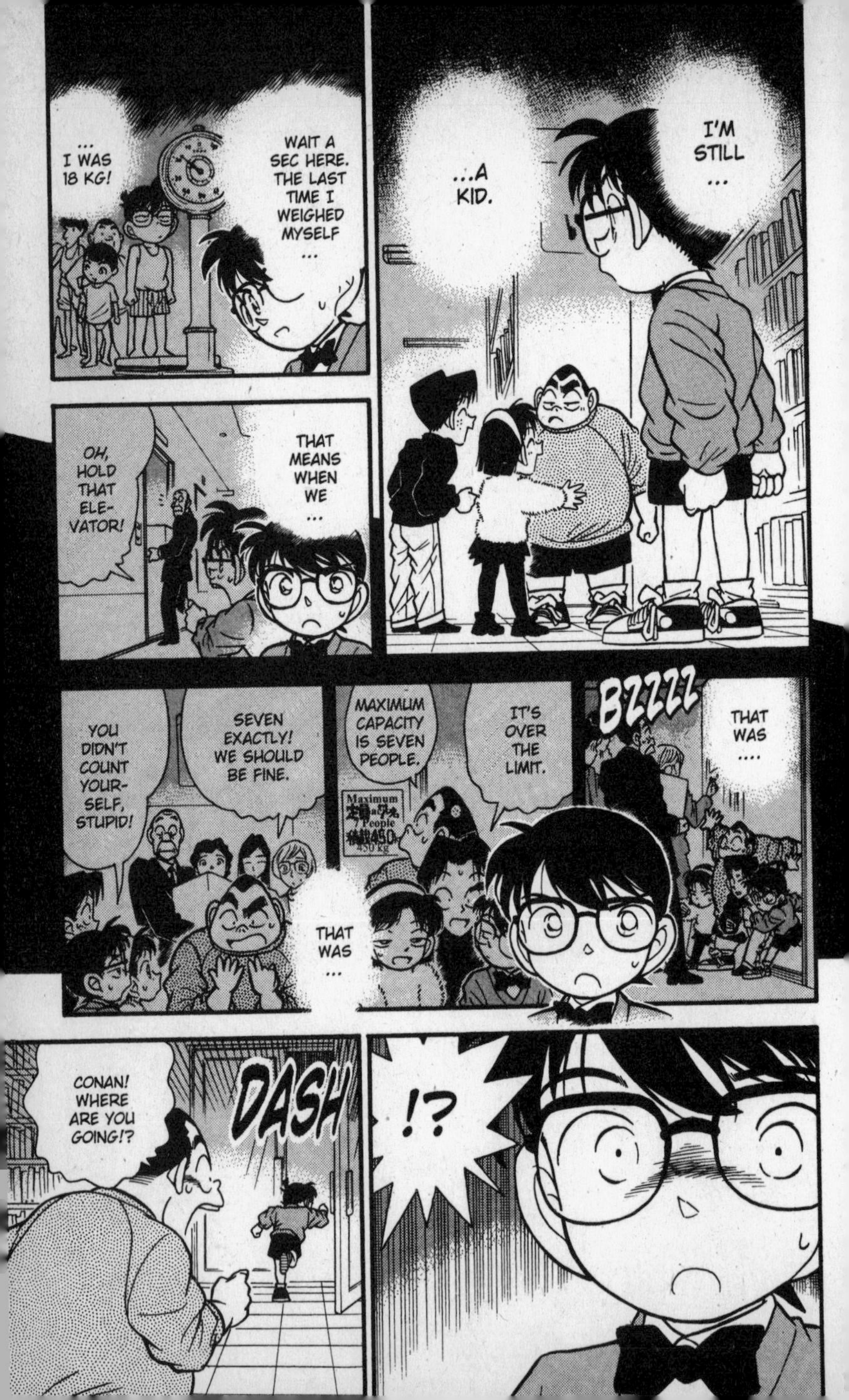
I'M STILL ...
...A KID.
WAIT A SEC HERE. THE LAST TIME I WEIGHED MYSELF ...
... I WAS 18 KG!
THAT MEANS WHEN WE ...
OH, HOLD THAT ELE-VATOR!
BZZZZ
THAT WAS ....
IT'S OVER THE LIMIT.
MAXIMUM CAPACITY IS SEVEN PEOPLE.
Maximum
7 People
450 kg
SEVEN EXACTLY! WE SHOULD BE FINE.
YOU DIDN'T COUNT YOUR-SELF, STUPID!
THAT WAS ...
!?
DASH
CONAN! WHERE ARE YOU GOING!?

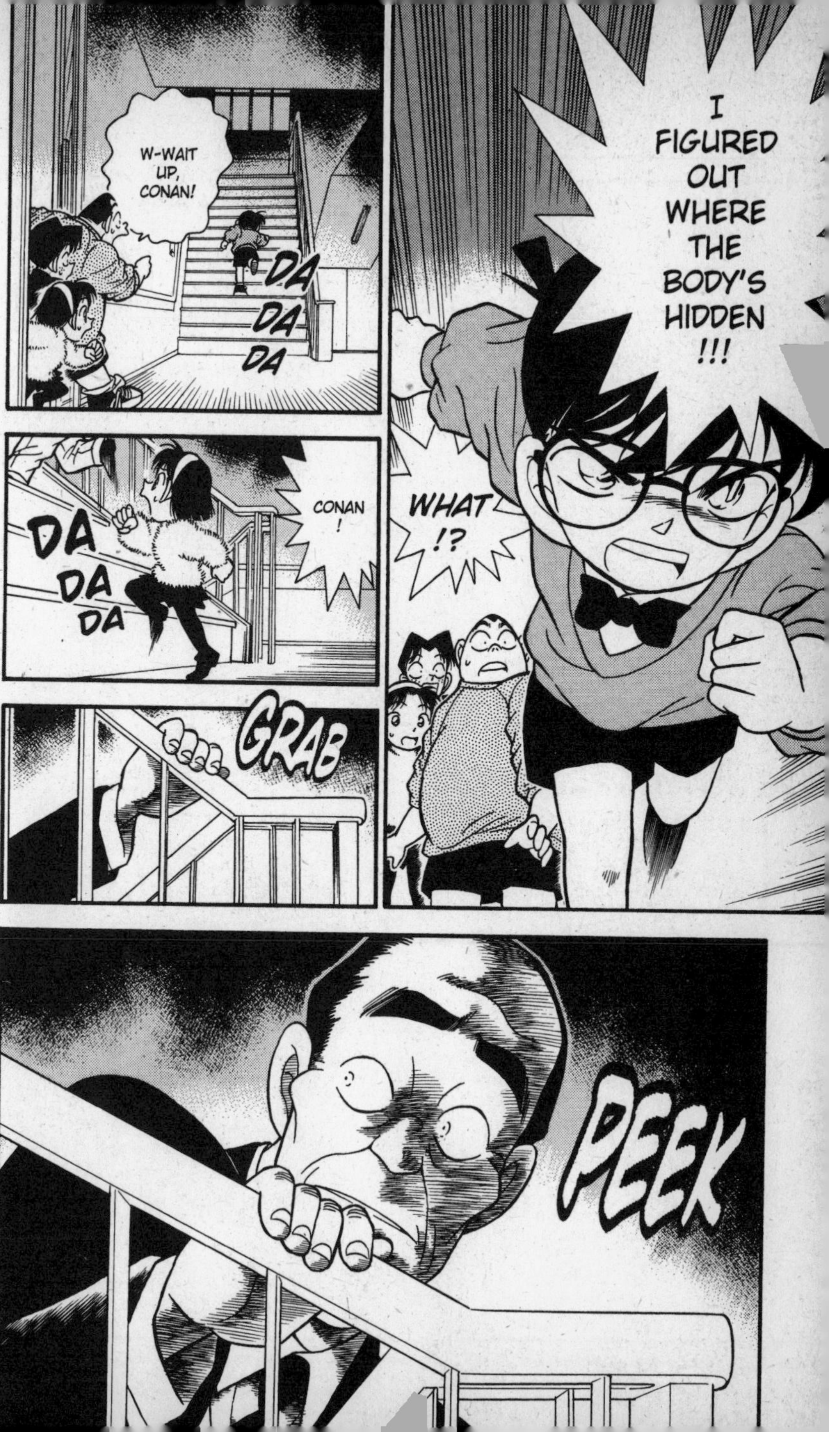
I FIGURED OUT WHERE THE BODY'S HIDDEN!!!
WHAT!?
W-WAIT UP, CONAN!
DA DA DA
CONAN!
DA DA DA
GRAB
PEEK

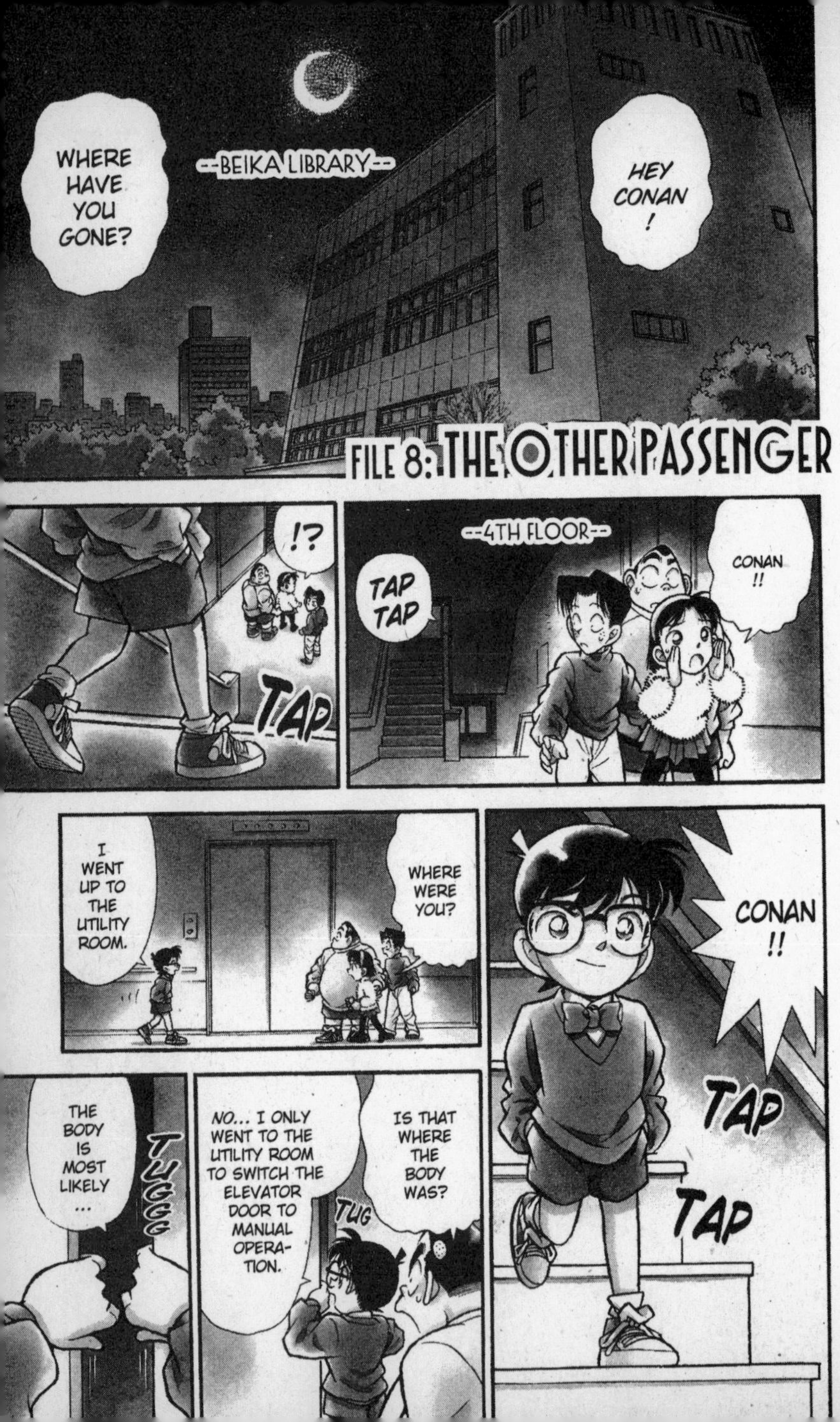
HEY CONAN !
--BEIKA LIBRARY--
WHERE HAVE YOU GONE?
FILE 8: THE OTHER PASSENGER
--4TH FLOOR--
CONAN !!
TAP TAP
!?
TAP
CONAN !!
TAP
TAP
WHERE WERE YOU?
I WENT UP TO THE UTILITY ROOM.
IS THAT WHERE THE BODY WAS?
NO... I ONLY WENT TO THE UTILITY ROOM TO SWITCH THE ELEVATOR DOOR TO MANUAL OPERATION.
TUG
TUGGG
THE BODY IS MOST LIKELY ...

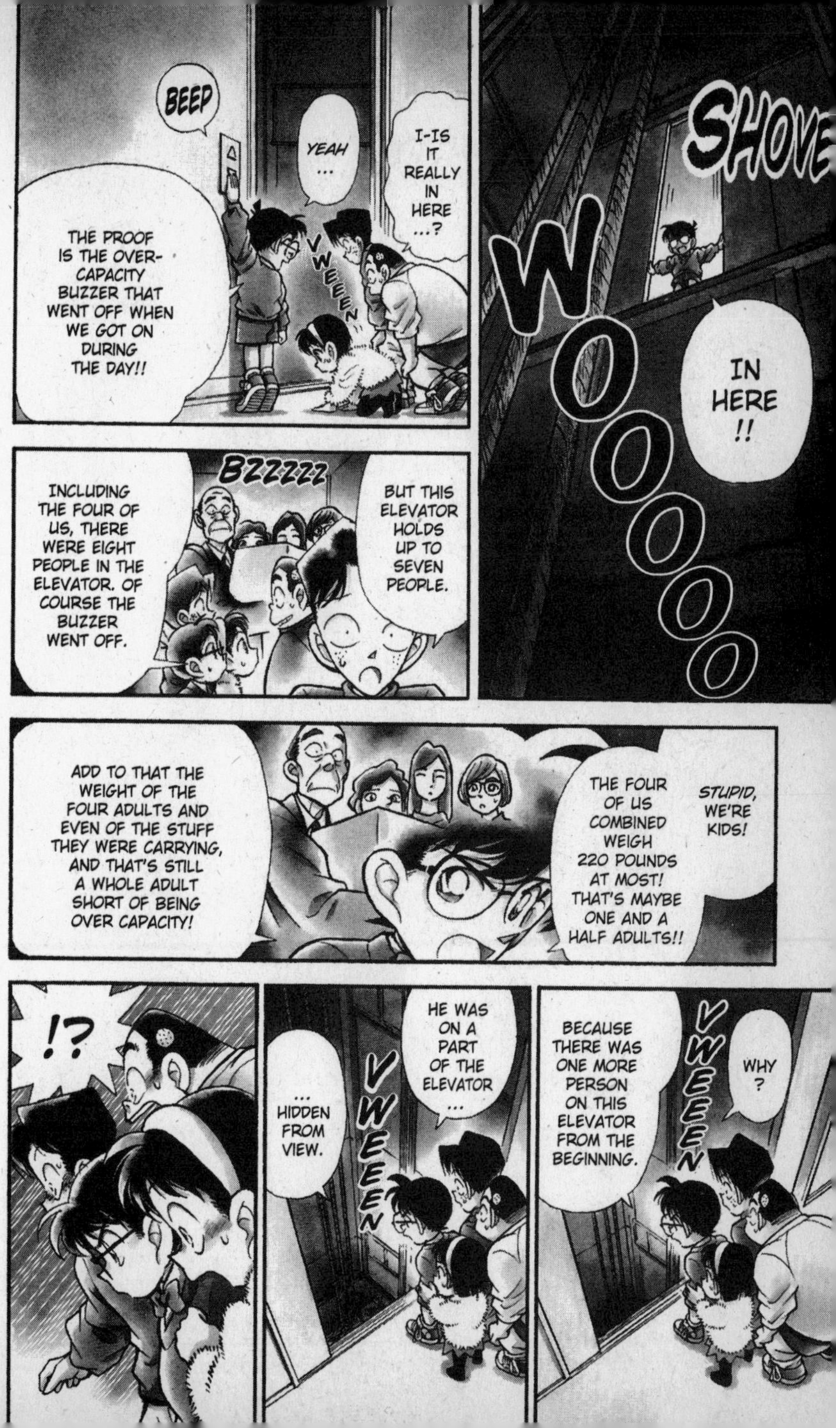
SHOVE
WOOOOOO
IN HERE!!
I-IS IT REALLY IN HERE...?
YEAH...
BEEP
THE PROOF IS THE OVER-CAPACITY BUZZER THAT WENT OFF WHEN WE GOT ON DURING THE DAY!!
VWEEEN
BUT THIS ELEVATOR HOLDS UP TO SEVEN PEOPLE.
BZZZZZ
INCLUDING THE FOUR OF US, THERE WERE EIGHT PEOPLE IN THE ELEVATOR. OF COURSE THE BUZZER WENT OFF.
STUPID, WE'RE KIDS!
THE FOUR OF US COMBINED WEIGH 220 POUNDS AT MOST! THAT'S MAYBE ONE AND A HALF ADULTS!!
ADD TO THAT THE WEIGHT OF THE FOUR ADULTS AND EVEN OF THE STUFF THEY WERE CARRYING, AND THAT'S STILL A WHOLE ADULT SHORT OF BEING OVER CAPACITY!
WHY?
VWEEEN
BECAUSE THERE WAS ONE MORE PERSON ON THIS ELEVATOR FROM THE BEGINNING.
HE WAS ON A PART OF THE ELEVATOR...
VWEEEN
...HIDDEN FROM VIEW.
!?

FILE 8: THE OTHER PASSENGER

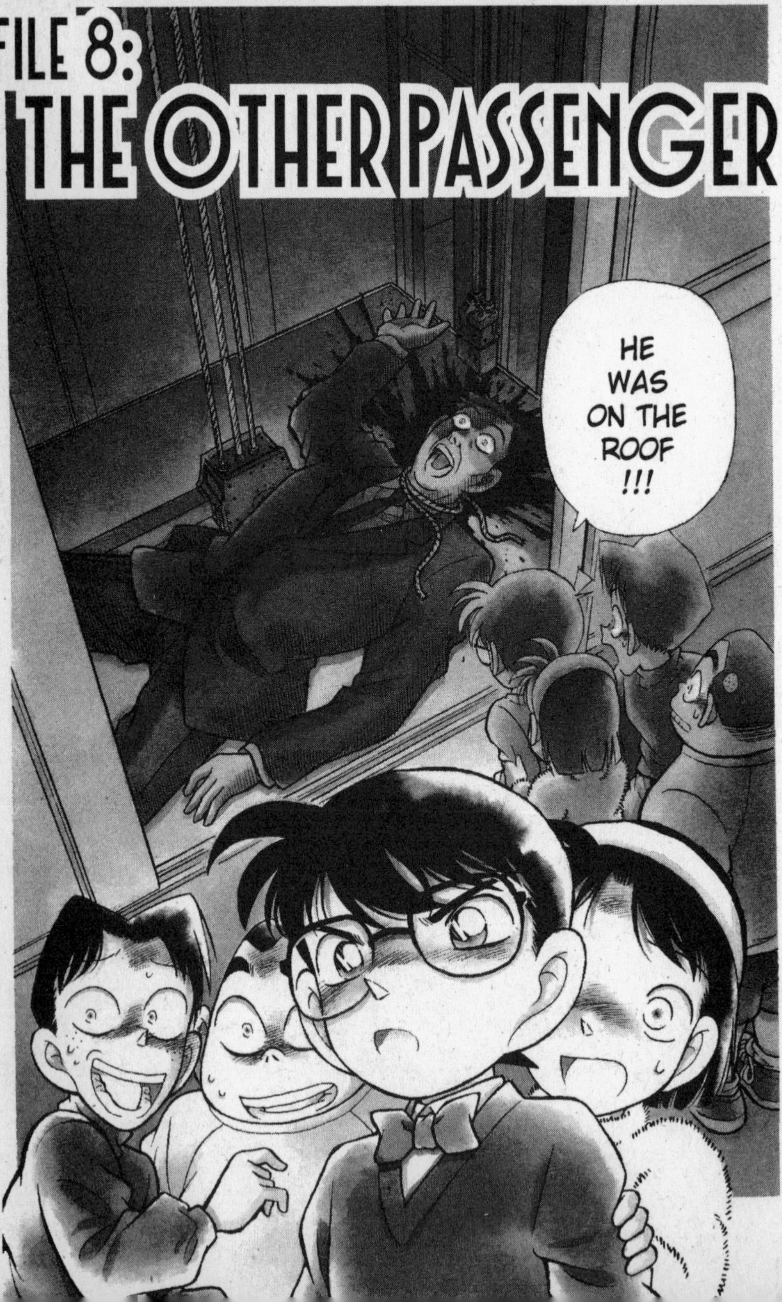
HE WAS ON THE ROOF !!!

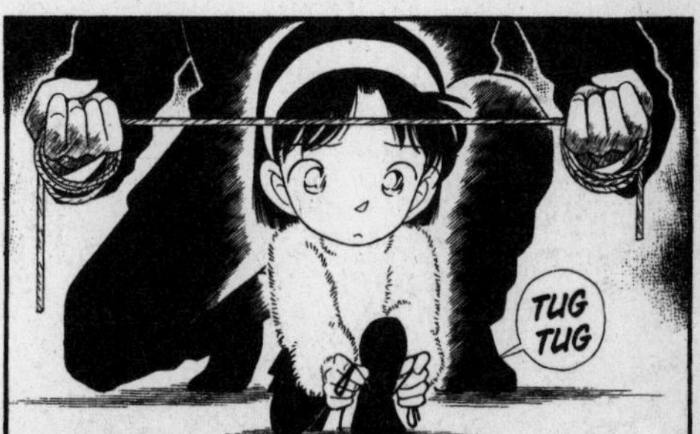
TUG
TUG

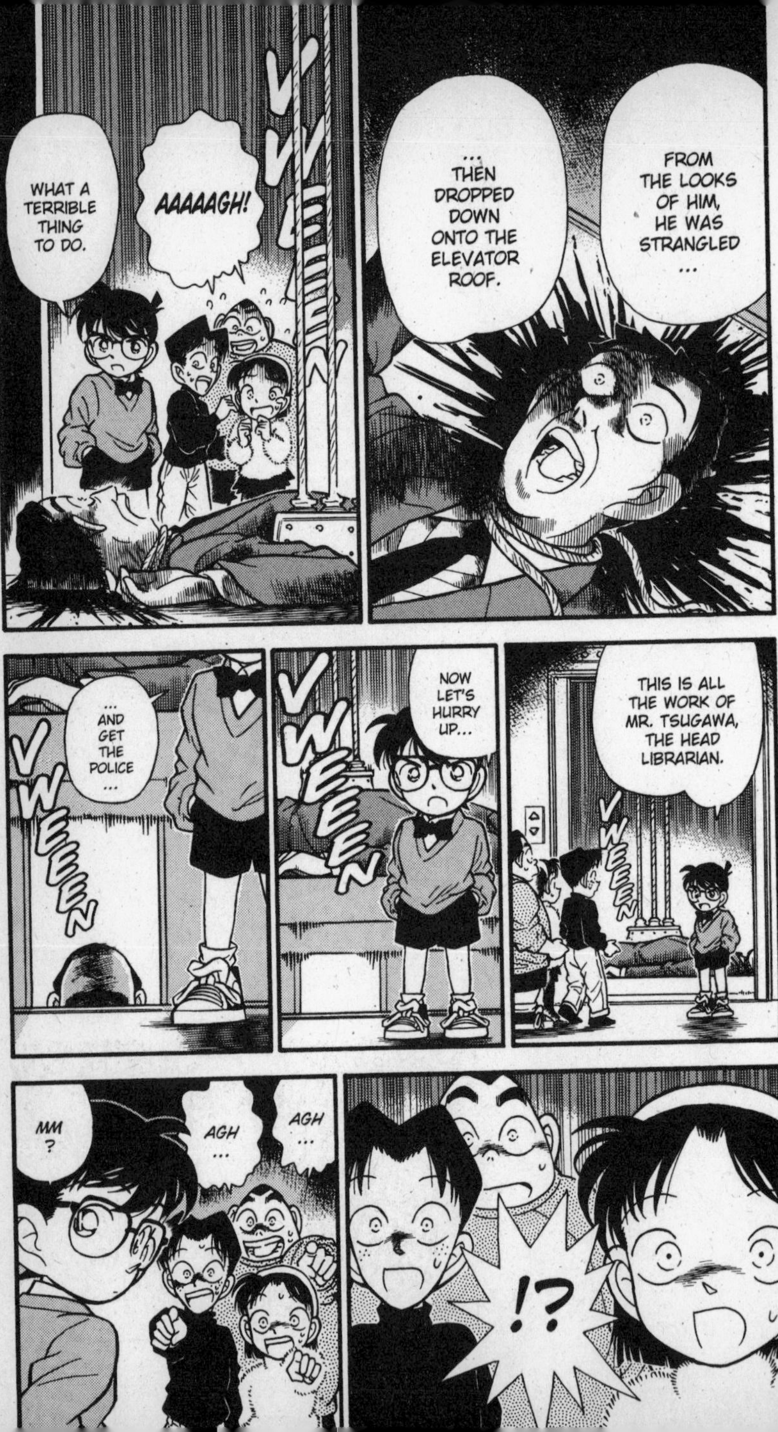
FROM THE LOOKS OF HIM, HE WAS STRANGLED ...
... THEN DROPPED DOWN ONTO THE ELEVATOR ROOF.
AAAAAGH!
WHAT A TERRIBLE THING TO DO.
THIS IS ALL THE WORK OF MR. TSUGAWA, THE HEAD LIBRARIAN.
VWEEEN
NOW LET'S HURRY UP...
VWEEEN
... AND GET THE POLICE ...
VWEEEEN
!?
AGH ...
AGH ...
MM ?

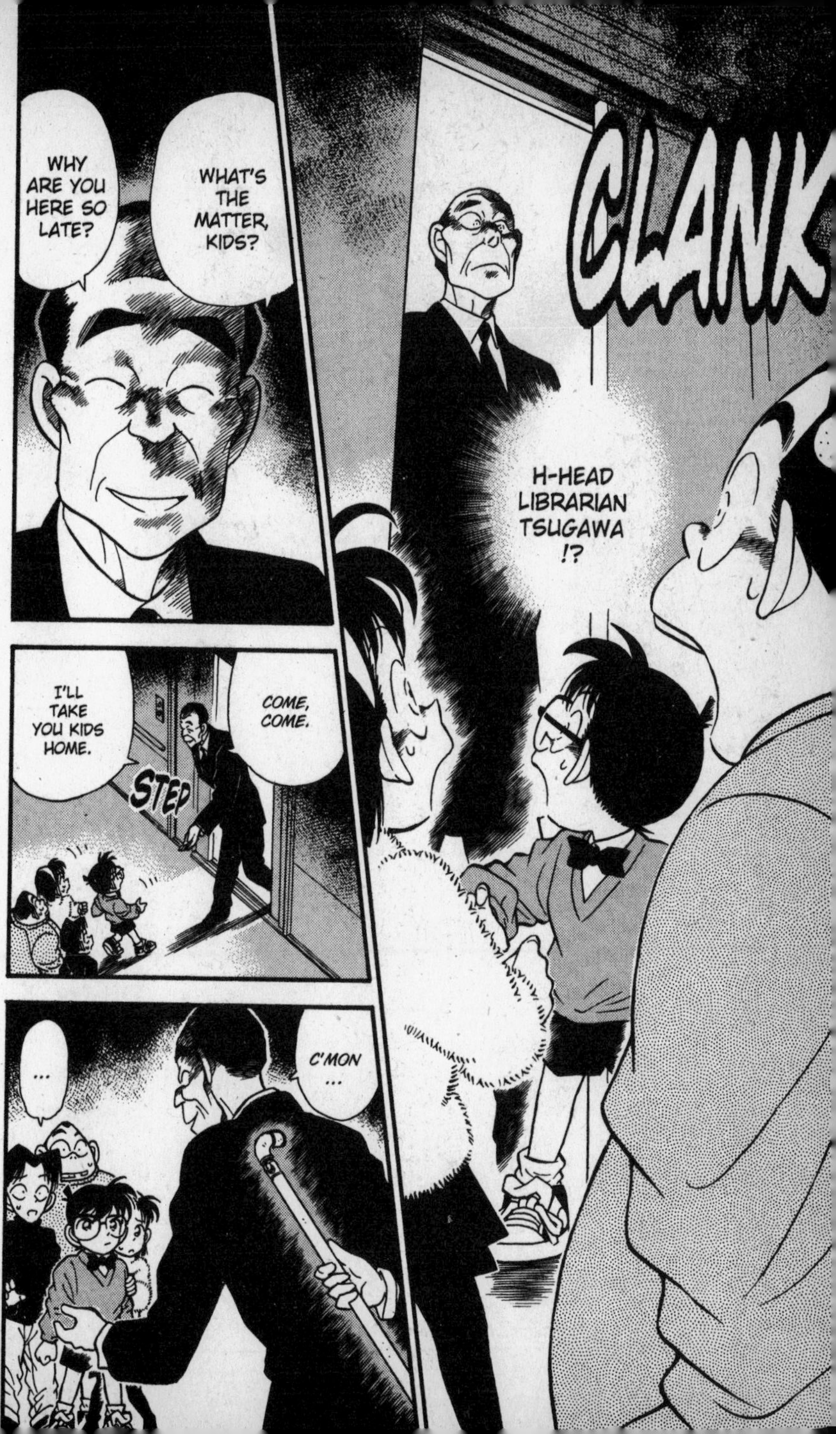
CLANK
H-HEAD LIBRARIAN TSUGAWA !?
WHAT'S THE MATTER, KIDS?
WHY ARE YOU HERE SO LATE?
COME, COME.
I'LL TAKE YOU KIDS HOME.
STEP
C'MON ...
...

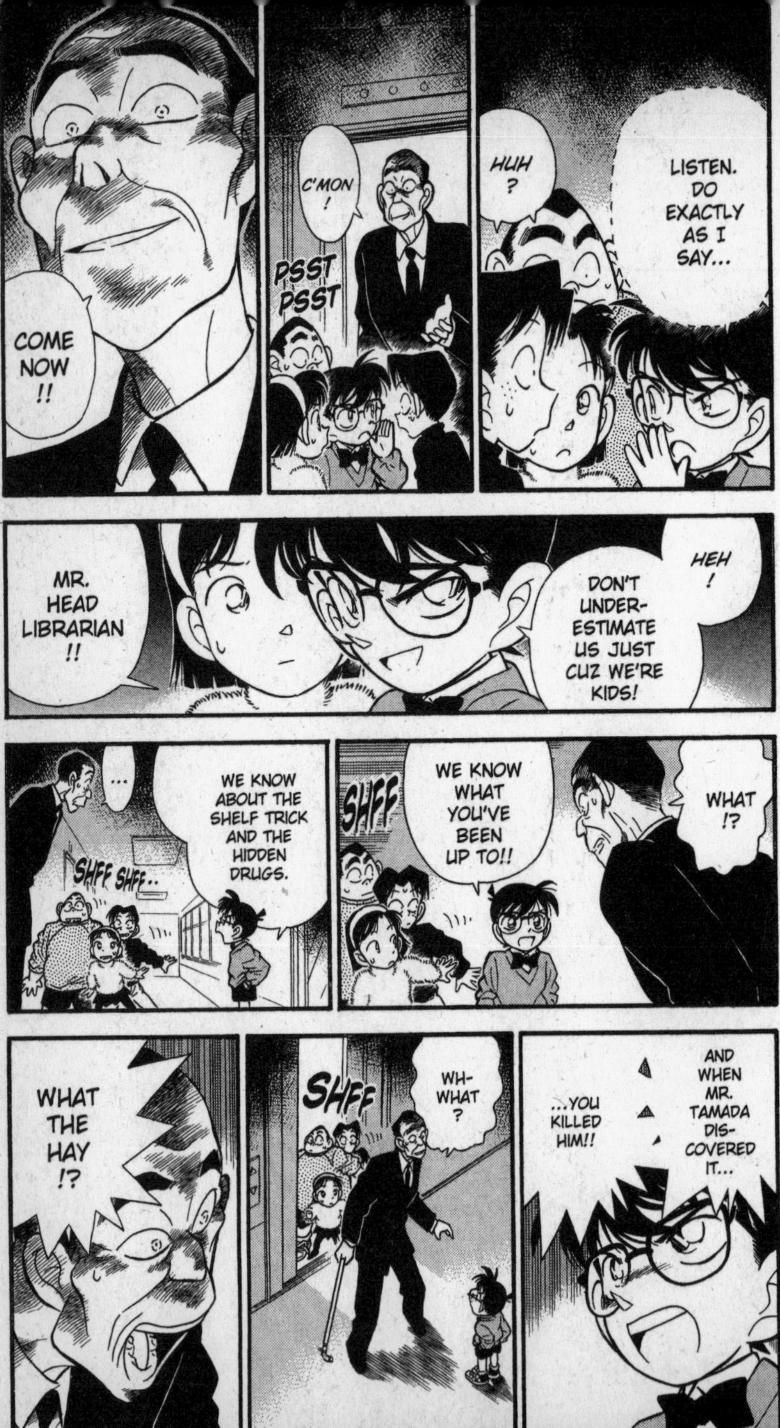
LISTEN. DO EXACTLY AS I SAY...
HUH?
C'MON!
PSST PSST
COME NOW!!
HEH!
DON'T UNDER-ESTIMATE US JUST CUZ WE'RE KIDS!
MR. HEAD LIBRARIAN!!
WHAT!?
WE KNOW WHAT YOU'VE BEEN UP TO!!
SHFF
WE KNOW ABOUT THE SHELF TRICK AND THE HIDDEN DRUGS.
...
SHFF SHFF...
AND WHEN MR. TAMADA DIS-COVERED IT...
...YOU KILLED HIM!!
WH-WHAT?
SHFF
WHAT THE HAY!?

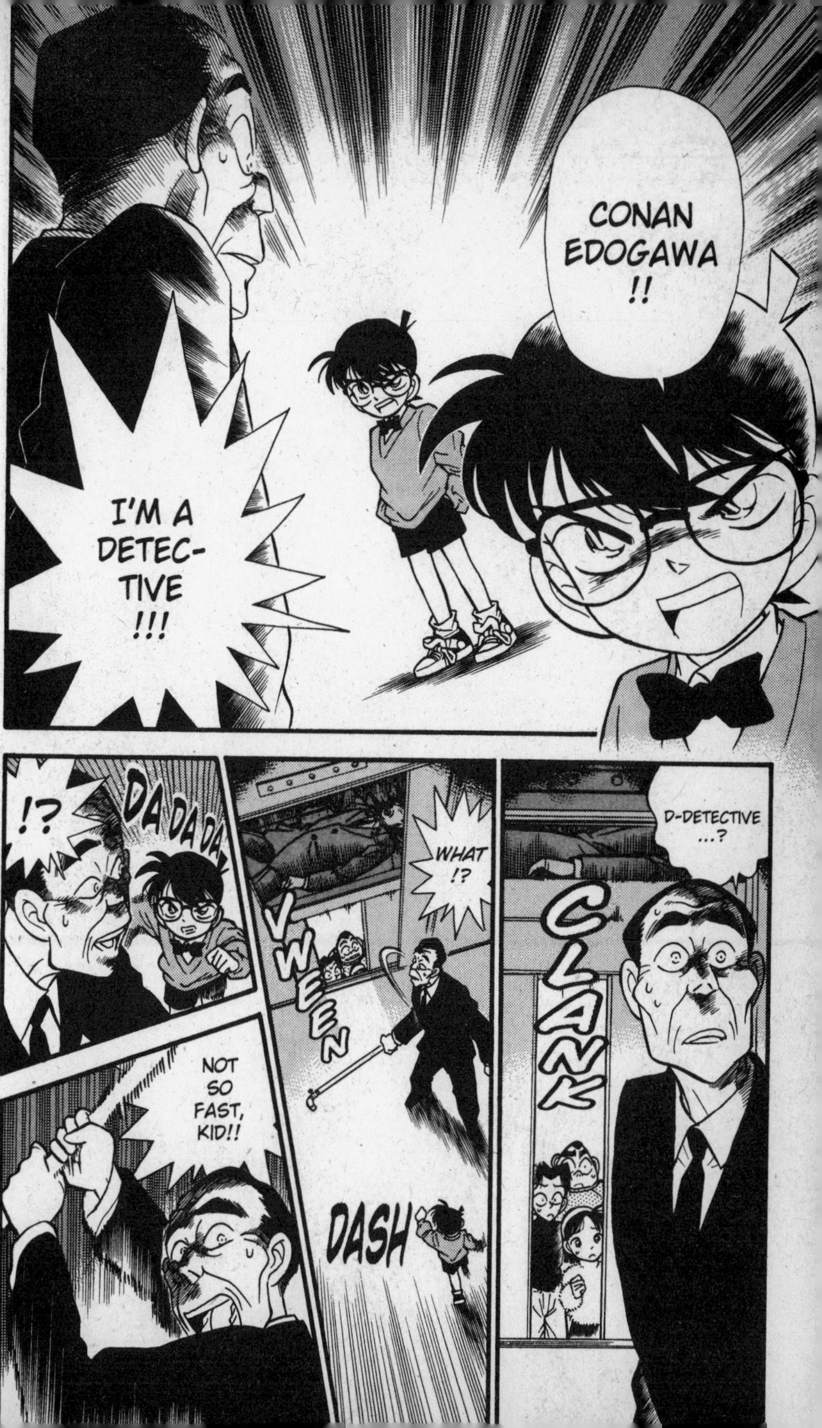
CONAN EDOGAWA !!
I'M A DETECTIVE !!!
D-DETECTIVE ...?
CLANK
WHAT !?
VWEEN
DASH
!?
DA DA DA
NOT SO FAST, KID!!

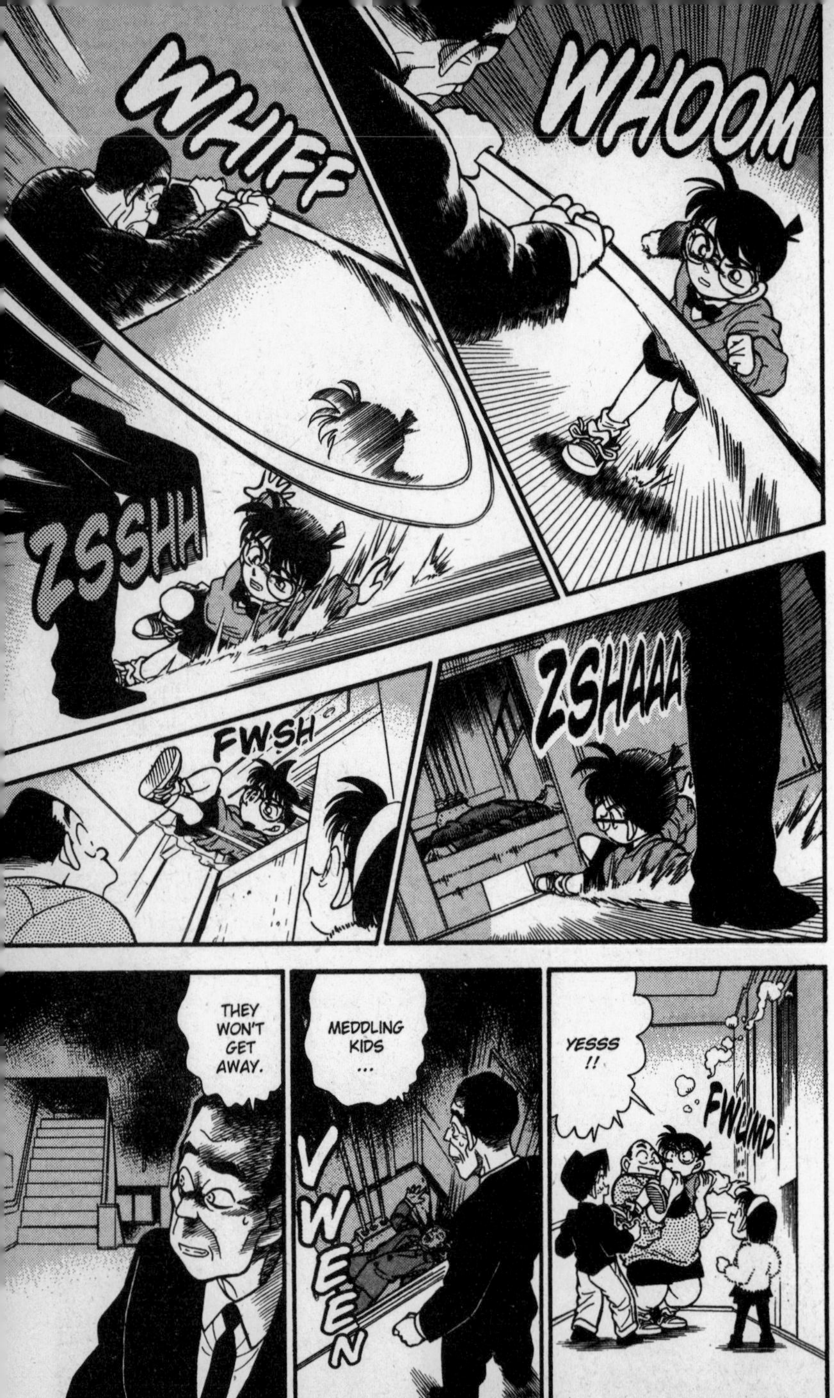
WHOOM
WHIFF
ZSSHH
ZSHAAA
FWSH
YESSS !!
FWUMP
MEDDLING KIDS ...
VWEEN
THEY WON'T GET AWAY.

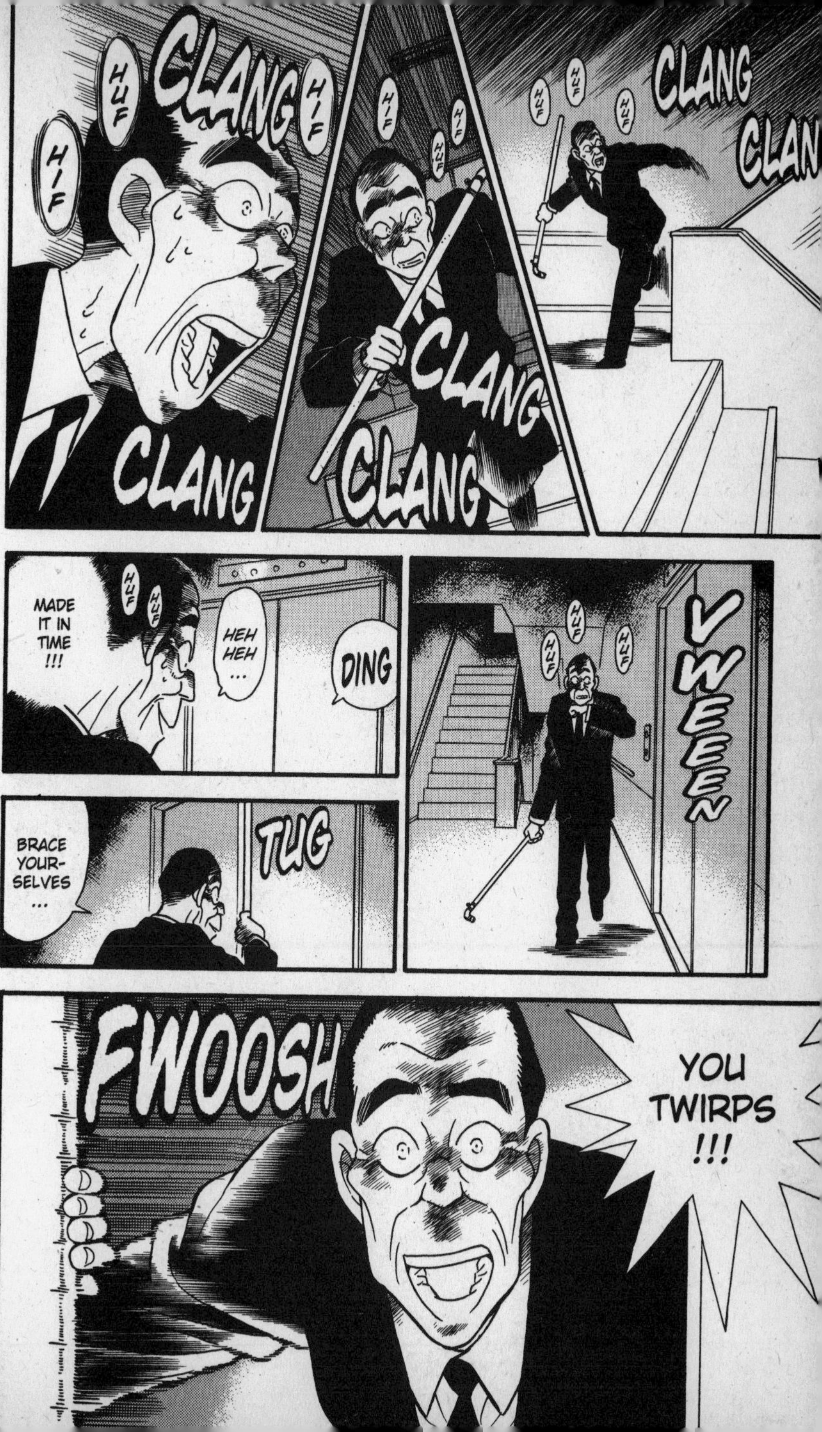
HUF
HUF
HUF
CLANG
CLAN
HIF
HIF
HUF
CLANG
CLANG
HIF
HUF
HIF
CLANG
CLANG
HUF
HUF
HUF
HUF
VWEEEEN
HUF
HUF
MADE IT IN TIME !!!
HEH HEH ...
DING
BRACE YOUR-SELVES ...
TUG
FWOOSH
YOU TWIRPS !!!

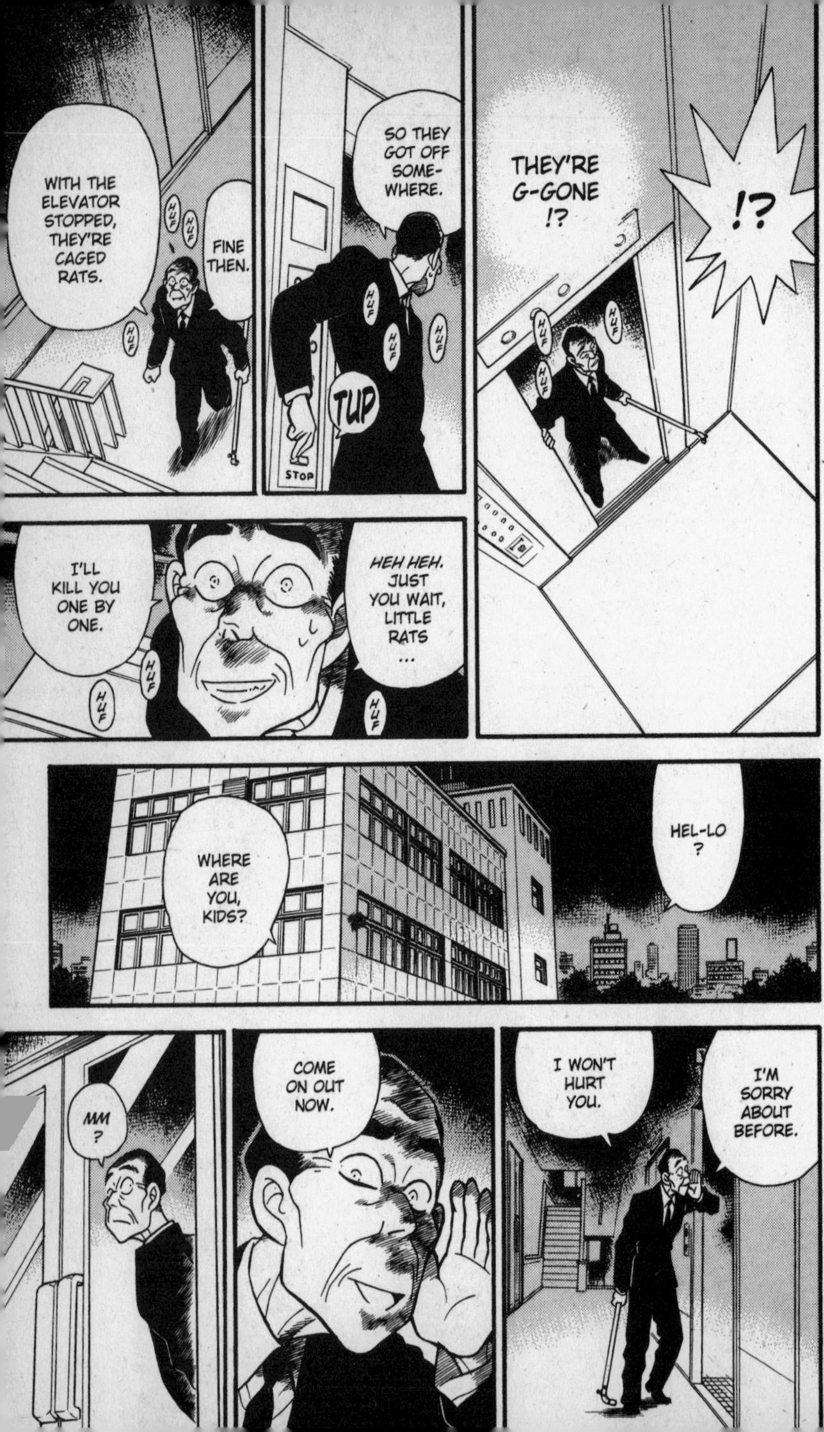

!?
THEY'RE G-GONE !?
HUF
HUF
SO THEY GOT OFF SOME-WHERE.
HUF
HUF
HUF
TUP
STOP
FINE THEN.
WITH THE ELEVATOR STOPPED, THEY'RE CAGED RATS.
HUF
HUF
HUF
HEH HEH. JUST YOU WAIT, LITTLE RATS ...
HUF
I'LL KILL YOU ONE BY ONE.
HUF
HUF
HEL-LO ?
WHERE ARE YOU, KIDS?
I'M SORRY ABOUT BEFORE.
I WON'T HURT YOU.
COME ON OUT NOW.
MM ?

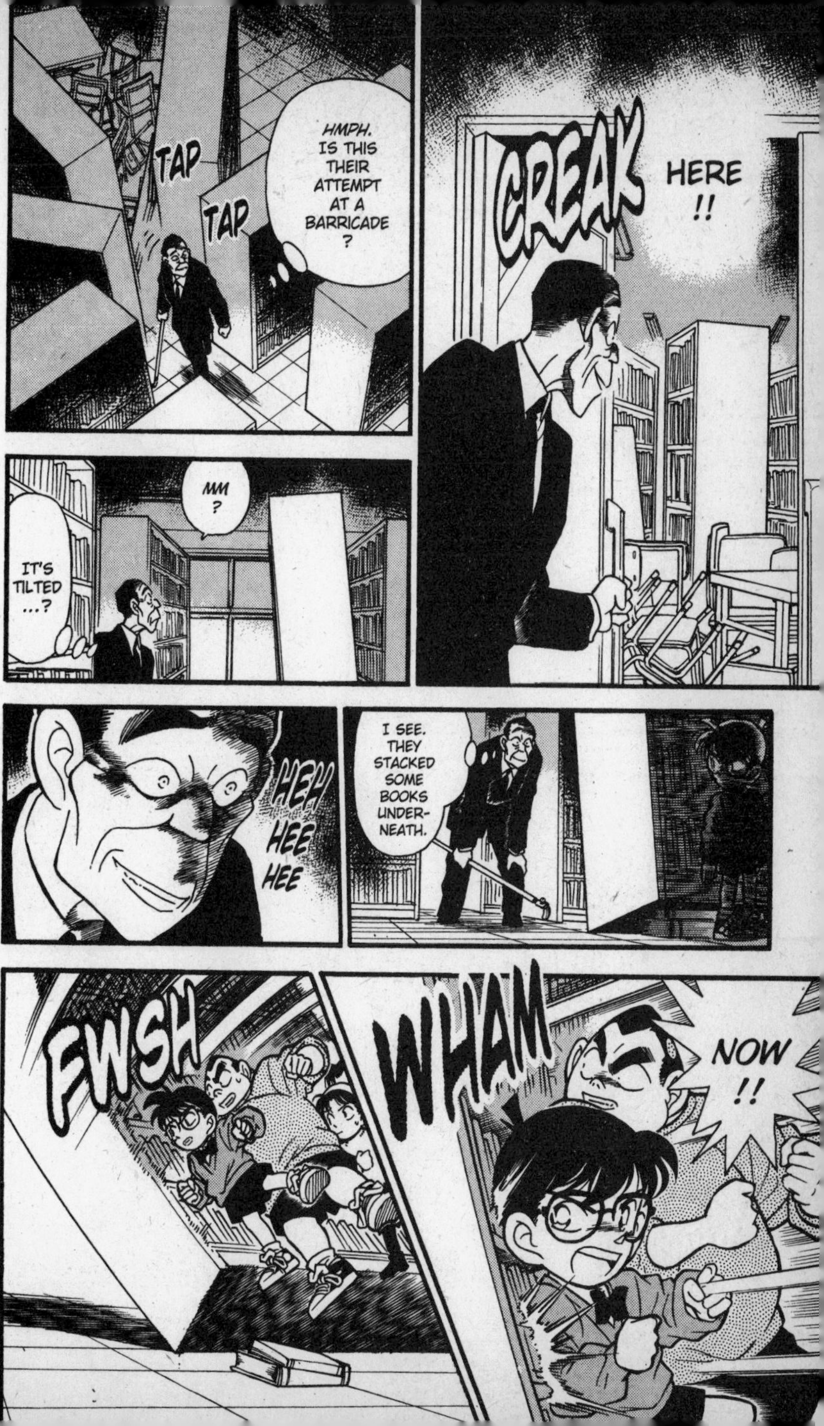
HERE !!
CREAK
HMPH. IS THIS THEIR ATTEMPT AT A BARRICADE ?
TAP
TAP
MM ?
IT'S TILTED ...?
I SEE. THEY STACKED SOME BOOKS UNDER-NEATH.
HEH HEE HEE
NOW !!
WHAM
FWSH

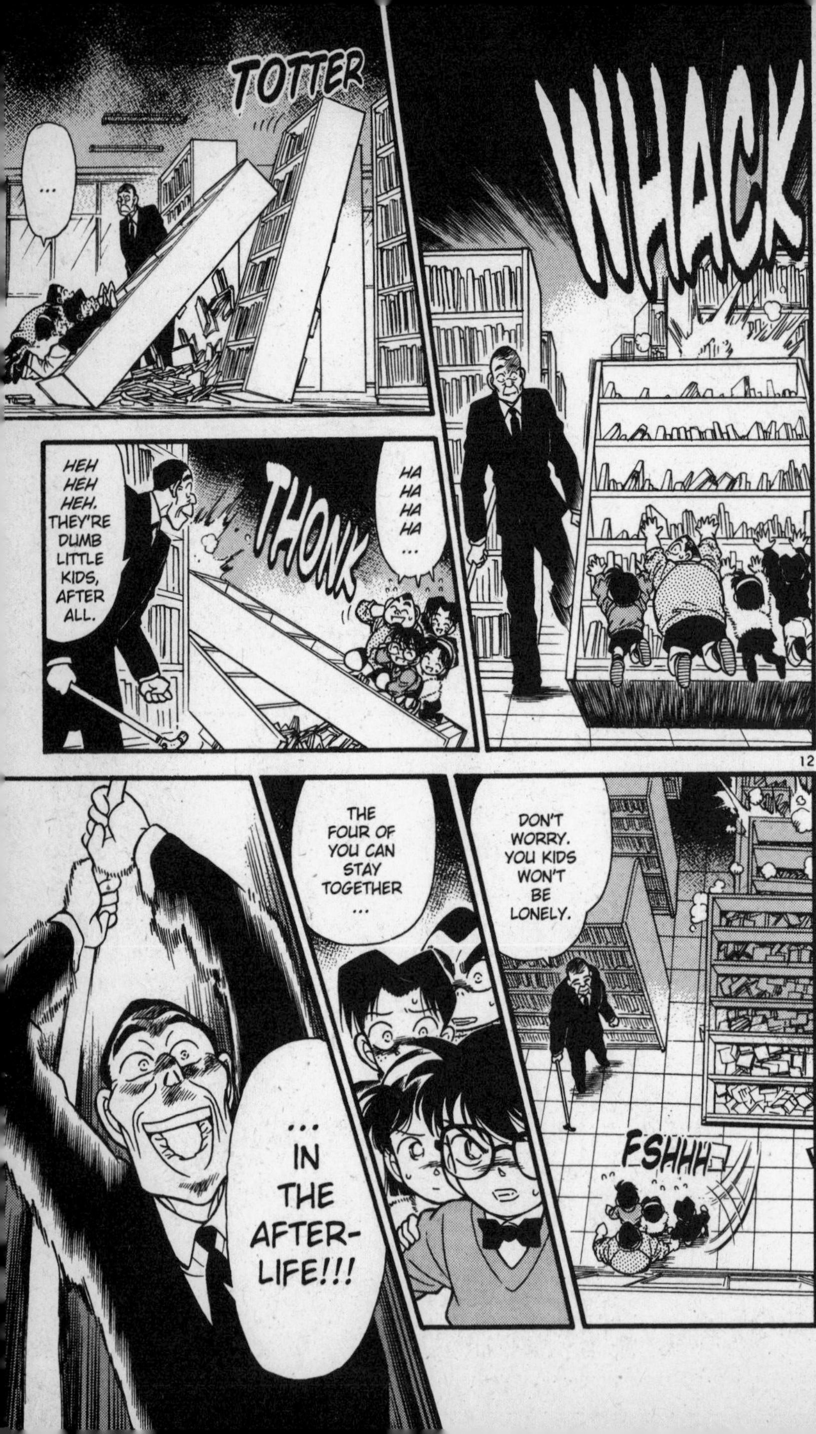
WHACK
TOTTER
...
HA HA HA HA ...
THONK
HEH HEH HEH. THEY'RE DUMB LITTLE KIDS, AFTER ALL.
DON'T WORRY. YOU KIDS WON'T BE LONELY.
FSHHH
THE FOUR OF YOU CAN STAY TOGETHER ...
... IN THE AFTER-LIFE!!!

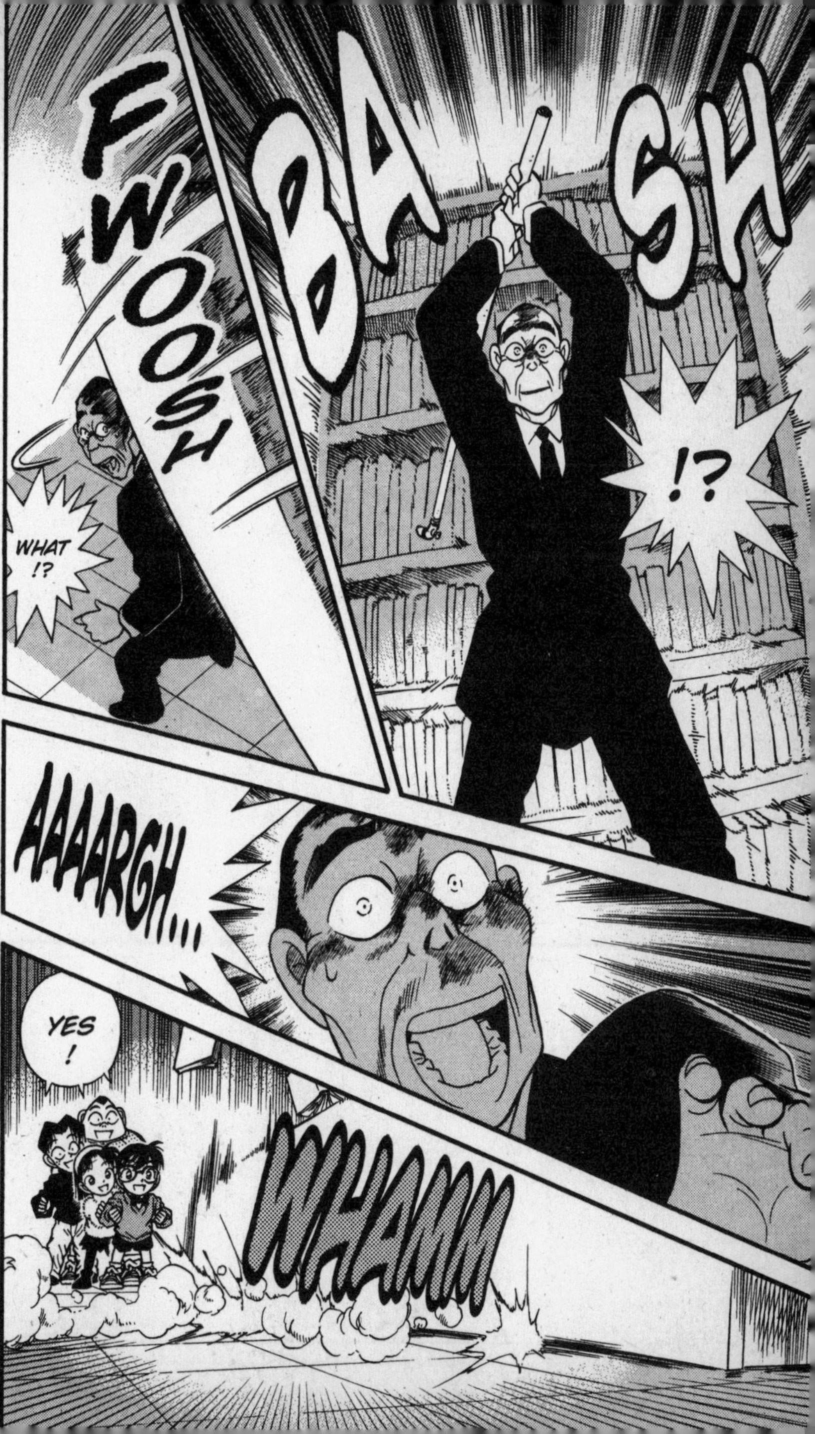
BASH
!?
FWOOOSH
WHAT !?
AAAARGH...
YES !
WHAMM

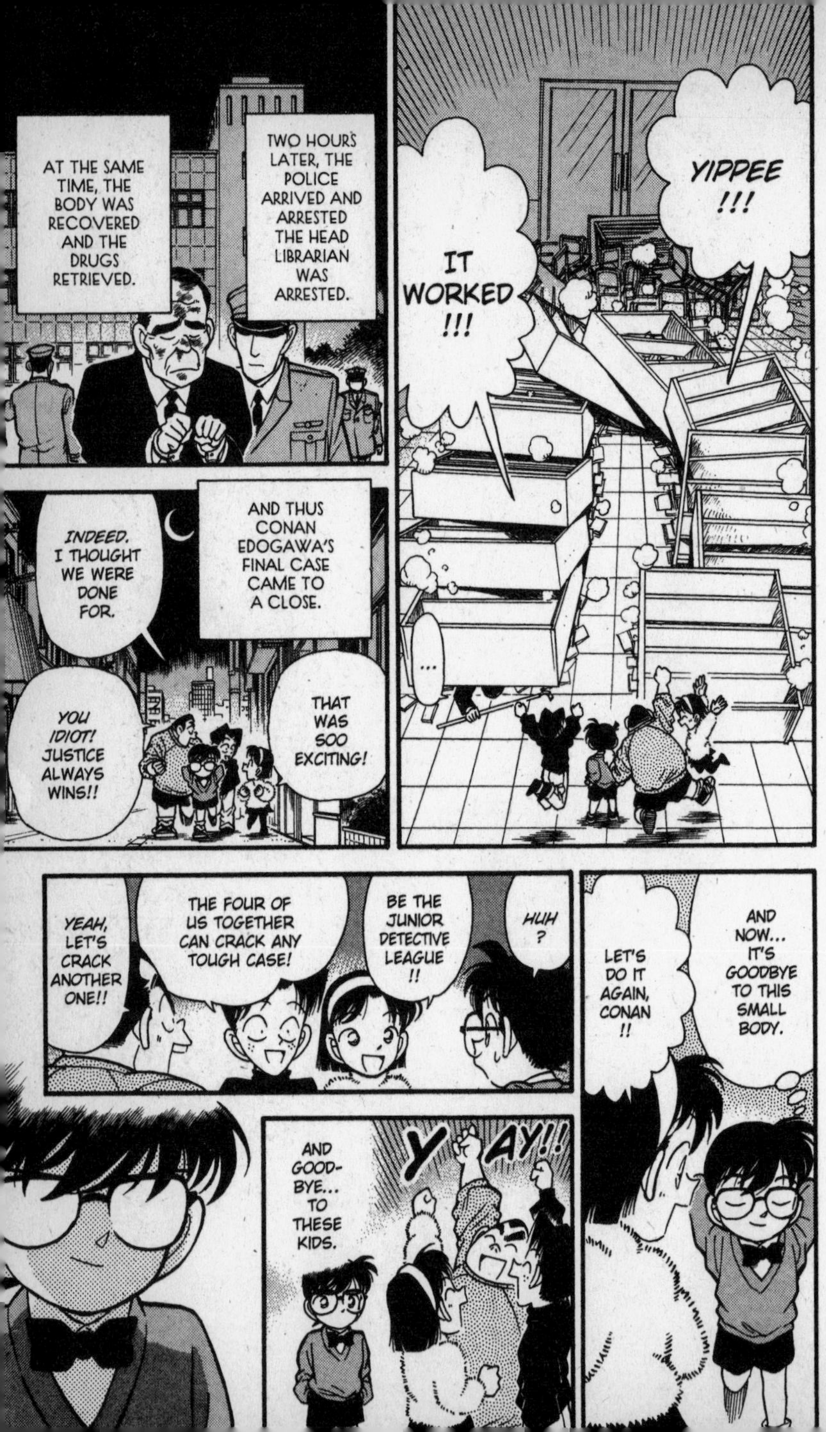
YIPPEE!!!
IT WORKED!!!
...
TWO HOURS LATER, THE POLICE ARRIVED AND ARRESTED THE HEAD LIBRARIAN WAS ARRESTED.
AT THE SAME TIME, THE BODY WAS RECOVERED AND THE DRUGS RETRIEVED.
AND THUS CONAN EDOGAWA'S FINAL CASE CAME TO A CLOSE.
INDEED. I THOUGHT WE WERE DONE FOR.
THAT WAS SOO EXCITING!
YOU IDIOT! JUSTICE ALWAYS WINS!!
AND NOW... IT'S GOODBYE TO THIS SMALL BODY.
LET'S DO IT AGAIN, CONAN!!
HUH?
BE THE JUNIOR DETECTIVE LEAGUE!!
THE FOUR OF US TOGETHER CAN CRACK ANY TOUGH CASE!
YEAH, LET'S CRACK ANOTHER ONE!!
YAY!!
AND GOOD-BYE... TO THESE KIDS.

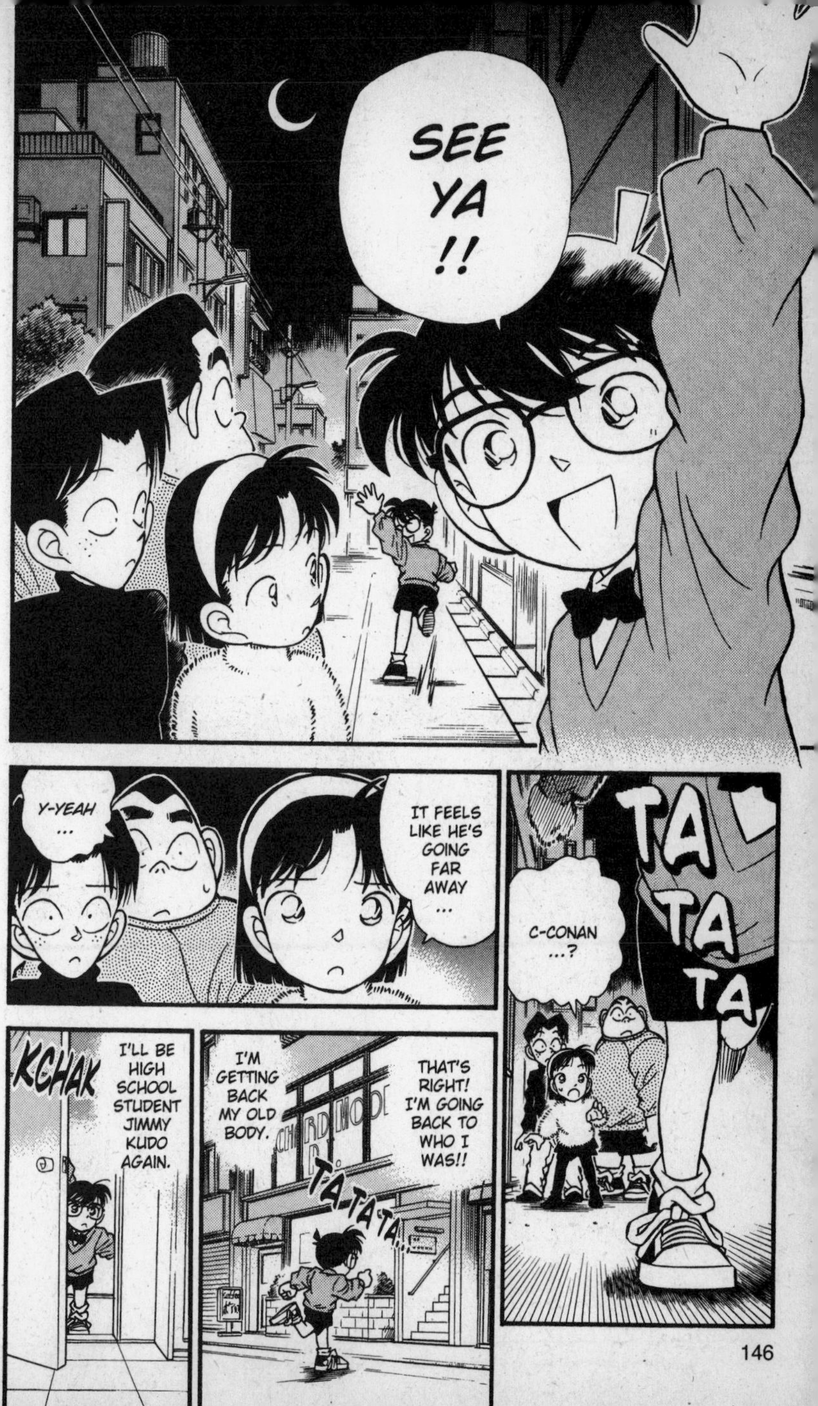
SEE YA !!
TA TA TA
C-CONAN ...?
IT FEELS LIKE HE'S GOING FAR AWAY ...
Y-YEAH ...
THAT'S RIGHT! I'M GOING BACK TO WHO I WAS!!
I'M GETTING BACK MY OLD BODY.
TA TA TA...
I'LL BE HIGH SCHOOL STUDENT JIMMY KUDO AGAIN.
KCHAK

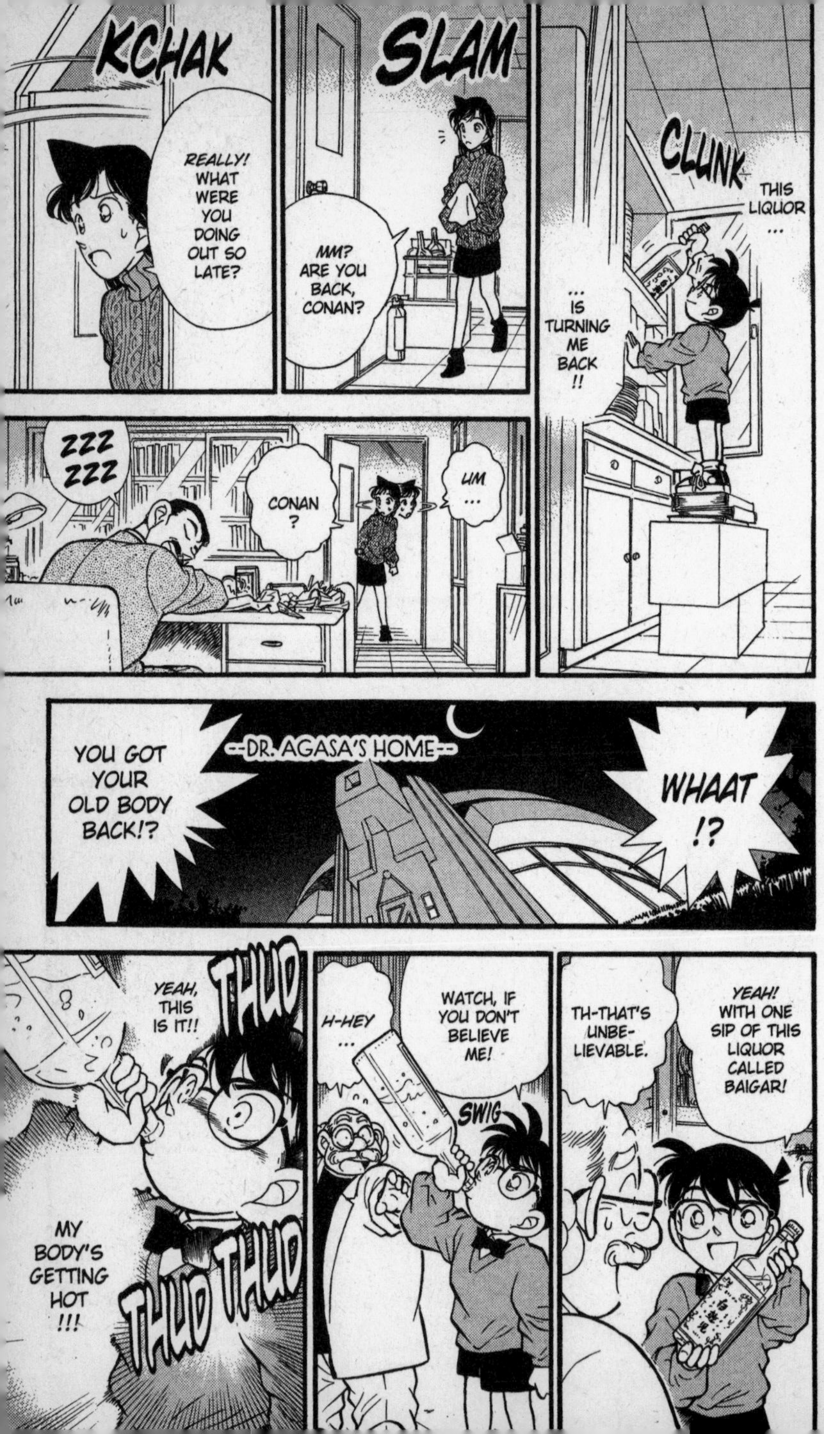
CLUNK
THIS LIQUOR ...
... IS TURNING ME BACK !!
SLAM
MM? ARE YOU BACK, CONAN?
KCHAK
REALLY! WHAT WERE YOU DOING OUT SO LATE?
UM ...
CONAN ?
ZZZ ZZZ
--DR. AGASA'S HOME--
WHAAT !?
YOU GOT YOUR OLD BODY BACK!?
YEAH! WITH ONE SIP OF THIS LIQUOR CALLED BAIGAR!
TH-THAT'S UNBE-LIEVABLE.
WATCH, IF YOU DON'T BELIEVE ME!
H-HEY ...
SWIG
THUD
YEAH, THIS IS IT!!
MY BODY'S GETTING HOT !!!
THUD THUD

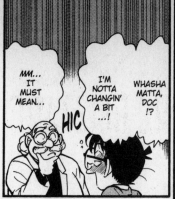

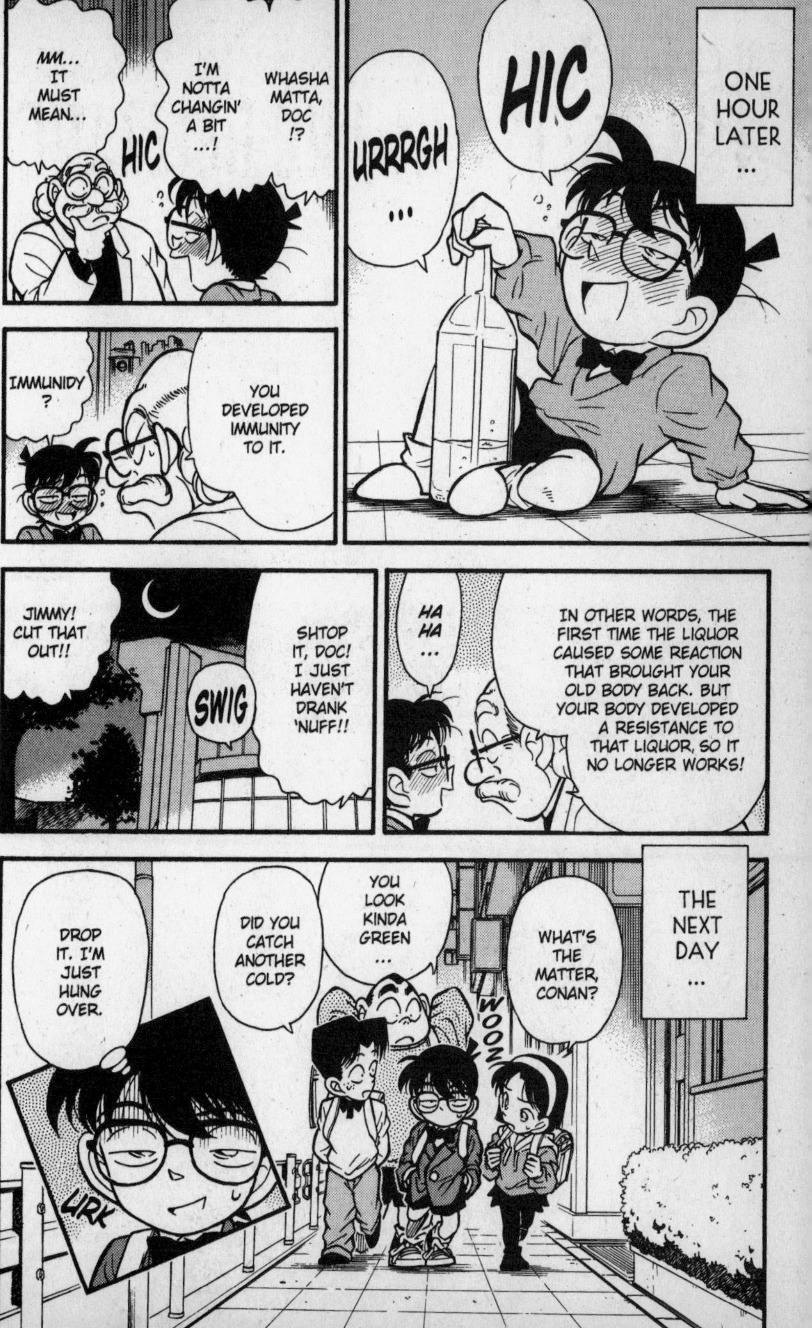
ONE HOUR LATER ...
HIC
URRRGH ...
WHASHA MATTA, DOC !?
I'M NOTTA CHANGIN' A BIT ...!
HIC
MM... IT MUST MEAN...
YOU DEVELOPED IMMUNITY TO IT.
IMMUNIDY ?
IN OTHER WORDS, THE FIRST TIME THE LIQUOR CAUSED SOME REACTION THAT BROUGHT YOUR OLD BODY BACK. BUT YOUR BODY DEVELOPED A RESISTANCE TO THAT LIQUOR, SO IT NO LONGER WORKS!
HA HA ...
SHTOP IT, DOC! I JUST HAVEN'T DRANK 'NUFF!!
SWIG
JIMMY! CUT THAT OUT!!
THE NEXT DAY ...
WHAT'S THE MATTER, CONAN?
WOOZ
YOU LOOK KINDA GREEN ...
DID YOU CATCH ANOTHER COLD?
DROP IT. I'M JUST HUNG OVER.
URK

FILE 9:
TRAGEDY IN THE BLIZZARD

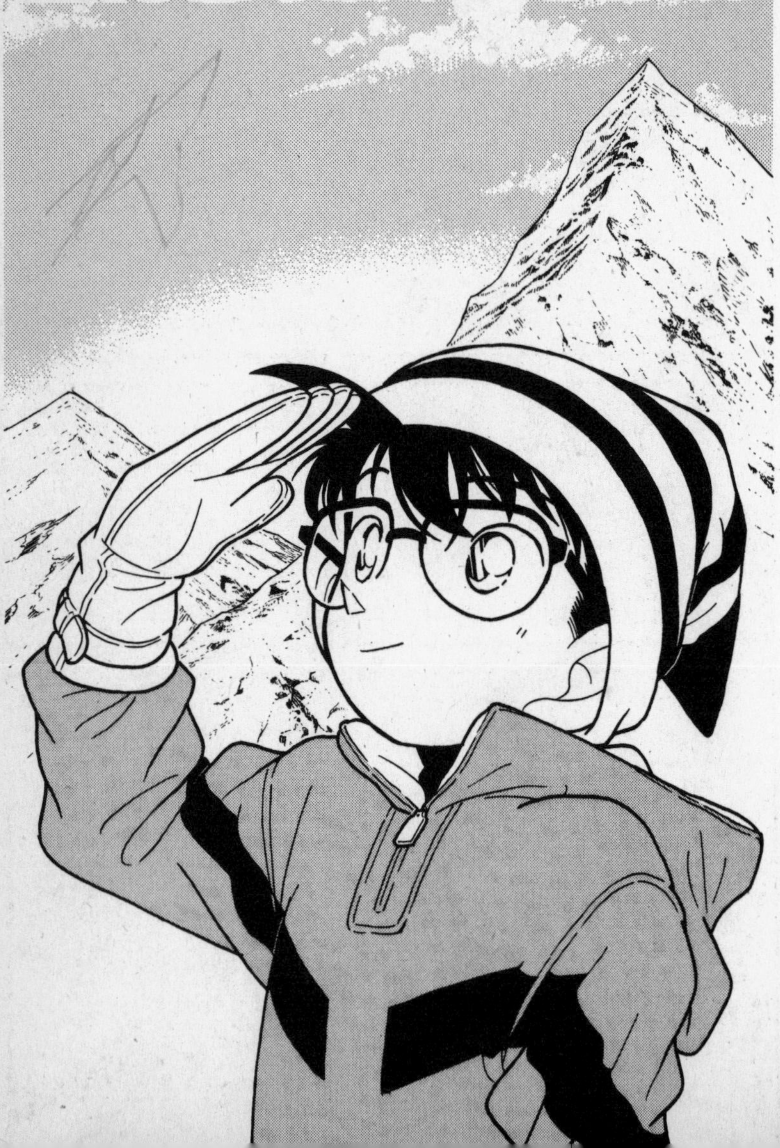

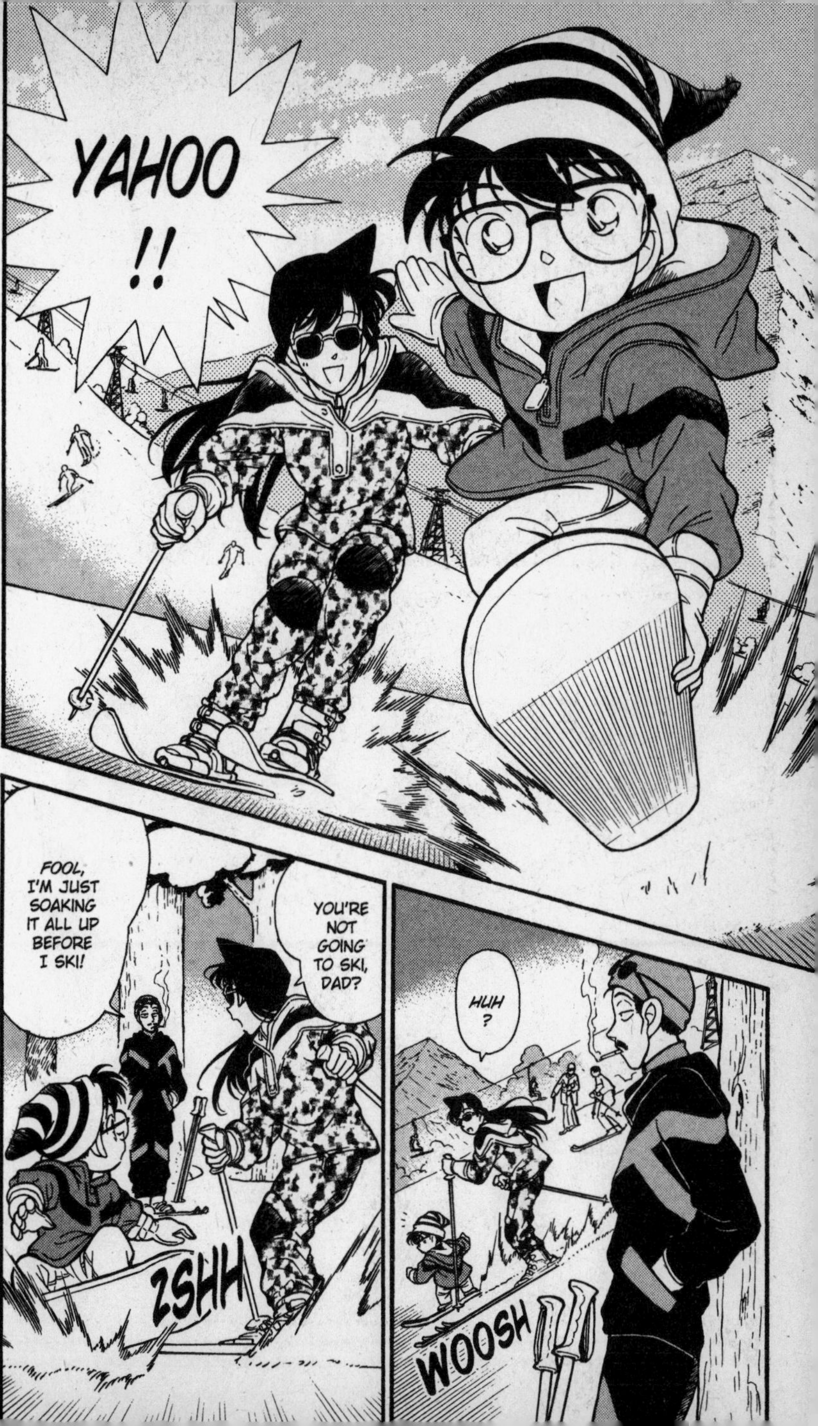
YAHOO !!
YOU'RE NOT GOING TO SKI, DAD?
FOOL, I'M JUST SOAKING IT ALL UP BEFORE I SKI!
ZSHH
HUH ?
WOOSH

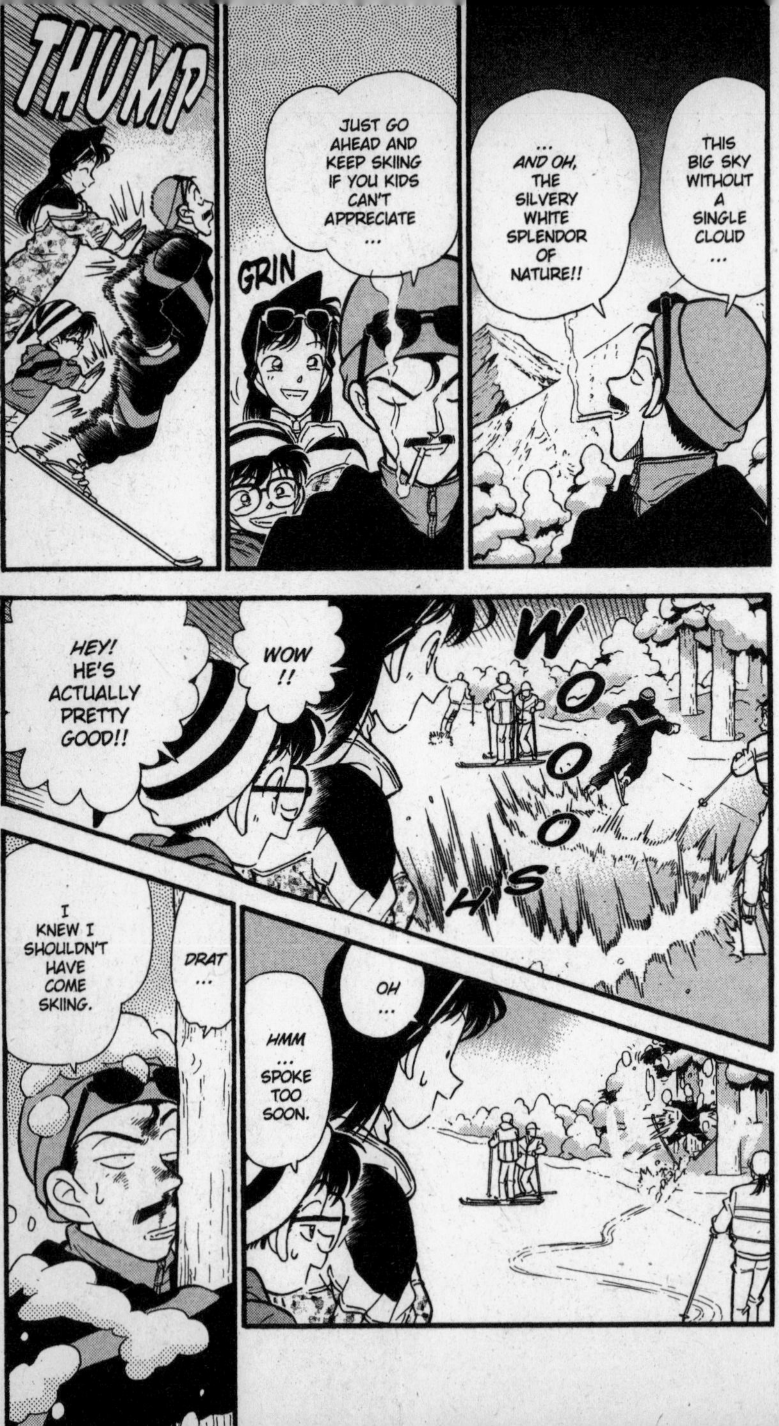
THIS BIG SKY WITHOUT A SINGLE CLOUD ...
... AND OH, THE SILVERY WHITE SPLENDOR OF NATURE!!
JUST GO AHEAD AND KEEP SKIING IF YOU KIDS CAN'T APPRECIATE ...
GRIN
THUMP
WOOOOSH
WOW !!
HEY! HE'S ACTUALLY PRETTY GOOD!!
OH ...
HMM ... SPOKE TOO SOON.
DRAT ...
I KNEW I SHOULDN'T HAVE COME SKIING.

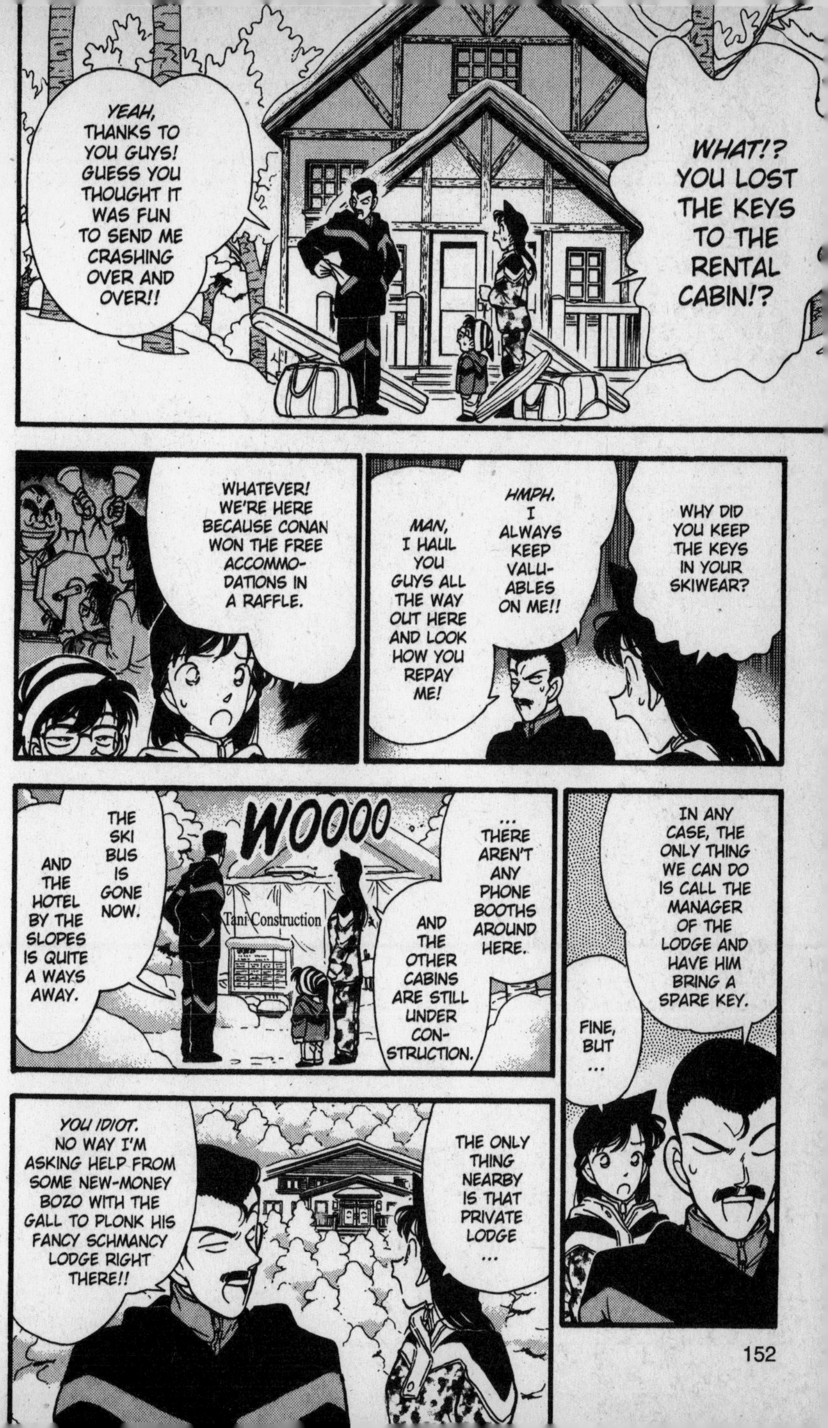
WHAT!? YOU LOST THE KEYS TO THE RENTAL CABIN!?
YEAH, THANKS TO YOU GUYS! GUESS YOU THOUGHT IT WAS FUN TO SEND ME CRASHING OVER AND OVER!!
WHY DID YOU KEEP THE KEYS IN YOUR SKIWEAR?
HMPH. I ALWAYS KEEP VALUABLES ON ME!!
MAN, I HAUL YOU GUYS ALL THE WAY OUT HERE AND LOOK HOW YOU REPAY ME!
WHATEVER! WE'RE HERE BECAUSE CONAN WON THE FREE ACCOMMODATIONS IN A RAFFLE.
IN ANY CASE, THE ONLY THING WE CAN DO IS CALL THE MANAGER OF THE LODGE AND HAVE HIM BRING A SPARE KEY.
FINE, BUT ...
WOOOO
... THERE AREN'T ANY PHONE BOOTHS AROUND HERE.
AND THE OTHER CABINS ARE STILL UNDER CONSTRUCTION.
Tani Construction
THE SKI BUS IS GONE NOW.
AND THE HOTEL BY THE SLOPES IS QUITE A WAYS AWAY.
THE ONLY THING NEARBY IS THAT PRIVATE LODGE ...
YOU IDIOT. NO WAY I'M ASKING HELP FROM SOME NEW-MONEY BOZO WITH THE GALL TO PLONK HIS FANCY SCHMANCY LODGE RIGHT THERE!!

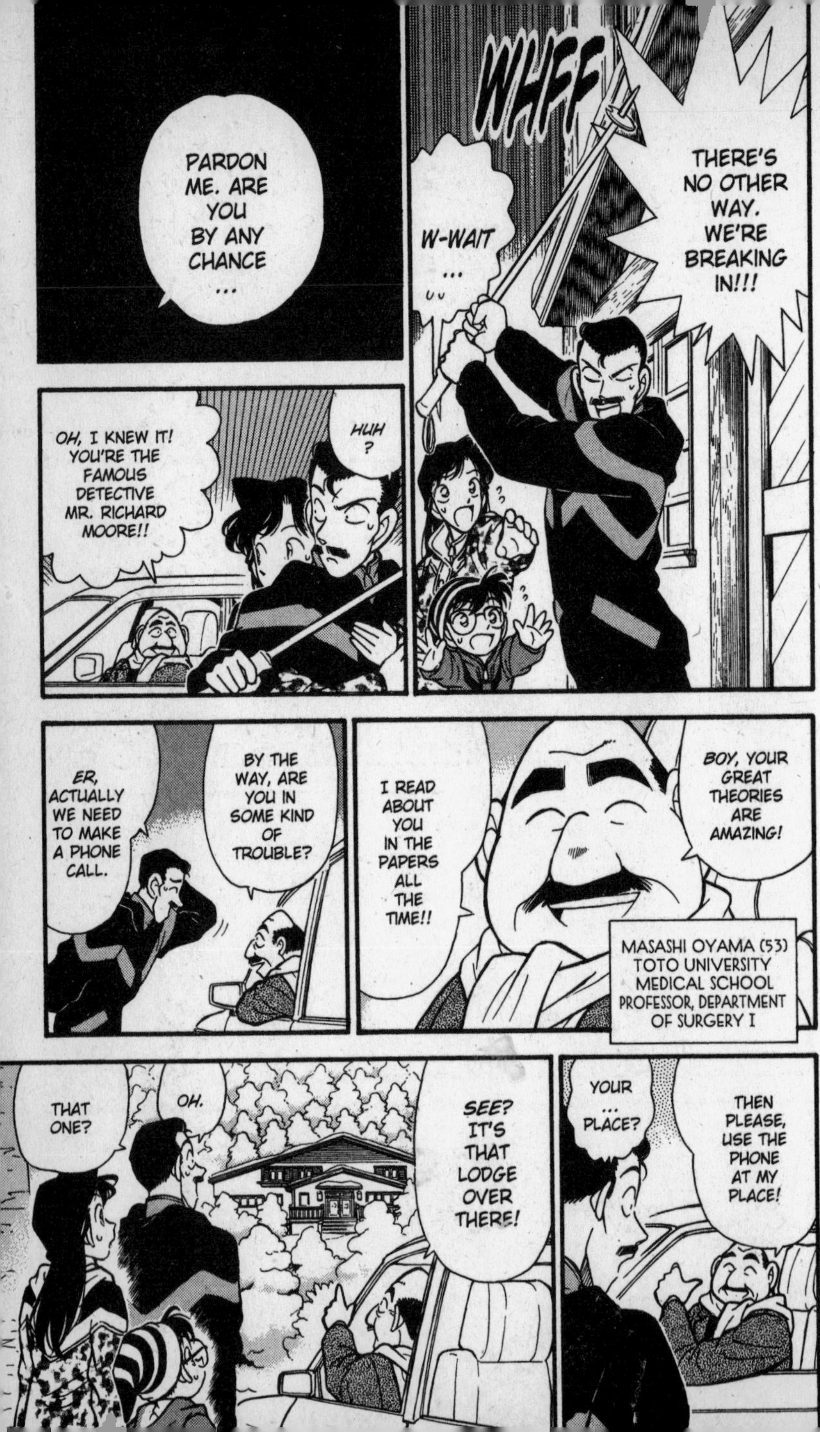
WHFF
THERE'S NO OTHER WAY. WE'RE BREAKING IN!!!
W-WAIT ...
PARDON ME. ARE YOU BY ANY CHANCE ...
HUH?
OH, I KNEW IT! YOU'RE THE FAMOUS DETECTIVE MR. RICHARD MOORE!!
BOY, YOUR GREAT THEORIES ARE AMAZING!
I READ ABOUT YOU IN THE PAPERS ALL THE TIME!!
MASASHI OYAMA (53) TOTO UNIVERSITY MEDICAL SCHOOL PROFESSOR, DEPARTMENT OF SURGERY I
BY THE WAY, ARE YOU IN SOME KIND OF TROUBLE?
ER, ACTUALLY WE NEED TO MAKE A PHONE CALL.
THEN PLEASE, USE THE PHONE AT MY PLACE!
YOUR ... PLACE?
SEE? IT'S THAT LODGE OVER THERE!
OH.
THAT ONE?

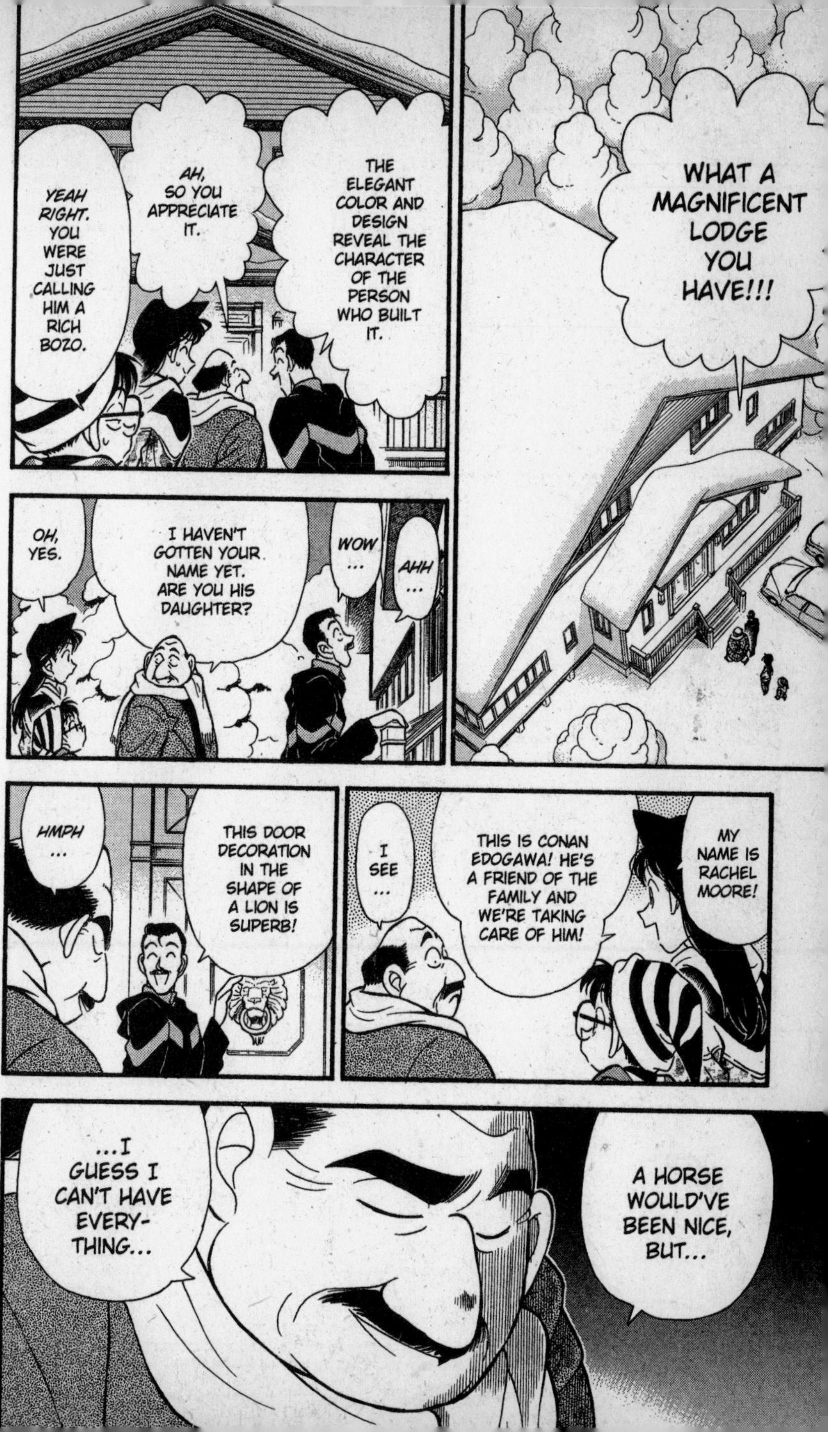
WHAT A MAGNIFICENT LODGE YOU HAVE!!!
THE ELEGANT COLOR AND DESIGN REVEAL THE CHARACTER OF THE PERSON WHO BUILT IT.
AH, SO YOU APPRECIATE IT.
YEAH RIGHT. YOU WERE JUST CALLING HIM A RICH BOZO.
AHH ...
WOW ...
I HAVEN'T GOTTEN YOUR NAME YET. ARE YOU HIS DAUGHTER?
OH, YES.
MY NAME IS RACHEL MOORE!
THIS IS CONAN EDOGAWA! HE'S A FRIEND OF THE FAMILY AND WE'RE TAKING CARE OF HIM!
I SEE ...
THIS DOOR DECORATION IN THE SHAPE OF A LION IS SUPERB!
HMPH ...
A HORSE WOULD'VE BEEN NICE, BUT...
...I GUESS I CAN'T HAVE EVERY-THING...

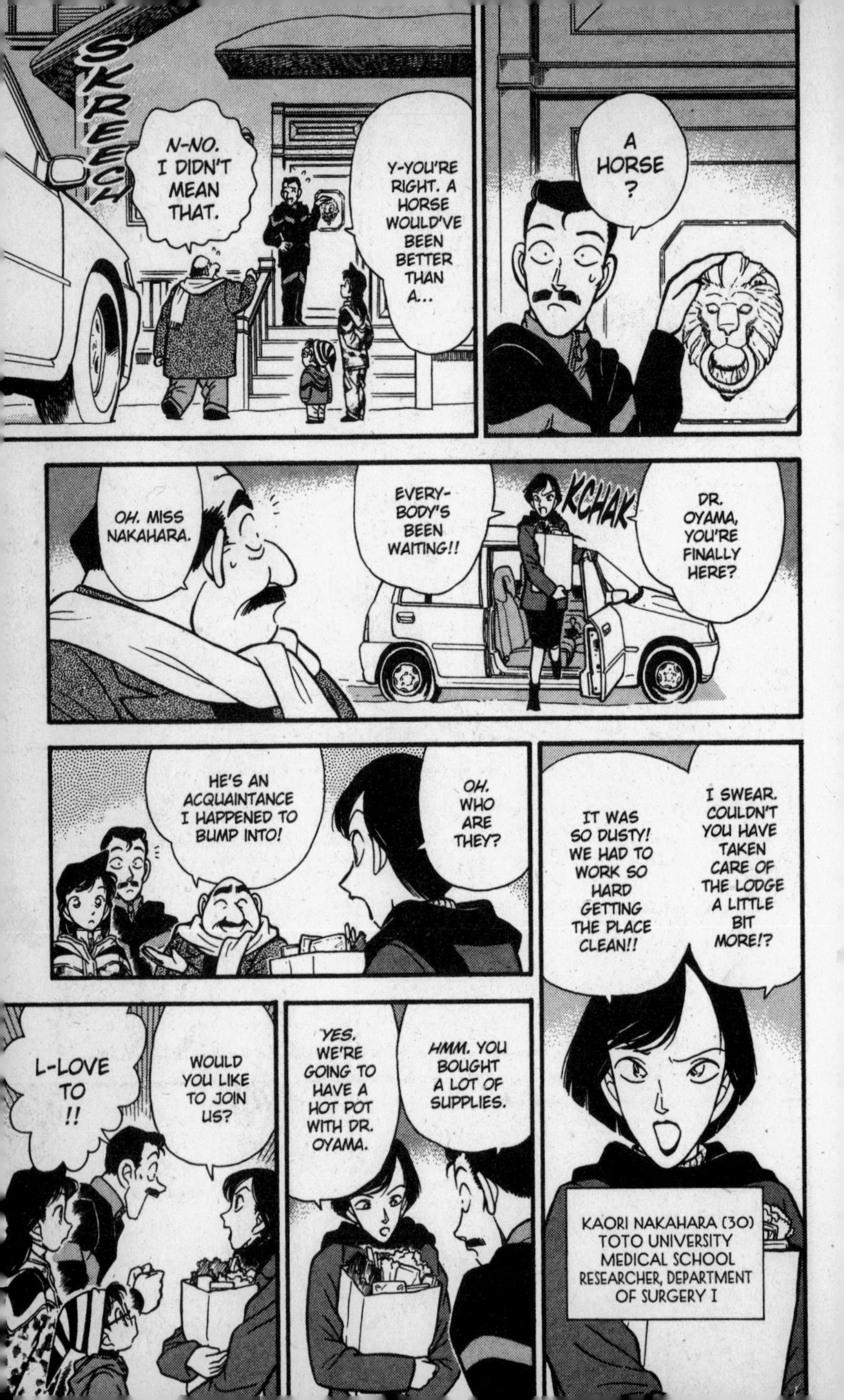
A HORSE?
Y-YOU'RE RIGHT. A HORSE WOULD'VE BEEN BETTER THAN A...
N-NO. I DIDN'T MEAN THAT.
SKREECH
DR. OYAMA, YOU'RE FINALLY HERE?
KCHAK
EVERY-BODY'S BEEN WAITING!!
OH. MISS NAKAHARA.
I SWEAR. COULDN'T YOU HAVE TAKEN CARE OF THE LODGE A LITTLE BIT MORE!?
IT WAS SO DUSTY! WE HAD TO WORK SO HARD GETTING THE PLACE CLEAN!!
KAORI NAKAHARA (30) TOTO UNIVERSITY MEDICAL SCHOOL RESEARCHER, DEPARTMENT OF SURGERY I
OH. WHO ARE THEY?
HE'S AN ACQUAINTANCE I HAPPENED TO BUMP INTO!
HMM. YOU BOUGHT A LOT OF SUPPLIES.
YES. WE'RE GOING TO HAVE A HOT POT WITH DR. OYAMA.
WOULD YOU LIKE TO JOIN US?
L-LOVE TO!!

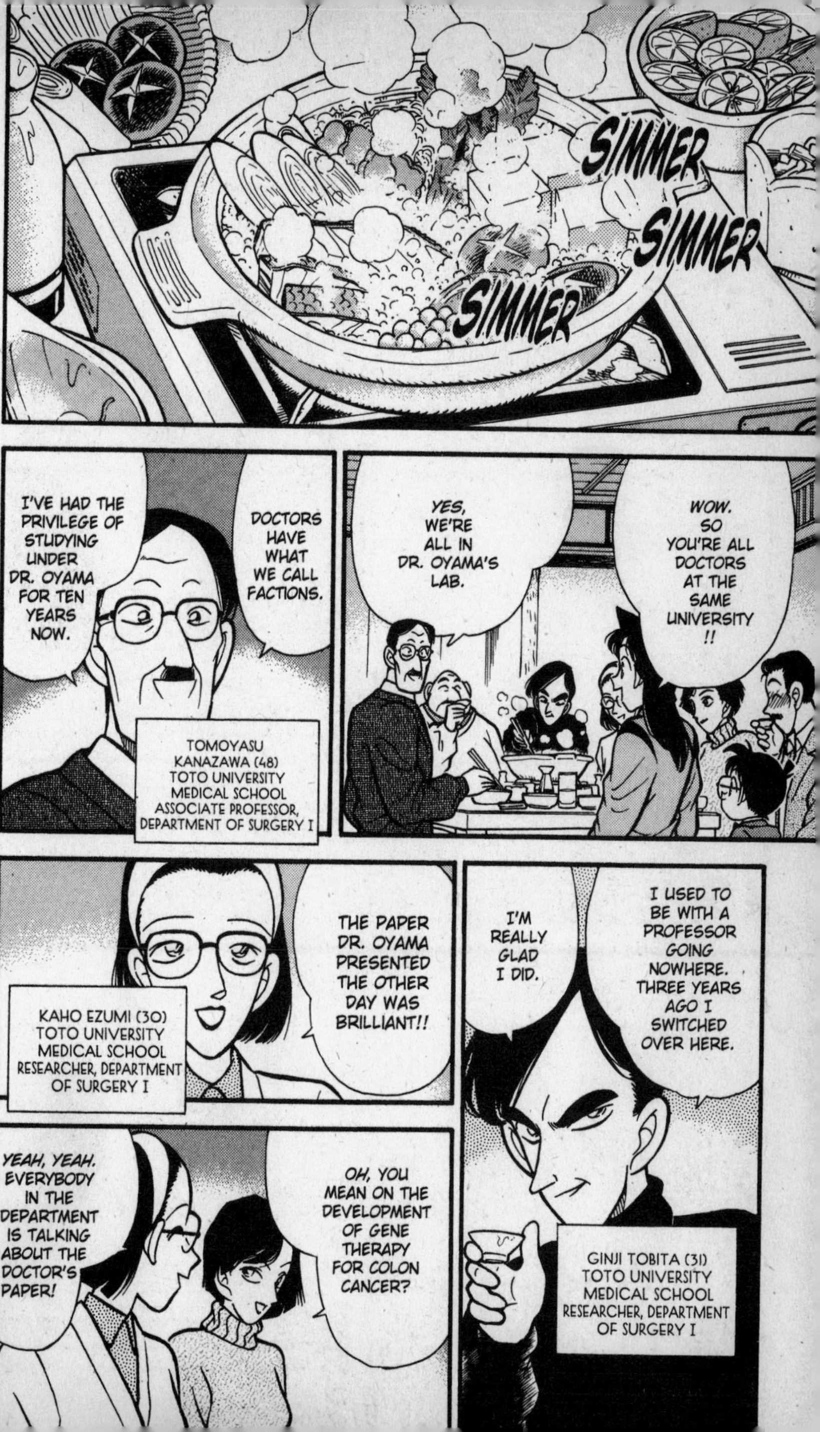
SIMMER
SIMMER
SIMMER
WOW. SO YOU'RE ALL DOCTORS AT THE SAME UNIVERSITY!!
YES, WE'RE ALL IN DR. OYAMA'S LAB.
DOCTORS HAVE WHAT WE CALL FACTIONS.
I'VE HAD THE PRIVILEGE OF STUDYING UNDER DR. OYAMA FOR TEN YEARS NOW.
TOMOYASU KANAZAWA (48) TOTO UNIVERSITY MEDICAL SCHOOL ASSOCIATE PROFESSOR, DEPARTMENT OF SURGERY I
I USED TO BE WITH A PROFESSOR GOING NOWHERE. THREE YEARS AGO I SWITCHED OVER HERE.
I'M REALLY GLAD I DID.
GINJI TOBITA (31) TOTO UNIVERSITY MEDICAL SCHOOL RESEARCHER, DEPARTMENT OF SURGERY I
THE PAPER DR. OYAMA PRESENTED THE OTHER DAY WAS BRILLIANT!!
KAHO EZUMI (30) TOTO UNIVERSITY MEDICAL SCHOOL RESEARCHER, DEPARTMENT OF SURGERY I
OH, YOU MEAN ON THE DEVELOPMENT OF GENE THERAPY FOR COLON CANCER?
YEAH, YEAH. EVERYBODY IN THE DEPARTMENT IS TALKING ABOUT THE DOCTOR'S PAPER!

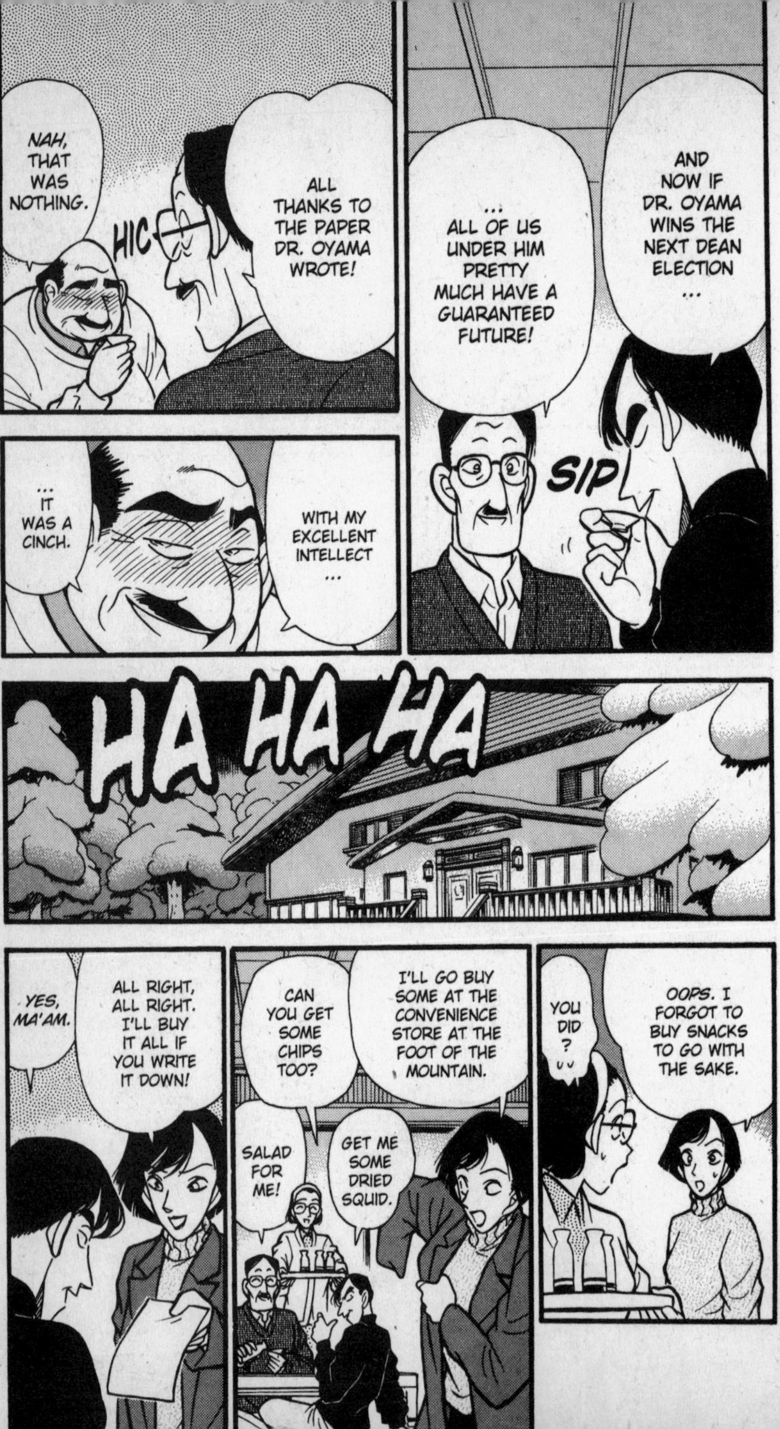
AND NOW IF DR. OYAMA WINS THE NEXT DEAN ELECTION ...
... ALL OF US UNDER HIM PRETTY MUCH HAVE A GUARANTEED FUTURE!
SIP
ALL THANKS TO THE PAPER DR. OYAMA WROTE!
HIC
NAH, THAT WAS NOTHING.
WITH MY EXCELLENT INTELLECT ...
... IT WAS A CINCH.
HA HA HA
OOPS. I FORGOT TO BUY SNACKS TO GO WITH THE SAKE.
YOU DID?
I'LL GO BUY SOME AT THE CONVENIENCE STORE AT THE FOOT OF THE MOUNTAIN.
CAN YOU GET SOME CHIPS TOO?
GET ME SOME DRIED SQUID.
SALAD FOR ME!
ALL RIGHT, ALL RIGHT. I'LL BUY IT ALL IF YOU WRITE IT DOWN!
YES, MA'AM.

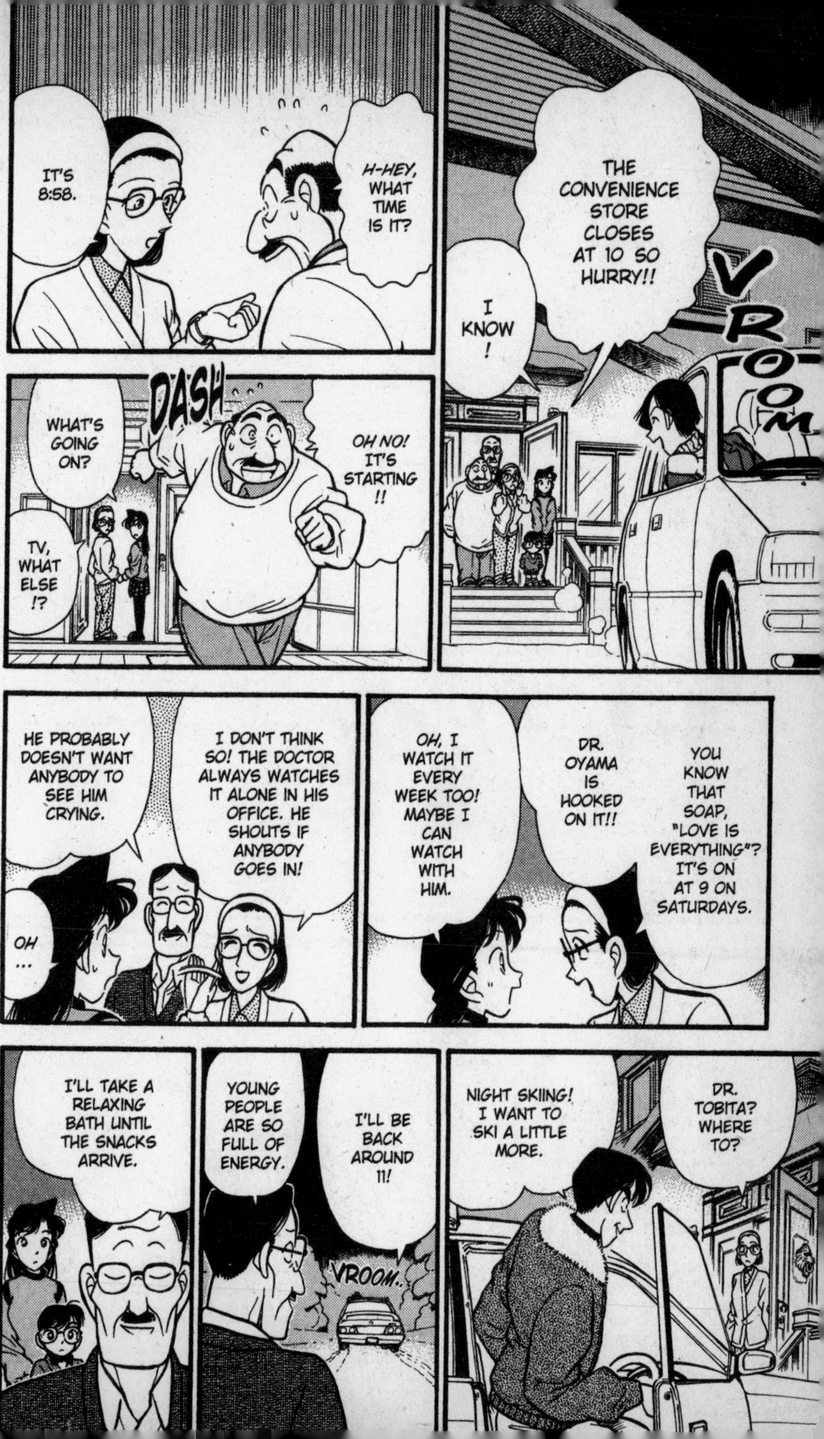
THE CONVENIENCE STORE CLOSES AT 10 SO HURRY!!
VROOM
I KNOW!
H-HEY, WHAT TIME IS IT?
IT'S 8:58.
OH NO! IT'S STARTING!!
DASH
WHAT'S GOING ON?
TV, WHAT ELSE!?
YOU KNOW THAT SOAP, "LOVE IS EVERYTHING"? IT'S ON AT 9 ON SATURDAYS.
DR. OYAMA IS HOOKED ON IT!!
OH, I WATCH IT EVERY WEEK TOO! MAYBE I CAN WATCH WITH HIM.
I DON'T THINK SO! THE DOCTOR ALWAYS WATCHES IT ALONE IN HIS OFFICE. HE SHOUTS IF ANYBODY GOES IN!
HE PROBABLY DOESN'T WANT ANYBODY TO SEE HIM CRYING.
OH...
DR. TOBITA? WHERE TO?
NIGHT SKIING! I WANT TO SKI A LITTLE MORE.
I'LL BE BACK AROUND 11!
VROOM..
YOUNG PEOPLE ARE SO FULL OF ENERGY.
I'LL TAKE A RELAXING BATH UNTIL THE SNACKS ARRIVE.

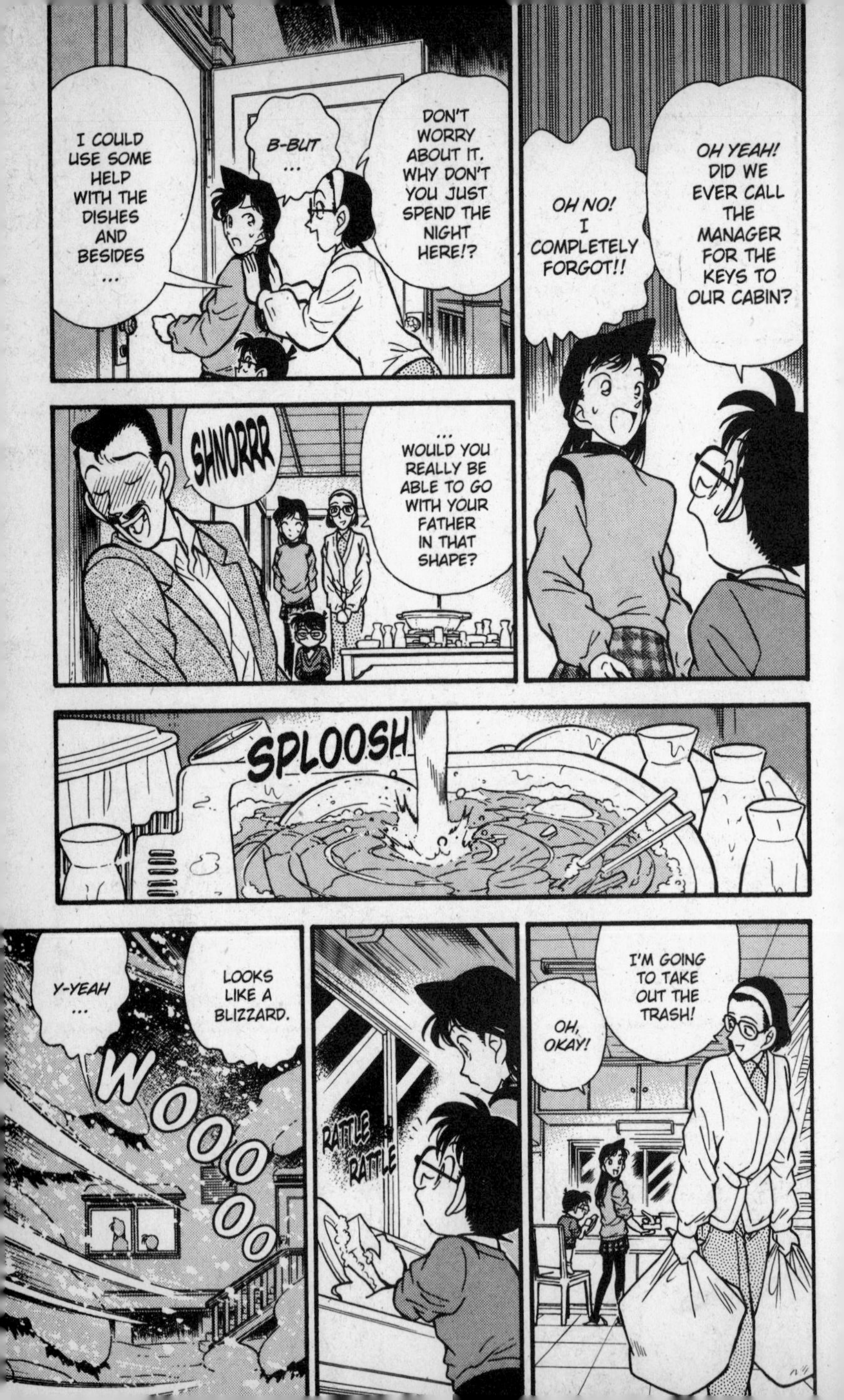
OH YEAH! DID WE EVER CALL THE MANAGER FOR THE KEYS TO OUR CABIN?
OH NO! I COMPLETELY FORGOT!!
DON'T WORRY ABOUT IT. WHY DON'T YOU JUST SPEND THE NIGHT HERE!?
B-BUT ...
I COULD USE SOME HELP WITH THE DISHES AND BESIDES ...
... WOULD YOU REALLY BE ABLE TO GO WITH YOUR FATHER IN THAT SHAPE?
SHNORRR
SPLOOSH
I'M GOING TO TAKE OUT THE TRASH!
OH, OKAY!
RATTLE RATTLE
LOOKS LIKE A BLIZZARD.
Y-YEAH ...
WOOOOO

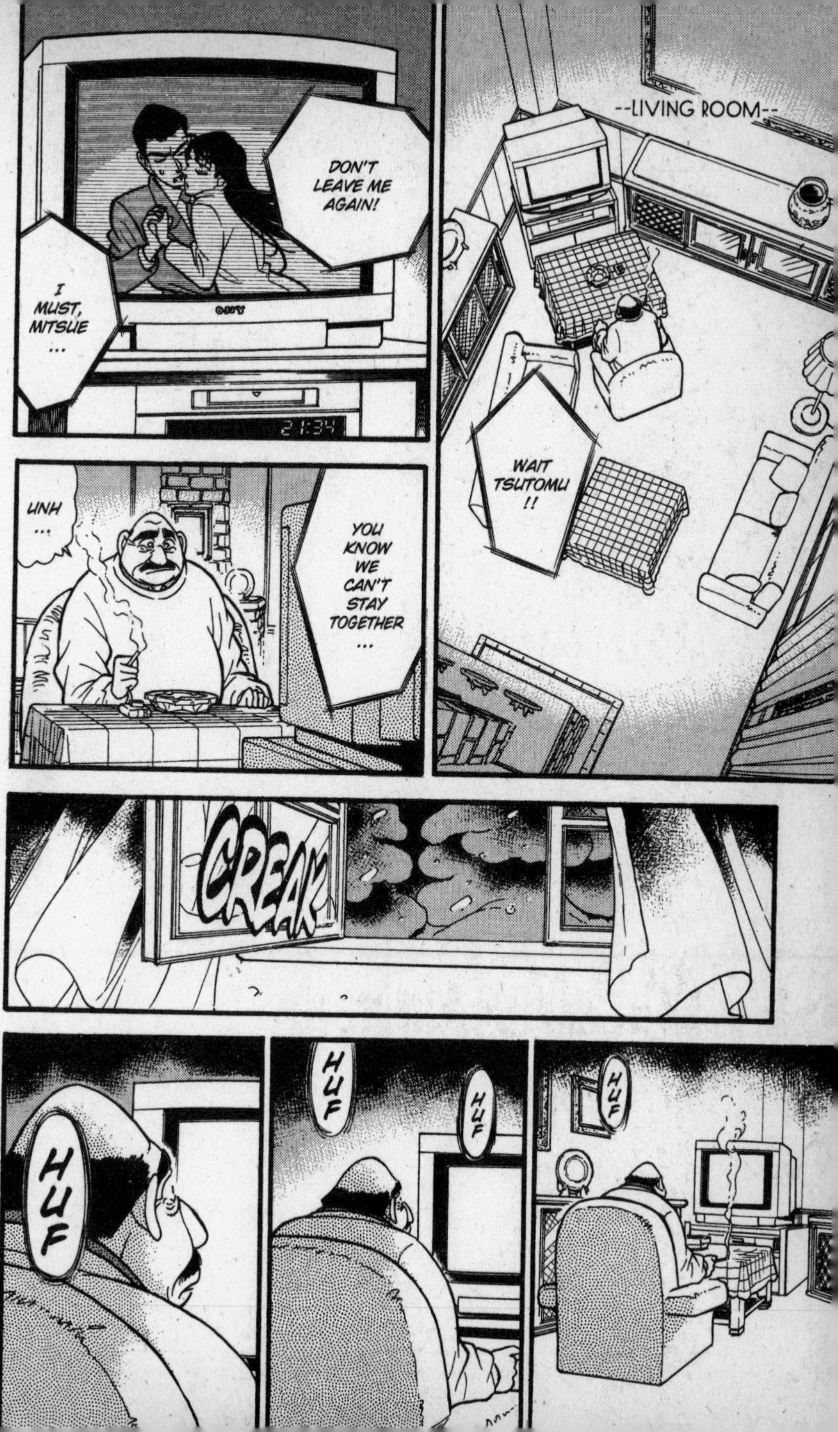
--LIVING ROOM--
WAIT TSUTOMU!!
DON'T LEAVE ME AGAIN!
I MUST, MITSUE ...
21:34
YOU KNOW WE CAN'T STAY TOGETHER ...
UNH ...
CREAK
HUF
HUF
HUF

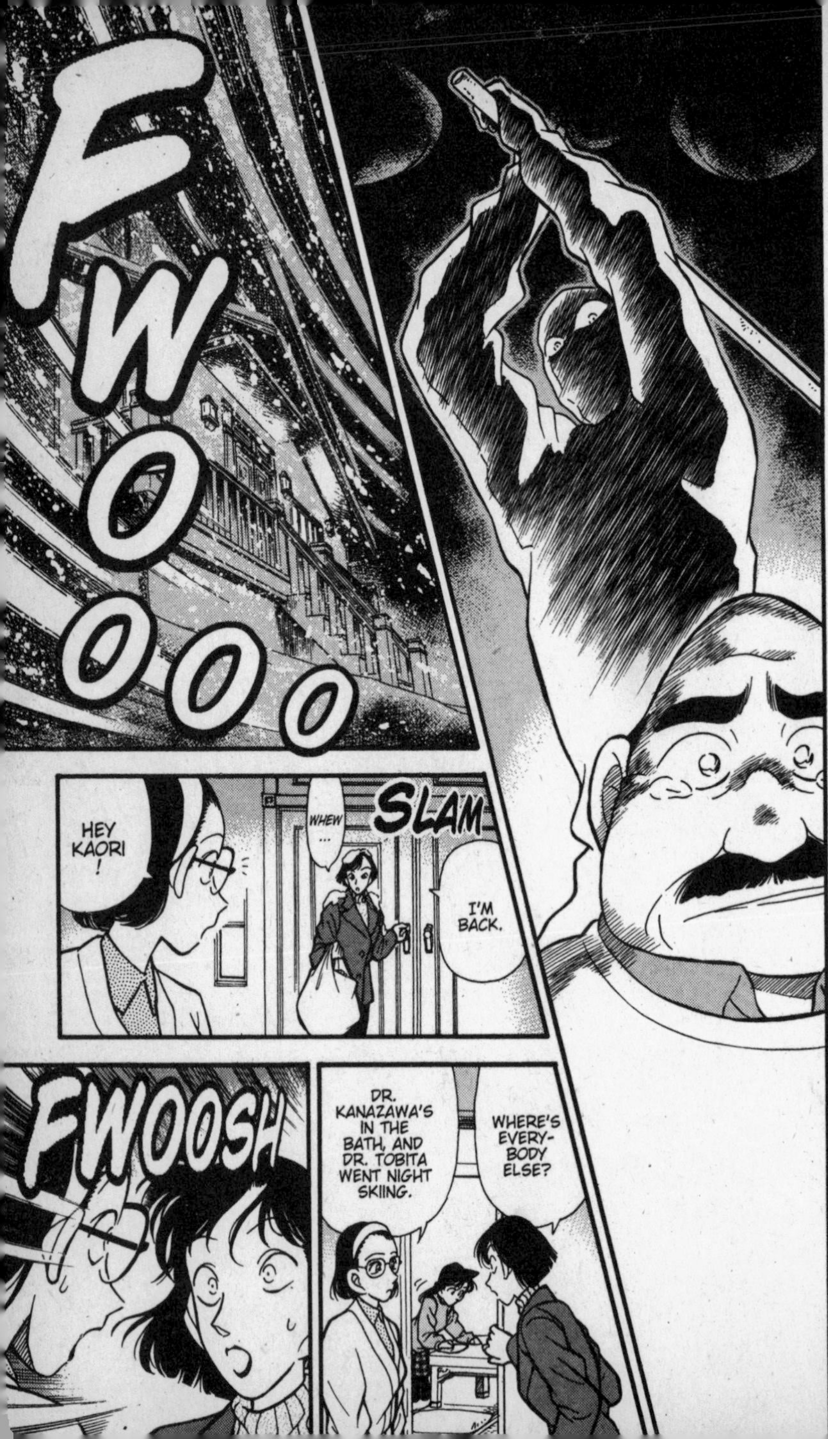
FWOOOO
SLAM
WHEW ...
I'M BACK.
HEY KAORI!
WHERE'S EVERYBODY ELSE?
DR. KANAZAWA'S IN THE BATH, AND DR. TOBITA WENT NIGHT SKIING.
FWOOSH

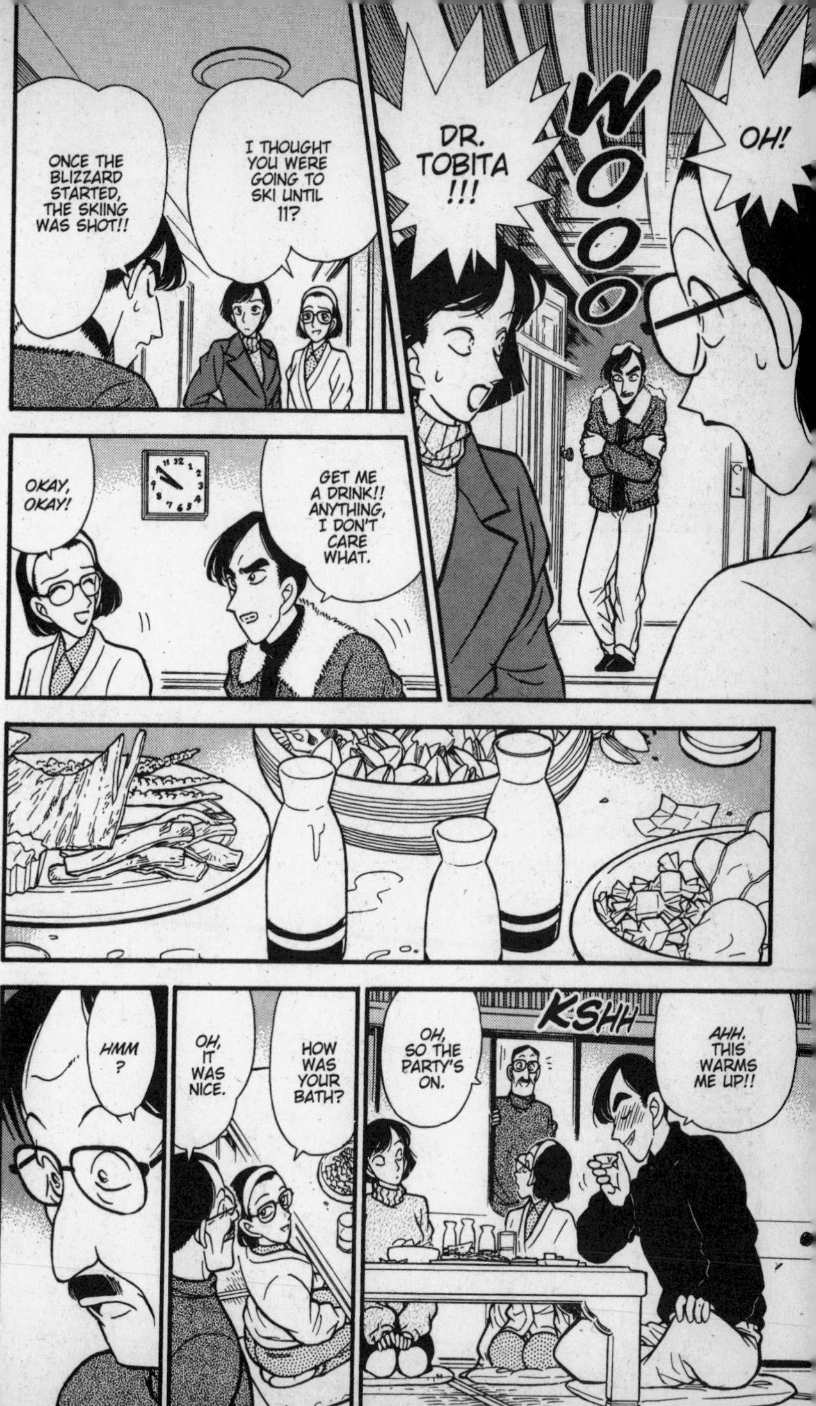
OH!
WOOO
DR. TOBITA!!!
I THOUGHT YOU WERE GOING TO SKI UNTIL 11?
ONCE THE BLIZZARD STARTED, THE SKIING WAS SHOT!!
GET ME A DRINK!! ANYTHING, I DON'T CARE WHAT.
OKAY, OKAY!
AHH. THIS WARMS ME UP!!
KSHH
OH, SO THE PARTY'S ON.
HOW WAS YOUR BATH?
OH, IT WAS NICE.
HMM?

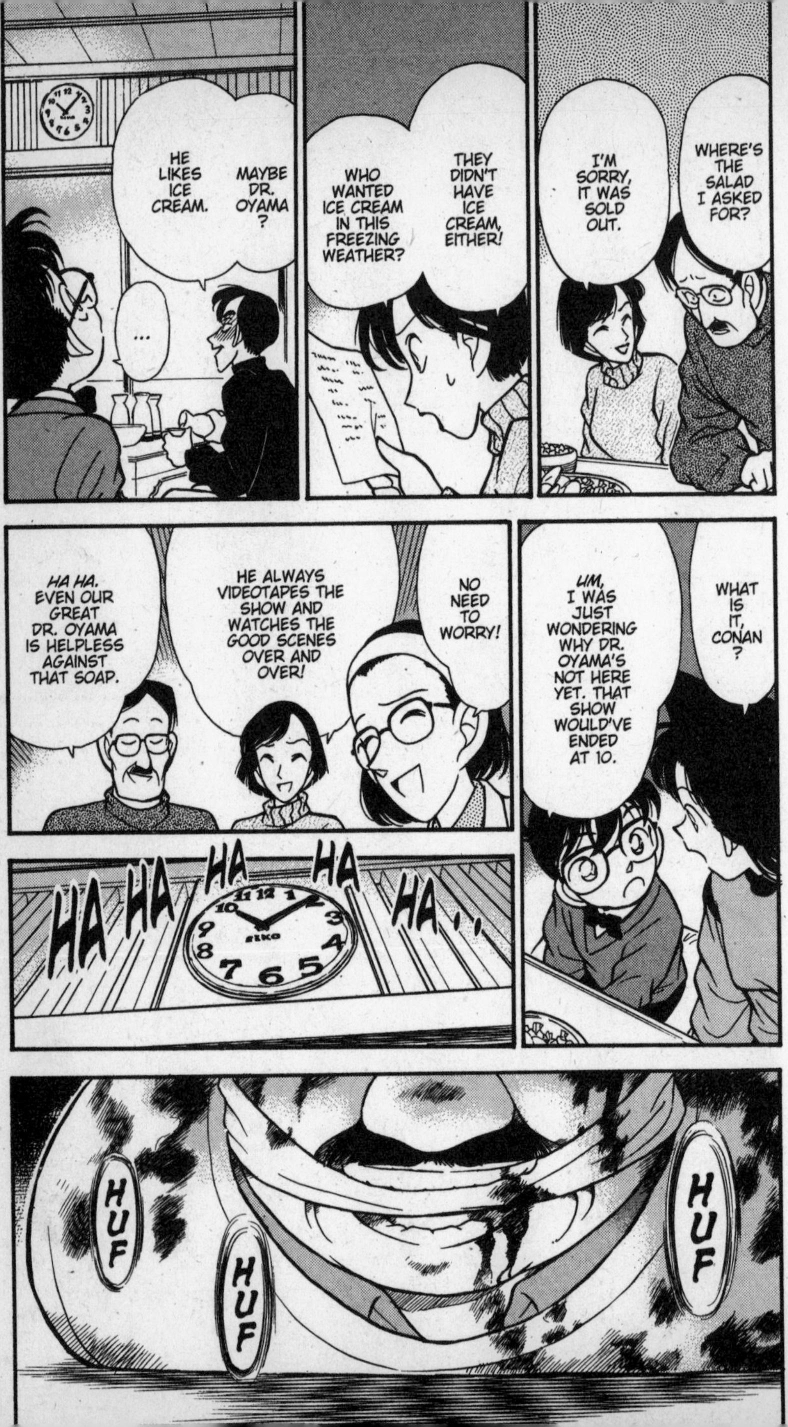
WHERE'S THE SALAD I ASKED FOR?
I'M SORRY, IT WAS SOLD OUT.
THEY DIDN'T HAVE ICE CREAM, EITHER!
WHO WANTED ICE CREAM IN THIS FREEZING WEATHER?
MAYBE DR. OYAMA?
HE LIKES ICE CREAM.
...
WHAT IS IT, CONAN?
UM, I WAS JUST WONDERING WHY DR. OYAMA'S NOT HERE YET. THAT SHOW WOULD'VE ENDED AT 10.
NO NEED TO WORRY!
HE ALWAYS VIDEOTAPES THE SHOW AND WATCHES THE GOOD SCENES OVER AND OVER!
HA HA. EVEN OUR GREAT DR. OYAMA IS HELPLESS AGAINST THAT SOAP.
HA HA HA HA HA..
HUF
HUF
HUF

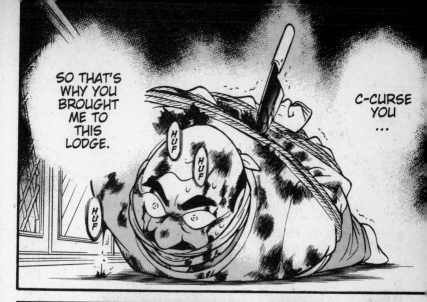

C-CURSE YOU ...
HUF
HUF
SO THAT'S WHY YOU BROUGHT ME TO THIS LODGE.
HUF
B-BUT YOU WON'T HAVE YOUR WAY.
THE DETEC-TIVE'S HERE ...
HUF
HIF
HUF
THE GREAT DETECTIVE RICHARD MOORE!!
H-HE'LL KNOW ...
... CUZ I'LL LEAVE HIM ...
HIF
HIF
HUF
HIF
HUF
... THIS MESSAGE !!!
WHAT? RICHARD MOORE?

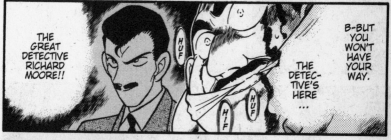

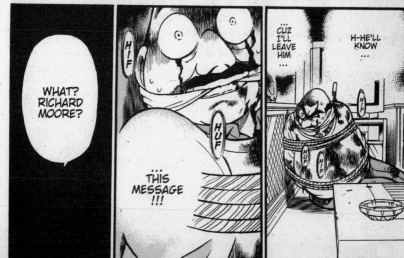

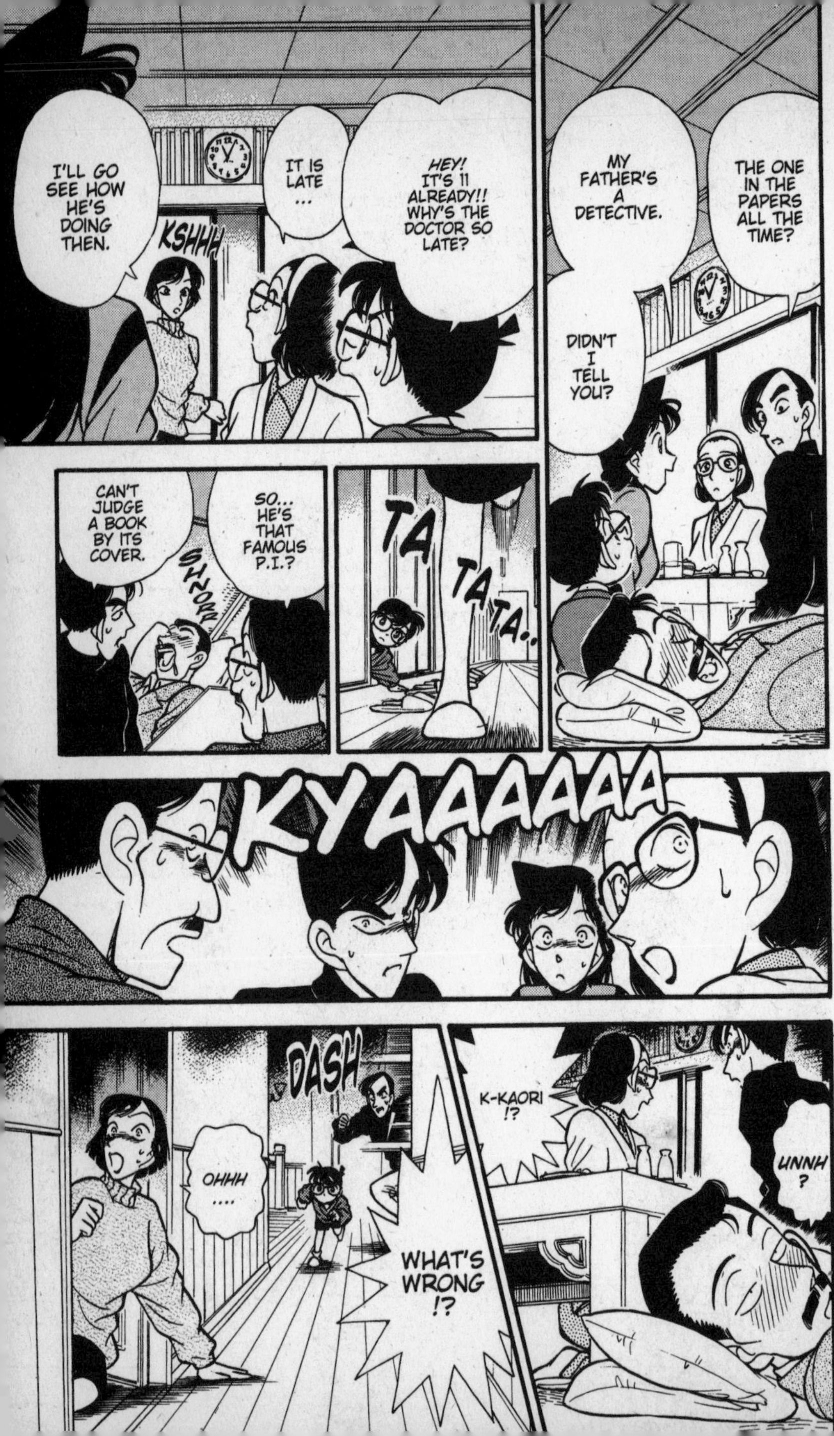
THE ONE IN THE PAPERS ALL THE TIME?
MY FATHER'S A DETECTIVE.
DIDN'T I TELL YOU?
HEY! IT'S 11 ALREADY!! WHY'S THE DOCTOR SO LATE?
IT IS LATE ...
KSHHH
I'LL GO SEE HOW HE'S DOING THEN.
TA
TA
TA..
SO... HE'S THAT FAMOUS P.I.?
CAN'T JUDGE A BOOK BY ITS COVER.
SHNORR
KYAAAAAA
K-KAORI !?
UNNH ?
WHAT'S WRONG !?
DASH
OHHH ....

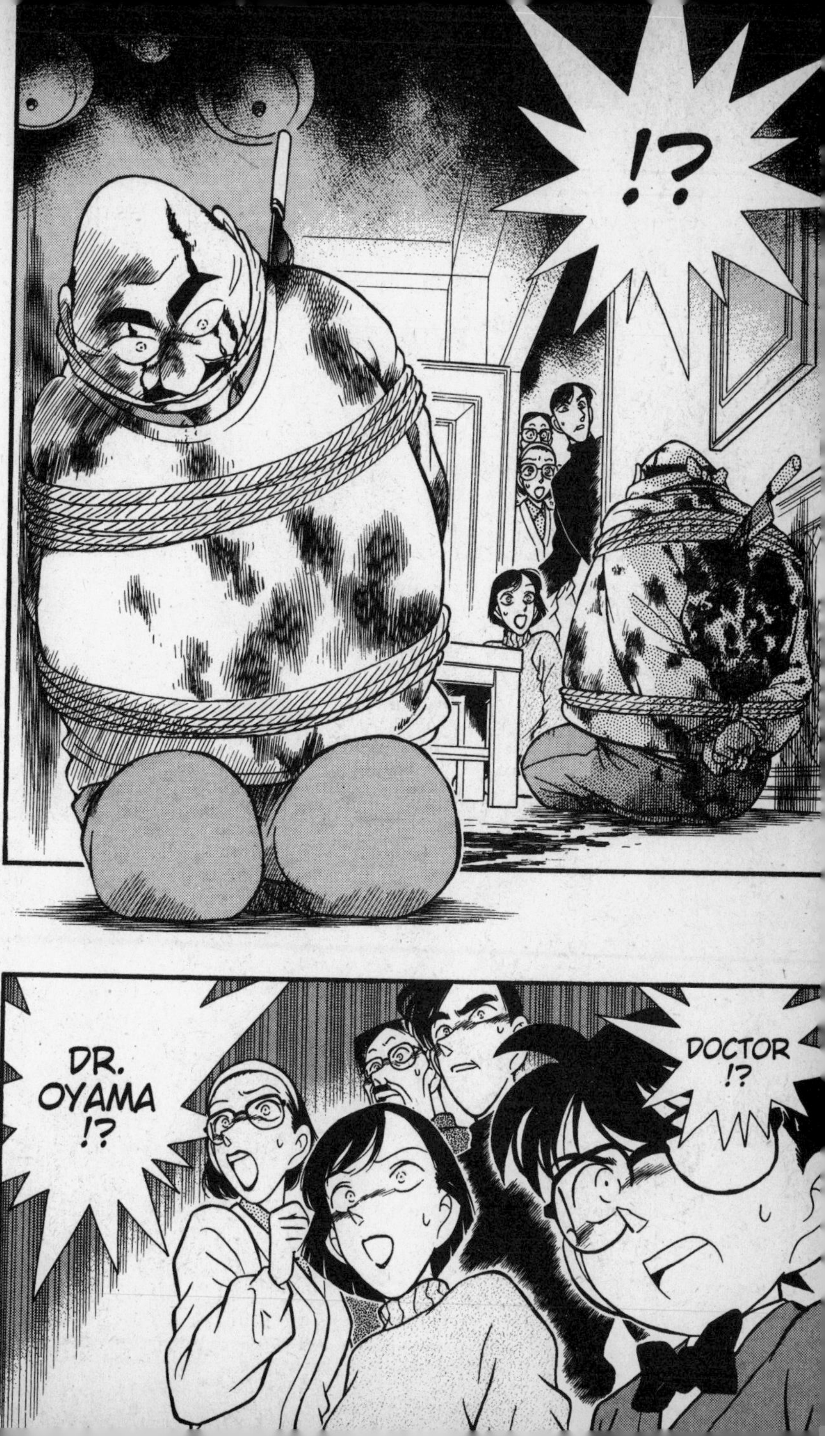
!?
DOCTOR !?
DR. OYAMA !?

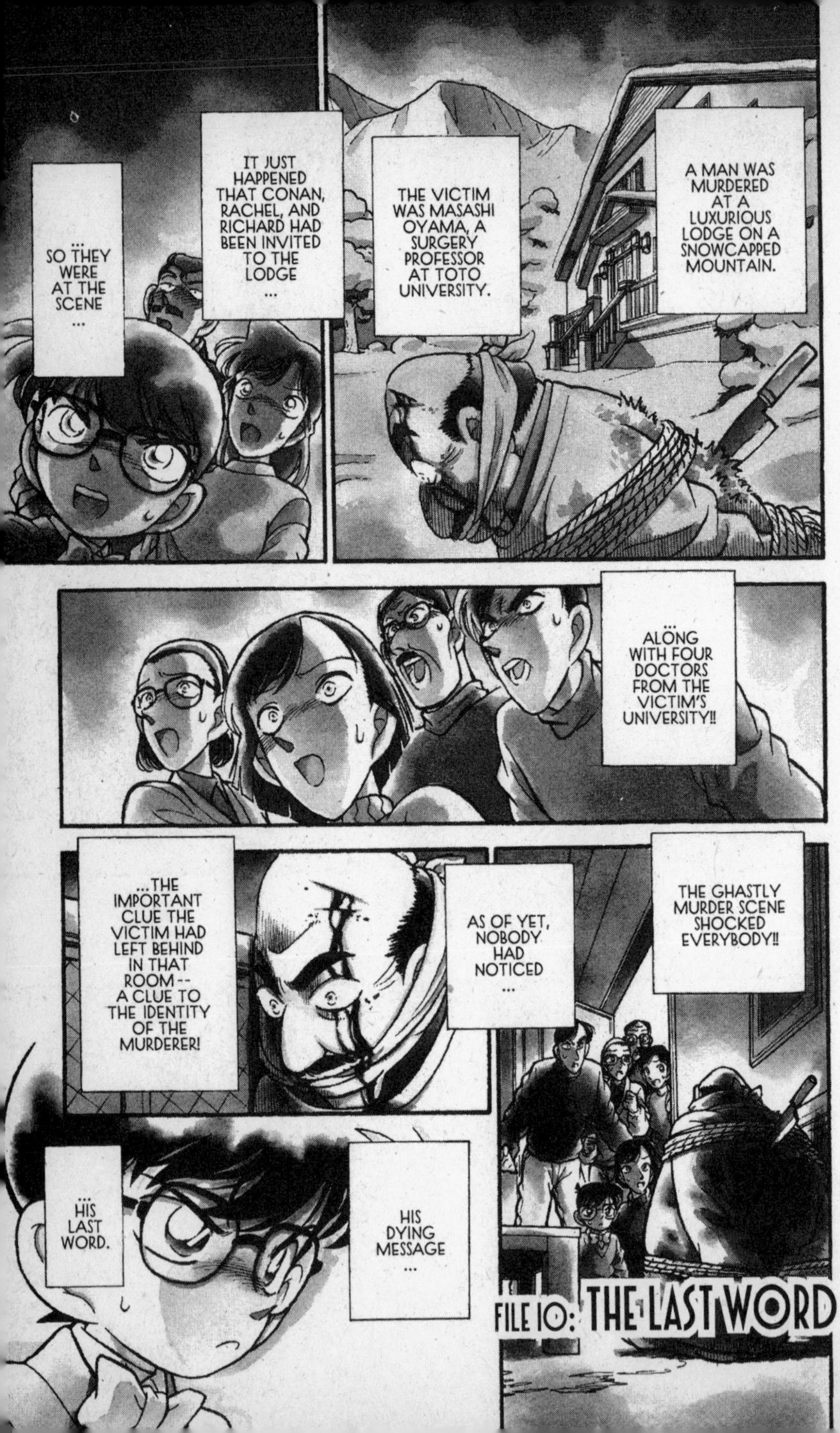
A MAN WAS MURDERED AT A LUXURIOUS LODGE ON A SNOWCAPPED MOUNTAIN.
THE VICTIM WAS MASASHI OYAMA, A SURGERY PROFESSOR AT TOTO UNIVERSITY.
IT JUST HAPPENED THAT CONAN, RACHEL, AND RICHARD HAD BEEN INVITED TO THE LODGE ...
... SO THEY WERE AT THE SCENE ...
... ALONG WITH FOUR DOCTORS FROM THE VICTIM'S UNIVERSITY!!
THE GHASTLY MURDER SCENE SHOCKED EVERYBODY!!
FILE 10: THE LAST WORD
AS OF YET, NOBODY HAD NOTICED ...
...THE IMPORTANT CLUE THE VICTIM HAD LEFT BEHIND IN THAT ROOM -- A CLUE TO THE IDENTITY OF THE MURDERER!
HIS DYING MESSAGE ...
... HIS LAST WORD.

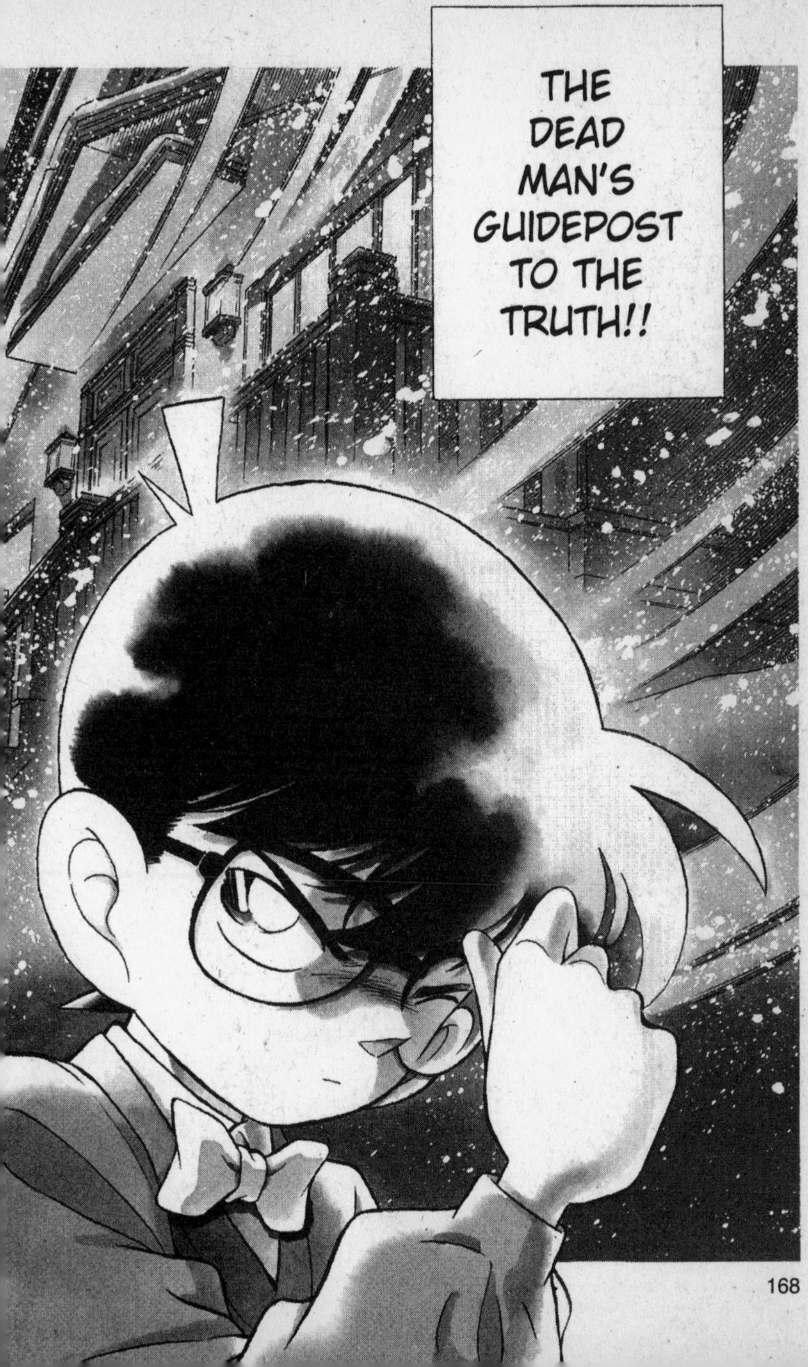
THE DEAD MAN'S GUIDEPOST TO THE TRUTH!!

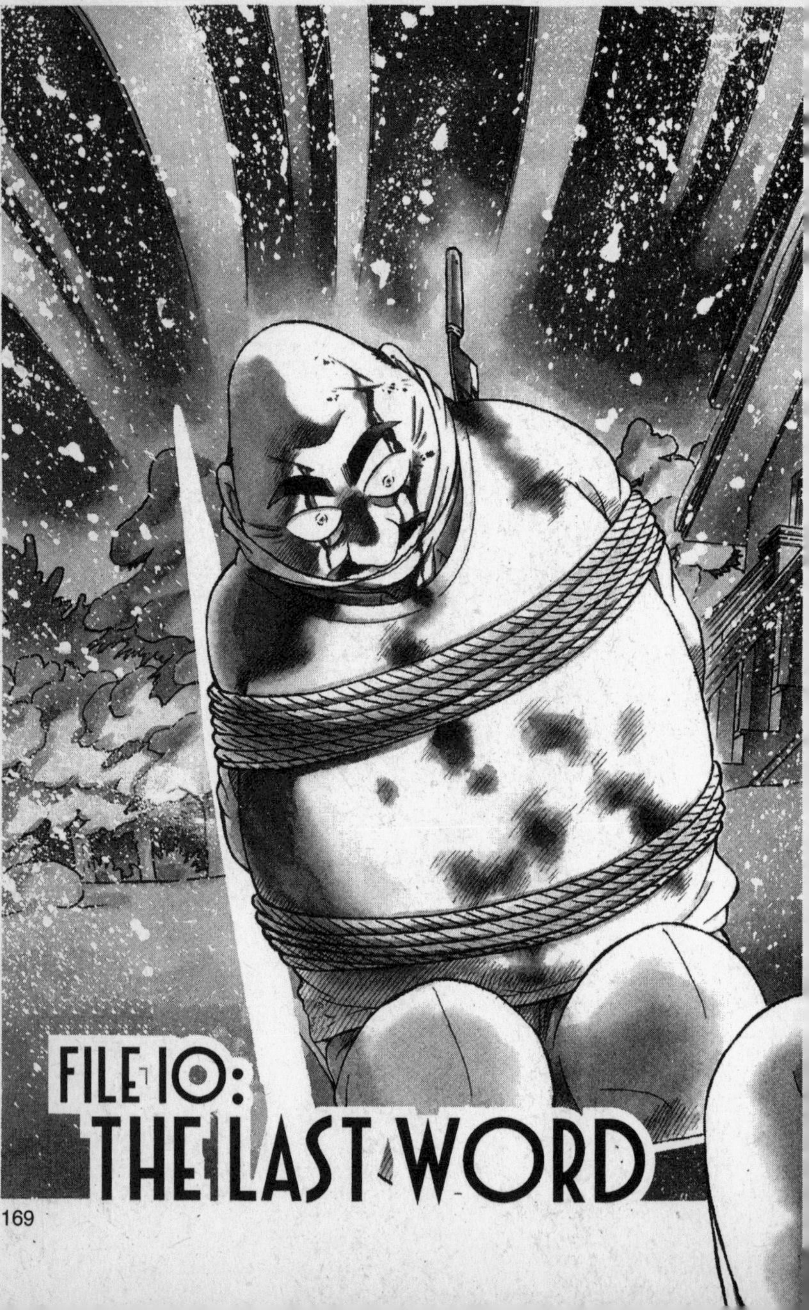
FILE 10:
THE LAST WORD

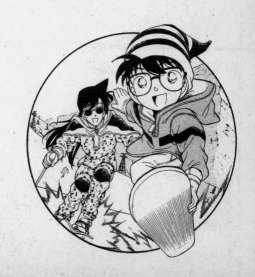

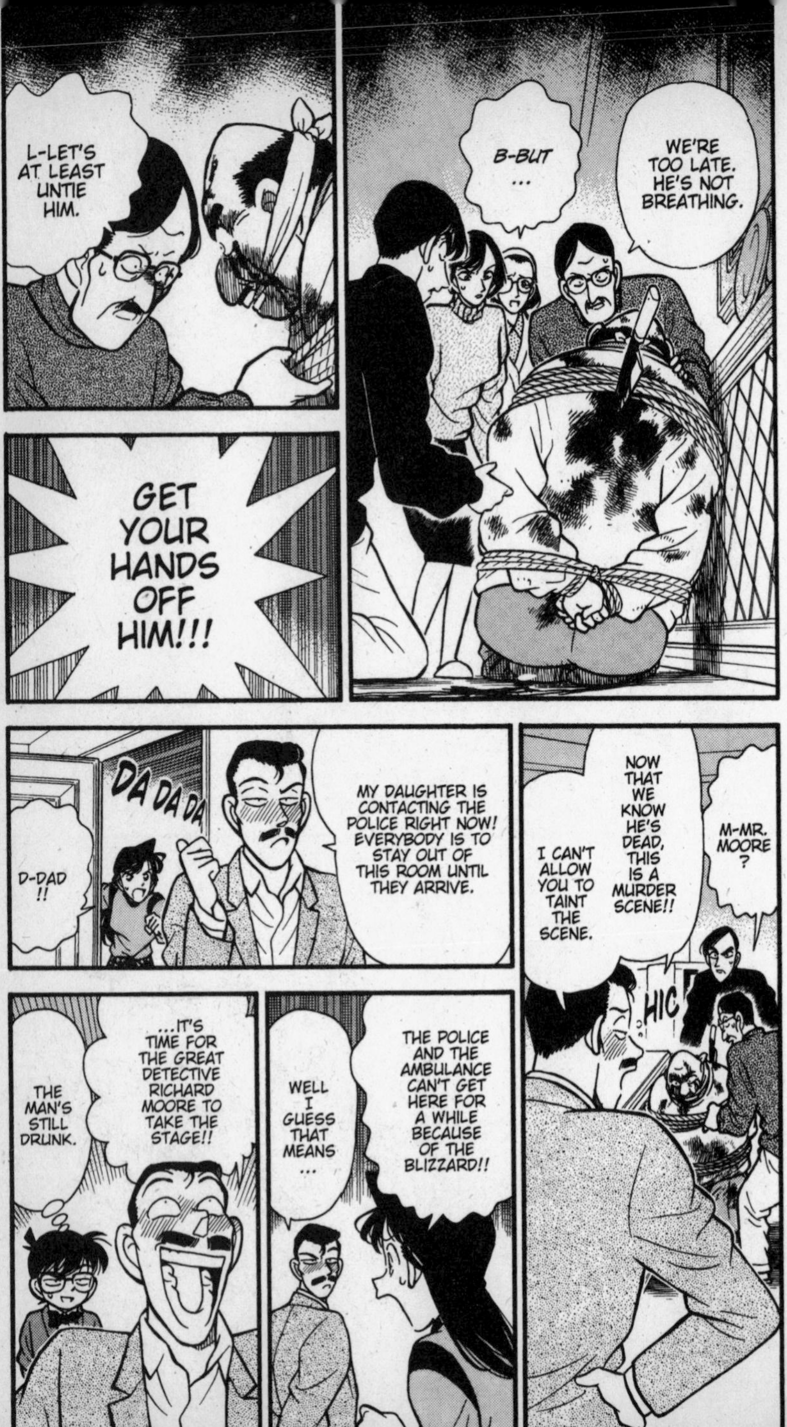
WE'RE TOO LATE. HE'S NOT BREATHING.
B-BUT ...
L-LET'S AT LEAST UNTIE HIM.
GET YOUR HANDS OFF HIM!!!
M-MR. MOORE?
NOW THAT WE KNOW HE'S DEAD, THIS IS A MURDER SCENE!!
I CAN'T ALLOW YOU TO TAINT THE SCENE.
HIC
MY DAUGHTER IS CONTACTING THE POLICE RIGHT NOW! EVERYBODY IS TO STAY OUT OF THIS ROOM UNTIL THEY ARRIVE.
DA DA DA
D-DAD!!
THE POLICE AND THE AMBULANCE CAN'T GET HERE FOR A WHILE BECAUSE OF THE BLIZZARD!!
WELL I GUESS THAT MEANS ...
...IT'S TIME FOR THE GREAT DETECTIVE RICHARD MOORE TO TAKE THE STAGE!!
THE MAN'S STILL DRUNK.

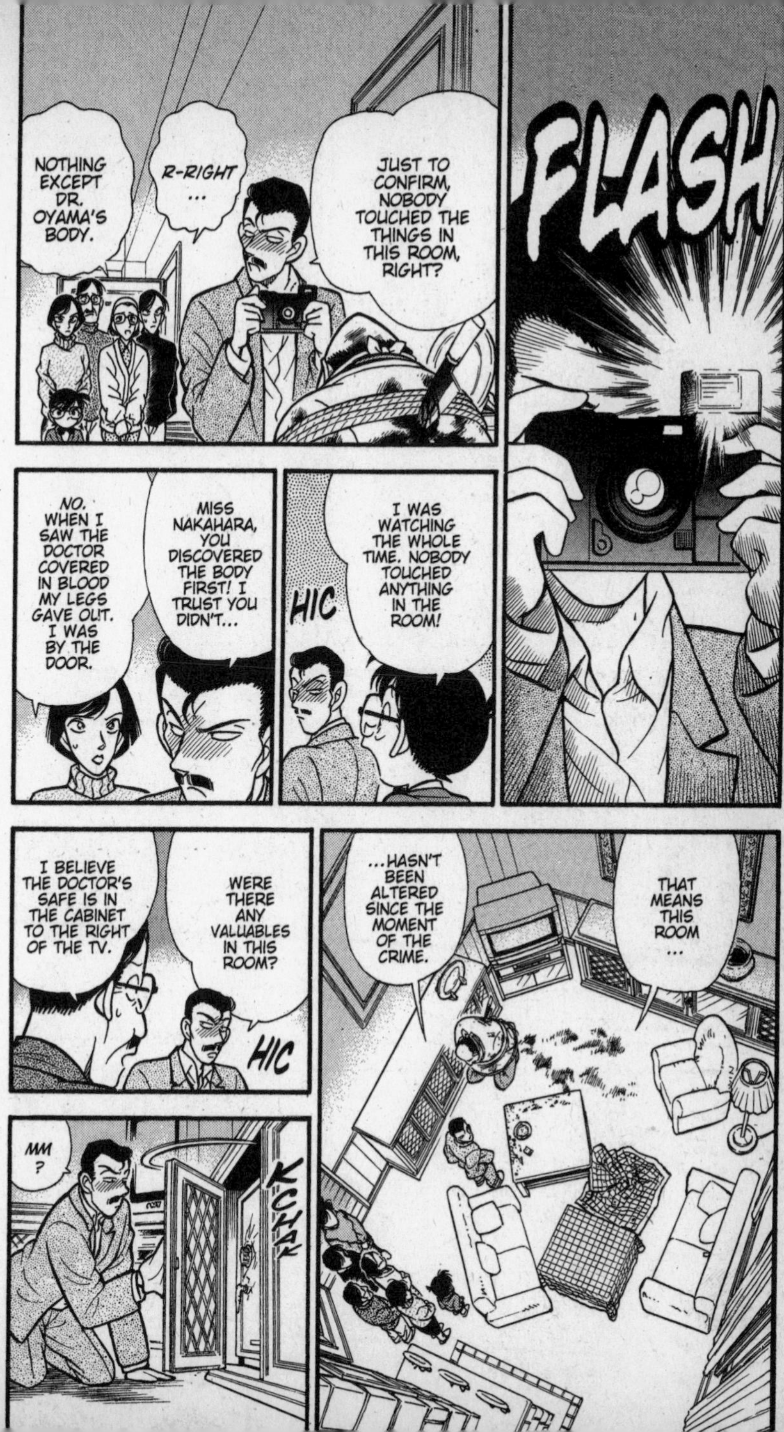
FLASH
JUST TO CONFIRM, NOBODY TOUCHED THE THINGS IN THIS ROOM, RIGHT?
R-RIGHT...
NOTHING EXCEPT DR. OYAMA'S BODY.
I WAS WATCHING THE WHOLE TIME. NOBODY TOUCHED ANYTHING IN THE ROOM!
HIC
MISS NAKAHARA, YOU DISCOVERED THE BODY FIRST! I TRUST YOU DIDN'T...
NO. WHEN I SAW THE DOCTOR COVERED IN BLOOD MY LEGS GAVE OUT. I WAS BY THE DOOR.
THAT MEANS THIS ROOM...
...HASN'T BEEN ALTERED SINCE THE MOMENT OF THE CRIME.
WERE THERE ANY VALUABLES IN THIS ROOM?
HIC
I BELIEVE THE DOCTOR'S SAFE IS IN THE CABINET TO THE RIGHT OF THE TV.
KCHAK
MM?

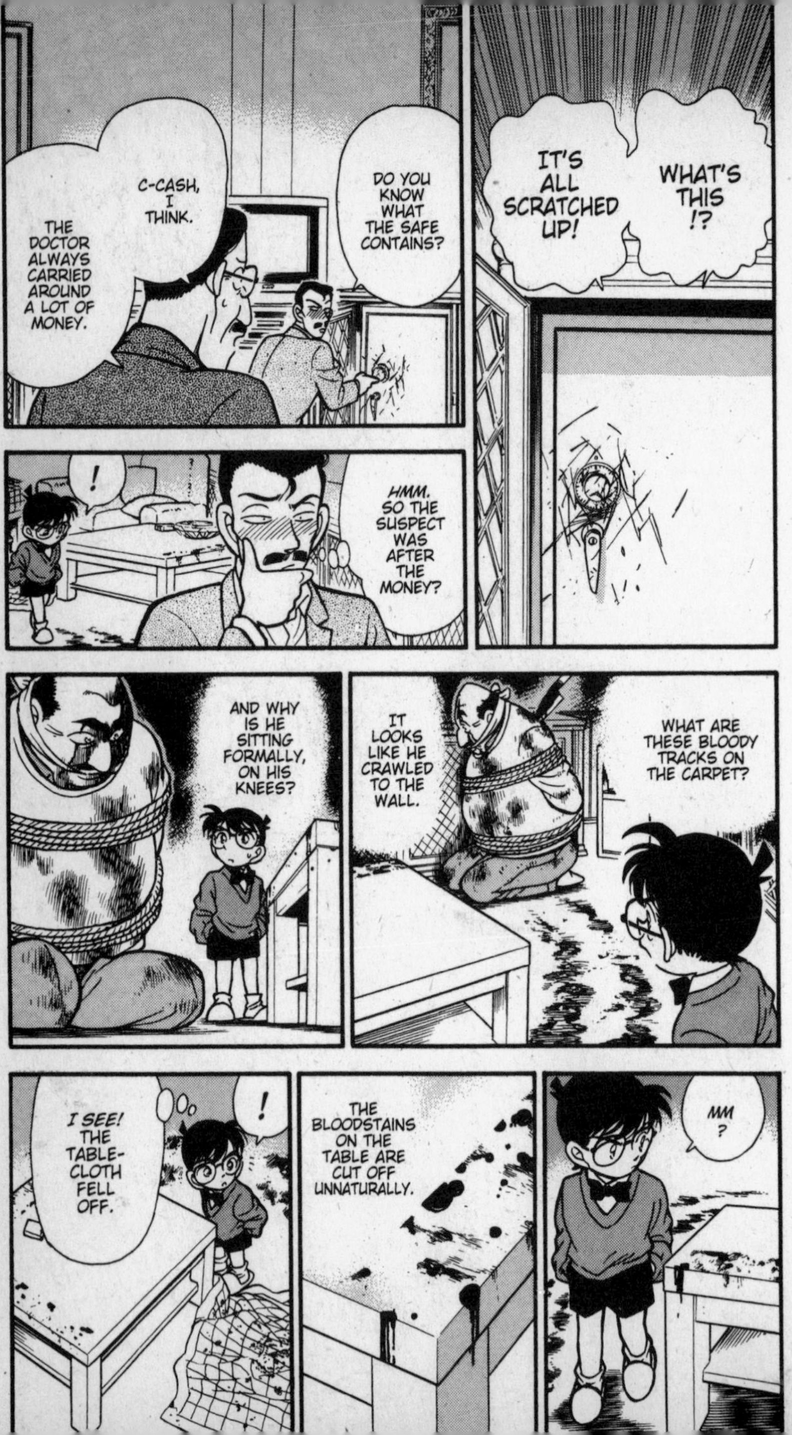
WHAT'S THIS !?
IT'S ALL SCRATCHED UP!
DO YOU KNOW WHAT THE SAFE CONTAINS?
C-CASH, I THINK.
THE DOCTOR ALWAYS CARRIED AROUND A LOT OF MONEY.
HMM. SO THE SUSPECT WAS AFTER THE MONEY?
!
WHAT ARE THESE BLOODY TRACKS ON THE CARPET?
IT LOOKS LIKE HE CRAWLED TO THE WALL.
AND WHY IS HE SITTING FORMALLY, ON HIS KNEES?
MM ?
THE BLOODSTAINS ON THE TABLE ARE CUT OFF UNNATURALLY.
!
I SEE! THE TABLE-CLOTH FELL OFF.

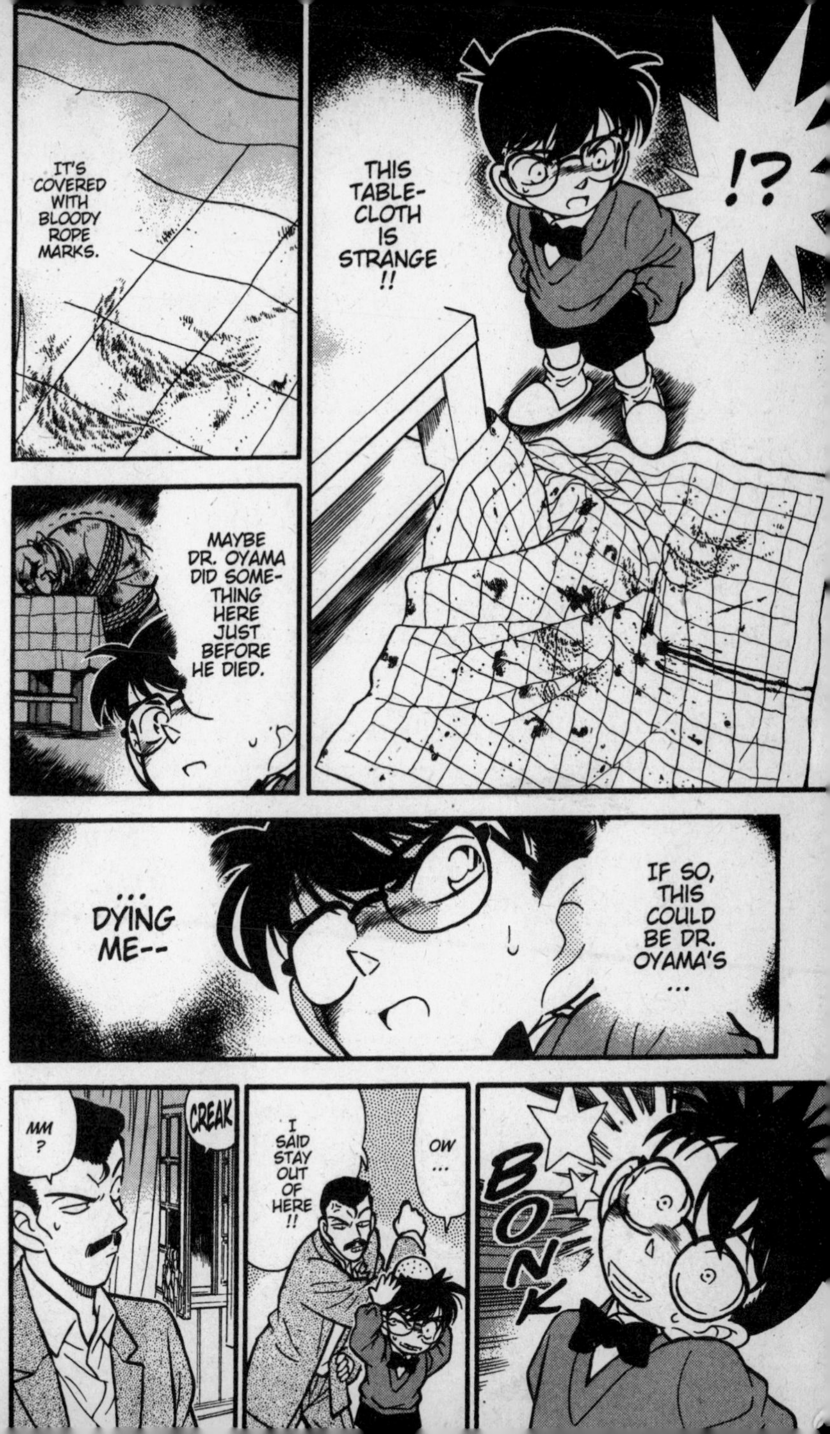
!?
THIS TABLE-CLOTH IS STRANGE!!
IT'S COVERED WITH BLOODY ROPE MARKS.
MAYBE DR. OYAMA DID SOME-THING HERE JUST BEFORE HE DIED.
IF SO, THIS COULD BE DR. OYAMA'S...
...DYING ME--
BONK
OW...
I SAID STAY OUT OF HERE!!
CREAK
MM?

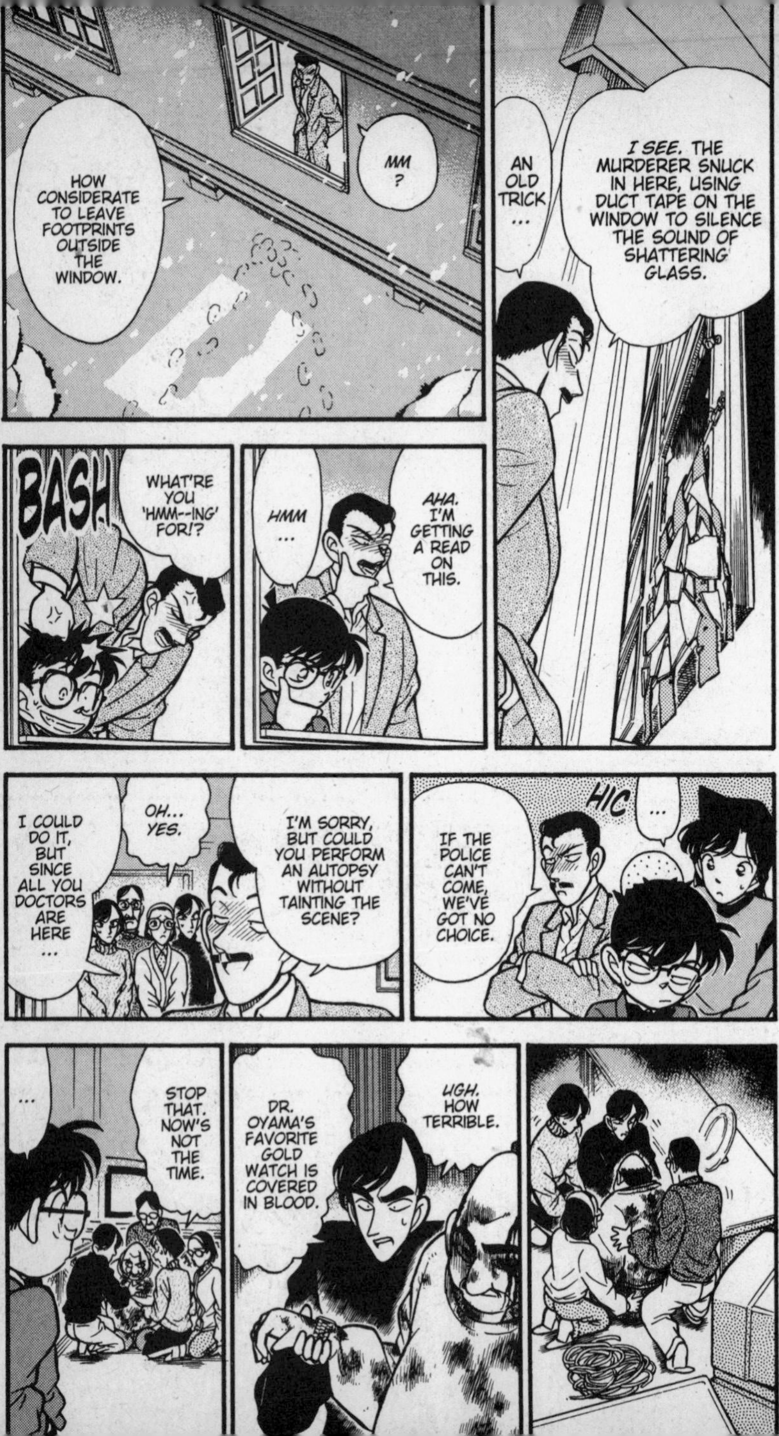
I SEE. THE MURDERER SNUCK IN HERE, USING DUCT TAPE ON THE WINDOW TO SILENCE THE SOUND OF SHATTERING GLASS.
AN OLD TRICK ...
MM ?
HOW CONSIDERATE TO LEAVE FOOTPRINTS OUTSIDE THE WINDOW.
AHA. I'M GETTING A READ ON THIS.
HMM ...
BASH
WHAT'RE YOU 'HMM--ING' FOR!?
...
HIC
IF THE POLICE CAN'T COME, WE'VE GOT NO CHOICE.
I'M SORRY, BUT COULD YOU PERFORM AN AUTOPSY WITHOUT TAINTING THE SCENE?
OH... YES.
I COULD DO IT, BUT SINCE ALL YOU DOCTORS ARE HERE ...
UGH. HOW TERRIBLE.
DR. OYAMA'S FAVORITE GOLD WATCH IS COVERED IN BLOOD.
STOP THAT. NOW'S NOT THE TIME.
...

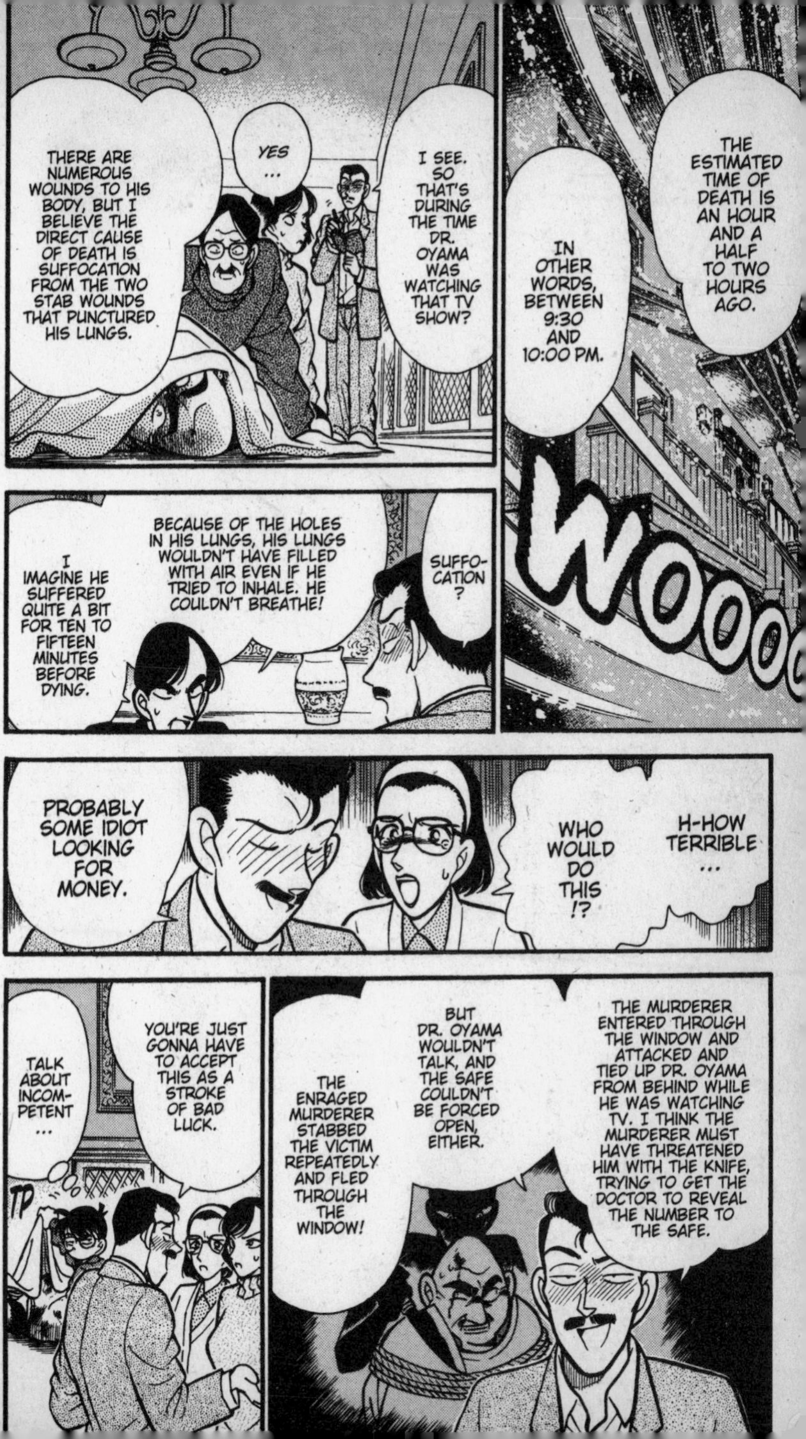
THE ESTIMATED TIME OF DEATH IS AN HOUR AND A HALF TO TWO HOURS AGO.
IN OTHER WORDS, BETWEEN 9:30 AND 10:00 PM.
WOOOO
I SEE. SO THAT'S DURING THE TIME DR. OYAMA WAS WATCHING THAT TV SHOW?
YES ...
THERE ARE NUMEROUS WOUNDS TO HIS BODY, BUT I BELIEVE THE DIRECT CAUSE OF DEATH IS SUFFOCATION FROM THE TWO STAB WOUNDS THAT PUNCTURED HIS LUNGS.
SUFFO-CATION?
BECAUSE OF THE HOLES IN HIS LUNGS, HIS LUNGS WOULDN'T HAVE FILLED WITH AIR EVEN IF HE TRIED TO INHALE. HE COULDN'T BREATHE!
I IMAGINE HE SUFFERED QUITE A BIT FOR TEN TO FIFTEEN MINUTES BEFORE DYING.
H-HOW TERRIBLE ...
WHO WOULD DO THIS !?
PROBABLY SOME IDIOT LOOKING FOR MONEY.
THE MURDERER ENTERED THROUGH THE WINDOW AND ATTACKED AND TIED UP DR. OYAMA FROM BEHIND WHILE HE WAS WATCHING TV. I THINK THE MURDERER MUST HAVE THREATENED HIM WITH THE KNIFE, TRYING TO GET THE DOCTOR TO REVEAL THE NUMBER TO THE SAFE.
BUT DR. OYAMA WOULDN'T TALK, AND THE SAFE COULDN'T BE FORCED OPEN, EITHER.
THE ENRAGED MURDERER STABBED THE VICTIM REPEATEDLY AND FLED THROUGH THE WINDOW!
YOU'RE JUST GONNA HAVE TO ACCEPT THIS AS A STROKE OF BAD LUCK.
TALK ABOUT INCOM-PETENT ...
TP

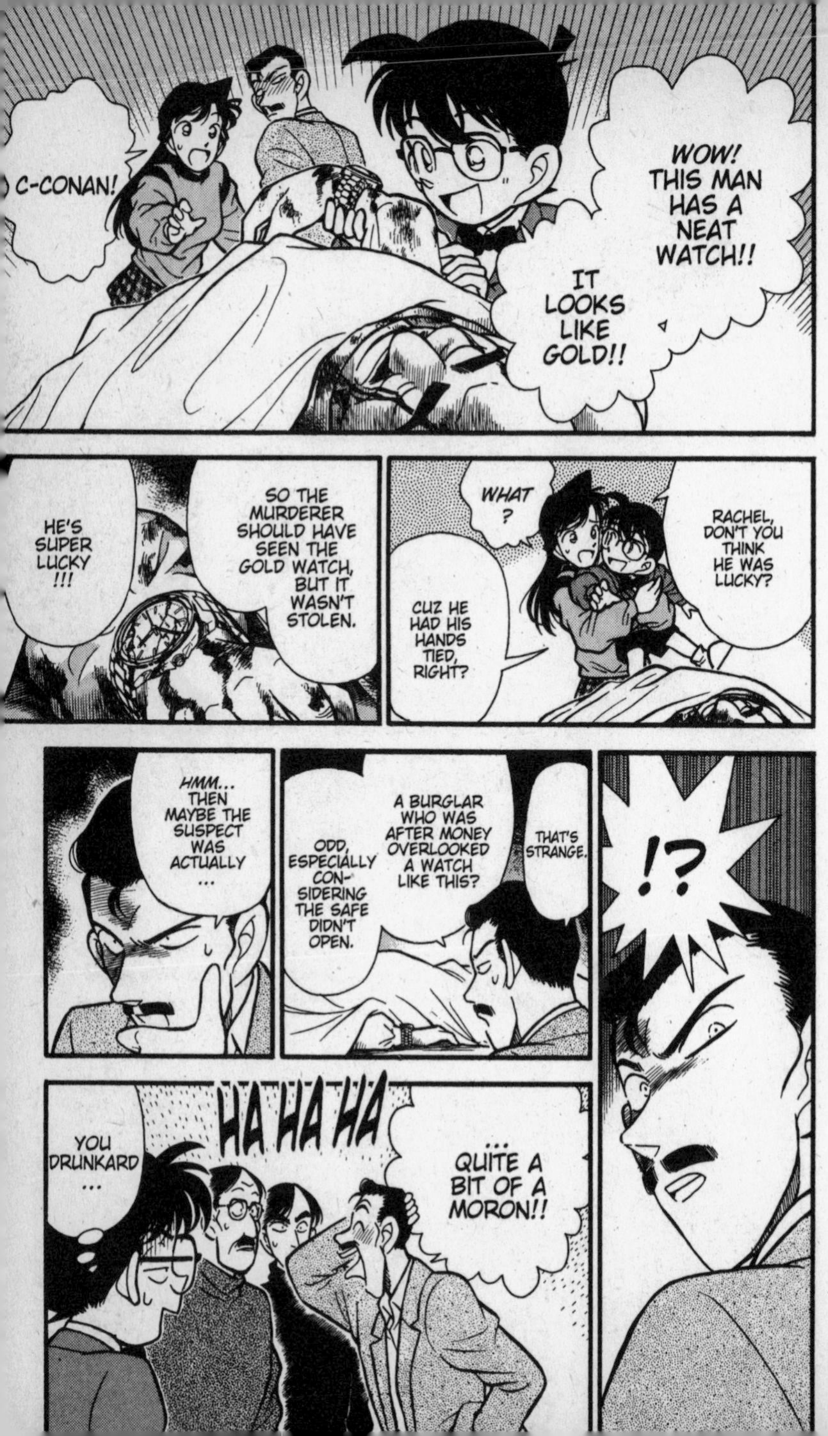
WOW! THIS MAN HAS A NEAT WATCH!!
IT LOOKS LIKE GOLD!!
C-CONAN!
RACHEL, DON'T YOU THINK HE WAS LUCKY?
WHAT?
CUZ HE HAD HIS HANDS TIED, RIGHT?
SO THE MURDERER SHOULD HAVE SEEN THE GOLD WATCH, BUT IT WASN'T STOLEN.
HE'S SUPER LUCKY!!!
!?
THAT'S STRANGE.
A BURGLAR WHO WAS AFTER MONEY OVERLOOKED A WATCH LIKE THIS?
ODD, ESPECIALLY CON-SIDERING THE SAFE DIDN'T OPEN.
HMM... THEN MAYBE THE SUSPECT WAS ACTUALLY ...
HA HA HA
... QUITE A BIT OF A MORON!!
YOU DRUNKARD ...

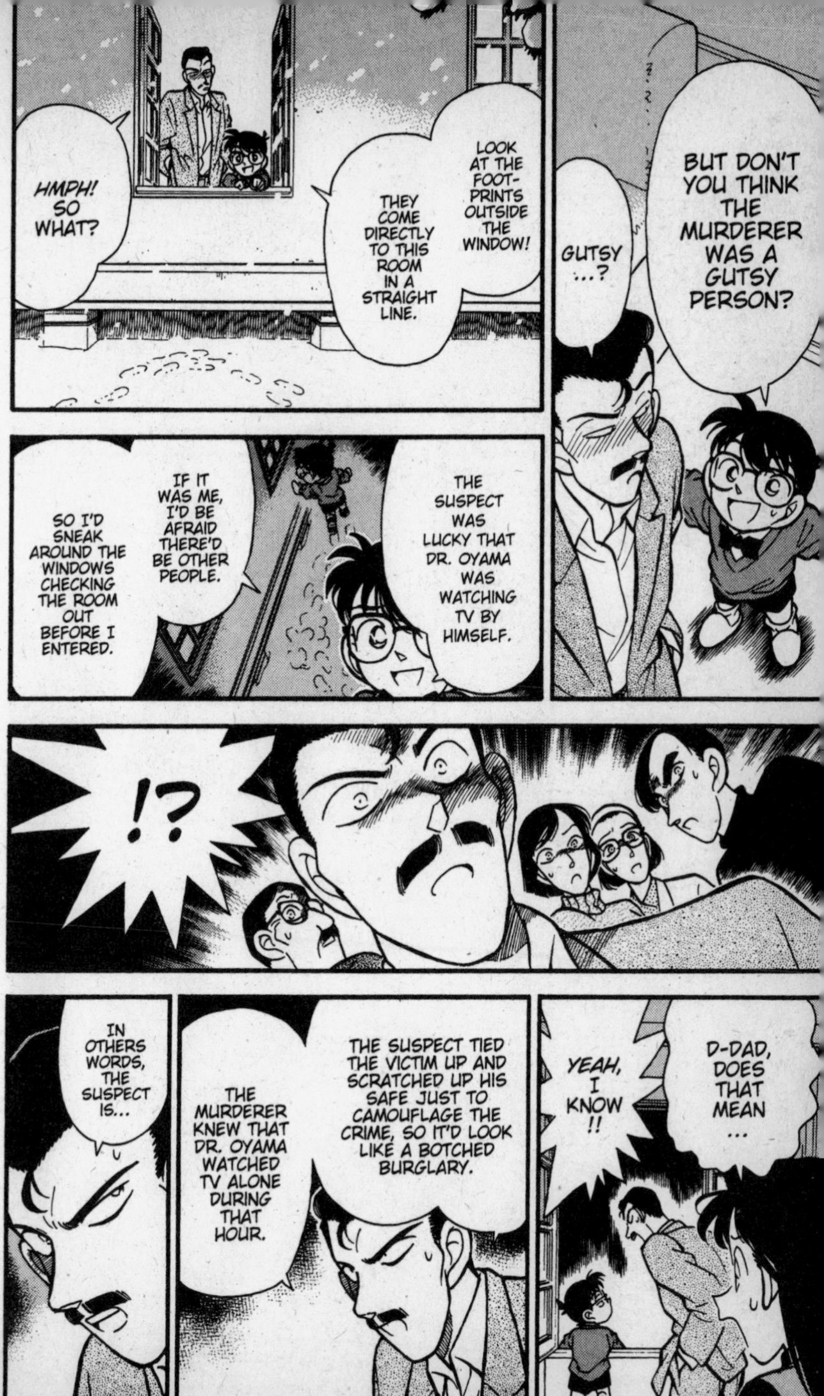
BUT DON'T YOU THINK THE MURDERER WAS A GUTSY PERSON?
GUTSY ...?
LOOK AT THE FOOT-PRINTS OUTSIDE THE WINDOW!
THEY COME DIRECTLY TO THIS ROOM IN A STRAIGHT LINE.
HMPH! SO WHAT?
THE SUSPECT WAS LUCKY THAT DR. OYAMA WAS WATCHING TV BY HIMSELF.
IF IT WAS ME, I'D BE AFRAID THERE'D BE OTHER PEOPLE.
SO I'D SNEAK AROUND THE WINDOWS CHECKING THE ROOM OUT BEFORE I ENTERED.
!?
D-DAD, DOES THAT MEAN ...
YEAH, I KNOW !!
THE SUSPECT TIED THE VICTIM UP AND SCRATCHED UP HIS SAFE JUST TO CAMOUFLAGE THE CRIME, SO IT'D LOOK LIKE A BOTCHED BURGLARY.
THE MURDERER KNEW THAT DR. OYAMA WATCHED TV ALONE DURING THAT HOUR.
IN OTHERS WORDS, THE SUSPECT IS...

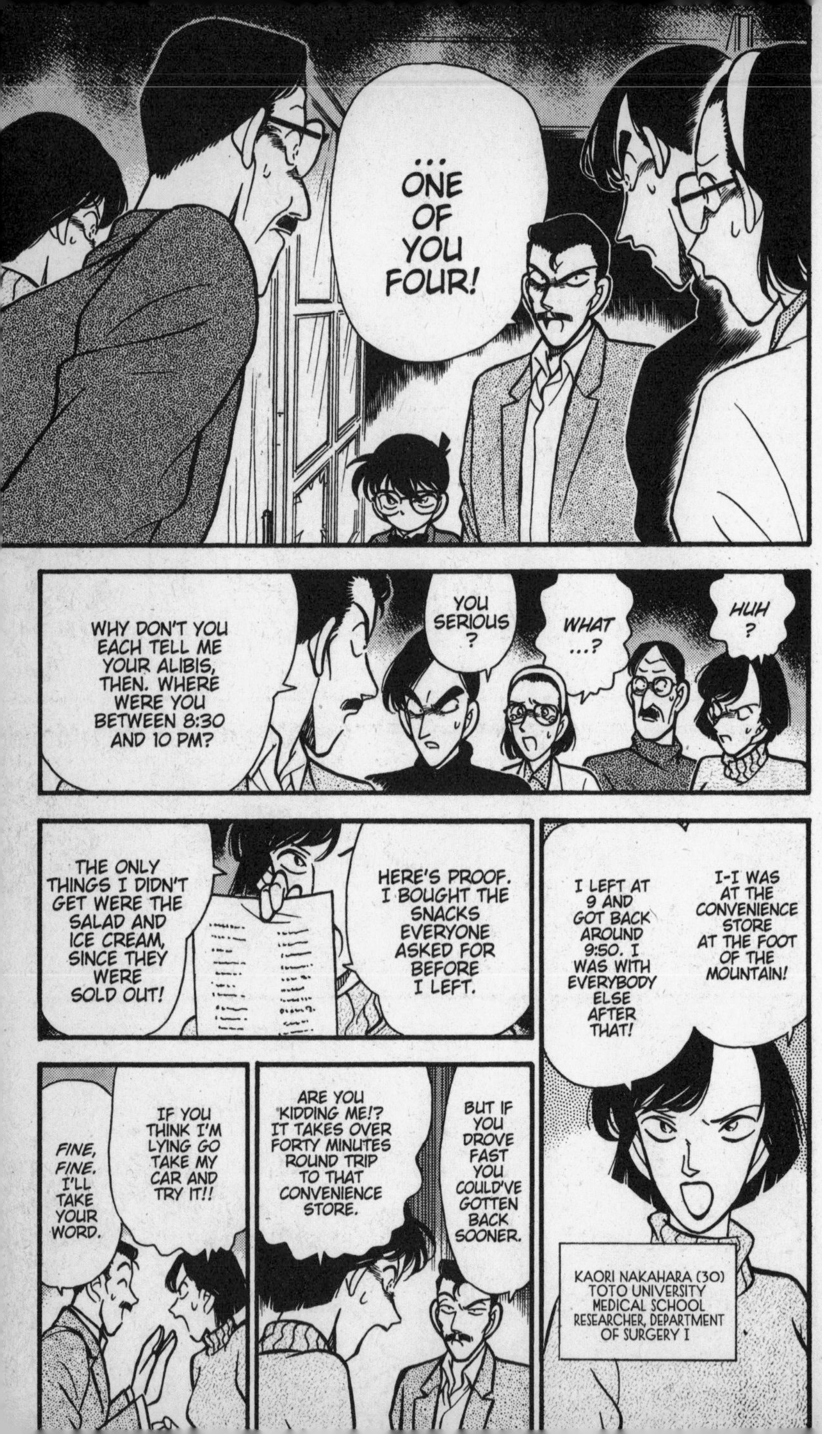
...ONE OF YOU FOUR!
HUH ?
WHAT ...?
YOU SERIOUS ?
WHY DON'T YOU EACH TELL ME YOUR ALIBIS, THEN. WHERE WERE YOU BETWEEN 8:30 AND 10 PM?
I-I WAS AT THE CONVENIENCE STORE AT THE FOOT OF THE MOUNTAIN!
I LEFT AT 9 AND GOT BACK AROUND 9:50. I WAS WITH EVERYBODY ELSE AFTER THAT!
KAORI NAKAHARA (30) TOTO UNIVERSITY MEDICAL SCHOOL RESEARCHER, DEPARTMENT OF SURGERY I
HERE'S PROOF. I BOUGHT THE SNACKS EVERYONE ASKED FOR BEFORE I LEFT.
THE ONLY THINGS I DIDN'T GET WERE THE SALAD AND ICE CREAM, SINCE THEY WERE SOLD OUT!
BUT IF YOU DROVE FAST YOU COULD'VE GOTTEN BACK SOONER.
ARE YOU KIDDING ME!? IT TAKES OVER FORTY MINUTES ROUND TRIP TO THAT CONVENIENCE STORE.
IF YOU THINK I'M LYING GO TAKE MY CAR AND TRY IT!!
FINE, FINE. I'LL TAKE YOUR WORD.

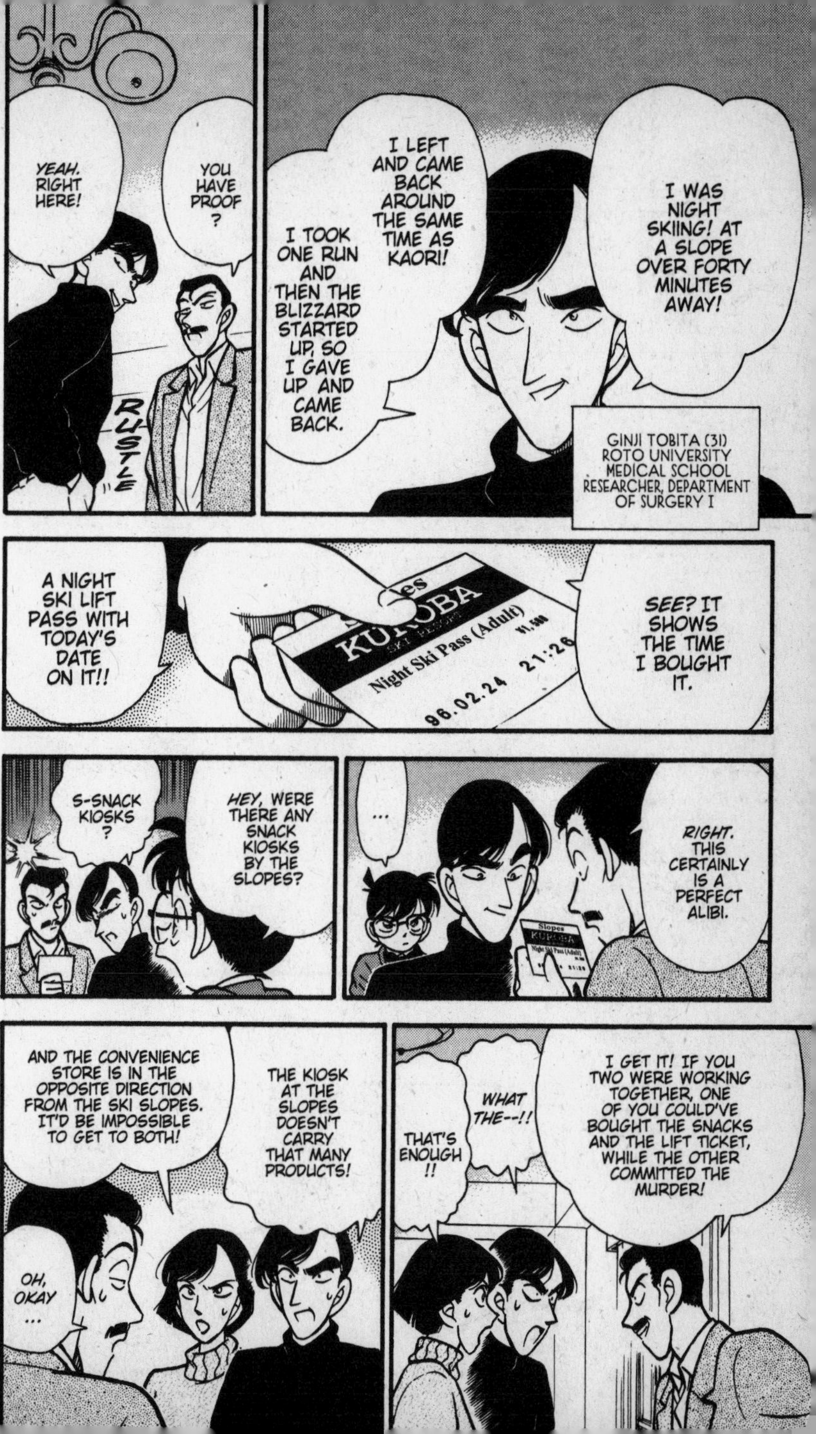
I WAS NIGHT SKIING! AT A SLOPE OVER FORTY MINUTES AWAY!
I LEFT AND CAME BACK AROUND THE SAME TIME AS KAORI!
I TOOK ONE RUN AND THEN THE BLIZZARD STARTED UP, SO I GAVE UP AND CAME BACK.
GINJI TOBITA (31) ROTO UNIVERSITY MEDICAL SCHOOL RESEARCHER, DEPARTMENT OF SURGERY I
YOU HAVE PROOF?
YEAH. RIGHT HERE!
RUSTLE
SEE? IT SHOWS THE TIME I BOUGHT IT.
Night Ski Pass (Adult)
96.02.24 21:26
A NIGHT SKI LIFT PASS WITH TODAY'S DATE ON IT!!
RIGHT. THIS CERTAINLY IS A PERFECT ALIBI.
...
HEY, WERE THERE ANY SNACK KIOSKS BY THE SLOPES?
S-SNACK KIOSKS?
I GET IT! IF YOU TWO WERE WORKING TOGETHER, ONE OF YOU COULD'VE BOUGHT THE SNACKS AND THE LIFT TICKET, WHILE THE OTHER COMMITTED THE MURDER!
WHAT THE--!!
THAT'S ENOUGH!!
THE KIOSK AT THE SLOPES DOESN'T CARRY THAT MANY PRODUCTS!
AND THE CONVENIENCE STORE IS IN THE OPPOSITE DIRECTION FROM THE SKI SLOPES. IT'D BE IMPOSSIBLE TO GET TO BOTH!
OH, OKAY...

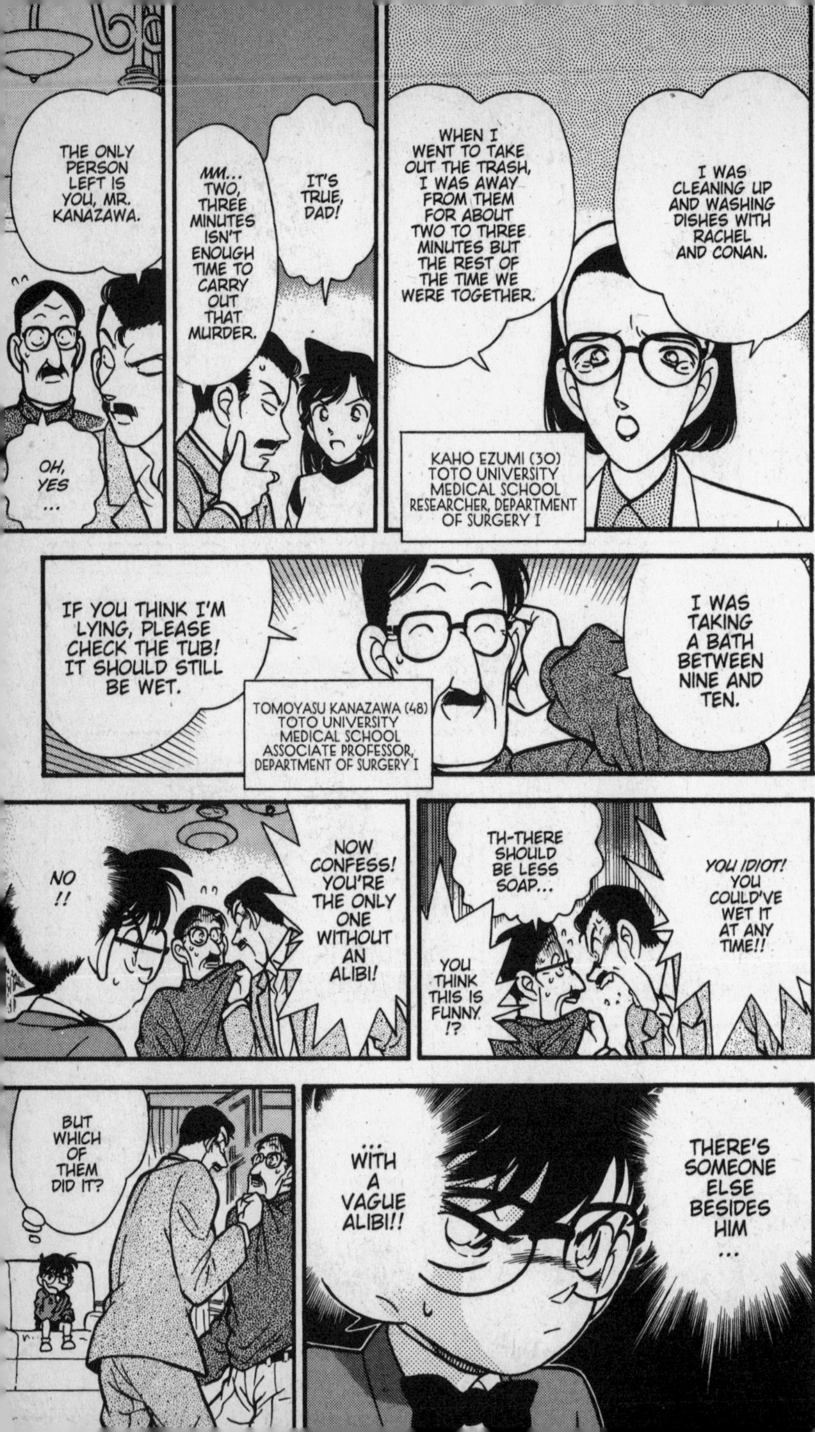

I WAS CLEANING UP AND WASHING DISHES WITH RACHEL AND CONAN.
WHEN I WENT TO TAKE OUT THE TRASH, I WAS AWAY FROM THEM FOR ABOUT TWO TO THREE MINUTES BUT THE REST OF THE TIME WE WERE TOGETHER.
KAHO EZUMI (30) TOTO UNIVERSITY MEDICAL SCHOOL RESEARCHER, DEPARTMENT OF SURGERY I
IT'S TRUE, DAD!
MM... TWO, THREE MINUTES ISN'T ENOUGH TIME TO CARRY OUT THAT MURDER.
THE ONLY PERSON LEFT IS YOU, MR. KANAZAWA.
OH, YES ...
I WAS TAKING A BATH BETWEEN NINE AND TEN.
TOMOYASU KANAZAWA (48) TOTO UNIVERSITY MEDICAL SCHOOL ASSOCIATE PROFESSOR, DEPARTMENT OF SURGERY I
IF YOU THINK I'M LYING, PLEASE CHECK THE TUB! IT SHOULD STILL BE WET.
YOU IDIOT! YOU COULD'VE WET IT AT ANY TIME!!
TH-THERE SHOULD BE LESS SOAP...
YOU THINK THIS IS FUNNY !?
NOW CONFESS! YOU'RE THE ONLY ONE WITHOUT AN ALIBI!
NO !!
THERE'S SOMEONE ELSE BESIDES HIM ...
... WITH A VAGUE ALIBI!!
BUT WHICH OF THEM DID IT?

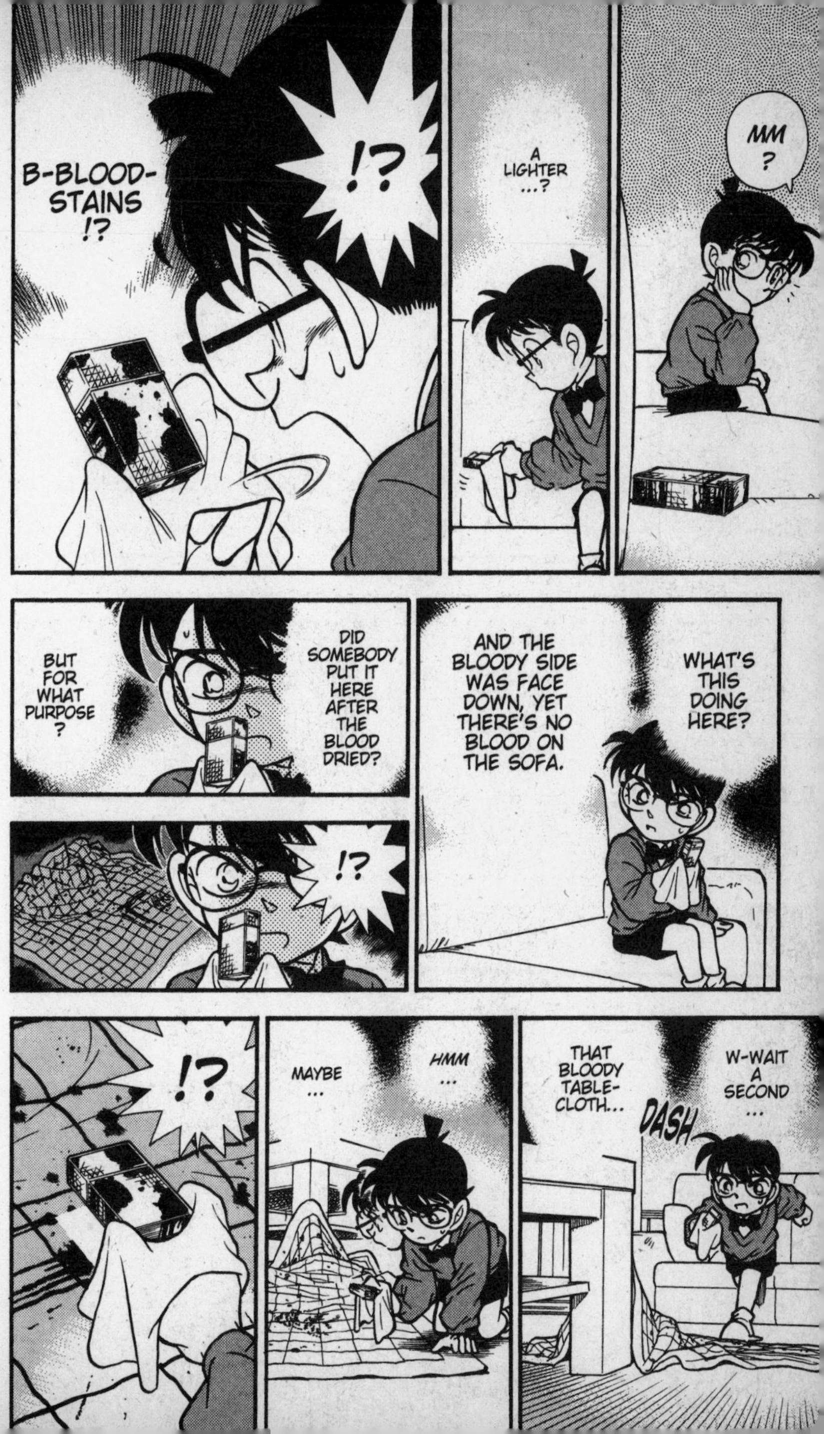
MM ?
A LIGHTER ...?
!?
B-BLOOD-STAINS !?
WHAT'S THIS DOING HERE?
AND THE BLOODY SIDE WAS FACE DOWN, YET THERE'S NO BLOOD ON THE SOFA.
DID SOMEBODY PUT IT HERE AFTER THE BLOOD DRIED?
BUT FOR WHAT PURPOSE ?
!?
W-WAIT A SECOND ...
DASH
THAT BLOODY TABLE-CLOTH...
HMM ...
MAYBE ...
!?

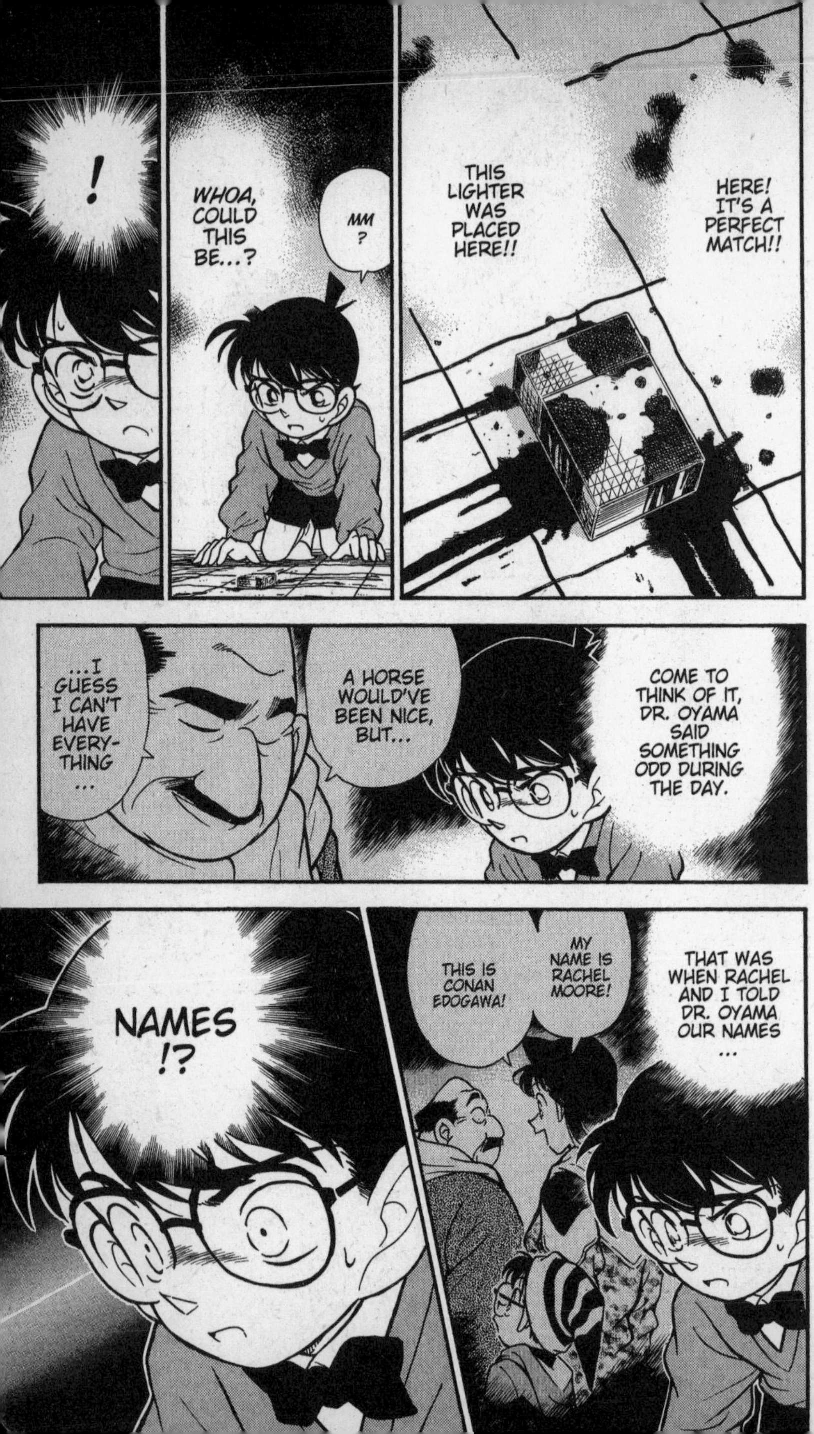
HERE! IT'S A PERFECT MATCH!!
THIS LIGHTER WAS PLACED HERE!!
MM ?
WHOA, COULD THIS BE...?
!
COME TO THINK OF IT, DR. OYAMA SAID SOMETHING ODD DURING THE DAY.
A HORSE WOULD'VE BEEN NICE, BUT...
...I GUESS I CAN'T HAVE EVERYTHING...
THAT WAS WHEN RACHEL AND I TOLD DR. OYAMA OUR NAMES...
MY NAME IS RACHEL MOORE!
THIS IS CONAN EDOGAWA!
NAMES!?

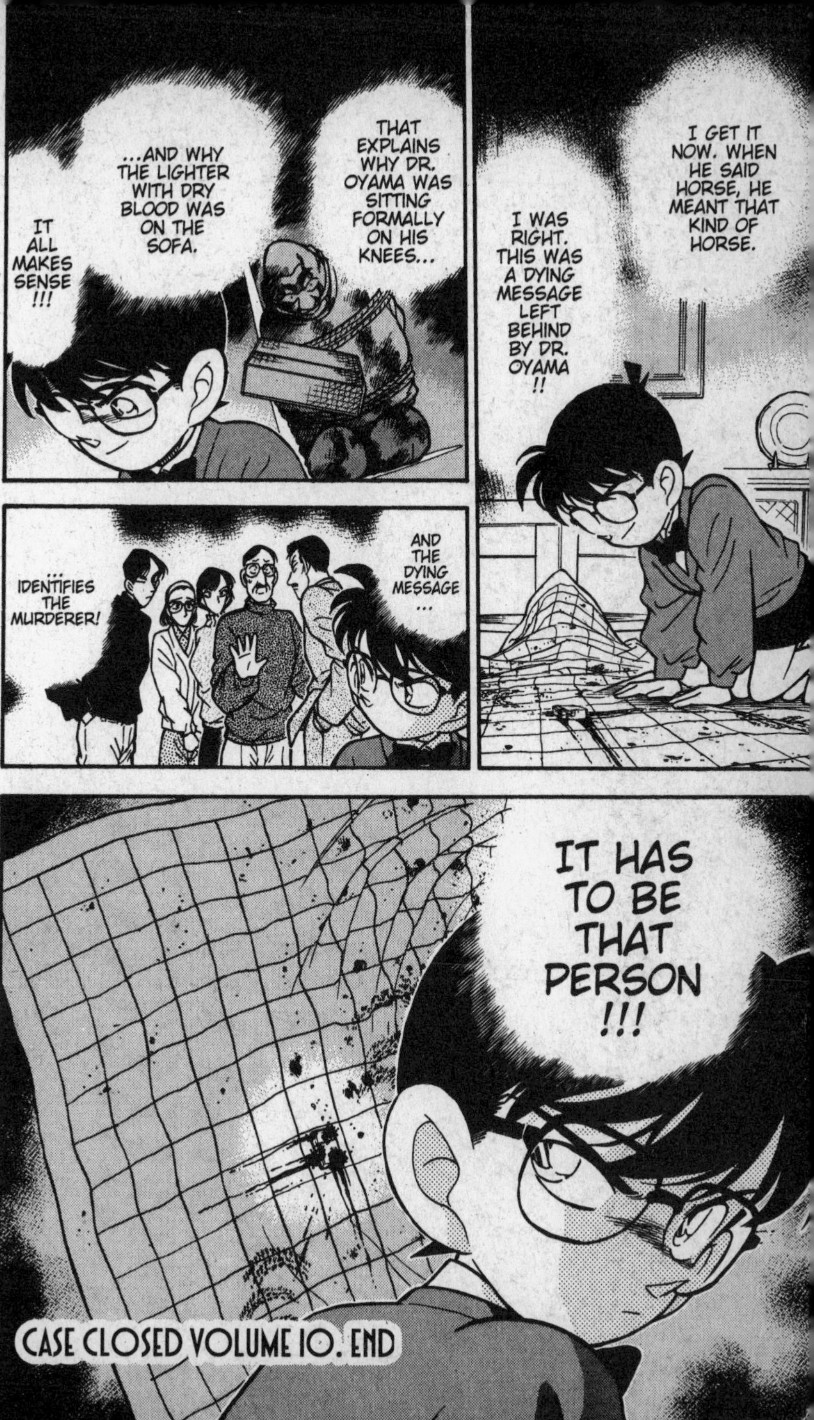
I GET IT NOW. WHEN HE SAID HORSE, HE MEANT THAT KIND OF HORSE.
I WAS RIGHT. THIS WAS A DYING MESSAGE LEFT BEHIND BY DR. OYAMA !!
THAT EXPLAINS WHY DR. OYAMA WAS SITTING FORMALLY ON HIS KNEES...
...AND WHY THE LIGHTER WITH DRY BLOOD WAS ON THE SOFA.
IT ALL MAKES SENSE !!!
AND THE DYING MESSAGE ...
...IDENTIFIES THE MURDERER!
IT HAS TO BE THAT PERSON !!!
CASE CLOSED VOLUME 10. END

Hello, Aoyama here.

Conan has finally reached ten volumes!!
In celebration, a character we haven't seen in a
while will make an appearance. You know, that
guy who was in volume one, that guy! It should
be fun trying to deduce who it'll be! ...But it
won't matter if you read this after reading the
book will it... (Hahaha...)

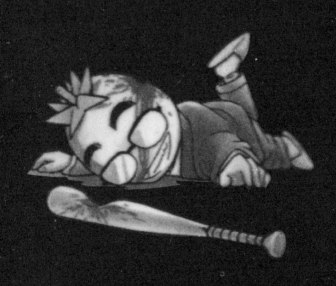

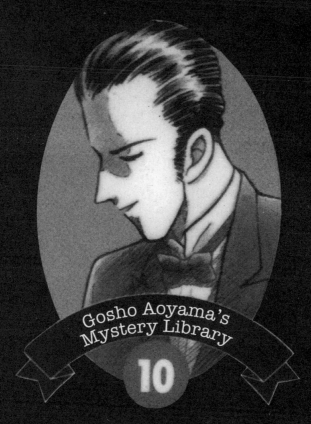

Gosho Aoyama's
Mystery Library

10

AUGUSTE DUPIN

Holmes, Poirot, Kogoro Akechi—there are many great detectives in the
world, but the original can be none other than August Dupin, who
Edgar Allen Poe created in 1841!! Auguste Dupin, a young gentlemen
and an impoverished aristocrat lives in seclusion, preferring the darkness of the night, and closing the blinds of the windows during the day
to read and contemplate under candlelight. His method of deduction
is observation and analysis. He can correctly point out what people
are thinking by observing their gestures and expressions. Even his
friend and narrator of the story 'I' is surprised. Yes...a pair is born—
the "genius detective" who solves cases logically and his devoted
"clumsy assistant" who records all his cases! Dupin appears in three
stories, but stuffed within these tales are the fundamentals of detective novels. This is the reason why Poe is called the "Father of
Mystery Novels." (I recommend *The Murders in the Rue Morgue.*)

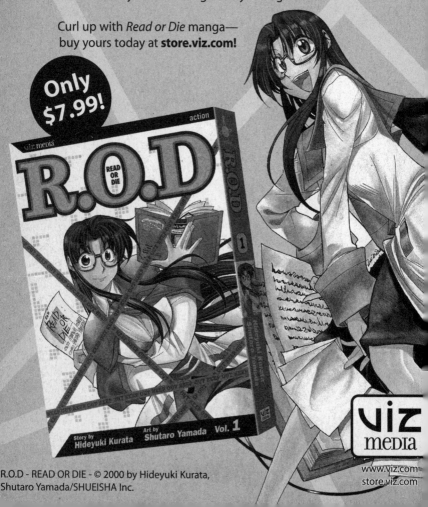

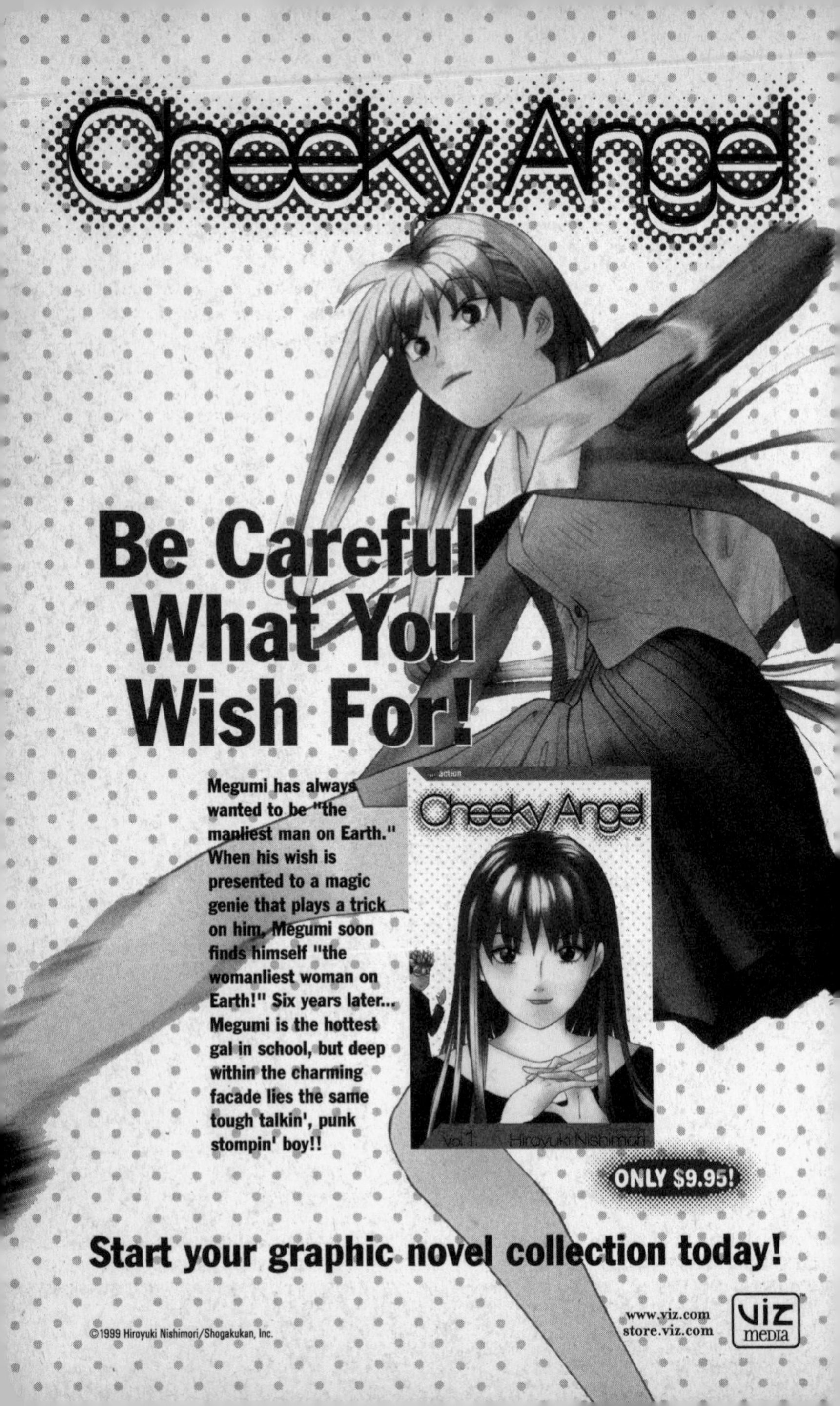
Cheeky Angel
Be Careful What You Wish For!
Megumi has always wanted to be "the manliest man on Earth." When his wish is presented to a magic genie that plays a trick on him, Megumi soon finds himself "the womanliest woman on Earth!" Six years later... Megumi is the hottest gal in school, but deep within the charming facade lies the same tough talkin', punk stompin' boy!!
Cheeky Angel
vol.1
Hiroyuki Nishimori
ONLY $9.95!
Start your graphic novel collection today!
www.viz.com
store.viz.com
VIZ MEDIA
©1999 Hiroyuki Nishimori/Shogakukan, Inc.

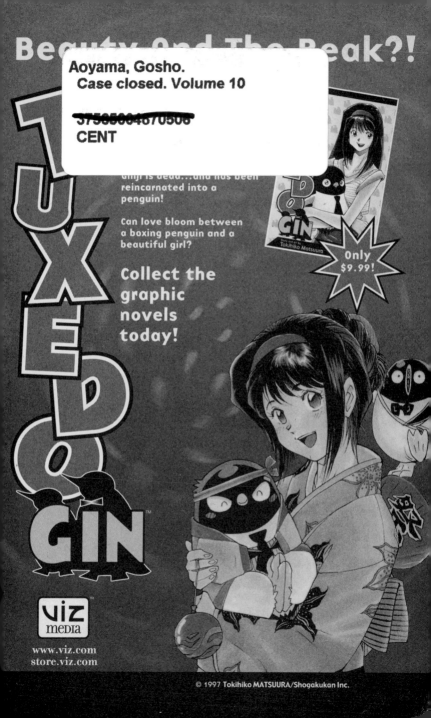

LOVE MANGA?   LET US KNOW!

☐ Please do NOT send me information about VIZ Media products, news and events, special offers, or other information.

☐ Please do NOT send me information from VIZ Media's trusted business partners.

Name: _____

Address: _____

City: _____ **State:** _____ **Zip:** _____

E-mail: _____

☐ Male ☐ Female **Date of Birth** (mm/dd/yyyy): ___ / ___ / ___ (Under 13? Parental consent required)

What race/ethnicity do you consider yourself? (check all that apply)

☐ White/Caucasian   ☐ Black/African American   ☐ Hispanic/Latino

☐ Asian/Pacific Islander   ☐ Native American/Alaskan Native   ☐ Other: _____

What VIZ Media title(s) did you purchase? (indicate title(s) purchased) _____

_____

What other VIZ Media titles do you own? _____

_____

Reason for purchase: (check all that apply)

☐ Special offer   ☐ Favorite title / author / artist / genre

☐ Gift   ☐ Recommendation   ☐ Collection

☐ Read excerpt in VIZ Media manga sampler   ☐ Other _____

Where did you make your purchase? (please check one)

☐ Comic store   ☐ Bookstore   ☐ Grocery Store

☐ Convention   ☐ Newsstand   ☐ Video Game Store

☐ Online (site:_____)   ☐ Other _____

How many ma... titles have you purchased ... year? How many were VIZ Media titles?
(please check o...

MANGA

- ☐ None
- ☐ 1 – 4
- ☐ 5 – 10
- ☐ 11+

How much influence do special promotions and gifts-with-purchase have on the titles you buy?
(please circle, with 5 being great influence and 1 being none)

1 2 3 4 5

Do you purchase every volume of your favorite series?

☐ Yes! Gotta have 'em as my own ☐ No. Please explain: ____________________

What kind of manga storylines do you most enjoy? (check all that apply)

- ☐ Action / Adventure
- ☐ Comedy
- ☐ Fighting
- ☐ Artistic / Alternative
- ☐ Science Fiction
- ☐ Romance (shojo)
- ☐ Sports
- ☐ Other ____________________
- ☐ Horror
- ☐ Fantasy (shojo)
- ☐ Historical

If you watch the anime or play a video or TCG game from a series, how likely are you to buy the manga? (please circle, with 5 being very likely and 1 being unlikely)

1 2 3 4 5

If unlikely, please explain: ____________________

Who are your favorite authors / artists? ____________________

____

What titles would like you translated and sold in English? ____________________

____

THANK YOU! Please send the completed form to:

VIZ media

NJW Research
42 Catharine Street
Poughkeepsie, NY 12601

Your privacy is very important to us. All information provided will be used for internal purposes only and will not be sold or otherwise divulged.